T0305239

PERILOUS WAGERS

Studies of the Weatherhead East Asian Institute, Columbia University

The Studies of the Weatherhead East Asian Institute of Columbia University were inaugurated in 1962 to bring to a wider public the results of significant new research on modern and contemporary East Asia.

PERILOUS WAGERS

Gambling, Dignity, and Day Laborers
in Twenty-First-Century Tokyo

Klaus K. Y. Hammering

CORNELL UNIVERSITY PRESS   ITHACA AND LONDON

First published 2024 by Cornell University Press

Library of Congress Cataloging-in-Publication Data

Names: Hammering, Klaus K. Y., 1980– author.
Title: Perilous wagers : gambling, dignity, and day laborers in twenty-first-century Tokyo / Klaus K. Y. Hammering.
Description: Ithaca : Cornell University Press, 2024. | Series: Studies of the Weatherhead East Asian Institute, Columbia University | Includes bibliographical references and index.
Identifiers: LCCN 2023046111 (print) | LCCN 2023046112 (ebook) | ISBN 9781501776410 (hardcover) | ISBN 9781501776427 (paperback) | ISBN 9781501776434 (epub) | ISBN 9781501776441 (pdf)
Subjects: LCSH: Masculinity—Social aspects—Japan. | Unskilled labor—Social aspects—Japan. | Gangsters in popular culture—Japan. | San'ya (Tokyo, Japan)—Social conditions—21st century. | San'ya (Tokyo, Japan)—Economic conditions—21st century.
Classification: LCC HN723.5 .H2664 2024 (print) | LCC HN723.5 (ebook) | DDC 306.0952—dc23/eng/20240129
LC record available at https://lccn.loc.gov/2023046111
LC ebook record available at https://lccn.loc.gov/2023046112

For my parents:
Reiko Yamamoto and Keld Hammering

Well, what is gambling, I should like to know, but the art of producing in a second the changes that Destiny ordinarily effects only in the course of many hours or even many years, the art of collecting into a single instant the emotions dispersed throughout the slow-moving existence of ordinary men, the secret of living a whole lifetime in a few minutes—in a word, the genie's ball of thread?

—Anatole France, quoted in Benjamin, *Arcades Project*

Contents

Note on Transliteration

This book uses the Hepburn system of romanization. It does not italicize Japanese words that have entered the English language, like *yakuza*, *tatami*, or *udon*. Rather, it defers to their conventional English form. At times, an italicized Japanese word may be introduced alongside its translation in parentheses, only to be replaced thereafter with its English translation. The terms that are retained throughout the text in their original form—like *otoko* (man)—constitute an intrinsic part of San'ya's world and resist translation. Quotation marks foreground the referential quality of words: "*hiyatoi rōdōsha*" (day laborers) are not just "day laborers"—in fact, the generic term *day laborer* (hiyatoi rōdōsha) denies these men their personhood as "men" (otoko), or rather, as otoko. For definitions of italicized Japanese words, see the glossary. Note also that, unless the person's name has become known in English—like Ken Takakura or Takeshi Kitano—I retain the original Japanese order of names, in which the first name comes after the family name, as Takakura Ken. All names of people from San'ya are fictive. Unless otherwise indicated, translations are my own.

INTRODUCTION

Although the lives of the men depicted in this book take place in the receding squalor of Tokyo's old skid row and day-laborer district, San'ya, nearly all these men were born and raised in the countryside and aftermath of World War II, on the devastated peripheries of postwar Japan. Their lives began in abject poverty, with sweeping blue skies and endless crystal-clear shorelines, for many, but not all the characters who appear in this ethnography grew up in the Okinawan islands during the 1950s, under US administration.[1] Their earliest memories include taunting US soldiers, hoping to catch a dime, spearing fish on the way home from school, snatching sugarcane from moving trucks, gliding down the giant slides of empty shipyards, domestic violence, divorce, suicides, thatch-roof homes, torrential storms, a mom doing construction work with a baby strapped to her back, and the final farewell that would take them to the *naichi* (mainland) of Japan as manual laborers with naught but the most lowly of social standing. Of one Okinawan island, Miyakojima, it was said that departing travelers would cast a string from the balcony of their ship to someone waving from the wharf, and they would let this string slip through their fingers. Thus, whether the lives that follow began in Okinawa or elsewhere on the margins of postwar Japan, the poignant violence and permanence of these originary displacements would haunt them forever after.

Nearly a half century later, these men would be eking out a living from construction work and welfare handouts, permanently displaced from their hometowns to metropolitan Tokyo. While the following account does not narrate the trajectories that landed them in the squalid bunkhouses of San'ya, nor the discrimination they encountered along the way, nor the decades of isolation that

would sever their relations with parents, spouses, and children, it seeks to facilitate an imagination of the manner in which they maintained sociality and dignity against the insurmountable odds of these histories. For this reason, the
portrayals hereafter are not concerned simply with the figure of the "day laborer"
or the geographic locale of "San'ya" but with the espousal of a vanishing set of
mobster virtues and the recurrent references made to this dignifying, virtuous
topos, just when the world of San'ya was coming to an end, because the deck had
been stacked against the San'ya man from start to finish. Having given his life to
construction work and other debased forms of labor, the resident of San'ya knew
that his time was nearly up, as his decrepit cityscape was indeed being demolished and replaced by tourist hotels and fancy apartment buildings. Precipitated
by impending death, this ethnography consists in the description of a final burst
of effervescence.[2]

It takes place primarily across two years, between 2011 and 2013, both at construction sites scattered across the northern margins of Tokyo and in the old *yoseba* (gathering place for laborers) of San'ya, said to have housed as many as fifteen
thousand male day laborers in the two decades following World War II.[3] Since
then, the population of San'ya has only diminished, especially so with the recessionary decades after the economic bubble burst in 1991.[4] In 2011–2013, active laborers in San'ya observed that there were probably fewer than fifty others working
in the area; official statistics on the black labor market are difficult to come by, and
if anyone had a lay of the land, it was the workers and subcontractors themselves.
Additionally, almost all these workers were in their fifties: "There are no young
people in this town," it was said. Indeed, the remainder of San'ya's populace was
considered either too old or physically unfit to labor. Living in the old two-story
wooden bunkhouses that still lined San'ya's back lanes, these men composed an
anonymous mass of rapidly declining individuals whose weekly routine consisted
in doing their rounds from the hospital, to the welfare office, to the gambling halls
in Asakusa, and to the convenience store. Even the many eateries, bars, or rather,
dive bars that used to pepper San'ya were becoming a thing of the past. If the daylaborer district was said to have once contained as many as five hundred eateries
and dives, in 2011–2013, there were no more than ten, and in 2018, there were five.
Once ubiquitous in day-laborer districts, only two of these were hole-in-the-wall
establishments that hosted illegal gambling and in which the clientele either stood
by the counter or sat about on chairs spread out on the pavement.[5] Since the 1990s,
moreover, not only had San'ya's bunkhouses been transformed into one-room occupancy, but the area had shrunk to one-fourth its previous size.[6] The inhabitants
of San'ya and their way of life were facing extinction.[7]

As much as the day laborer or the district of San'ya, which now encompasses
no more than a one-kilometer-square area, this book is concerned with the fan-

tasy of a transgressive masculinity intimately intertwined with the honorable mobster (yakuza) values of old and, specifically, with how an *otoko* (man) conducts himself when backed against the wall. It is as much about "day laborers" (*hiyatoi rōdōsha*), labor, labor power, and the disposability of labor power at construction sites as it is about the embodied references made by one group of active workers in San'ya to the vanishing yakuza virtues represented by underdog characters like those of Ken Takakura (perhaps the most well-known Japanese actor of yakuza characters in the West), Andō Noboru, or Sugawara Bunta, and it is about the fact that, if one happens to be invited up one of the steep, narrow, dark staircases that lead through unlocked partitions into the musty interior of a third-floor San'ya apartment, one suddenly feels oneself transported onto the set of a 1970s Japanese yakuza movie. The windows are shaded, but streaks of light nevertheless penetrate the room, giving it a twilight hue by lighting dirty, frayed tatami mats, as well as a row of laundry, shirts, and pants hanging from a pole stretched across the ceiling. Across from a sink and gas stove, the bed is aligned against the windows, beside which stands a small table with a dysfunctional alarm clock, a TV that works when you hit it, and a 2.7-liter bottle of cheap shochu. During the summer, it gets as hot as 40° C in this apartment, but there is no air conditioner, and so the fan is running and the windows are always open, outside of which a mouse can be seen scuttering across the electric wires into the bunkhouse on the opposite side of the street. The occupant of this flat works occasionally at construction sites. But his primary source of income is welfare, and on account of his age (sixty-two), the city ward has approved his move from a bunkhouse into an apartment of his own. After decades in San'ya, he still goes by an assumed name, ostensibly because he was running from the law when he first arrived in the area, and he is known not only for his underworld connections but for his hot temper and tendency to pull a knife in confrontations. While he speaks with another man of Okinawan descent, I look out the window, pretending not to hear, because the conversation concerns a longtime mutual acquaintance who is suspected of having started injecting meth (*shabu*). In joking imitation of the three wise monkeys—"see no evil, hear no evil, speak no evil"—the tenant looks at me and covers his mouth, ears, and eyes, and eventually the conversation moves on to lighter topics like baseball or movies, of which a stack of some twenty DVDs lie next to the TV. As I sift through them, I am told that I can have any one, including the porno, but not Takakura Ken, and sure enough, the stack is composed almost entirely of yakuza movies, be it *Battles without Honor and Humanity*, *New Battles without Honor and Humanity*, or less canonical fare featuring Tanba Tetsurō, Kitaōji Kin'ya, or Matsukata Hiroki. While the names of such actors and their films may be unfamiliar outside Japan, in San'ya they constituted the Japanese counterpart to the American *Godfather* series, the narrative of

which everyone I knew had internalized and made their own. Notably absent
from their repertoire were references to contemporary actors like Takeshi Kitano,
whose characters embody the shamelessness of the mobster underworld. For if
anything, theirs was a world grounded in nostalgia for the early decades of the
postwar and for the vanishing values of shame, honor, and the upstanding otoko.

What one most often hears upon entering one of San'ya's eateries or dives,
therefore, is the blaring voice of a man singing karaoke against the backdrop of
stools spread about three or four tables, a menu pasted onto the walls in the form
of greasy handwritten pieces of paper, a cramped kitchen, counter, concrete floors,
and retrograde TVs screening either the lyrics or the boat and horse races. Often
tipsy if not drunk, the man will not be singing pop songs, however, but *enka* from
the '60s, '70s, and '80s in which the hardships and virtues of an otoko (man) are
given poignant expression, and not surprisingly, the sentimental themes of these
songs resonate with the lives of the men who sing them: of leaving the countryside to find work in the city, of long-lost loves and family, of loneliness, of longing
for the good times, and of perseverance.[8] But just as the objective market conditions that necessitated the violence of these displacements stay tacit in the lyrics, so
too, the men I came to know in San'ya rarely spoke of the wounds that they themselves had incurred over time. In fact, the masculinity that they espoused was one
that frowned upon excessive self-indulgence and that displaced the failures induced by the economy into the excesses of camaraderie, gambling, and the occasional brawl. Much as the solitary gangster flings himself against his adversaries in
the final scene of a Japanese mobster movie rather than back down, the San'ya
man was more likely to hurl himself against denigrating circumstances in what
Georges Bataille has described as a "real *charge* of the passions," only to perish.[9]

In this way, an otoko enacted his bravado precisely when he was in the direst
of straits, out of luck, cash, or friends to rely on without compromising himself.
Before physical deterioration set in, the moment of his appearance, or the moment of seeking to be recognized on his own terms, not as a disposable "day laborer" (*hiyatoi rōdōsha*) but as an "otoko" (man) in his own right, coincided
with the moment of his disappearance, and in 2011–2013, this was also the predicament in which the district of San'ya found itself. For while men in San'ya had
lived under conditions of economic and social insecurity decades before the
bubble burst in 1991, earning their livelihood from day to day, it would not be until
well into the twenty-first century that the district was dying as surely as the demand for its laborers had disappeared. Perched upon the precipice, its remaining
workers had time for one more blast.

Calling them *toppamono*, or "devil-may-care types," the former construction
worker, mob member, and investigative journalist Miyazaki Manabu has described this destructive character of individuals in San'ya in his best-selling

autobiography. At once contemptible and respectable, this character is possessed by a nearly reckless disregard for general propriety and for the consequences of transgressing its norms. But while he is a man who resorts to "bulldozing" his way onward—"a man who charges forward without actually knowing where he is going"—it must be underscored that the actions of this individual earn its bearer recognition especially when they are paired with consideration for those with less social prowess, and this entails that he will sacrifice himself for others.[10] Hence, the character that Miyazaki calls the devil-may-care type may not know precisely where he is going, but he is certainly aware of the potential costs necessitated by his actions. It is the risks he exposes himself to that confers respectability on this person, and for this reason, he knows where he is most likely to wind up: in debt, jail, or dead. The construction worker and gambler of whom I write acts on account of the risks he incurs. Rather than bend his convictions, he prefers to die early.

It has been seven years since I lived in San'ya, and Akira, my confidant and primary interlocutor, has been true to his word.[11] Back then he was still stout, witty, and convivial over drinks, stood straight on his feet, occasionally going to work at construction sites, taunting the police whenever he got the chance, and ready to engage in physical altercations, even if it resulted in a jail stint. Now, at the age of sixty-two, he totters with a cane. If I had not witnessed his gradual physical and mental deterioration, Akira would be virtually unrecognizable. His cheeks have gone sallow and cavernous, reminiscent of the full-blown puffs he gives to cigarettes, like the gulps of shochu he takes with his medication. His chest has become hollow, his back bent, and his body unhealthily lean. Akira now wears the same urine-stained clothes every day, and before the ward assigned helpers to clean his apartment twice every week, his room was in an unimaginable state. Because he has called the ambulance one too many times, the nurses at Asakusa Hospital have sanctimoniously informed him that he has been placed on their "blacklist," meaning that the hospital will not accept him in case of an emergency. Scared of collapsing after a bout of drinking, Akira now shuffles his feet while waiting for a taxi, as if a child holding in a wee, and when he arrives home, he has to climb a steep concrete staircase from which he has fallen unconscious. Most devastating of all, his eyes have taken on that vacant aspect which can be encountered in so many of the men who wander aimlessly about San'ya, dosed on a mixture of medication, sedatives, and liquor.

Indeed, Akira is one among many. Tamura, for instance, passed away during my stay in San'ya, at the age of fifty. Unlike others, he was fortunate enough to have been volunteering at the local NPO (nonprofit organization), meaning that staff members sought him out and discovered his body shortly after he stopped showing up. So too, Hayashi died in his room, reputedly from a brain hemorrhage.

When I left San'ya, he appeared to be in much better shape than Akira, but then he started drinking day in, day out, until it became a common sight to find him sleeping naked on the streets. Had it not been for the rumor that a neighbor had called the police regarding the odor emanating from his room and that his body had been disposed of by the ward, nobody would have known of his death, at the age of fifty-eight; it could only be presumed that Hayashi's ashes had been handed to his estranged wife and daughter. Then there is Kentarō, who refused to see the doctor even when his stomach swelled abnormally and his robust arms withered. In fact, Kentarō continued to drink even after he had been diagnosed with cirrhosis of the liver, resulting in multiple emergency trips to the hospital, until he coughed up so much blood that the ambulance staff told his cousin he might not make it. On the following day, he became so enraged by the condescension from nurses and doctors that he proceeded to pull out his IV needles and walked out while telling his cousin to take him to another hospital. Having had this brush with death, Kentarō no longer drinks but is a skeleton of his former self.

And this is much the same way that San'ya itself appears today. Once a bustling city of day laborers, the district has become a ghost town of shuttered stores and high-rise hotels that cater to tourists oblivious to its historical and social significance. Last year, in 2017, the *mama-san* (an older female proprietor or manager) of the eatery Iseya died of cancer. This year, the decades-old pachinko parlor Atariya was razed to the ground (figure I.1), and a few months ago, the overhang to San'ya's shopping arcade, Iroha, was removed along with its anachronistic, colorful entryway placard and its faded banner depicting *Tomorrow's Joe* (*Ashita no Joe*) anime characters—a series from the '60s and '70s that relates the rise to boxing fame of the delinquent youth of San'ya, Joe, under the tutorship of his alcohol-prone coach.[12] Remarking that Iroha had been rendered "butt naked"— for many homeless people sleep in the arcade, where illegal gambling and drinking also take place—the removal of San'ya's signature, shielding overhang caused people I knew to lower their heads and ponder where they would drink once the proprietors of the last two hole-in-the-wall dive bars passed away. Soon, only Tamahime park would be left.

This book, therefore, begins and ends with death. It ends with death because the sociality it depicts, when life had "been good" among one group of workers, had fractured over the course of two years and because many of its characters are dead today. But the book begins with death because it was the imminence of death that instigated the conduct that I describe, conferring necessity upon it by preceding it as its cause. Predominantly the outcome of unrestricted working conditions and excessive alcohol consumption, the San'ya man had seen his predecessors die, and he knew that what awaited him was third-rate treatment by the state, the medical establishment, and a lonesome death. Long before words

FIGURE I.1.   The old pachinko parlor Atariya, before its demise.

like *neoliberalism*, *precarity*, or *abandonment* came into vogue, the state had consigned men in San'ya to an economic insecurity in which the extraction of what Marx called "absolute surplus value" could be maximized.[13] Save during the bubble economy, when wages and spendings were said to have been truly extravagant, conditions had been put into place such that their bodies were worked to their physical limit, while they were compensated just enough to live from day to day, or even less; most certainly, the forms of labor through which they were made to earn their living, of which cleaning radioactive materials is perhaps most scandalous, were not designed to protect the longevity of workers.[14] For men in San'ya composed a reserve army of labor that could be discarded without consideration for their reproduction. As alienated from general society as from their opposite gender, the San'ya man had virtually no prospects of marriage and children, and biopolitics had been dispensed with in the area. During its heyday, the district's labor force had been successively replenished by victims of the economy, and now that San'ya was disappearing, the insecurity that had conditioned its way of life for over half a century had become generalized to the population at large. As if overnight, Japan Inc. of the bubble era had degenerated into a land of economic insecurity and, for a brief moment after the nuclear meltdowns at Fukushima Daiichi Nuclear Power Plant, of nuclear gypsies.[15] But this is also precisely why the death of places like San'ya demand attention, because lest the wreckage that history has always already left behind is forgotten, these places disclose the truth of surplus extraction and capitalism and signal the future for a nation in which the inexhaustible violence of capital accumulation has been unleashed on the general populace.[16]

In fact, not unlike Japan's multibillion-dollar sex industry, San'ya was forgotten before the ongoing nuclear catastrophe in Fukushima and remains evermore forgotten today. While the old day-laborer districts of Japan availed the nuclear industry of laborers decades before the "human-made accident" (*jinsai*), the lives of these men have not changed in its aftermath. Notwithstanding momentary discussions of "nuclear laborers" and "nuclear gypsies" after the meltdowns, the paltry financial sources that previously provided aid to San'ya have since diverted their funds to Japan's northeastern coast.[17] Yet when the Fukushima-born antinuclear activist Mutō Ruiko addressed a crowd of sixty thousand half a year after the tsunami, she also raised the plaintive cry, "Please don't forget Fukushima," warning against and presaging a future in which Fukushima, too, has become forgotten.[18] Of course, while the mass media may have forgotten about Fukushima, the academic bandwagon continues to attend to its golden goose—"Fukushima"—but neglects to address the *general* formation of state recognition that has been marshalled to contain or eliminate backtalk in Japan today, the effects of which have long been evident in the old day-laborer districts, where the association of labor with uncleanliness and death triggers shame before general society, compelling individuals to silence. So too, during the course of COVID-19 and the 2020 Olympics, San'ya's population of ageing men was one of the most vulnerable in Tokyo, and it should be recalled that San'ya was where homeless people were shuttled and confined prior to the celebrated Summer Olympics of 1964.[19] Much as it has been observed that the stigma of radiation exposure is not new to Japan, it must be acknowledged both that such stigmatization drives victims beneath the threshold of public visibility and that the structure of this containment is not limited to second or third generations from Hiroshima or Nagasaki or residents of Fukushima. Be it radiation work, construction work, sex work, or so-called 3K work—*kitsui* (severe), *kitanai* (dirty), and *kiken* (dangerous)—the relationship between state ideology and a whole gamut of marginalized labor forms calls for interrogation.

Given the fear of contagion that surrounds such labor forms and places like San'ya in their affiliation with death, their containment can be identified as the effect of a certain rhetoric akin to that which surrounds and constitutes the negativity of "drugs." It was in a state of fearful attraction and repulsion at the possibility of breach that outsiders once entered San'ya, and one must, indeed, still be careful of sharing drinks on the street or at dive bars because tuberculosis can be contracted through contact. On the other hand, veterans of San'ya themselves employed a rhetoric of drugs to explain the addictive lifestyle that it offers, remarking that "once you taste" San'ya, you "cannot give it up." This was also the reason that, when younger men entered the district, some senior members of my group urged them to return to their families or to find employment appropriate for a CV, lest they burn their bridges. For while the initial appeal of San'ya consisted in anonymity, escape, and, for able-bodied young men, an income without strings attached, the passage of time and habitual alcohol consumption made it increasingly unlikely that these individuals would return to a life in general society. An autobiographical account by Tsukada Tsutomu, an outsider to San'ya, is even titled *This Is Why I Cannot Quit San'ya*.[20] Writing in 1997, Edward Fowler observes that San'ya

> suggests a kind of moral degeneracy to mainstream Japanese which is anathema to their way of life. An acquaintance became visibly disturbed when I told him that I was frequenting this section of Tokyo. "I wouldn't waste my time there if I were you," he told me. "You don't want to get dragged down in the mire." In the eyes of my Japanese acquaintance, San'ya was not simply an eyesore, a blot on Tokyo's image, but a festering wound capable of infecting any passerby foolish enough to come in contact with it.
>
> San'ya, then, might just as well be considered a state of mind as a slum. Or, more properly, "states of mind," for the meaning of this neighborhood is clearly not the same for the resident (or even the different categories of resident) and nonresident. For the latter, who rarely if ever sets foot in the area and is left simply to imagine it, San'ya is a filthy repository for men whose personal world has gone awry, the result of individual excess or error; for the former (at least for the day-laborer resident), it is a refuge—a symbol of defeat, perhaps, but at the same time a cradle of opportunity which holds the possibility, however slim, of a second chance in a society that is most stingy with second chances.[21]

In 2011–2013, after the collapse of the bubble economy and the recessionary decades that followed, construction work had all but disappeared from the area, and outsiders contemptibly called San'ya a "welfare town."[22] In a transition that Tom Gill has documented in San'ya's counterpart in Yokohama, Kotobukichō, second chances had become nonexistent, and the "degeneracy" that previously attached to San'ya had become compounded by the notion of taxpayer's money wasted on the excessive habits of unemployed lowlifes.[23] Never mind that inhabitants of San'ya literally built Tokyo or that their welfare dependence owed largely to the conditions of labor they had been placed in by the municipality and state. But men in San'ya were themselves likely to concur with the diagnosis that they had brought their situation upon themselves and to admit that, to add to the conglomeration of vices already concentrated in the district, illegal "drugs" and especially injected methamphetamines were consumed by its residents behind closed doors (as elsewhere in Japan, I might add). The needle, as Derrida has said, epitomizes the diseased and infectious quality, indeed, the danger and impropriety of drugs.[24] In the interest of eliminating these improprieties, it might be observed, as one American nurse of many decades of experience in San'ya did, that what these men need is a twelve-step program to cure their alcoholism, that is, a program to replace an unruly and unacceptable addiction with an ever more sinister addiction rooted in dominance by and obsequiousness to the Western torchbearers of Alcoholics Anonymous.[25] Either way, the resident of San'ya is stiffed. More often than not, he therefore mimics compliance before welfare officers and doctors, seeking to secure what he requires to survive, and reverts to excess upon his return to San'ya. However suicidal this excess may be, it garners him recognition within the confines of San'ya. Shielded there from the judgment he incurs in general society, the veteran of San'ya transforms the infectious symptoms of his defeat into a repulsive sign of empowerment.

Condensed as much in the excesses of gambling, drinking, fighting, or the piles of garbage that could be seen in San'ya, the conventional form of such signifiers had long been associated with traditional tattoos (*irezumi*), the missing pinkie, and the knife scar across the cheek, each of which indicates mobster affiliation. Much as traditional Japanese tattoos have captured the fascination of the West and have admittedly taken on a new meaning for Japan's younger generations, who may sport such tattoos just because they like them, in San'ya, these signs nevertheless signified avowal of current or past outlaw status and a code of conduct that opposed upstanding society, prompting wariness among outsiders. Of course, more often than not, tattoos or missing pinkies conceal yet another man who castigates himself for having let his loved ones down and with whom one can converse as easily as with a salaryman. But the fact of the matter was that even the men I came to work with (many of whom had spent years in the yakuza) were circumspect in the public bathhouses (*sentō*) of the nearby red-light district, Yoshiwara, where the yakuza also came to bathe and that a hush descended on eateries when the local mob entered. And it was in its association with this outlaw world that San'ya itself occupied the place of a constitutive negative in the social imaginary, threatening general propriety while holding it in its thrall. In the excesses of working hungover at construction sites, only to carouse, gamble, and, given the chance, womanize, San'ya was located at the margins of the social bond of statist propriety. It was only by virtue of expelling the useless and heterogeneous elements of San'ya that the propriety of "general society" (*ippan shakai*) could establish itself, constituting San'ya, in turn, as a menacing entity of its own.[26] As if they were caught in a symbiotic relationship, the necessity of the mobster underworld was, in fact, explained to me with reference to ineluctable logics of negation and containment, like yin and yang, or "shadow" (*kage*) in the presence of "light" (*akari*). But to harness the power of this negativity, the veteran of San'ya could not charge headlong into death: if he was to enable signification, he had to limit his expenditures, and herein resided the difficulty of his predicament.[27] Because his conduct was grounded in excess, he always ran the risk of undoing his reputation by drinking or gambling too much, by selling meth too flagrantly, or by inflicting disproportionate injuries on his adversary in a brawl, and for this reason, his enactment of masculinity was prone to collapse into bombast, failure, and compulsive repetition.[28] In short, the very impropriety of San'ya necessitated its own code of conduct, its own propriety, and its own improprieties. A genuine otoko adhered to a chosen "path" or "way" (*michi*), thus "seeing things through" (*suji o tōsu*), and if he was not only steadfast but considerate and perhaps even selfless in this transgressive enactment of justice, it secured him the place of a dependable personage.

Emerging from within differences that had been expelled from society, the sheer abjection of San'ya precipitated the formation of a sociality that constrained excess through the demand that an otoko demonstrate consideration for his "buddies" (*nakama*) and, in so doing, conferred dignity in place of failure. Emblematized in the figure of the upstanding otoko, this not only entailed that a respectable person refrained from embroiling others in brawls too many times, from repeatedly borrowing or failing to return money, or from humiliating himself over drinks but that, when the occasion arose, he sacrificed himself for others. In this way, it was precisely where the signifier of equivalent value—the commodity form—had created the most abject circumstances that the desire to be recognized in one's singular and irreplaceable value materialized, and it is the enactment of this aspiration that I try to intercept and decipher, without committing the violence of replacing it with the artifice of the ethnographer. Across the death-inducing activities of labor, gambling, and staking oneself for one's buddies, this ethnography seeks to restore the qualitative heterogeneity of the skilled "artisan" (*shokunin*) by depicting a cast of individuals embracing a masculinity that sought to counteract the violence of the market and their containment in negativity.[29] As much as the theory that undergirds the writing that follows, my concern is to give imaginative space to the social world of San'ya as I encountered it and to the specific individuals who composed this world.

As of old in San'ya, this cast was constituted by a troupe of incorrigible and rambunctious characters. For not only did men in San'ya hail from the entirety of Japan, if not occasionally from Korea, China, or the Philippines, but many of the differences that were otherwise self-consciously set aside in adherence to a standard Japanese identity could be met in the open, whether that be a regional accent, a queer identity, or an ethnic affiliation. Disabilities were an all-too-common sight, be it a speech impediment; harelip; missing finger, limb, or eye; a gammy limb; a limp; scars from workplace accidents or physical altercations; or a host of less identifiable mental disabilities. On any regular night, the small crowd that gathers at an outdoor dive may include a former yakuza member; someone just released from jail, be it for drugs or murder; or an Okinawan worker for whom such stories are old hat and who prefers to banter with the regular clientele of middle-aged women, one of whom sleeps on the streets and another of whom has a reputation for shoplifting. And in the course of the evening, a stream of others passes by the dive, greeting customers in passing, sitting down to gossip, talk about work, or exchange goods, and the nameless group of regulars, whose speech is often slurred or unintelligible on account of alcohol and medication, begin to take on individual features. At some point, the homeless man who lives in a tent by the Sumida River may also stop by on his way back from the supermarket, or a member of the local mob may bicycle by to receive an envelope from the owner. Unlike the crowd that hangs out drinking by the old labor union, the individuals who frequent this hole-in-the-wall have no overt political affiliations. Most likely, everyone here spurns leftist ideology in favor of an antediluvian right-wing ideology that involves emperor worship and self-sacrifice. In fact, it was at this hole-in-the-wall dive bar that I met the group of men from Okinawa (and mainland Japan) with whom I came to work at construction sites. In their first account, the sacrifice of Okinawa during World War II and its subsequent handover to the American forces was transformed into a narrative in which the Okinawan islander claimed Japanese identity by having renounced more than anyone else. Yet, on occasion, these men did converse among themselves in their native tongue—which varied from island to island—and they recognized brethren islanders from their accents.[30] In what follows, I refer to this conglomeration of men from Okinawa and beyond alternately as a social entity in the abstract, as "the group," or as "the guys," to signify the intimacy and loose affiliation among a slew of individuals in whose orbit I slowly came to be included. Finally, as this cast of characters approach their curtain call, I refer to them once more as "the troupe."

Rather than the anti-state sentiment that might have been expected among individuals who had been systematically exploited by the state, what the men I write of shared was the precondition for secondary elaborations of sociality to take place, namely, the fact of their failure in the eyes of their families and general society. Nearly every one of the guys had severed their family relations when they first arrived in San'ya, which, if anything, marked the end point of a trajectory of failed masculinity. They were the long-lost sons, husbands, and fathers who had trouble supporting even themselves and who were no longer expected to provide for others. If it happened once every few years that a daughter or son called asking for money, they might have been able to spare ¥10,000 ($100), but that was it, and with the passage of time, they had become increasingly isolated within the stigma of San'ya. After years of making acquaintances and manipulating the system to their advantage (getting welfare while working secretly), it had become well-nigh impossible for these men to leave behind the familiarity of San'ya for the alienation and hazards of striking out in society at large, and this entailed accepting what San'ya had to offer: giving up on the prospects of finding a spouse or reestablishing family relations. Circumscribed by the shame of retrograde working conditions, welfare status, and the fact of residing in a bunkhouse, it was thus from within the conditions of their defeat that the group sought to maintain "dignity" (*iji*).

As much as theory, the chapters of this book consist in an exposition of these conditions and of the people who endured them.[31] Readers should be aware that, in the interest of legibility, I have embedded my theoretical framework in the narrative and that explicit elaborations of theory and their import for cultural anthropology, critical theory, and East Asian studies can be found in the endnotes. Alas, industry standards have disallowed footnotes. Readers interested in theory will therefore find the rest of this introduction helpful, as it provides a road map to the chapters that follow. But readers who desire a straightforward narrative are encouraged to move on to chapter 1. While the theory that underpins this book deals with questions of labor, exchange, and value; honor and shame; temporality and desire; gender and personhood; or state recognition and violence, the book is equally dedicated to enabling an ethnographic imagination of social life as it was lived by a specific handful of men in San'ya—however impossible it may be to put oneself in the subject position of someone else.

Here, my understanding of subjectivity and the "subject" draws largely on psychoanalytic theory and its postulate that sociality derives its normative force from the organization of lack or insufficiency. If a constitutive split did not separate us from our identification within a social and symbolic order, there would be neither desire nor an aspiration to overcome our insufficiencies by meeting the expectations of the sociality that constitutes our world. For men in San'ya, this would originally have entailed becoming self-sufficient caretakers of their families and children, but not only had they fallen short of this expectation. They had failed miserably, beyond the point of return, and herein lies the crux of my argument, because once your place within sociality has assumed the irrevocable and enduring character of utter abjection, you cannot but reference other social forms. It is either that or becoming stuck endlessly in shame, guilt, and self-recrimination. Having been denied even the organization of insufficiency that constituted you as a social being, you are, in fact, predisposed to being hailed into another sociality, as Akira had been when he was released from years in jail on a manslaughter conviction and was approached by the yakuza. This was also partly why San'ya had been so popular among NPOs, leftist labor unions, and religious organizations and also partly how I forged my relationship with the guys.

It cannot be emphasized enough, however, that the countersociality of San'ya had well and truly been contained and that this containment was the effect of a normative, statist gaze that forced undesirable elements beneath the threshold of public visibility. There was no escaping the shame of failed masculinity, save in San'ya, where the abandonment of families could be iterated as a successful assertion of masculinity. For this reason, the analytical categories I privilege are not those of a sovereign suspension of the law, abandonment to the vagaries of the market, or bare life but, rather, state recognition, commodification and absolute surplus extraction, and language. For language and desire persist in places that appear to have been reduced to bare life.[32] And there can be different subject positions or secondary organizations of lack within language, particularly so in places that have been expelled from general society.[33] Moreover, the violence that circulated in San'ya owed its source to the state, because much as San'ya was described as a "lawless zone" (*muhō chitai*), its circumscription was grounded in a dialectic of recognition in which residents and especially welfare recipients had no choice but to be recognized in accordance with municipal demands—a recognition that entailed a negation of every other aspect of his person.[34] As I hope to unpack, this recognition was a complicated thing, for while many men were undoubtedly ashamed and compliant on first seeking welfare or medical services, what they had to master over time was the mimicry of shameful need and, in so doing, to replace shame with shamelessness. In this way, they became witness to a doubling of their social personas so that their reputations within San'ya were refracted, in turn, as "acts" or "performances" (*engi*) that could nevertheless be imposed on their interlocutors for a moment of mutual recognition to arise.

Enacting outlaw codes of masculinity in face of economic and social depredation is by no means a Japanese phenomenon. Among others, Jason Pine, Elliot Liebow, and Philippe Bourgois have shown how the failure by stigmatized men to retain a dignified job may give rise to forms of sociality that confer "respect" where other means of recognition have been denied.[35] This book is also preceded by a tradition of urban ethnographies of Tokyo, especially of its *shitamachi* (low-city) district, of which San'ya forms a part, and it is preceded by academic work focusing on labor and gender beyond mainstream Japanese society.[36] But its theoretical scaffolding is poststructural and psychoanalytic, expanding on writings that have explored the nexus between fetishism, failure, repetition, and historical conditions that induce violence.[37] As such, the theory and subject matter of this book resonate with anthropological work on precarity and so-called neoliberal conditions of global labor.[38] The point of departure of this book, however, is not the insecurities of everyday life but the certainty of an early death. In the imminence of premature death, the book focuses on leftovers from Japan's "miraculous" economic recovery from World War II—day laborers—and it asks how one group of postwar day laborers sought to secure sociality and dignity under statist conditions that had written them out of history and consigned them to oblivion.[39] If anything, the book shows how the most precarious of acts— gambling, in many iterations—can create a sociality that divests state recognition of its power.[40] In his insatiable desire to expose himself to shock, harness experience, and create social values that transcended individual life, the day laborer I write of therefore emerges as a poet of modernity.[41] Insofar as the trope of gambling pervaded his everyday life, he created accountability in insecurity, dignity in abjection, and through the mutual recognition of his peers: the singular value of his person in a world that dictated his obsolescence.[42]

Much as this book focuses on a group of marginalized men in Japan, however, their values take part of a global configuration of patriarchy in late modern capitalism. In fact, misogyny was an intrinsic part of the drinking scene in San'ya, where Chinese waitresses could occasionally be fondled and where sexism converged with racism. I deal with this scene explicitly in chapter 4, in terms of Gayatri Chakravorty Spivak's critique that imperialist, patriarchal discourse legitimates itself by claiming to save racially different women from their male counterparts.[43] Moreover, while there was a modicum of hospitality toward sexual differences among the men that I worked with, the book concludes with an outburst of transphobic violence that was triggered by the appearance of a transgender person. As Susan Stryker has pointed out, the ambiguity of gender points up the constructed character of sexual difference, not to mention of sex itself, and in so doing, it threatens to unleash the normative violence of the social order.[44] Sexual difference was, indeed, constitutive of the masculinity that I describe, be it in bars with Chinese waitresses or at construction sites, but it is the performative character of this masculinity that this ethnography seeks to bring forth, both in its honorable, self-sacrificial aspects and in the violence that would maintain the boundaries of its identity.[45] It should be noted, however, that one of the most influential characters in this book was a woman. For as Miyazaki Manabu writes: "Beneath its macho exterior there is a matriarchal aspect to the yakuza world and maternal principles exert a powerful influence."[46] As the figure of authority in San'ya par excellence, her male partner, in turn, was impeccably faithful to her, and he himself might be witnessed bowing his head for and introducing a Chinese man to an employer, so as to secure them work. Indeed, "the guys" may have been close cousins to "the lads" of England, much as the

FIGURE I.2.   David Wojnarowicz, *Untitled (Falling Buffalos)*, 1988–89, gelatin silver print. Copyright David Wojnarowicz Estate. Courtesy of the David Wojnarowicz Estate and PPOW, New York.

gun-slinging cowboy might be identified as a counterpart to the knife-wielding otoko, but the possibilities raised by their ethos for hospitality should not be dismissed. Already expelled from upstanding society, this book attempts to give imaginative space to this ethos. Drawn from the universe of Japanese historical drama (*jidaigeki*), theater for the masses (*taishū engeki*), yakuza movies, karaoke (specifically, *enka*), and an abiding fantasy of the honorable outlaw mobster who sets aside capitalist self-interest, the specificity of San'ya resided in the trope of the otoko as a man who, by adhering to his sensibility of shame (*haji*), protected the weak and sacrificed himself for others.[47]

Nonetheless, in a social world that did, in fact, draw upon a genealogy of stereotyped forms of outlaw honor, it is difficult to escape the exoticizing and ghettoizing closure of Japanology and Japan, and it is for this reason that I turn to an image (figure I.2) that may appear to have everything to do with the United States and nothing to do with Japan but that, in my reading, has everything to do with San'ya. This untitled photograph by David Wojnarowicz depicts buffalo, suspended in a moment before their death, careening as they tumble over a cliff.

The photo captures as if in slow motion the nearly vertical progression of the buffalo, as the head of the first has entered the upper-left corner, the second lifts its legs above the precipice, the third charges down the cliff, head lowered and legs assembled beneath it for one last burst of energy, and the fourth floats pathetically in midair, upside down, freefalling toward death. If not also the plight of society at large and our contemporary universe, this black-and-white image metaphorizes the self-destructive conduct of individuals in the absence of proper medical care and social recognition, and in so doing, it acts as an indictment of the state and as a portrayal of the defiance that is the subject of this book.[48]

Chapter Outlines

Chapter 1, "Setting Out 'Yama,'" illuminates San'ya's place within the social imaginary of Japanese society. Set in 2011–2013, when the majority of this book takes place (except chapter 5 and the epilogue), it explicates a structural opposition between the world of active day laborers and the world of nonprofit organizations, where residents had to be docile to receive medical care. In sum, this introductory chapter delineates the structure of state recognition that confines San'ya's inhabitants to San'ya. But it also exposes their excessive lifestyles, which repelled this normative, statist gaze.

Chapter 2, "The Day Laborer," examines the day laborer in terms of his experience of time at the construction site, the materiality of this workday, and the violence of his commodification. The chapter describes subcontracting practices that precede work, detailing dynamics between the street-level subcontractor, the paucity of work, welfare recipients, and persons who relied entirely on construction work for their income. The chapter describes the 3K work—dirty, dangerous, and demeaning labor—demanded of laborers from San'ya, from digging holes next to a thirty-ton excavator to operating a concrete vibrator during cement work. Although the chapter demonstrates how physical power and technical expertise translated into the skill of an artisan (*shokunin*) within San'ya, where conversations undid the distinction between skilled and manual labor, it shows how San'ya's laborers were used to complete the most undesirable tasks. By focusing on the materiality of the day laborer's working day and its mediation by the wage, the chapter discloses how surplus extraction dictated that workers deaden themselves to interruptive material contingencies and that they repress the specter of inevitable accidents. Finally, the chapter explicates how, as the abstract measure of bodily expenditure, laborers depleted their energies under a capitalist temporality that was oriented toward the future in a future anterior mode in which the workday *will have* ended.[49]

Chapter 3, "Gambling," shows how the temporality of gambling supplemented that of the working day, doubling the death-inducing form of the subsistence wage with the dream of singular winnings, such that the form that robbed work of content—money—was transformed into the wish of acquiring an incommensurable value. By building on the distinction between labor and play as expenditure without production, the chapter shows how gambling sought to rejuvenate the body's nerves and, thereby, to reclaim the time lost to manual labor by transforming it into a "narcotic."[50] Compounded by the illegal character of gambling dens in San'ya, the chapter demonstrates how it was the near misses and intoxicating risks that propelled the gambler. Finally, it shows how group members held each other accountable for debts incurred through gambling, as creditors in San'ya considered the reliability of the group before lending to individuals. In sum, the chapter considers gambling as a solicitation for recognition—a solicitation that sought to master the abjection of San'ya by countering the death-inducing form of the subsistence wage and transmuting the modern passage of empty time into an experience of contingency that created debt and sociality.

Chapter 4, "Forbearance," begins with the circumstances of a manslaughter conviction that redirected the life of the book's primary character, Akira. By considering some of the wounds that led people to come to San'ya, the chapter links the stigma of San'ya to the state and to the shame of having failed as men and fathers. More importantly, the chapter describes how the containment of San'ya ensured that violence was made to circulate within San'ya rather than being returned to its source: the state. As such, the violence of physical altercations could assume an inexhaustible character, threatening to spill into an excess that embroiled everyone, and the chapter shows how, as in gambling, it was consideration for one's fellows that constrained excess. Forbearance had to be practiced in any form of conduct. As a dramatic enactment of masculinity, fighting referenced an honorable social code that predicated that an otoko constrain himself in consideration of the group. In San'ya, such consideration was emblematized in the senior figure of the group and his spouse, whose apartment provided a space of hospitality. The chapter concludes by considering this space of hospitality in distinction to a local nonprofit organization, where welfare recipients bowed their heads to receive food. The chapter thereby prefigures the moment when active day laborers had to set aside their dignity to go on welfare. In conclusion, it describes the physical and mental effects of Akira's misdiagnosis, which the nonprofit helped him receive: "schizophrenia."

Chapter 5, "Disintegration," tracks the individualizing effects of the labor market and, in so doing, considers San'ya as a space of accelerated obsolescence and death. The chapter revisits the group one year after I concluded fieldwork, in 2013, when construction work had gone scarce and when there were lingering resentments over debts and money. Nowhere was this more evident than in the collapse of the group's rotating savings and credit association, in which members met once every month, each contributing ¥10,000 ($100) to a pool that one person pocketed on a rotating basis. As a sign of the group's largesse, the association began to crumble when members found it too risky, believing that others would renege on their obligations. Slowly but ineluctably, the market violence of "every man for himself" crippled the social fabric of the group. In addition, as the chapter unpacks in the details of a trip to hospitals under the influence of delirium tremens, individuals eventually had to submit themselves to state welfare and, therefore, to give themselves to be recognized as docile recipients, in accordance with the demands of welfare officers, or state recognition. The chapter unpacks how fear of death forced active workers to accept their condition of dependence as welfare recipients, and it demonstrates how state recognition handed individuals into its power. Moreover, when welfare recipients grew older, it was common for the municipality to move them from bunkhouses into isolated apartments, sometimes far from San'ya. The chapter recounts how one member of the group died in such an apartment. Having considered San'ya in relation to state welfare, illness, hospitals, death, and the violence of state recognition, the chapter concludes with the missed funeral of a San'ya resident and volunteer at the nonprofit organization.

The epilogue offers a lyrical conclusion to the book, as it takes the reader back to Miyako, the hometown of Akira, where he visited his mother's tomb for the first time, in 2015. The chapter reflects on the regrets of a lifetime lived in adherence to a transgressive masculinity, as everyone had become increasingly weak, and it attends to two key moments in which the heteronormative masculinity of San'ya was undone. The first moment was a transphobic assault on a crossdressing person who had ventured into the Iroha arcade. I consider this incident with reference to the writings of Susan Stryker and Sandy Stone, as an attempt to preserve a "pure" gender identity.[51] The second moment was Akira's suicide attempt by disembowelment.

Fieldwork or the Force of Coincidence

My time in San'ya began volunteering at a decades-old NPO, Sanyukai, located in the heart of the area. While the staff was aware of my purpose in San'ya, I entered its world as a volunteer who made *omusubi* (rice balls) and *bentō* (lunchboxes) three mornings every week and, in the afternoons, handed them out to homeless people along the Sumida River, which flanks San'ya to the east.[52] Most of my time was spent in the kitchen, by the Sumida River, and outside the NPO, where mainly middle-aged men sat on benches smoking and waiting for the free lunch that was given upstairs. It was thus in the narrow passageway outside the NPO that I was able to overhear stories unrelated to the NPO, albeit altogether related to San'ya, and it was there that I met Akira Norio, a veteran of San'ya and volunteer whose health had forced him to quit construction work and go on welfare. A treasure trove of lived experience and knowledge of San'ya, Akira had an extraordinary ability to converse with just about anyone, from the local yakuza to destitute homeless people, and it was through Akira that I was able to connect with the remaining day laborers of San'ya. Thus, I started witnessing workers when they came back from construction sites; however, it was only when I went to work with the group that I ceased to be just a novel fixture in their evening life and realized that they were no longer filching drinks off me. The period of total immersion in this life—working four days per week, waking at six or earlier, coming back at six or later, and then drinking, gambling, eating, sleeping (sometimes all in the same room), and waking, only to work more—continued for six months and a little less regularly for another six months thereafter.

It could be said that the writing of this ethnography itself arises out of the coincidence of a fateful encounter at the interface between Sanyukai and its men outside, where the containment of San'ya was abrogated. There, on the raggedy tatami floors of the NPO, volunteers from without San'ya would gather every Wednesday and Thursday for snacks, juice, tea, and coffee with the local men after an afternoon of food handouts, and it was at these meetings that Akira—a self-professed *pūtarō*, drifter, vagabond, or vagrant—would elicit the laughter of all and sundry, as if he were a professional jester in their midst. For as the famous mobster-turned-actor Andō Noboru has noted, there is an affinity between the yakuza (mobster) and *yakusha* (actor). Thus, Akira remained silent as staff cashed in on the joke, sometimes slapping Akira's head from behind, while shouting, "You're stupid, stupid!"—that is, until they learned that he had been diagnosed with a brain tumor. Over time, it would be Akira's refusal to remain in place at the NPO that ensured his "expulsion." But it was his refusal to observe propriety in yet another sphere, namely, that of the construction workers, that enabled my entry on the scene, because by bowing his head for me—a contemptible "researcher"—he staked and imposed himself on the others. Backed by his resolute inflexibility, the source of this ethnography resides in that act.

A demolition worker, right-wing emperorist, and professional extortionist in his past, Akira embodied a conduct that has been described by Benjamin: "The destructive character knows only one watchword: make room."[53] Consigned to tumble and freewheel toward death, this destructive impulse would ultimately be subverted into strife, self-destruction, and right-wing politics among most of the characters in this book, and thus, the power of state discourse would carry the day. But in the excesses of their demand for recognition, the troupe transmitted an urge that would have poisoned the smothering propriety that accomplished their social expulsion and death. Like San'ya, they were doomed to begin with, but therein arose the urgency of one last gamble, and that is their gift.

SETTING OUT "YAMA"

San'ya, the old day-laborer district of Tokyo, or Yama, as veterans of San'ya call it, has long since passed its heyday as the hub for construction workers servicing the central metropolis and its environs.[1] Accounts vary from person to person regarding when work started to grow scarce in the area: five years, ten years, fifteen years, twenty years ago—but the story everyone tells is one of excess. There was once so much work and so many workers that the main thoroughfare of San'ya, Namidabashi (which translates as the "bridge of tears"), was blocked every morning by throngs of street-level labor brokers and laborers. Between six and eight, from Monday to Saturday, the five-hundred-meter stretch of Namidabashi was so packed with workers, brokers, and their minivans that cars could not pass through. In fact, there was such an excess of work available that you could take your pick by going from broker to broker, asking about the work and wages, and settling on your preference.[2] Such was the surfeit of work and workers that even drunkards sleeping on the sidewalk would be hauled into the backs of minivans by brokers seeking to fill their quota of workers for the day and thereby to maximize their cut of workers' wages. Likewise, the daily wage was an exorbitant amount of money. It was not unusual for a scaffolder to earn the equivalent of two thousand dollars in less than one week. But upon returning from the construction site where the scaffolder had passed the nights in a sleeping bag hoisted high on a skyscraper, the entirety of those wages would be squandered on food, liquor, women, or gambling in a display of camaraderie and generosity as superabundant as the labor market from which his wages had originated. Indeed, after these expenditures, it was quite common for men to incur debts to local eateries or to their friends.[3]

The cycle of work (*shigoto*) and play (*asobi*), of monetary accumulation, bankruptcy, and dependence on others, was thus perpetuated and repeated. In the mythic San'ya of old, laborers disposed of money, reaped from the exhaustion of their bodies, with a recklessness that seemed to signify inexhaustible funds, squandering it to the point of indebtedness through activities that were as destructive as the labor from which it was obtained. But while the high-rise buildings and fancy apartment blocks of Tokyo remain standing, San'ya and the men of San'ya have been reduced to dilapidation, age, and illness. Today, practically every *doya* (bunkhouse) expressly built to house laborers in San'ya is fully occupied, and these bunkhouses continue to line San'ya's backstreets, called the *doyagai*.[4] The famous Palace Hotel stills stands along Namidabashi, and countless small bunkhouses with their characteristic horizontal, rectangular window slats, two per floor (one for the top bunk, one for the bottom), can still be found lining its backstreets.[5] But many of the bunkhouses, particularly those flanking the main thoroughfare of Namidabashi, have been converted into cheap, shiny hotels catering to tourists and businessmen. Meanwhile, in the back alleys, the aging tenants of the old bunkhouses no longer do construction work to earn their livelihood but are mainly on state welfare. Akira, a San'ya veteran whom I met volunteering at an NPO, says that at least one person passes away every day in San'ya. Indeed, ambulances are a common sight in San'ya's backstreets, as are drunken bodies passed out on the cement amid garbage and the smell of piss. In fact, in 2012 the five-hundred-meter stretch of Namidabashi is empty between the hours of six and eight. If anyone can be seen going to work, it is but a few solitary figures, seeming stragglers, heading toward Minami-Senjū train station between seven and eight. They would be inconspicuous and unidentifiable, if it were not for their stuffed backpacks, loaded with a workman's tools, or their standard-issue work clothes. The only other figures to be seen in the early morning on Namidabashi are a small crowd of middle-aged men sitting on chairs spread out in front of a cheap, open-air sushi bar, drinking from pint glasses of shochu mixed with green tea or water and ice. On the corner of Namidabashi and a narrow side road, the sushi bar only opens in the early mornings, rotating its hours with the next-door, hole-in-the-wall dive bar run by Mutō, to which customers return in the evening to drink and gamble on boat races screened on a small TV, standing on a shelf in the upper left corner of the boxlike, all-but-bare-necessities bar counter.

San'ya has acquired the reputation of that place where backpackers on a shoestring stay or where good-for-nothings on welfare blow away public funds on liquor and gambling, and with the strained national economy, the negative image of San'ya has only been compounded in recent years by mass-mediated incidents of people abusing the welfare system to their advantage.[6] During the two years I lived in Hashiba, adjacent to San'ya, I was reminded countless times by friends, family, and others outside San'ya of what kind of environment and what type of person is encountered in San'ya. One person simply winced when I said I was living close to Minami-Senjū Station. A friend could not divorce San'ya from the image of being "dangerous" and insisted that she would "absolutely not go," adding that the situation of men in San'ya was "their own fault": a burden to society and others who work to support themselves. Making objects of the men in San'ya, one psychologist I met observed that their habits of drinking and gambling exhibited the pathological characteristics of "addiction." But the most virulent of all preconceptions was expressed by individuals who had never been to San'ya or, for that matter, to its counterparts of Nishinariku or Kotobukichō in Osaka and Yokohama—namely, that San'ya had simply become a place where foreign backpackers come to sleep, as if "Yama," which did not exist to begin with, had been wiped off the map and out of history.

Whether consciously or not, such reactions suggest that San'ya has been disavowed in the Japanese imaginary and that it is inextricably linked to practices and signifiers long ago relegated to the margins of modern Japan. Indeed, San'ya is located in a marginal section of the premodern "low-city" (shitamachi), where the "commoners" (shomin) of the Edo period once lived. A little more knowledge of the area reveals that Minami-Senjū Station stands next to a former execution ground and that San'ya is flanked to the southwest by Yoshiwara, the largest red-light district of the Kantō region, and to the south by Imado, a neighborhood associated with the Buraku minority, considered outcastes during Japan's feudal period.[7] Not surprisingly, the day-laborer district of the modern construction industry is located next door to the center of Tokyo's sex industry, and while discrimination against Buraku people continues to inform decisions regarding employability and marriageability, San'ya has become a space of the unsanitary, of the dying, and of the dead, whom it was once the role of Buraku to dispose of.[8]

Yet each of the above preconceptions is true to a certain degree. San'ya can be dangerous since men fight in San'ya; on occasion there are stabbings and, at least once per year, a murder of or by an acquaintance.[9] Likewise, the San'ya man can be found drinking from five in the morning, sometimes to the point of death, and gambling when the chance presents itself. What accounts for the necessity of such reactions, however, and no doubt also the joy of the psychologist working in San'ya, is the normative violence by which the social requires and establishes itself vis-à-vis that which it is not. Hence, one need not have been to San'ya in order to judge it: one must merely know what it stands for, the associations it triggers, and its impropriety. Complicit with the medical and the political, an economic principle dictates the separation and confinement of certain types of individuals to San'ya, be they the criminal, the disabled, the psychotic, the terminally ill, the addicted, the unemployable, and other figures marginal to modern Japan, like the Buraku, the Okinawan, the Chinese, or the Korean.[10]

In an uncanny reversal, however, San'ya reveals itself as a mirror image of general society otherwise hidden.[11] For in the containment of economically unprofitable elements of general society, these same elements have been recycled in a way that has accelerated the death of these human elements, as they are set to work at the most menially demanding labor, in a confinement that limits expenditures to the momentary consumption of liquor and the practices of gambling. San'ya gives the lie to general society, because when a man in San'ya is called "unusable" (tsukaenai), no one makes a secret of the fact that he may be or is dying, which many men were, and this is what is most unsettling about the associations it calls forth: it discloses the truth of capitalist Japan and the violence with which this truth is repressed. In fact, during the heyday of the 1980s bubble economy, it was the smell of San'ya that triggered immediate repugnance, of urine and feces in the gutters and of piles of uncollected garbage.[12] To act as if places like San'ya do not exist, or as Akira phrases it, "to put a lid on what stinks" (kusai mono ni futa o), is to instantiate the social structure that consigns San'ya to oblivion and death. Every veteran of San'ya knows that the murders and deaths that happen in San'ya are not reported in the mass media. It used to be that the bodies of deceased men in San'ya, anonymous in the official registry and with no kin to claim them, were appropriated by hospitals for experimentation, only to end up as skeleton specimens in university classrooms.[13] In this way, the human costs of Japan's postwar economic recovery have been swept under the carpet.

Today, now that the chapter seems to be closing on San'ya, it would constitute no less of an injustice to claim that its story is finished. For the social structure that consigns San'ya to death is alive and well in this claim, and the reality that faces San'ya now is none other than the catastrophic aftereffects of untrammeled commodification and of the excessive lifestyles of men with nothing to lose but their dignity.

On the Other Side of the Bridge of Tears

No doubt, the men in San'ya have grown circumspect in their spendings after their primary source of income, construction work, all but vanished. But the old sign warning drivers to beware of drunk men sleeping on the street still stands, slightly askew, by the corner of Namidabashi and Meiji-dōri road. The entryway to the Iroha arcade (figure 1.1), between the old liquor store called Nodaya and

FIGURE 1.1.   The entryway to the Iroha arcade, San'ya's main thoroughfare.

the once-militant union for day laborers and homeless people, Sōgidan, is littered with one-cup sake cans and liquor bottles spewing out of temporary aluminum trash cans alongside piles of garbage.[14] Here and there, someone is passed out drunk, like a dead, stray body enveloped by the smell of piss rising from the street. From almost five in the morning until late evening, a small crowd can be found drinking there, its members switching in and out as the day progresses.

Just a few meters inside the canopy that covers the Iroha arcade, a two-by-two-meter mat has been placed in front of one of the many shuttered stores. Kept in place by red traffic cones when nobody is there, the cardboard mat marks the spot where Gīn runs his gambling joint. In the afternoons and early evenings, four to five figures huddle silently over a deck of *hanafuda* (flower cards) spread out on the mat as they divine the winning eight or nine, in plain sight of police cars that silently circulate the streets.[15] Gīn, a diminutive person dressed in tweed pants, collared shirt, and his signature Scottish touring cap, reputedly also runs the distribution of drugs in San'ya, consisting primarily of injected meth. For whatever reason, his hands are always covered in Band-Aids and sores.

Beside Gīn often sits Yamamori, a man who shows that he has been in the yakuza for years by allowing his traditional, elbow-length tattoos to emerge from below the sleeves of his T-shirt, and if there is any doubt, the scar of a knife wound across his cheek reinforces this image.[16] Indeed, the silent gesture of slashing a forefinger across the right cheek, accompanied only by the word "this," is used to signify the yakuza in San'ya, for while many are very well acquainted with yakuza, if not actual or past members of the mob, the word *yakuza* is not lightly spoken but merely indicated by this gesture. An incorrigible gambler, always upping the stakes, and a bad boy of intimidation and vulgar ostentation, Yamamori also makes a show of his money. Having won repeatedly at the races, Yamamori would sport a wallet stuffed with ¥10,000 bills (approximately $100) so that the wallet was brimming with a wad two to three centimeters thick. Of course, only a few weeks later, the bills were no longer in his wallet since, as he matter-of-factly said, they had been put in his savings account. Moreover, Yamamori was rather careful in his use of cash, saving his public spending for moments in which everyone could witness his lavishness. He thereby went counter to the spontaneous spectacles of generosity still to be seen on Sundays: when the main horse races are screened, winners helplessly announcing their winnings, followed by cash gifts and expenditures that frequently leave winners penniless by the end of the day. Yamamori seemed to seize every opportunity to use his "outlaw" (*autorō*) appearance and manner, sometimes purely for the fun of it, by intimidating outsiders to San'ya. When during the course of a taxi ride with Yamamori and two others the taxi driver expressed uncertainty regarding where we wished to go, Yamamori took the opportunity to harangue the driver with a string of invectives lasting the entirety of our ten-minute journey: "You don't know where it is? It's on your fucking tab then! I'll fucking kill you, you hear!?" Meanwhile, the two others told the taxi driver where to go, tiredly remarking to Yamamori to "let it rest," and when we finally got out, Yamamori himself paid the fare from his bulging wallet. In the tram ride afterward, he made such a loud mockery of our group that oncoming passengers scurried past for the end of the compartment. Nor, for that matter, did Yamamori's intimidation tactics merely amount to the empty tantrums of an adolescent fifty-year-old. The threat of physical violence that they implied was real. One time, an older woman had to restrain him with the plaintive words "You'll kill him," as he persisted in beating an already blood-bespattered and unconscious man.

Yamamori was a former yakuza, and through his connection with Gīn, he surely felt connected to and therefore entitled by the local yakuza organization (the Kanamachi-ikka), yet the arrogant behavior he exhibited was precisely the kind that could land him in serious trouble with prominent figures in San'ya. In fact, it had "been agreed in advance" that Yamamori, a so-called member of Matsuda's "group," would not "lay a hand" on Kentarō or Rikiishi of the so-called Okinawa-gang (Okinawagumi).[17] On several occasions, it had been the very abuse of iconography associated with the yakuza that had triggered Rikiishi or

Kentarō to go on a rampage, putting the other party in place by beating the hell out of them. Coupled with a haughty attitude, the revelation of traditional body tattoos could prompt rage and, possibly, long-term hospitalization, not to mention the ousting of an adversary from San'ya, for it was not simply that Rikiishi or Kentarō could not tolerate the puffed-up entitlement that accompanied traditional tattoos. The abuse of yakuza iconography stained values of justice, self-sacrifice, and hospitality that they associated with a vanishing underworld and therefore necessitated that they reestablish the proper order of things.

Yamamori's style of vulgar ostentation must be counterposed to another type of self-conduct to which deference was accorded in San'ya. This opposing term can be located in the senior figures of the Okinawa-gang, Takeda-san, and his partner, "Nē-san" (older sister), as everybody addressed her. Like Yamamori, Takeda-san had once been a member of the yakuza, but he did not flaunt it. Though it was difficult for Takeda-san to dissimulate the fact that he was once in the mob—since he was missing three fingers, two from above the middle joint and one from below it, indicating that they were cut no less than five times—I spent almost an entire year working with him, moving in and out of changing rooms, without once noticing (as someone later pointed out to me) that Takeda-san's body was covered in tattoos. No matter how hot it was, Takeda-san always wore a white, cotton, long-sleeved shirt thick enough to conceal his tattoos, and it was only from intimate friends that one learned that Takeda-san had been lieutenant (*kashira*) for an eminent yakuza leader from his hometown of Fukuoka, known by anyone with the slightest knowledge of the yakuza, and that Takeda-san was on the list of individuals against whom the local yakuza (again, the Kanamachi-ikka) was not permitted to raise a hand. Contrary to common lore that members of the mob cut their fingers over contraventions that they themselves had committed, it was said that Takeda-san had lost his fingers to take the blame for those working under him. In Akira's words, this made Takeda-san an "incredible person." Takeda-san and Nē-san were thus recognized for their effortless tact, elegance, discretion, and the humility with which they interacted with everyone, showing the same modesty and deference regardless of social difference. Combined with the aura of Takeda-san's past, the everyday conduct of Takeda-san and Nē-san operated as cause of the esteem with which they were regarded. Takeda-san and Nē-san took care of everyone, inviting them home for endless meals and drinking. They were present when someone was put in jail and always exhibited consideration, such that it was said that "everyone is indebted to" them. One word from Takeda-san, who had himself made a practice of the dictum that nothing is more important than one's buddies (*nakama*), and potential schisms within the group were resolved.[18] Even other senior members, like Kentarō, a burly, fifty-seven-year-old, no-nonsense worker who ensured the availability of work for everyone through his presence at the construction site, would set aside differences and make peace, if so asked by Takeda-san.[19]

In their power to resolve constitutive and seemingly insuperable tensions between factions and individuals, Takeda-san and Nē-san occupied a mythic place in the atomized social world of Yama. In the absence of Takeda-san and Nē-san, social relations in the Okinawa-gang might well have split and devolved on the economic principle of every man for himself, devoid of hierarchy, deference, generosity, and buddies. Contrary to Yamamori forcibly pulling rank for his own purposes and abusing the iconography of the yakuza world, Takeda-san actualized a principle of selflessness in the name of the individuals he cared for and for those to whom he held social obligations. Like the Caduveo face painting of which Claude Lévi-Strauss writes in *Tristes Tropiques*, Takeda-san and Nē-san embodied symbols of sociality par excellence, and the respect accorded to them actualized the dream of individuals searching for social institutions they might have, if the individualizing violence of the market did not obstruct their formation at every turn.[20] In San'ya, it was the principle of masculine sociality itself that was sought so that the quality of person, status, and history were repeatedly emphasized in an insistent and pervasive reversal of the individualizing labor market, which reduced men to the quantitative value of their wage and imposed an objective condition of existence that compelled them to sell their labor as segregated units. Perhaps the disruptive and individualizing violence of the labor market could not be resolved, but it could certainly be concealed with a dream of sociality, hospitality, and self-sacrifice for the weak, which was, indeed, inscribed on Takeda-san's body in the condensed form of his missing fingers and his hidden traditional tattoos, the power of which would only be revealed and wielded in the name of justice and sociality. For this reason, much as Takeda-san formed a counterpoint to the loud and self-centered Yamamori, and much as Takeda-san was loosely a "member" of the Okinawa-gang, his figure transcended exclusive affiliation. It was common practice for Nē-san and him to invite all and sundry home, thence unifying the Okinawa-gang with the Matsuda-group and, in the embrace of hospitality, imposing peace on individual tensions.

Such gatherings, however, were almost exclusively composed of men. While the absence of romantic engagements made it appear that there were no women the guys would have brought along anyway, one day Takeda-san himself stated the gendered basis of these gatherings. When Suzuki, the only worker with romantic successes, suggested that he bring his girlfriend along to introduce her to me, Takeda-san dismissed the suggestion, asking rhetorically why Suzuki would bring his girlfriend to a gathering "of otoko." An exception was made to this rule when my foreign partner was invited home. She and I wined and dined with the group, and Takeda-san paid exceptional hospitality to her, ignoring my presence beside her. But it was Nē-san's presence in the adjacent room and kitchen that established Takeda-san's eminently self-effacing authority.[21] While her social position among the guys must be distinguished from that of the female proprietors of the snack bars and eateries they frequented in the evenings, the attentions of these women was necessary to affirm the trope of the otoko.[22] Takeda-san was deferential and respectful to everyone, regardless of gender, but the hospitality of an otoko was grounded in sexual difference.

It was these visible practices and the deference with which Takeda-san treated everyone, be it the owner of an eatery or the homeless people in Iroha, all of whom knew Takeda-san, that earned him the praise, given behind his back and never in his presence, of being a "man's man" (otoko no otoko). It was not simply the trope of the otoko but of embodying the vanishing values of a specific world of men—namely, those of old-style yakuza—that earned Takeda-san his respect, bestowing him with that inescapable aura that attached to his person no matter where he went. On this note, it was common for men in San'ya to describe their relations in yakuza terms: shatei, meaning "younger brother" or "underling," and aniki, meaning "blood brother" or, more literally, "older brother."[23] When I asked Kentarō why, aside from daily conduct, such high esteem was given to Takeda-san, his response was brief to the point of being hasty, as if he did not want to be caught in an indiscretion. First, he recounted the circumstances under which he had met Takeda-san. More than a decade ago, Rikiishi, an underling to Takeda-san, had challenged Kentarō to a fight: "You wanna take me on?!" It was Takeda-san who put a stop to this by interjecting his body between the two, insisting that Kentarō was the senior figure and that Rikiishi back down. Second, Kentarō made direct reference to Takeda-san's former life in the mob by stating that Takeda-san "knows everything about such things," that is, concerning the intricacy of hierarchy in the mob world. It was no coincidence that Takeda-san, guarantor of sociality and honor in the "lawless zone" of San'ya, embodied in practice the knowledge that was ascribed to his mythic past. The trope of the otoko reinstated sociality where it was lacking, but it also threatened to undo the propriety of "general society" by exceeding the negativity and shame that confined San'ya to San'ya.

The normative force of acting like an upstanding otoko rendered the lives of the old-guard San'ya man and almost any active construction worker antithetical to the philanthropic mission of nonprofit organizations operating in San'ya. Indeed, the very notion that men in San'ya need help could not run more counter to the "self-reliance" (jiritsu) predicated by the idealized otoko, and for those on welfare, the contradiction of asserting masculine independence consisted in their dependence on the state. But it was precisely this dependence that was relegated to the outside of Yama in the performance and assertion of masculine self-reliance. By the same token, the once-powerful labor union for day laborers and homeless people, Sōgidan, had acquired the trappings of asinine ideological interests that could not be further from the imperative of looking after oneself and one's group: prancing down Namidabashi every Friday morning with a red flag and speakerphone, preaching the renunciation of war and liberation for workers across the world. Participating in a demonstration or lining up for food handouts (*takidashi*) fell outside the purview of men even remotely affiliated with the workers of the Okinawa-gang or Matsuda-group.[24] Takeda-san was not even aware that the oldest nonprofit organization in San'ya, Sanyukai, operated a medical clinic offering free services. His lack of basic knowledge testified to the split between the adjacent worlds of the active construction worker and of Sanyukai, hidden in an alleyway only one hundred meters from Mutō's hole-in-the-wall, where the guys drank.

But a medical clinic offering free services would have served the needs of no one more so than the active construction worker. Along with the homeless men and women, although primarily men in blue tents along the Sumida River, individuals without recourse to welfare or health insurance were most likely to be found among the active construction laborers of San'ya. At least a quarter of the active workers I became close to were receiving welfare, including Takeda-san, Shōkawa (both sixty), Saruma, or Akira (in their midfifties), none of whom declared their income and, thus, were illegally supplementing their meager welfare (approximately ¥100,000 per month, or $1,000) and running the risk, if found out, of losing this support altogether.[25] The latter prospect was dire, as it would most certainly leave some on the streets and others working excessively with a sick body, which was bound to shut down. Notably, no one expressed shame over receiving welfare except Akira while he was at Sanyukai, who had a brain tumor and was strictly forbidden by doctors to do manual labor (other people's tax money, Akira said); the others appeared to echo Kentarō's explicit principle that "you take what you can get," because it would have been well-nigh impossible for the worker in his fifties or sixties to earn a living at manual labor, given the scarcity of work and the fact that many of the guys were ill. Others, like Rikiishi, Norihisa, Maku (in his seventies), Kentarō, and Matsui, were all registered for "out-of-work aid" (*abure teate*), which was designed specifically to sustain the livelihood of day laborers, and received a maximum of ¥50,000 per month ($500), provided that they worked.[26] Then there was Suzuki and Matsuda, the respective *tehaishi*, or street-level labor brokers, for the Okinawa-gang and Matsuda-group, who were each said to earn as much as ¥500,000 ($5,000) every month simply by doing the work of *tehai*, that is, of brokering labor at the last interface between employers and laborers.[27] And then there were people like Tetsu, who lived in a tent by the river; Sawamiya, who traveled between San'ya and Nishinariku in Osaka, depending on work availability, and faked the loss of his ticket upon arrival (by explaining to station staff that he had traveled from the closest station, the trip could be made for ¥150, about $1.50); Riku, who refused to seek any help from the state and, to everyone's surprise, decided to cut off state aid when it turned out he didn't have cancer; the twenty-eight-year-old Wakami, who earned his living flat out, working five days every week, and who spent the rest of his time at slot machines; the two who worked for the subcontractor company, Tenjima, for ridiculously cheap wages, having gone into debt to the yakuza and were housed in a dorm (*ryō*) or the confinement of a *takobeya* (literally translated as an "octopus room") while they worked off their debt; and the countless other nameless figures, oftentimes picked off the street or the environs of Minami-Senjū Station by Matsuda, who would use them as convenience demanded, slashing half their wages in the process.[28] Except for those indebted to the mob or those running from the law, it was entirely possible to work the system to earn welfare benefits or, for Wakami, to get out-of-work aid. Yet Sawamiya, like many others, did not wish to have his whereabouts known to his family in Okinawa, and the first thing the ward office would do was to contact his next of kin. As for Wakami, he could not have been bothered to register himself for out-of-work aid, although even he, after two years, was feeling the toil of working every day. At some point, the inevitable was bound to happen: injury at work, for which construction companies were most unlikely to compensate workers, particularly day laborers.

Sanyukai

People would start gathering in the narrow, twenty-five-meter back alley that flanked the entryway to Sanyukai at ten every morning, slowly amassing over the next two hours as they stood or sat on white plastic benches lining the alley, until lunch was served on the second floor at noon. Almost without exception, this amorphous gathering of people comprised men in their fifties and above, although, on occasion, and later toward noon, someone younger in their thirties or twenties might appear. And sometimes Yasuko, who lived in a tent in the nearby Tamahime Park, made her way out to the benches, asked for tea from the reception area at the top of the five stairs leading up to the entry, and sat back down to chat loudly and indiscreetly about whatever she wanted; she had an unmistakable presence with a nasal voice and bulging layers of homeless clothing. Otherwise, it was rare, indeed, to see any women at Sanyukai, and if they did come, it was for an appointment with the doctor that day, after which they promptly left. Apart from that, it was in the company of a man, like the homeless, tanned, meek woman with glasses who seemed to push her bearded father around in a wheelchair all day, sleeping in the streets of Asakusa at night.[29] Not once during the year and a half I volunteered at Sanyukai did I see anyone but the regular crowd of men go up to the second floor to eat. Thus, the crowd of men outside sat and waited for lunch. Some would smoke, dropping ash in the aluminum ashtrays interspersed beneath the benches, while others engaged in inconsequential conversations. Favorite topics included the latest news, the weather, sports, and perhaps even—although the subject of gambling was consciously avoided—the latest horse races. The generic character was that of a man in his midfifties, dressed in grayish pants, a plain collared shirt with an equally plain vest or jacket in winter, and low-budget, black plastic shoes or jogging gear. Most often, this figure would be silently hunched over on the benches, alone. Given the signal for lunch, he would walk upstairs, eat without uttering a word, maybe even bow in passing to the staff downstairs, and head home. At one o'clock, when the Sanyukai kitchen stopped serving lunch, the alley outside would often be empty.

A clear hierarchy structured the provision of meals because it was none other than the head of Sanyukai, a stocky European man with decades of experience working in San'ya as a Catholic philanthropist, Guy-san, who decided and indicated whether someone would be given a meal. Once lunch had been prepared upstairs, he would do so by walking the alley and signaling to individuals with his index finger, most often calling them by their name, to go eat. Because the tatami room upstairs only seated twelve, six at each table, only twelve men could go up at a time, and Guy-san would have to repeat this process of signaling individuals to go up. The tatami dining room always had a small TV switched on, usually to the NHK news (Japan's largest public broadcaster), during lunchtime. Its walls were decorated with posters and photos of Sanyukai's past activities, some Christian missionary artwork, colored pencil drawings of children's anime figures by Kawaii (one of the men outside who professed to being mistaken for a woman), and collections of four-leaf clovers collected by Aokan, who lived in a tent by the Sumida River and claimed that trillions, literally trillions, of ants paraded through his tent in summer. One wall of the dining room was stacked waist high with donated rice bags, many from Fukushima; another led to the staircase up- and downstairs and would become so crammed with shoes that there was hardly space to walk. Last, there was a toilet adjacent to the dining room, a small closet, and a doorway and counter opening onto the two-by-five-meter kitchen where the cooks, almost all women, would stand and chat after serving lunch. When one group had finished eating, which for some regulars involved thanking and flirting with the cooks when giving back the dirty plates, the next round was sent up to eat, often clashing with down-coming traffic on the narrow staircase. Finally, Guy-san would go up to eat and sit at a table surrounded by the regulars he appeared closest to—called the "Guy-san group" by the kitchen staff—which invariably included Izumo, Numaja, Amai, and Akira. Those who could not make it up the stairs either because they were in a wheelchair or were truly "homeless" and were not asked up, ostensibly for hygienic reasons, were given lunch boxes to take with them. It rarely happened that there was not enough food to go around, since the number of people outside would rise and fall with the time of the month, enabling the staff to anticipate how many meals would be needed. In the mornings, Guy-san would give the kitchen staff a number that varied from twenty to thirty at the beginning of the month to sixty or so at the end of the month, when welfare allowances had all but run out.

This daily gathering of men outside Sanyukai produced a spectacle of need and, in so doing, confirmed the necessity of the service Sanyukai provided. The kitchen kept track of the number of individuals who came to eat every day, commenting as they wrote the numbers down on the fridge calendar that there "were not so many" or "a lot" on that day. Likewise, the rare occasions when there were so many people that Guy-san had to lower his head and turn the last away became the subject of much gossip. But with the exception of the one or two homeless persons who came to eat, almost all the people waiting outside were receiving welfare, and the same went for the people who frequented the clinic. As the Sanyukai staff confessed in interviews, at least 80 percent of the individuals who regularly came to Sanyukai were already welfare recipients. It should also be added that, with the occasional exception of Akira, virtually none of these men were active construction workers, who constituted a separate social formation on the other side of San'ya. In other words, everyone who ate lunch at Sanyukai (many of them daily) were receiving a monthly allowance of approximately ¥100,000 ($1,000) and, as welfare recipients, already had access to medical care from hospitals and doctors, gratis. For these men, Sanyukai provided additional aid in getting through the month by easing the constraints of welfare.

In an online Sanyukai blog entitled "Daily Events," it is regarding these men that a long-term staff member declaims on the mission and everyday task that faces the staff: "What can we ourselves do for the person, right in front of us now, 'with difficulty' in some aspect? What can we do for this person that will be 'most for their own good'? While listening to their talk one by one, we ourselves respond through trial and error."[30] What enables this line of inquiry, materialized by the threshold at the top of the five stairs leading up into the Sanyukai entryway and the knee-high table from behind which a staff member serves tea, to the right of which the enclosed clinic was located behind yet another partition, is the division of "we" or "us" (*watashi tachi*) from "this person" (*kono hito*). Hence, from inside the back alleys of San'ya, Sanyukai instantiates the structural division that confines San'ya to San'ya, and what is at stake in this "consultation" work is the place of Sanyukai itself, grounded in the ostensible coincidence between an individual in need or "with difficulty" (*komatteiru*) and what the NPO can "do for" (*shiteageru*) this person. Notably, the direction of "doing for" is as unidirectional and downward as the act of serving tea. Gifting functions, above all, to confirm the place of Sanyukai staff as providers of that which the men outside desire. Sanyukai desires to be desired.[31] But this question—what does the other want from me?—is posed from both sides. Even before the individual ascends the steps to Sanyukai, they know the institution will ask—"What can we ourselves do?"—and to make their visit a success, they have internalized this question, so that they can give the institution what it wants from them. In short, the man from San'ya knows that he must be able to answer properly, that is, to be recognized in accordance with Sanyukai's demands, which is to say that he must confirm that Sanyukai is needed by confessing that it can give him what he needs. As a lacking individual "with difficulty," he is interpellated into a structure of desire in which he is "right in front of" an institution that designates itself in terms of the collective "we." This is the structure of shame, and thence the Sanyukai staff member continues: "It's not just people who come for the clinic; people who somehow want to get off the street and return to a normal lifestyle come over and over for consultation."[32] Individuals not only come to Sanyukai when they need medical services: they come and they come "over and over," desiring the "normal lifestyle" (*futsū no seikatsu*) that Sanyukai can provide. Notwithstanding that many homeless people did want to get off the streets, whether or not they desired the return to a "normal lifestyle," replete with work, family, bills, and the alienation of a one-bedroom apartment, was rather questionable. In fact, the homeless people by the Sumida River had already turned down an offer made by Sumida and Taitō Wards, in an effort to clean the river area, to move into apartments.[33] Aokan seemed quite content with his trillions of ants every summer, showing his face at Sanyukai every few weeks, watering his many plants, and walking the stretch between Tamahime Park and his blue tent, laden with water bottles. As for Tetsu, the scaffolder who also lived in a tent by the river, he was clearly saving money to repay his debts, although he was later diagnosed with cancer, as other homeless people before him had been, refusing to seek help until it was too late. Nevertheless, the general desire was ascribed to these "homeless" of wanting to return to a "normal lifestyle," and the "consultation" by Sanyukai emerged as the site at which lack was produced, internalized, and individualized through a process of "listening" that uncovered the preexisting needs of the individual.

More often than not, however, what the Sanyukai staff encountered was a mimesis of the desire to be "normal" (*futsū*), since proximity to the institution came with its benefits. Whether the men outside truly needed the meal upstairs or not, Sanyukai staff themselves postulated that many were pretending. On the one hand, Sanyukai could not do enough to be desired by a group of men who were already receiving welfare and had recourse to aid from other NPOs, and on the other, the men outside had to perform their desire before an institution that doubted them. Their state of lack or of being "with difficulty" demanded an impossible confirmation that would give necessity to the existence of Sanyukai.

The spectacle of the crowd gathered outside Sanyukai thus served a dual purpose. Because showing up on the dot at noon and expecting to receive food would have been outright shameless, the men gave themselves to be seen waiting two hours, and in doing this, they invested a proper amount of time in a shameful place that validated Sanyukai as provider. In fact, for newcomers who may have had a consultation but whose faces were still unfamiliar to the staff, there was no choice but to arrive early and be noticed because meals were served to individuals in the order in which they had arrived and only by permission of the staff, who approved those who were allowed upstairs and, on rare occasions, declined others. And during especially busy times of the month or year, when everyone was low on funds, it was especially important to arrive early since there might not be enough meals to go around. At least initially, there was genuine shame in having been reduced to the point at which one had no choice but to wait two hours to receive a meal, and the exterior signs of this shame were presented in the form of silence and having one's head lowered. Sanyukai was, indeed, the first stop in San'ya for most individuals who had recently been laid off and forced to go on welfare. Over time, however, occupying the shameful, individualized place of waiting in front of Sanyukai mandated that shame be displaced with a shameless performance of shame that legitimated the philanthropic mission of the institution. In return, the men outside got a meal, and thereby, each party was more or less satisfied. In short, although some men undoubtedly felt ashamed, they had to disguise the shamelessness that was required to perform the shame of waiting two hours for a free lunch, and this was made ever more apparent when men who had just eaten at Sanyukai were seen making a beeline for a second free lunch at a second nonprofit organization: going from curry at Sanyukai to udon noodle soup in Tamahime Park.

There were, indeed, certain rules that had to be observed at Sanyukai, the contravention of which could earn one a bad name and, with it, the loss of one's privileges. For example, the staff had implemented a "no drinking" policy during work hours, in accordance with which anyone drinking or drunk was frowned upon or, if obstructively so, was ousted from the Sanyukai alleyway. There was an implicit, additional proviso to this policy under the condition of which one could remain at Sanyukai: in the interest of safety, fighting was not tolerated. If fights broke out, which regulars and staff said happened much less over recent years, they were instantly broken up, and when a staff member was punched by a newcomer, the police were summoned. Thus, Kubota, a decades-old volunteer at Sanyukai and resident of San'ya, noted how differently some people behaved when they were not at Sanyukai. In contrast to the figure of obsequious helplessness they presented at Sanyukai, these men would start brawls and go wild when they were in other parts of San'ya. It was as if their behavior conformed to the geographic location of Sanyukai, on the opposite side of Namidabashi from Iroha. But when members of the Kanamachi-ikka passed through the narrow alley, as if it belonged to them in their sharp business suits and shiny, expensive black shoes, silence would descend in a reminder that perhaps the alley did not belong to Sanyukai. None of the staff, for that matter, ever ventured beyond the confines of Sanyukai and into San'ya proper. It was to the staff of this sanctuary from San'ya within San'ya, however, that the men outside had to present an idealized, pliant, and docile image of themselves as was desired and thus rise in favorability. Waiting two hours might have secured a stranger a meal, but additional steps were necessary to become known by name and to gain access to additional privileges, like Friday and Saturday parties, when alcohol was served, and it was only intimacy with the staff that guaranteed these privileges.

Akira, a volunteer of three years, said that the ritual of waiting should be abolished in favor of a token system. That way people could pick up a numbered ticket, come back for lunch, and go home without the headache of having to wait two hours. But such a system would have gotten rid of that nonrelation—each aspiring to occupy the place of the other's desire—in which Sanyukai's social world consisted and would have overturned the hierarchy in which Sanyukai, the apparent provider, ultimately emerged as the duped and dependent party.[34] Because it was not shame but shamelessness that was precipitated by the process of waiting two hours outside. Hence, the active construction worker never went to Sanyukai. To endure the shame of the two-hour wait, one could "know no shame" (*haji shirazu*).

On the other side of Namidabashi, Akira had become close with his peers from Okinawa in the Okinawa-gang, and together they would take issue with the attitude of Sanyukai, disclosed in the phrase: to "do *for*." Having neither computer proficiency nor access to the internet, the guys had not picked this phrase up from Sanyukai's blog but happened to use it to depict the activities of the NPO. Redolent with condescension, in that the verb to "do *for*" inscribed a hierarchical relation in which the giver goes out of his way to do something *for* another, the guys would flip the phrase to restore the proper order of things, saying: "It isn't 'doing *for*,' is it! It's '*being allowed*' to!" In their eyes, Sanyukai was "arrogant" for entering on their turf and presuming to do something *for* them. Rather, Sanyukai was "being allowed" (*sasete moratte iru*) to be in San'ya. In permitting its presence, it was the residents of San'ya who were doing something *for* Sanyukai.[35]

On a hot summer morning, Akira brought some of these members of the Okinawa-gang to Sanyukai for medical check-ups. Rather than wait in the alleyway for their names to be called—that is, together with the regular crowd waiting for lunch—Akira, Rikiishi, Shōkawa, and Kentarō removed themselves a distance of some twenty meters to the end of the alley, where they stood facing one another, leaning against an electric pole, sipping green-tea shochu from cans. Every once in a while, the obese and round Izumo, ensconced as always at the bottom of the entryway steps, would shoot a quick, nervous glance at the guys from Okinawa. Guy-san, too, would turn to look at their figures down the road, muttering, "Okinawa-gang." For Akira, the visitation and personal entourage functioned as a double demonstration of his influence. On the one hand, Rikiishi, Shōkawa, and Kentarō would recognize his pull at Sanyukai, which enabled him to set up appointments for them without the routine hassle of having to approach and ask the staff personally. On the other hand, Sanyukai was made to witness the other world of construction workers, masculinity, muscle, and flagrant disregard for Sanyukai etiquette to which Akira was connected and by which Sanyukai appeared to be disconcerted, if not also threatened. Akira acted as the guarantor that the guys would be seen in the clinic, regardless of the fact that they were drinking. In fact, the Christian nurse had popped her head out of the clinic earlier in the morning to kindly ask the guys to hold off alcohol, since they were—"for once"—getting a checkup, and there was no reason for it to be wasted. Nonetheless, there the four of them stood with shochu in their hands, except Akira, who refrained, and because they stood at the far end of the alley, when each of their turns came the Sanyukai staff member called their names from inside the entryway, as he usually did, but for lack of response, stuck his head out the entryway and tried once again—"Shōkawa, please come in!"—only to have to put his slippers on in final frustration, shuffling into the alley to call their names one last time. Oblivious and caught up in their conversation, yet somehow sure that someone's name had been called, Shōkawa then looked at me, pointing stupidly at his own face with his index finger—saying "me?"—and waited for a confirmation. When I had confirmed with the staff that Shōkawa's name had been called, the latter set aside his drink and, sporting what appeared to be the best demeanor he could muster, dawdled down the alleyway, climbed the stairs up into the clinic, and bowed profusely as he crossed the threshold. Next came Rikiishi, carrying the weight of his upper body up the stairs, bowing curtly at the threshold, and crossing into the clinic.

Besides the consultation itself, the medical checkup could obviously not take place because the guys all had alcohol in their blood. This became the subject of much gossip at Sanyukai in the days after. What was this behavior, to show up at the clinic drinking?[36]

Akira and the members of the Okinawa-gang embodied the afterlife in the present of San'ya, as it had been in its heyday. On the one hand, the group, or gang, was composed of a group of men that worked together for various construction companies and for whom Suzuki acted as tehaishi, though it was his older brother, Kentarō, who had the reputation and connections that secured steady work availability. On the other hand, the Okinawa-gang constituted a loose group of drinking buddies whose central figures, many of whom were from Okinawa, pulled a slew of other figures into its orbit. In this way, Norihisa and Rikiishi were both central members of the Okinawa-gang but were employed as scaffolders for a separate company. Shōkawa, too, had another buddy who provided him with work as an ironworker. In the evenings and especially on Sundays, when everyone got together for the horse races, sometimes even going to the Okinawan restaurant in Asakusa, Gajū-Maru, the members of the Okinawa-gang could be seen drinking here and there in San'ya, be it at Sakura, Iseya, Hikari-Sushi, Chūfukuro, or on the street by Mutō's hole-in-the-wall. Nor, for that matter, were the working arrangements set in stone. Anyone could work as a *dokata* (navvy) with Kentarō, and if work was scarce for the others and they needed the money, it was not unusual for Suzuki to send Shōkawa, Rikiishi, or Norihisa to work as navvies with Kentarō and the other regulars.[37]

Akira himself did not work at first, having only recently become intimate with the Okinawa-gang through an encounter at a San'ya dive bar, where he noticed that Saruma, Kentarō's cousin, was speaking with a Miyakojima accent, an island off Okinawa proper, where Akira, too, was born. Nor had Akira been long in San'ya on this occasion, returning to it after several years in Kotobukichō in Yokohama, where he had put himself to use at an illegal gambling joint. The suicide of a friend and the fact that his face had become too known prompted his return to San'ya, where he had first come to seek work fifteen years earlier, when he had been put on probation for infighting by the Nibikikai, a defunct yakuza organization for which Akira had worked for ten years, specializing in what he called *kiritori* (extortion). Though he had not told anyone about his past, this past was part of what made his personality so attractive to others, especially at Sanyukai: never showing "weakness" (*yowami*) and fearlessly staking himself and his reputation for those around him. When he tried to kill himself, it was also this machismo, turned ludicrous, that led him repeatedly to contend that he would have succeeded had the knife been sharper. Inside the last few years, Akira had, in fact, been diagnosed with a brain tumor that could not be extracted. Together with other physical ailments, this prevented him from engaging in any form of strenuous physical labor or, for that matter, from finding employment, and it required that he be on medication all the time.

Hence, I first met Akira at what would otherwise have been the unlikeliest of places, Sanyukai, where he volunteered to keep himself busy, or as he himself explained: to "do his best" (*gambaru*). At the time of our first meeting, Akira was fifty-four years old. Standing some 160 cm, with a stocky, stout build but a slightly protruding belly, Akira's physique bespoke his younger days when, as he put it, his muscles had been "bulging." At the time of our encounter, Akira had also been sober for an entire year, since he had been told by doctors to abstain from liquor, due to his health. This was to change drastically, however, after a concatenation of events that included a falling out with Guy-san and the passing away of Akira's older sister, for whom—though he did not say so—Akira was not able to mourn because he did not have the funds to travel to the funeral in Okinawa. Even if he had had the money, he might not have been welcome.

The most painful things were thus unspoken in San'ya. Indeed, the precipitating, structuring events that had originally prompted individuals to come to San'ya—unemployment, crime, illness—were not dwelt upon but passed over during drinks in moments of pregnant silence. The men, be it at Sanyukai or in the Okinawa-gang, rarely if ever mentioned what effectively kept them in San'ya, namely, the absence of a family or wife, children or parents. Their "connections" (*en*) with spouse, children, and parents had "been cut" years, if not decades, ago. One exception to this rule was Suzuki, himself a relative newcomer to San'ya three years earlier, where he had come to join Kentarō after leaving his wife and grown kids. Every month, Suzuki would send money to his mother in Okinawa, and throwing guilt on Kentarō by reminding him of this, Kentarō would retort: "Who would send money to that bitch?!" Likewise, Akira would occasionally say that he had "left Okinawa behind for good."[38]

One day, after returning to Sanyukai from a few weeks abroad, I found Akira as vivacious as ever, typically transforming the daily atmosphere by exercising his penchant and skill of making others laugh at his inanities. But while I had been gone, he had gotten into a brawl in the Iroha arcade and wore a chest strap to hold his fractured ribs in place. As it turned out afterward, his injuries included a fractured disk in the spinal column, in spite of which he continued to volunteer at the nonprofit organization, overseeing its menial tasks by hauling luggage back and forth.

As Akira explained what had happened, he had "lost it" or "gone amok" (*abareta*) in the Iroha arcade after learning that his older sister had passed away. He had let a sarcastic comment slip about someone at a dive bar, after which he was confronted by the man and two others, demanding that he compensate for his words. When I noted that it might not have been necessary to fight over this, Akira explained that with some people, "it doesn't matter how much you apologize." The three men had not backed down even after Akira apologized. What they wanted was "money." In what would be described as a "man's dignity" (*otoko no iji*), Akira had refused to lower himself to this demand, promptly taking the matter outside, and woken up in the hospital. He said he was pretty sure that he had taken one of the guys down, though there had been three of them. Akira whisked off the suggestion that these men were still around, saying that they were probably scared, "hiding somewhere." The police had, in fact, asked Akira if he remembered who had done this to him, to which he had feigned ignorance. Pointing to an old knife wound on his throat, he added that he had not informed on the person who had done this either. That was what it meant to be an otoko, and he had a reputation to uphold in San'ya.

My first real encounter with this world of San'ya, of fighting and reputations, took place on the eve of the yearly Sumida River fireworks festival. At this stage, I had yet to work and see the labor at construction sites that constituted the inescapable and otherwise invisible backdrop to the enactment of masculinity in San'ya. Aside from an occasional beer with various individuals at Mutō's hole-in-the-wall, I had not yet even been introduced to the group or met Takeda-san. This was my first full-on exposure to the heady, boisterous atmosphere of a night in San'ya, replete with an introduction by Akira and the politely dismissive response that I would continue to meet until well after I started working with the group:

> I thought I'd catch Akira and his buddies by the corner dive, but it was closed. When I then headed over to Iroha, there was Akira standing beside Suzuki in the middle of a small crowd, beside the entryway to Iroha, under the roof beside the gambling sheets. Akira standing there in his sports shorts, brown slippers, and white plain T-shirt. Sushi had been put out for the guys on the gambling sheet, and Akira was helping himself. The fireworks were over. The corner dive had been closed early because of the fireworks, they said, and they'd been watching it from the street. You could see it even better from there, Akira said, raising his arms big to show the fireworks. He'd been drinking, but not that much. We all headed to Sakura afterwards, and a regular party was going. Suzuki's brother—who ended up sleeping at my place—was sitting by the far end of the counter, having just ordered curry. He said he didn't want a drink because he'd eat curry and then just head to sleep. I gave him a glass of beer nonetheless. The karaoke was going. Around ten guys— more, twelve or so—were sitting at the two tables across from the counter.

Suzuki's older brother had been working all day, in the heat, Akira had said. I learned a lot of new names last night. Makoto with the real downcast, somber eyes, but kind looking. He recalled how he'd spat blood, how blood had come out everywhere, from his nose, his mouth, his piss. He "thought he was going to die." So he'd gone to Sanyukai, because he had no insurance card or anything. He'd said that twice: that he has no insurance card. On that day, the doctor hadn't been there and only the psychologist was there. Makoto said he was on real good terms with him. But on that first day, since the doctor hadn't been there, they had started asking about his parents. He'd broken down in tears. The conversation—with Akira at our side—continued on toward how Makoto has come through his work seeing people around him reach that point where they cannot continue to work anymore. Their bodies won't hold. They're at their limit. He's seen this happen around him repeatedly. Coming up real close to my face, he ran his finger along his cheek to delineate the yakuza's cut, and said that those he works for are primarily of that sort. The place was real lively while we were having this conversation. Someone came over to me and showed me photos of Makoto naked. Makoto had just said, indicating beneath his shirt . . . that because he'd been working with the mob, or for the mob, he had tattoos. The photos on this other guy's phone showed Makoto from the back, covered from the hips to the neck. He had actually said it with a sad expression, that he'd covered his body in tattoos. Akira started speaking . . . saying to Makoto, "you're at the limit," and why don't you "make it easy for yourself." Suggested that Makoto come to Sanyukai, where they would get him registered, etc. Akira had said to check out Makoto's head, which was, indeed, covered in scars. He'd been through a lot, Akira seemed to say. I think he used the word "bullied." But this person, Makoto, "can see things," like Akira can. Here, in this world, you meet people who can see, Akira seemed to say. Makoto nodded. . . . Makoto had a wooden cross around his neck that he'd been given by some priest. He held it up between his fingers. Akira said Makoto wouldn't give that up for a million yen! Makoto nodded. . . . Right after we'd gotten into the place, Akira had pulled me from the counter to introduce me to the guys by the table. There were so many, I'd been shy and tried to avoid. But Akira headed straight in and introduced me in front of everyone to Takeda-san—later, I learned, the don of the neighborhood—saying who I was, what I was doing, and, bowing his head, saying: "Please take care of him." A couple of times he said it. It was Akira's way of saying "I vouch for this guy," and of using his credentials for me. Now, I can't let

Akira down either. In any case, I think I was acknowledged by Takeda-san, as the talk turned to another person who had also come to San'ya to work and write on it. Takeda-san was wearing what might be mistaken for pajamas elsewhere, but white thin cotton top and matching bottom, with a zip-up—open—at the neck. Like something you'd wear before going to sleep, just out of the bath. He had a lean, slightly sallow face, but good complexion and kind-looking. Later, Akira said—whispering to me behind his upheld palm—that this is an "incredible person." With real emphasis. "Just look at his hands," he said. And sure enough, Takeda-san was missing three fingers. One on his right hand. Two on his left. Akira said he had not done this on account of himself, but that he had done it to take the fall for those under him. That's why, Akira said, that people bow their heads to him when he walks down the street. Makoto agreed with Akira when he said that "he's a real gentle person."

It was real crowded, and at the very beginning, they'd gotten an arm wrestling match started. . . . This guy—Sho something was his name—was apparently real strong—everyone said so—so the guys took turns. Everyone, including Akira, lost. The guys saying, "Come on! Come on!" A real show. This one big guy, though—looked like a boxer with big nose and hefty upper body; whom, I was told, likes bright colors like yellow or the red shirt he was wearing—won. Kept showing off his muscles, flexing them jokingly, saying he'd won against the guy everyone had lost to. When the other tehaishi—Matsuda—showed his face at the entryway, though, this big brawly, joking guy sprang to his feet within an instant and charged. Before I knew it, two or three guys—Takeda-san restraining the boxer—had gotten in between the two, to keep them from fighting. Akira said this happened hundreds of times and just kept talking.

When we left the place, everyone followed Takeda-san and two others—a curly haired woman who was also drinking in there and a man called "the gangster guy"—to the cab and bowed to him before he got in. Akira effusively. Like watching the mob leader step into the cab with his entourage, and those below him bowing away.[39]

THE DAY LABORER

The working day starts early for construction workers in San'ya. Most construction sites begin the day with radio calisthenics and a general meeting at eight o'clock, by which time laborers must have changed into their work clothes and be ready to work. This means that workers must arrive in the changing rooms by seven thirty and that, depending on the location of the construction site, some of which can be up to two hours from San'ya, workers have to leave their apartment or bunkhouse between five thirty and seven o'clock in the morning. Solitary figures on the early-morning train platform, they head to work before the morning rush hour—often in the opposite direction from central Tokyo, because the up-and-coming residential sites are to be found in the nearby prefectures of Chiba or Saitama—and by the time they get back to San'ya, more than twelve hours will easily have passed. If they have to work again the next day, this leaves them with three to four hours to drink, eat, and maybe even go to the local bathhouse.[1]

San'ya itself still moves to the rhythm of the construction worker's workday. As a strange but telling survival from the days when Namidabashi was thronging with laborers looking for work, the "morning market" (*asa ichi*) or "thieves' market"—as it is also called, since many of the objects on sale are said to be stolen—thrives between six and seven o'clock every morning, from Monday to Saturday. Within this hour, the side streets flanking Tamahime Park are lined with rows of temporary stalls, and a thin crowd of men saunters through them. Practically any kind of secondhand object can be found on sale in these backstreets. Certain stalls specialize in clothes—T-shirts, collared shirts, pants, and jackets—others in decorative trinkets disposed of long ago (be it porcelain statues, glassware animals, or a plastic figurine of the anime character Doraemon), all with that dusty, worn look of having been through the trash. Other stalls specialize in old magazines, porn magazines, DVDs, CDs, and VHS and music tapes, and still others specialize in handyman tools, and yet others in obsolete electronic goods, including tape recorders, CD players, analog box TVs, mini handheld TVs, and radios, switched on to air the morning news against the sound of static. A MacBook might even be on sale amid the curios and bric-a-brac, all sharing the musty air of having long ago fallen into disuse.

The entire morning market is illegal. Under normal circumstances, stall owners require a permit from the police to run stalls in a public space, but none of the stalls of the morning market has applied for this. Instead, stall owners of the morning market pay a percentage of their monthly earnings as a protection fee to the local yakuza organization, the Kanamachi-ikka, which presumably manages the extralegal aspects of the market so that it can persist. Underneath this umbrella of protection from the local mob, another black market flourishes: the market for prescription medication, so the San'ya man can peddle the surfeit of medication he receives from the hospital or purchase medication for high blood pressure or pain killers, depending on what is laid out for sale. Only once during two years was the morning market raided by the police, a few days after which the stalls were up and running again.

The morning market formalizes an array of barters and exchanges that occur between the men in San'ya every day. It was common for the guys to circulate DVDs between themselves, to give work clothes to each other, and to take over any miscellaneous objects that had become redundant. So too, it was common for the sick on welfare—for whom medication was free—to distribute their pills liberally to their buddies. After a routine visit to the hospital, painkillers, pills for high blood pressure, sleeping pills, stomach pills, and what not were handed out as promised. The next day, so-and-so might come along, exclaiming that such-and-such pill had "worked," sticking his palm out in a demand for more.

On the Black Labor Market

Once and if the exchanges left the sphere of friendship and gifting to make it onto the black market, where objects took on the character of commodities proper, the trick was to turn a profit from objects that had far passed their date of obsolescence. In form, this was no different from the labor market of San'ya, whose labor was composed of men in their fifties or sixties or older, almost all on welfare and mostly bearing some kind of physical ailment, suggesting that they should not be working at a construction site in the first place. It was therefore no coincidence that the content of work circulated to San'ya workers was, as Akira put it, of the sort that no one else wanted to do. Nor was it a coincidence that, shortly after the Fukushima Daiichi Nuclear Power Plant disaster, posters had been put up on electric poles in San'ya advertising work cleaning rubble (*gareki*) in Fukushima Prefecture.[2] Like the objects for sale at the morning market, the workers of San'ya had been disposed of once and could readily be disposed of altogether. Indeed, oftentimes the circulation of secondhand objects occurred side by side with work and liquor. When workers of the Okinawa-gang came back from work between six and seven o'clock in the evening to report to Suzuki—dirty, tired, and with a can of beer, one-cup sake, or plastic cup of shochu in their hand—Suzuki would be well into his third or fourth *mizuwari* (shochu with water and ice) in front of Mutō's, gambling on boats with one eye, writing down names of workers with another as he assigned them to construction sites, and self-medicating his perennial stomach ache by dropping painkillers filched off Akira. Thus, the working days would repeat.

If they did not say so, the daily lifestyle of the guys attested to the fact that they privileged money, liquor, and excess over health and that they sacrificed the latter for the former. Moreover, the guys were well aware of the low regard in which they were held: pinpointing the "problem" of San'ya to "disposability" (*tsukaisute*) and noting straight out, albeit in private, that they were considered akin to "human garbage." Nonetheless, the dominant code of conduct was such that a real day laborer put cash, and therefore the excesses of liquor or gambling, before health.

It was not just their bodies, however, but their lives that were staked in the determination to persist in their expenditures: an exchange in which the day laborer would emerge as the losing party. Marx thus begins his famous chapter on the "working day" by pointing out both the limits and the insatiable drive of capital to accumulate surplus value, reaped from the bodies of workers. Capital does this by maximizing the length of the working day, while paying workers only enough to ensure their reproduction. And while the commodity of labor contains an irreducible negativity in the laborer, who can raise their voice in objection, the equivalent *form* of surplus extraction goes unquestioned.[3] Thus, the effects of commodity exchange carry the day.

As a matter of course, everyone in the group had complaints relating to work, but it was only when they had come into another source of income, like winning at the races, that the guys ceased to work. The construction site might be too far away, like Kami-Fukuoka in Saitama, which was two hours by train, or the subcontracting company might be unreasonable, like Futomaki, which did not let its workers take breaks on time. The content of work could also be physically grueling and pointless, as at one construction site where the top coordinator demanded that every single rock be cleared off the ground before cement could be

filled in. Navvies consequently spent all day lifting rocks in the blistering summer heat, but no one complained, except under their breath and among themselves. Even Kentarō, who could recall laborers walking out en masse during the
bubble economy of the 1980s, acceded to ridiculous demands knowing that too
much backtalk might cost everyone their income. Work was undergone by necessity, and it was self-evident that this was what an otoko did, for "work" did not
refer to any kind of work but to work in which one "moved the body."[4] As I was to
learn when I asked Kentarō and Akira whether they would ever bring a woman
(*josei*) to work, the response was an immediate no. Realizing that I might be asking if I could bring someone along, Kentarō notably pulled back, only to reply
that, yes, there were some carpenters who worked as families and that I could
bring someone along as long as I took care of her. Otherwise, the response was
unequivocal. They would let me carry her burden, but I could not recommend a
woman for work in my absence. The laborers of the Okinawa-gang were exclusively men, and it was from manual labor that an otoko derived his worth. Referring back to his own experience one evening, Akira addressed Kentarō:

> AKIRA: What would you do if you couldn't work?
> KENTARŌ: I'd kill myself.

An otoko shorn of labor power was worthless, and though he did not mention it
on this occasion, Akira had, in fact, tried to take his own life years earlier when
he had been deemed unfit to work by his doctors.[5] He would recount how it used
to be that recipients of welfare were frowned upon and excluded from social activities. Now, all this had changed, and San'ya had become a "welfare town."
Yet, by a certain irony, it was welfare that enabled men in San'ya to persist in their
excess-driven lifestyles, whereas the worker with neither welfare nor insurance
had to eke out a living and borrow.

For the guys on welfare, the sale of their labor was therefore akin to making a
surplus off an object on the black market. In the Okinawa-gang, the income of
¥12,500 ($125) per day constituted cash in excess of their monthly allowance from
the state: something extra. In fact, as a man at Sanyukai noted when Akira had
started working with the Okinawa-gang, it was illegal not to report earnings in
excess of one's welfare. Ostensibly, the reason for this was that monthly allowances
had to be recalibrated in accordance with one's income. But reporting income in
excess of welfare could result in a diminution of one's total monthly finances—
welfare was reduced by a larger amount than one earned!—which functioned as a
veritable disincentive to report one's earnings and encouraged men to put themselves to use on the black market.[6] On the other hand, there was a real risk involved in not reporting earnings, because welfare was instantly cut if the failure to
do so was confirmed. The ward office could find out about this by two routes. The

first involved an "informant" (*chinkoro*) in one's immediate environment who told the office that so-and-so was working. The second involved the ward office sending an employee out on a home visit or an undercover operation to investigate or confirm whether someone was in fact earning extra income. Ward employees were said to spy on a variety of infractions, including alcohol consumption as well as pachinko and other gambling. Welfare recipients who worked thus led a stealthy existence, wary of the watchful eye of the state and of neighbors who might notice their early-morning departures, heavy bags, and late returns. Indeed, everyone knew of others losing their welfare because someone had reported them. One day, Akira was accosted in front of his bunkhouse by four ward employees who questioned him regarding work. In fact, Kentarō had been receiving welfare until the ward discovered that he was working on the side. Now he had become "envious" of others on welfare, Akira would say, and spent their money as if it was public property. As a tacit rule, it was known that Akira or Shōkawa were both on welfare and could be turned to for funds that were never returned. But by the end of the month, they, too, had run dry in frustration. Whether on or off welfare, the guys never had enough cash to go around. Yet the most disadvantaged was the worker with neither welfare nor the assistance of out-of-work aid.

The periodical nature of work for the Okinawa-gang made it almost impossible to sustain a reliable income without welfare, save for a few core workers. For one, no one knew how many workers would be needed the following day. This decision came by phone every day around four or five o'clock in the afternoon, from Barasawa, who paid Suzuki a monthly fee to round up workers and thereby acted as the middleman between the tehaishi, Suzuki, and the subcontractor, the Tenjima Company, which was hired, in turn, by the Seichō Corporation to build apartment blocks. Secondly, there were periods, sometimes of months, when there was very little work, be it because the group had fallen into ill repute, because Seichō had chosen to go with competitors, or because there was no construction in progress. And even if there had been enough work to go around for everyone, work as a navvy was so taxing that only the youngest and fittest could manage five days per week. Kentarō himself seemed to manage this only by directing work and abstaining from hard physical tasks as much as possible. At the age of twenty-eight, even the youngest of the group, Wakami, said he could work a maximum of only four times per week.

In the absence of a contractual relationship with employers, flexibility was required of the Okinawa-gang, which had to provide workers in accordance with fluctuating demand. Too many consecutive days of work was as much a problem as too little work, and it was in tacit recognition both of this shifting nature of work availability and the necessity to capital of an idle pool of labor—Marx's "reserve army of labor"—that Taitō Ward had instituted a system to compensate laborers for days on which work, as the guys would say, was not "coming around."[7] Out-of-work aid required day laborers to work at least thirteen days per month, for which their employers signed off in a stamp book (at times, even if they were not working), and in return for these working days, they were guaranteed thirteen days on which the ward gave them ¥7,500 ($75). This was far from sufficient, however, to carry workers through thirty days when there was no work at all. By midmonth, the money would be gone. Thus, the group would wait for a dose of work that no one else wanted to do or once the foundations of the buildings had been dug by navvies (*dokata*), and the scaffolders (*tobi*), ironworkers (*tekkinya*), and carpenters (*daiku*) had taken over the upper stories, for the two or three days per week when the navvies were called to do the cement. Alternatively, they would wait for April, when the new fiscal year arrived, and construction companies invested in new sites. In prolonged dry spells, the guys were starved for work, any work at that.

These provisional conditions of work forced the laborer to shift from tehaishi to tehaishi. If work grew scarce in the Okinawa-gang, the individual had no recourse but to find other means of income or borrow, and it was for this reason that the maintenance of an individual reputation and personal connections assumed paramount importance for the laborer in San'ya. The reputable worker was not only reliable, meaning that he showed up for work as promised, like the borrower was good for his word to return money, but possessed vast experience and commanded a versatile repertoire of skills. For such a reputation could secure work for both oneself and one's acquaintances. Hence, Kentarō not only knew all about work as a navvy but had worked in other fields of construction (originally carpentry) and was able to perform and direct a range of tasks beyond the immediate demand of the workplace. On one occasion, he even maneuvered the excavator, grinning from behind the wheel because he did not have a license. In short, if Kentarō was on-site, the director could expect tasks to be completed expediently and without any fuss. For this reason, Kentarō said, it was necessary for him to be physically present at the construction site and to leave the work of *tehai* for Suzuki.[8]

For those who had acquired an established reputation, like Kentarō, the necessity of self-reliance presented itself in the guise of "freedom" (*jiyū*). For all the headache that the inveterate drinker, womanizer, and braggart that Suzuki was, Kentarō would scornfully say that he had been "free" before Suzuki came since it had just been about "himself" (*jibun*). On top of this, Suzuki had invited along their salaryman-gone-insolvent cousin, Saruma, unversed in the ways of San'ya. With Suzuki and Saruma in San'ya, Kentarō was held accountable for them in spite of himself and, though he was loath to admit it, felt obliged to look out for them. Yet what Kentarō expressed as "freedom" of "self" disclosed an objective necessity of the economic order in San'ya that might render Kentarō as redundant as it already had other workers marginal to the Okinawa-gang. When work was scarce under Suzuki, some laborers obviously had to seek work elsewhere.[9]

But Suzuki would take it personally when workers, for whatever reason, perhaps even on a whim, switched to another tehaishi. Kentarō would say of Suzuki, who had only been in San'ya three years (one as a navvy, two as a tehaishi), that he "does not understand" that it is normal for individual workers to switch tehaishi as they wish. It had always been this way in San'ya, but this was not only social convention: the logic of the market dictated such practice. Yet Suzuki, tehaishi of the Okinawa-gang, and Matsuda, tehaishi of the Matsuda-group, had set up a working relationship such that each would borrow workers from the other. If Matsuda was short of workers, he would ask Suzuki, and vice versa; and the payment for each worker adhered to the standards of the group from which they came. Such an arrangement between the tehaishi made it impossible to switch between groups and, to the eventual demise of both Suzuki and Matsuda, produced the appearance and belief that specific individuals belonged to one and not the other, because it was always an option to get away from the duo by seeking work elsewhere. Finally, Suzuki assumed such an attitude of self-importance that he demanded a finder's fee from anyone who went to work for another tehaishi, because Suzuki had presumably facilitated the connection in the first place. When Suzuki exposed his senior by ten years and veteran ironworker, Shōkawa, to such proprietary behavior, Kentarō at long last exploded.

That workers were at liberty to switch tehaishi *if* they could find other means of income sometimes made it difficult for tehaishi to maintain an available pool of labor, and this problem of reliability was compounded by the low work ethic in San'ya. Kentarō would repeatedly lament that if only he could get together a steady and reliable group of laborers, it would be possible to really get business going, but the paucity of work availability was mirrored in the inconstancy of workers. Matsuda especially seemed to suffer from temper tantrums because workers simply did not show up for work as promised. This was called to "open a hole" (*ana o akeru*), news of which reached the tehaishi when the others arrived at the construction site and could not find or reach so-and-so. Then, Matsuda or Suzuki, hungover from the night before, would have to get on the phone either to reach the individual in question or to find a replacement. But it was usually to no avail. The repetition of such instances made it nearly impossible to build a reputation at the workplace such that demand for the group remained continuous, and it was the tehaishi who felt the brunt of this drop in reputation. But the group suffered as a whole, as well, because work might not be circulated to them in the future or because the directors realized that certain tasks could be performed with one less person and, as a result, decided to lessen the number of workers. Of course, Suzuki and Matsuda bore no small responsibility for opening holes, particularly when this resulted from overextending their obligations to various subcontractors. The reputation and income of the tehaishi stemmed directly from the number of subcontractors he provided laborers for, and Suzuki bragged of receiving payment from three out of the five subcontractors operating in San'ya. In addition, as a favor, he secured workers for the other two subcontractors—a relation that could easily evolve into an obligation if Suzuki, as he was wont to do, decided to pocket an extra paycheck every month. On the one hand, this increased work availability, but it did so for a group of workers whose dependability was erratic at best. Suzuki had to cultivate a list of connections that exceeded the maximum number of workers on any given day, which ranged from zero to twenty, and there were a number of reasons why someone might not be able to or agree to go to work when Suzuki asked them. Some of the guys were not picking up their phone or did not have one. Others might have switched to another tehaishi, since work had been scarce with Suzuki. But most frequently, they simply did not want to go, which led to a comical exchange between Suzuki, pressured to fill his quota, and another man who had just gotten back from work, started drinking, and begun feeling good about the next day off. Someone might not want to work because they had worked all week and were tired. Others might have won at the races, and still others declined since, by the time Suzuki, who was also drunk, got around to phoning them, they could not fathom the prospect of waking the next day.

It was common lore in San'ya that everyone sometimes missed a day of work. To a certain extent, this was anticipated and forestalled by the tehaishi, who could force so-and-so to take one day off, so as to prevent them from making promises they would not keep. Suzuki knew, for instance, that the lean and seemingly tireless fifty-seven-year-old Riku, who ran the show with Kentarō, would eventually hit his limit and go on a drinking spree for days on end, sleeping outside in the Iroha arcade, and Suzuki would have a replacement ready for this eventuality. But even Kentarō, who liked his drink as much as the others, would sometimes show up for work late or not at all. Indeed, everyone, even Takeda-san, had days when they neglected to work as promised. At the construction site, workers from San'ya consequently had a reputation for unreliability. When it was said in the changing rooms one day that the navvies were a man down (Kentarō), the identity of the culprit was confirmed by a rhetorical question—"Yama?" as if to suggest that the guy from San'ya was most likely to flake—and a nod. On one occasion, Kentarō had spent the entire previous evening persuading Shōkawa to work because they were a man short, but upon arriving at the station in the morning, Shōkawa, who had been suffering from a backache, changed his mind and made a U-turn to his bunkhouse. This was called "flaking on work" (*tonko suru*), and supposedly, the work of *tehai* in the heyday of San'ya had taken place in the mornings since that way, tehaishi could ensure that workers were awake, sober, and prepared to work.

The real problem was not that the guys would drink every evening: that occurred without exception, although many kept it moderate if they had work the next day. In fact, everyone worked hungover, and Kentarō would note that by the time work finished at five o'clock, the hangover would be wearing off just in time for another drink. The real problem was that everyone knew that they were, in any case, "disposable" labor from San'ya and that they were employed as a means to conclude the most disagreeable part of construction work, sacrificing their health in the process. Akira would say over and over again of work, and of liquor, that "it only destroys the body." Nevertheless, as if to contradict himself, "work" was what an otoko did: a discourse that emerged out of labor as an act of creative destruction and that negated the negativity of death in which a man's worth was measured exclusively in terms of the daily wage, for which one paid with one's life. At the margins of the nation, the day laborers of San'ya were exposed to the most brute effects of capitalist surplus extraction, in which, as Marx says, the commodity of labor power is reduced to a minimal value, expending their labor power unto death. But grounded in their work expertise, the discourse of the otoko sustained and added to this objective order of the economy. For an otoko went "his own way" (*jibun no michi*) and replaced its monetary relation with a principle of sociality, hierarchy, and honor of the marginal outlaw, embodied in the figure of Takeda-san.[10] At the end, everyone would die, but the narrative detour of being an otoko held the contingency of death, materialized daily in the exchange relation, at bay. Likewise, the veteran worker was called an "artisan" or quite simply "skilled" (*ude ga tokui*), and with a statement that pardoned the occasional act of flaking on work—"This is, after all, Yama"— San'ya's day laborers disclosed the truth of productivity and discipline to consist in expendability.[11] What was the point, after all, of going to work?

There was a difference, however, between feeling guilty and shamefaced for failing to go to work one time and blazing a trail of failures. Some men developed a reputation of not showing up, leaving a string of irreparable relations behind as they hopped from tehaishi to tehaishi. Like debts that could not be returned, such burned bridges eventually prompted individuals to disappear from San'ya, but so too did scarcity of work and low wages.

Makoto, for instance, vanished from San'ya overnight. Although he had been speaking of joining the yakuza, everyone had witnessed his deteriorating physical condition from liquor and overwork. Stumbling about town drunk, with a black eye from fighting and leaving his wallet lying about, Matsuda, his tehaishi, had to implore him to put his valuables in his room when he was drinking. Yet it was common knowledge that, like for everyone else in the Matsuda-group, ¥2,000

($20) was docked from Makoto's pay as *pinhane* (finder's fee) for Matsuda each time Makoto went to work.[12] With only ¥8,000–¥9,000 left for daily expenses, Makoto was just eking out enough to pay for transportation, meals, drinks, and his bunkhouse (which he paid by the day). Kentarō noted that Matsuda had "been like that from way back," and it went without saying that taking *pinhane* was what the work of a tehaishi was all about: that surplus or excess pocketed from each laborer. Suzuki and Matsuda were pimps of the construction trade. Unlike the objects on sale at the morning market, however, it was generally (albeit tacitly) recognized in the Okinawa-gang that Matsuda's "system" of extracting surplus from everyone was excessive. There were certain limits to be observed. Even if Makoto had assented to the conditions, the deduction was far from fair, and Makoto consequently emerged as a symptom of the order of equivalent exchange between a tehaishi and his workers, which was made to appear fair; most certainly, no one told Matsuda to his face that he was ripping off workers.[13] Indeed, if Makoto, who was situated relatively high in Matsuda's hierarchy of workers, was docked ¥2,000 per day, it was not unheard of that Matsuda would take half the pay of some homeless person given a day of work. Hence, the subject of Makoto had become "taboo" (*tabū*) in the days following his disappearance, because it suggested that Matsuda, who was enraged, had brought the matter upon himself. It was bound to happen that workers quit. And it happened on a number of occasions that members of the Matsuda-group vanished. One man who had been entrusted with the wages of six or seven others pocketed the cash and left without a word, and it was similarly a regular occurrence that guys in the Matsuda-group would not show up for work. If this occurred repeatedly, as it did in the case of Kon-chan, everyone would begin to wonder when Matsuda's fuse would blow. Damage control involved beating the culprit with a metal baseball bat that Matsuda and Suzuki had stowed away in a storage space by Mutō's hole-in-the-wall, along with worker's gear (safety belts, helmets, chainsaws, tools, etc.). Physical violence constituted a recognized means of meting out punishment and reestablishing authority. Hence, when Makoto phoned Matsuda a year later and reappeared in San'ya, Akira had to ask Matsuda not to batter Makoto. But Makoto showed up walking with a cane. During his absence, he had suffered a brain hemorrhage and had lost mobility in half his lower body. People said it had been the "liquor." Having gotten on welfare and relocated to another ward, Makoto rarely came to Yama afterward.[14]

The demise of the Matsuda-group came when Matsuda himself suddenly disappeared from San'ya. Over the years, Matsuda had built quite a reputation as a tehaishi in San'ya, with the guys and workers, the Kanamachi-ikka, and the police. He himself stayed in a cheap, ¥2,000 bunkhouse by the Iroha arcade, cutting a stocky figure as he could be seen after two in the afternoon, cycling about Yama on a *mama-chari* (mom bike), dressed in jeans, beach sandals, and a plain collared shirt or T-shirt. He had silver jewelry hanging around his neck, showing through the opening at the top of his shirt, and never went anywhere without his cell phone. Over the years, he had gotten fat about the waist, which lent him a comical air, paired with a quick-witted, almost nasal voice and laughter. He was always on the phone and always rushing off to attend to matters that required his immediate attention. Unlike Suzuki, whose workers were paid at the construction site, Matsuda paid his guys upon their return from work; sporting this cash in a bundle of ¥10,000 ($100) bills strung together with a rubber band, which was entrusted (albeit in an envelope) to someone close if Matsuda was not around to pay workers himself. In effect, Matsuda acted the part of the boss-caretaker, and it therefore came as little surprise when he announced the opening of his own construction company in the spring of 2013: Sanja Kensetsu, it was called, with an office right off the Iroha arcade, next to a run-down dive with mice (figure 2.1). The opening was accompanied by an invitation list and formal invitation letters. Everyone attended the opening event at a karaoke bar on Namidabashi, but in the following months, Matsuda increasingly stopped picking up the phone when Suzuki or Kentarō called for workers, relegating this task to one of his innumerable minions at the office (on the office number). He started traveling, mixing business with pleasure, and A-4–size cheap colored ink-jet photos of Matsuda appeared here and there in San'ya, on the inside walls of the dive bar, Sakura, in front of a takeaway lunchbox counter, or posing in baggy working pants and baseball cap before a primordial tree on Yakushima Island. Yet another poster showed Matsuda standing and smiling in front of his office, with the tacky slogan "to work = life" (*hataraku = inochi*) printed alongside his cell phone number. Having discovered, he said, a rock formation that accelerated the process of decontamination in soil, Matsuda also began going to Fukushima to engage with nuclear decontamination work, repeatedly appearing in a business suit in the Iroha arcade, tired out after a day on the bullet train. He started hanging out with professors from Tōdai (Tokyo University), conversing with them about nuclear decontamination, and alongside this, he seemed to be working on a project to export water-cleansing equipment to Burma and was enlisting Akira—who just shook his head in private and politely deferred on the matter in public—to act as head of a new NPO in San'ya. Yet everyone in the Okinawa-gang knew from the beginning that Matsuda spread himself thin as tehaishi and that, regardless of his extensive connections, he tended to use an especially unreliable labor base. The setup with Suzuki did not improve matters either, because Suzuki would only take ¥500 as *pinhane*, contrary to Matsuda's minimum ¥2,000. Hence, when a Matsuda crew member worked side by side with Suzuki's guys at the same construction site, the former was made painfully aware that he was doing the exact same work as the latter but was receiving one-fifth less

FIGURE 2.1.   One after the other, San'ya's old dive bars were being shuttered.

in wages. In the absence of a contractual relationship, Matsuda treated his workers as if they were his own. Less than a year after the inauguration of his new company, Sanja Kensetsu, however, Matsuda's crew members consolidated, objected to his conditions of labor, and refused to work. Shortly thereafter, Matsuda disappeared from San'ya. Everyone knew he had fled, because the Kanamachi-ikka sent its people out looking for him, asking everyone if they had seen Matsuda or knew where he was: Matsuda had disappeared with a debt of ¥30,000,000 (approximately $300,000) to the Kanamachi-ikka, a sum that would cost him his life if they located him.

As Akira had predicted from the very beginning, Matsuda was "finished." Kentarō, too, had foreseen this eventuality, as he reiterated the principle of the worker in San'ya, stating that the collapse had been bound to happen because the enterprise had been based on making a claim to an informal network of workers as one's own. But the San'ya man moved about according to his own whims, and in the absence of a formal contractual relationship that dissimulated the exploitative relationship of the tehaishi to the laborer, the availability of other means of income would crumble any attempt at forming a hierarchical institution in the name of self-interest. The individualizing order of the economy was to prevail.

But the informal and personal relations between the tehaishi and his workers also made for an economy of favors and obligations that far exceeded cash compensation for services. This was especially the case under Suzuki when work was abundant. The provision of work would itself assume the form of a gift, in that Suzuki was thinking of the well-being of the worker by giving him work. When ten or more guys were being sent out on a regular basis, Suzuki was able to expand this thoughtfulness beyond the core workers in the Okinawa-gang to anyone who required work (those not receiving welfare) and was recognized as "usable" (*tsukaeru*) at the workplace. Thus, when I started working, the first thing Suzuki told me was that if I desperately needed work, I could call him, and he would make it happen. He said he kept track of who worked how many days per week and how much they needed to get by. Takeda-san constituted an exception to the rule that the core members were off welfare, and he had grown frail over the years so that hard manual labor had become an increasing challenge for him; perhaps it was for this reason that he seemed to put all the more heart into the tasks he was assigned. A principle of seniority in the network of social relations necessitated his regular inclusion in the work group, though Takeda-san was subordinate to Kentarō at the workplace itself and was inescapably included in the every-man-for-himself market logic that would ultimately work to unravel sociality and group cohesion. By the same token, Suzuki emerged as a kind caretaker of the group when work was abundant, although economic necessity would one day lead the group to disband. Akira always did say: "Just watch, it won't last." Yet, likewise, he would note of Suzuki that he had a "genuinely kind" side; akin to Takeda-san and Ne-san's hospitality, this aspect of Suzuki's personality appeared unmotivated by immediate self-interest. Ideally, Suzuki thus rotated workers by taking into consideration the fatigue and financial needs of "everyone" (*minna*) and thereby ensured income for core workers without overwork. On the other hand, the guys tried to make sure to go, since "opening a hole" put the income of everyone at stake and served as a direct rebuff of Suzuki's consideration. Work was inscribed in a network of obligations on which the financial viability of the group as a whole and of Suzuki depended. Suzuki's reputation as tehaishi was heightened along with that of his workers, which, in turn, enabled him to provide more work. But this generosity was inscribed side by side with an egotism, the propensity toward which resided in both Suzuki's personality and the economic logic of being a tehaishi. Of course, Takeda-san *never* permitted egotism to rear its head, and it was from this self-effacement that he derived his undeniable respectability, authority, and power. But Suzuki would declare that the way things worked was that his own reputation would "rise" in accordance with the quality of work performed at the site. Via the vine of subcontractors above Suzuki, news reached him regarding the performance of his workers, leading Suzuki to have favorites. Wakami's tireless proficiency at all tasks reflected well on Suzuki—subcontractors put in requests for Wakami—and led Suzuki to send Wakami to construction sites that were of most significant income for the group.[15] When Wakami's only next of kin passed away, it was also Suzuki who did the rounds, collecting cash from everyone to pay Wakami for the bullet train and the working days he had missed. In another similar incident, Suzuki had moved in with his girlfriend and, because his room was now empty, decided to give it (all expenses paid) to an eighteen-year-old youngster who was having domestic problems. Assuming the role of a father figure, Suzuki urged the young man to take advantage of the place and to go to work, but the setup ended in a disaster when, having neglected to take care of the room, the eighteen-year-old was kicked out by Suzuki—clothing, luggage, and everything hauled into a garbage can on the street.

The scale of Matsuda's operations enabled him to act in a far more official capacity on behalf of his own crew and the Okinawa-gang. In fact, whenever someone wound up in the local, giant three-story police box in San'ya—nicknamed the "Mammoth" in the old days, on account of its size—it was Matsuda who stepped in and would use his reputation to fix a release, whenever he could. Sometimes a release could be achieved when two parties had been fighting. As he did later when Akira and Shōkawa were in custody for two weeks because the other party to a dispute refused to drop suit, Matsuda met with police officers outside of visiting hours and convinced the other party (whom he knew) not to press charges. This relieved everyone, including the local police, of the headache of prolonged detention and possible jail time. In fact, it was common practice for the police in Yama to let matters like fighting slip: brawls happened all the time, and so long as these were confined to San'ya, the police preferred to "turn a blind eye" (*mite minu furi*) and avoid the hassle of detaining someone or making an arrest.[16] In this way, Matsuda generated indebtedness not only with the Okinawa-gang, who would have been hard put to find someone to mediate, but with the police. Yet, contrary to Suzuki's moments of generosity, which had the air of disinterest to them, Matsuda's every act appeared in retrospect to have been motivated by some calculation of self-interest. When Matsuda received word that my partner was in town, he promptly put in a reservation for us to drink and dine on the house at the members-only bar on the twenty-eighth floor of the Asakusa View Hotel. By far the tallest and most opulent building in the Asakusa area, this was an invitation that was eagerly and genuinely presented and could not be turned down without causing insult. There was nothing to do but accept—even Akira said "there is no problem"—and so my partner and I stepped into a dimly lit bar on the twenty-eighth floor with a panoramic view of Asakusa and Tokyo's newest tourist attraction, the 640-meter-tall

Skytree. A waiter approached us in a tuxedo, presented us with menus, and proceeded to set up a table before us, on which he lined up six 1.5-liter bottles of shochu ordered from Kyushu. Taken aback by the ghastly juxtaposition of five-star luxury to San'ya, we were left to wonder at the connection between the disparate worlds.

As I discovered when I became unwillingly embroiled in Matsuda's world, the connection was the yakuza. After our visit to the Asakusa View Hotel, Matsuda increasingly started to relate his business schemes to me, calling me over the phone to schedule informal meetings at Sakura during which he expatiated in frenzied fashion about his plans to export water-cleansing equipment to Burma, his relations with a professor at Tokyo University who specialized in nuclear radiation, and the mystical rock formation (he had a sample in his office) that, unbeknownst to the scientific world, had magical properties that would accelerate nuclear decontamination. When he asked for my help, I said that I would aid as best I could. But I declined when he repeatedly and insistently requested that I accompany him to Fukushima Prefecture to oversee his decontamination projects. Disappointed, Matsuda finally relented and noted that he understood I was "afraid" of radiation, while I was left to ponder why on earth he would have wanted to bring me along in the first place. As a cultural anthropologist, I had no expertise in any of his ventures, and it was only after some time that I realized that Matsuda was angling to buttress his projects with the appearance of authority in just about any shape or form. For him, it sufficed that I was affiliated with a prestigious university in the United States and that he could speak of me and introduce me to others as his associate. This happened one evening when I had been asked to attend a meeting of all the participants in Matsuda's project, some of whom had flown in from Kyushu (the southernmost of Japan's four main islands) to meet on the twenty-eighth floor of the Asakusa View Hotel. Replete with a shady yakuza man in his midfifties who reminded me that I had previously dined on his tab there (I had not known), construction work subcontractors, company owners and businessmen from Fukushima, Matsuda's hoodlum (*chinpira*) sidekicks dressed in cheap suits, and a PhD student from the United States, this meeting was a burlesque masquerade of legitimate business concerns, in which everything was discussed from making contact with the military in Burma to decontamination in Fukushima and providing Fukushima Daiichi Nuclear Power Plant with workers:

> I had changed into a collared shirt and sweater to go. I waited before entering the lounge on the 28th floor of Asakusa View Hotel . . . but I arrived a little too early and entered the lounge only to find a bunch of senior intimidating figures in suits—including the dark figure of Mr. X—

exchanging calling cards. I felt decidedly out of place and waited for Matsuda outside, until he arrived shortly after with two younger men dressed
in cheap business suits. One looked decidedly punkish with hair sticking
straight up. Both were overweight, with heavy black circles under their
eyes. Otherwise, everyone seemed like real businessmen, that is, with the
exception of Mr. X and Matsuda, the latter of whom came in his regular
clothes, cellphone strapped to his belt. There were some 13 of us, some of
whom had come from Kumamoto and some of whom were affiliated
with this company, Hisugawa. The topic of the day was water-cleansing
technology—to be exported on the back of Naniwa company to Burma—
and related to this, the decontamination of radiation using this rock
called "minakami green." A bogus possibility, no matter how you looked
at it, but these men were really trying to sell the idea. . . . Photos were
circulated of Mr. X in Myanmar, standing in a line beside a military man
and his subordinates, all in military uniform. There were comments
made amongst everyone regarding how they really were in military uniform. Throughout the four-hour meeting, a 75-year-old technician and
owner of the rights to the technology spoke most of the time, getting on
Matsuda's nerves, saying that he had not heard about this or that. He especially freaked when he heard Naniwa company's name mentioned,
because he had had his rights stolen from them before. . . . It took a lot of
persuading from Matsuda to slowly get him onboard. You could tell,
though, that what this man really wanted—over and above Burma—was
to get inside TEPCO [Tokyo Electric Power Company] to clean the water.
It was a spectacle of someone wanting a piece of the pie—hard figures
were quoted—since Naniwa has monopolized the decontamination work
in Fukushima. Thus, he was really excited to get to know the TEPCO-
affiliated professor whom Matsuda and Mr. X knew. But Matsuda warned
him to stay clear of suggesting any business plan to the professor—this
relation had to stay purely "research"—because otherwise it would alien-
ate the professor from them. There was also talk of how most of the decontamination work is being done by workers from the outside of
Fukushima, and how they knew of locals from Fukushima who would be
eager to do that work themselves. This conversation struck a particularly
bad note with me, causing me to remember news articles stating that
decontamination workers simply do not have the necessary expertise to
do their jobs. As the night progressed, the three main figures at the end
of the table—Matsuda, Mr. X, and the owner—proceeded to get increasingly intoxicated, vivacious, and talkative, while the remainder of us
stayed silent.[17]

Too close for comfort, this meeting nevertheless provided the clearest picture I would get of the intersection of San'ya with the sordid corporate interests of construction companies, the yakuza (which hosted the meeting and financed Matsuda), and government funds. Matsuda was the brains behind both the project and the stitched-up assemblage of parties present, most of whom had not met each other before, and Mr. X was his benefactor. Obviously, there were no day laborers present. In fact, during the meeting, Matsuda was receiving phone calls from his minions back in the office regarding Suzuki, who had called to ask whether Matsuda could spare workers for the following day (this was about when *tehai* was taking place back in San'ya). Exasperated, Matsuda told them to deal with it by themselves and hung up. He clearly had more important matters to deal with. For the conglomeration of vested interests at this meeting constituted precisely the group of interests that labor unions in San'ya had fought against in the 1980s: a tehaishi in cahoots with the yakuza, construction companies, and, by extension, the state.[18] When Matsuda and the others above spoke of providing workers to Fukushima Daiichi Nuclear Power Plant, this was a conversation that was purely concerned with pocketing money that would accrue to them in return for supplying labor, that is, with taking easy money that would not go to workers.[19] And whether or not there was any merit to exporting water-cleansing equipment to Burma, the notion of a mystic rock formation that could accelerate nuclear decontamination was a lie. At the end of the day, when the pretense to philanthropy had been set aside, every one of the schemes discussed at the meeting above focused on taking funds that had been made available by the state, be it for decontamination in Fukushima or inside Fukushima Daiichi Nuclear Power Plant, the contracting of nuclear laborers, or the large-scale business alliance between Japan and Burma.

Thankfully, this meeting at the Asakusa View Hotel was the one and only occasion in which I was asked to meet Matsuda's business associates. Soon after, I left Japan for the United States, and when I returned, Matsuda had already fled from San'ya and from his debt to the mob, which he had been repaying by cutting the wages of his workers. But before this happened, I was privy (yet again) to the difficulties of navigating the political relationships of Matsuda's world, into whose orbit I had been forcibly pulled, or so I felt, by a display of generosity. One day I had entered Sakura:

> The place was packed. Sitting across from Akira, next to Suzuki, was a face that I had seen before. Big burly body. Equally big, comical face with a slight beard. Akira introduced me to Ikari, a member of the Kanamachi-ikka. "Ikari, Kanamachi-ikka," he said. Jokingly, Akira asked Ikari if he wouldn't "go nuts" at Sanyukai, where Akira had re-

cently gotten into a quarrel. Or if he wouldn't put on his black mobster suit and pay Sanyukai a visit to ask whether Akira was there. Ikari jokingly flexed his shoulders and muscles in response, as if preparing for action. It was a little afterwards that I felt like I had to be careful about what I said. Akira mentioned that I had gone to this meeting with Matsuda, and that I was going to meet this professor from Tokyo University. Ikari then asked me—indirectly, jokingly, but not really—to fill him in on this this professor, whom one of his friends had introduced to Matsuda. He said that he had already heard a little about this professor, but—blinking at me—would I not fill him in? I had to say that I was just there to help and not in a position to judge or know. I thought to myself: what if Matsuda hears about this conversation.[20]

Suzuki, too, had his way of showing off his largesse, albeit in a more down-to-earth, if unrefined, vulgar, and innocent way. He bragged of how he had "become famous in this town" after rumors spread of his fighting exploits, crowing about how, one day, the crowd by Mutō's hole-in-the-wall had parted like the ocean before him. Indeed, Suzuki dominated the scene by Mutō's, transforming the alley into a reception ground for the group as they got home, bought drinks, reported on how it had gone, and waited to be assigned sites for the following day. Notably, Matsuda, too, was known for never having lost a fight, but his manners were crafty, functional, and sober, as opposed to Suzuki, who perorated drunkenly on having become the most well-known tehaishi in San'ya. Extending his fingers to demonstrate how many subcontractors he had pocketed, Suzuki would continue, oblivious of Kentarō's frown, all the while drinking shochu with an air of self-entitlement and acting as if he was the only tehaishi who could provide the group with work. To make matters worse, Suzuki was also an incorrigible and successful womanizer, to the comical bewilderment of the Okinawa-gang, all of whom wished for romance but could not fathom how Suzuki always managed to have an affair going, and once even with a graduate of Tokyo University! And Suzuki was a terrible spendthrift, carelessly spending money as a sign of his influence and frequenting the neighboring red-light district, Yoshiwara, where he would easily blow ¥50,000 or ¥60,000 ($500 or $600) in one evening.

If not deriving from real egotism, projecting the image of an intimidating personage was an intrinsic part of the tehaishi role. Suzuki's most important task was to make sure that the correct number of workers went to work, and to ensure this, it had to be known that the failure to show up would carry consequences. This was particularly the case with new and unknown workers, with whom Suzuki would initially meet to lay down the terms of work, which included a warning of how angry he would become if they failed him but also an expla-nation of the many benefits they would receive (more work) if they did well. At times, especially with younger workers in their early twenties, Suzuki made it sound like he was offering them the opportunity of a lifetime, explaining how they could slowly work their way up, and he was forgiving at first, as were the others, when eighteen-year-olds had trouble getting up in the mornings and opened a hole. In the final analysis, however, the failure to comply had negative consequences for the Okinawa-gang as a whole, and on occasion, Suzuki, too, meted out physical retribution—the "chokehold," he called it—before giving someone a last chance. One did not go back on promises made to Suzuki.

Regrettably, Suzuki finally accepted money from so many subcontractors that he had trouble meeting the daily demand for workers. This happened much to Kentarō's distress, since it overworked the group and because, by foregoing the money, Suzuki could have maintained the relation at the level of favors that would have increased work without obligations. Combined with Suzuki's liquor habit, which started when he woke in the afternoon and approached two liters of sho-chu per day, egotism led Suzuki to make himself accountable for services that he could not provide. On the one hand, he was earning the money that had always been the sure sign of his standing in San'ya. Every worker paid him ¥500 ($5) as *pinhane* from their wages, in addition to which he received a minimum of ¥50,000 ($500) per subcontractor as a flat monthly fee, and he was in the habit of bragging that his income exceeded ¥400,000 (approximately $4,000) every month. On the other hand, Suzuki's liquor habit would force him to renege on his promises to subcontractors and the Okinawa-gang, spelling his downfall as a tehaishi.

Unlike the old days when tehaishi lined up at Namidabashi in the morning to pick their workers, Suzuki and Matsuda concluded their work between the hours of four and seven the previous evening. Except on Saturdays, Suzuki received a call from subcontractors when construction sites concluded the day, between four and five o'clock, after which Suzuki began his work of *tehai*. In addition to the number of workers required, the subcontractors informed Suzuki what type of worker (navvies, scaffolders, ironworkers) to assign and what kind of work they would do. Because the Okinawa-gang was composed mainly of navvies, the labor of which almost anyone could do, requests primarily came for navvies, but if other laborers were needed, Suzuki had acquaintances at hand.

It was important that Suzuki assign to sites workers who could be "used" (*tsu-kaeru*) at the given tasks. To ensure this, Suzuki generally paired inexperienced men with experienced workers so that the latter could instruct the former. For example, if *konkuri* (cement work) was scheduled, it was necessary that at least two workers knew how to use the vibrator that enabled the concrete to flow on the top floor and that at least one worker knew how to take care of things on the floor below, as cement seeped through the walls and often spilled out the cracks. Three extra workers were then required: one to join the worker on the floor below, one to hold the heavy wires of the vibrator, and one to clean the steel rods protruding from the top floor. To do his job well as tehaishi, Suzuki consequently had to possess proficient knowledge of the skills required of specific tasks and had to know which of the guys could do what. But Suzuki had only worked for one year as a navvy alongside his brother Kentarō, who had four decades of experience. As a result, Suzuki was criticized for lacking the expertise necessary for his work, and as he expanded his obligations to subcontractors, he came into the habit of pairing any number of inexperienced workers with experienced workers like Kentarō, such that the latter was overburdened. Because Kentarō cut such an intimidating figure that anyone would "listen to" (*iu koto o kiku*) him, as Suzuki noted, grouping newbies with Kentarō became a quick-fix solution to fixing the numbers for the following day, especially as Suzuki got progressively drunk and desperate to settle the tehai. It was not unusual, however, that tehai continued late into the evening and that, as a last resort, Suzuki had to wake up early in the morning to scout a stranger lingering by the train station. Otherwise, Suzuki did not show his face in the mornings, save on the rare occasion when he had to introduce new workers. Yet even this became more and more infrequent as Suzuki preferred to sleep in until the midafternoon.

As a rule, Suzuki could be found at a designated spot in San'ya, from which he did his tehai. By making it known where he would be between four and seven o'clock, by which time the tehai had generally concluded, Suzuki made himself available to anyone who wished to seek him out in person and to workers who did not have a cell phone. It also allowed him to welcome back workers, to check in with them as he assigned them to new sites or gave them the day off, and to collect his ¥500 *pinhane*, or for that matter, any money he had lent them, so they could pay for their transportation and lunch. Sitting in a designated spot also enabled the Tenjima company's middleman to find Suzuki easily in order to hand him the transportation money for the following day, which was a flat ¥500 per person: the same as Suzuki's *pinhane* or his daily liquor allowance.

Emblematized in the figure of the tehaishi, the meeting place for Suzuki and his crew was far more than functional because it condensed the excesses of work, alcohol, and gambling. During the spring, summer, and early fall, and with the exception of that brief period when the seventy-year-old Mutō was jailed for running an illegal gambling operation, this meeting place where all the returning workers of the Okinawa-gang congregated after work was the narrow street in front of Mutō's hole-in-the-wall. A one-minute walk from Suzuki's bunkhouse, Suzuki would arrive around four, pull up a wooden stool, and wait for the phone to ring. Dressed in flip-flops, shorts, and a T-shirt, he would sit with a glass of

Mutō's cheap Daigoro shochu with water and ice, placed on the ramshackle table beside him, alongside two sheets of paper: one of that day's statistics on boat racing—and after he had received calls from the subcontractors—another of a list of construction sites with numbers written in parentheses next to them. Suzuki would move his eyes, distracted, between the box TV in the upper left-hand corner of Mutō's hole-in-the-wall and the race stats. Eyeing the races and shouting at the regular drunks—of which there were always five or six, lounging about chatting, talking to themselves in their own worlds, or passed out on the cement—to get the hell out of the way when they blocked his field of vision, Suzuki would shift back to the statistics after the races concluded, talk to Akira, or pick up the phone. Every time he shifted to pick up the statistics or to fill in another name on his list of workers, Suzuki would put on his sharp-looking red reading glasses, which made his face look distinctly like that of an out-of-place accountant on the grimy street. Every once in a while, he would receive a phone call or put one in, almost just like he placed ¥500 bets with Mutō, who sat behind the counter and wrote numbers in his ledger. Sometimes tehai ended with one phone call, as when the number of workers and locations matched up with the day that was just concluding. Then, Suzuki could put in a single call to the guys, who were still at the construction site, and tell them to repeat the routine the next day. More often, however, the tehai continued into the evening, as dusk fell and members started coming back, sometimes alone, sometimes in pairs or groups, dirty, tired, and carrying backpacks laden with clothes, tools, and safety belts.

The street in front of Mutō's hole-in-the-wall was then transformed into a veritable thoroughfare for workers, especially when Matsuda was also doing tehai from the same place, trading workers with Suzuki. At Mutō's, the guys would have another drink (their second, at least, after work), standing about, sitting on a chair if they could find one or on the ground in small groups. They would buy 'drinks for one another, which called for reciprocity, and they would gamble before splitting up and leaving for the next dive bar. After he started working, Akira would always observe of this daily celebration, as he would of every occasion with the guys, that he was left without a penny after all the rounds of drinks and gambling. "No matter how much, there is never enough money" (*ikura kane ga attemo tarinai*). Kentarō, too, would make an unknowing gesture as to where exactly all the money went, raising his palms upward to the sides and tilting his head. The only way not to spend the entirety of the daily wage from that day was to go home.

Alongside the drinking and gambling, it was normal for confrontations to take place, for fights to break out, and for the cops to pay the crowd a visit, if only to warn them that complaints had been issued and to be careful not to block the passage of cars. The cops were well aware that the entire conflagration of activities was illegal, beginning with Mutō's boat racing, for which he had no license and was backed by the yakuza (which also made the gambler criminally responsible). This was likewise the case for the dive bar, Sakura, where Suzuki would do his tehai during the winter months and where boat racing bets were also accepted, backed by the mob. Thus, it befell Suzuki and Matsuda to pay the Kanamachi-ikka monthly for the right to work in their "territory" (nawabari). As a matter of pride, Suzuki was thus a "sworn brother" (kyōdaibun) with a man in the Kanamachi-ikka. Once every month, their shiny, black van could be found parked outside Sakura, in which a driver in a black suit waited for Suzuki. But the Okinawa-gang declined to take on work directly from the Kanamachi-ikka, as it entailed too many complications. Indeed, when rumors started to circulate regarding well-paid work at Fukushima Daiichi Nuclear Power Plant, this work was to be acquired through the Kanamachi-ikka.

At the Construction Site

Work started at eight o'clock in the morning at the construction site, but workers would arrive as early as seven to sit, smoke, read the sports newspaper (which contained the gambling statistics), and while away the time that remained after changing into work clothes. If it was their first time at a construction site, they tried to arrive especially early to stay on the safe side. Only a few of the guys, like the twenty-eight-year-old Wakami, who commuted in his work clothes, or Kentarō, when he had had a late night, would arrive last minute or late to work. There was thus almost always time for a cigarette, a nap, light breakfast, and maybe even a quick game of cards.

At eight o'clock, the general assembly began in a clearing with radio calisthenics. Introduced in 1928 to commemorate the emperor, the same cheery music with instructions aired all across construction sites in Tokyo and, no doubt, all of Japan, at eight every morning. The crowd of workers did their stretches in construction gear in sync with the music, facing a central platform before which the foremen, identifiable by their green denim clothes, also did stretches.[21] At most sites, the workers and overseers alike did their calisthenics half-assed, but *not* doing them was not an option. Kentarō just pointed his fingers downward, wriggling them with his back upright, when he was actually supposed to be reaching for his toes. The exertion was in any case impossible, since he was as stocky and round as a penguin. Yet, at certain sites, the calisthenics took on an explicitly disciplinary function. To put me in place before work began, one work leader slipped up behind me during the calisthenics and told me to do them "firmly." At another site, it was daily practice to line workers up for calisthenics according to their specialization—navvies, scaffolders, carpenters, electricians, machinists—all seated in separate rows on dinky little plastic chairs before and after calisthenics, and during the stretches themselves, one of the foremen walked around, watching the workers while occasionally telling them to bend their knees properly. Hardly any surprise, at this site it was also the foremen who decided when workers took breaks, and it was explained to me that the top foreman was so strict that he would single out workers who were not doing the stretches seriously and make them repeat the exercises alone after the morning assembly. Once the assembly concluded, a solitary figure might thus be doing the calisthenics alone to nonexistent music.

The meeting itself began after calisthenics. Workers then picked up their helmets, safety belts and equipment and lined up in the queue of their profession. They self-identified in accordance with their specialization, referring to each other as navvies, scaffolders, carpenters, operators, or electricians.[22] At some sites, new workers were even made to introduce themselves on a microphone in front of the crowd, stating their name and subcontractor. Then the foremen took turns outlining the tasks for the day and the safety precautions that needed to be taken. They explained where the heavy machinery—excavators, dump trucks carrying away soil, cranes, cement trucks—would be moving. On rainy days, the slipperiness of the soil and the danger of falling into the trenches was emphasized. In the summer, when it got as hot as forty degrees Celsius, workers were told to take precautions against heatstroke, to keep well hydrated, and were reminded how many workers had already been carried off from heatstroke. If an accident or death had recently occurred at a company site, workers were especially urged to ensure "safety" (anzensei).[23] Once the foremen had spoken, workers gathered in groups of four or five to go over the tasks of the day again, to reiterate the safety precautions, and to verify that everyone's safety gear was in order. The foremen walked around while this took place, listening in, and as if this were not enough, a single worker was finally called in front of everyone to summarize the tasks and safety precautions, a prospect many of the guys dreaded: public speaking. At last, everyone retired to the changing rooms for a quick rest and smoke before actual work started at eight thirty. Workers were only spared this morning assembly (chōrei) when cement work was scheduled, since navvies then had to be ready once the concrete trucks arrived, and thus they prepared for this during the morning assembly.

The haphazard means of approving the medical condition of workers were revealed at an additional introductory meeting for new workers, after the assembly. It was at this meeting that workers were required to submit their blood pressure readings to receive approval for work. Since the foremen did not observe the laborers when they took their blood pressure (the monitor was in another room), it was common practice for everyone in the group who had high blood pressure—that is, almost everyone—to submit a false reading. For if the upper reading was above 160, workers were denied permission to work. Consequently, when the guys arrived at a new construction site en masse, the first matter of business was for the twenty-eight-year-old Wakami or myself to take four or five readings and hand them out to the group. It would have posed a problem for both workers and foremen if most workers were disqualified on account of high blood pressure, and so the foremen turned a blind eye to fake blood pressure readings. By so doing, they also retrojected responsibility for health consequences on the individual himself: everyone worked at his own risk. Indeed, no one even raised an eyebrow when five men in their midfifties presented identical blood pressure readings of 120/80.[24]

Thus, three to four times per week, the guys in the Okinawa-gang were consumed by the work of a navvy, which involved a number of tasks that, at least in theory, could be done by anyone. For work as a navvy required no license and paid less than many of the other lines of construction work. Many in the group did, in fact, have licenses to work as scaffolders, which paid more on account of the danger for which the scaffolder assumed full responsibility, but they would reluctantly admit that anyone could work as a navvy, regardless of age and physical condition.[25] At least in appearance, this was a form of labor that Marx referred to as "unskilled labor" and that disclosed a strict hierarchical division not only between manual and mental labor, which was all too evident in the difference between the foremen who never raised a finger and everyone else, but between the "skilled" worker and the "unskilled" navvy, whose work could be undertaken by anyone.[26] Of course, for the guys, their labor was certainly "skilled" and thereby masculine labor, for this was labor, they said, that women could not do, and it was undeniable that the expertise of veteran workers increased productivity at the site and enhanced demand for the group. To a certain degree, even the work of a navvy retained the character of a unified craftsmanship that demanded experience, knowledge, and expertise, and perhaps this differentiated it from work that might have been undertaken at an assembly line.[27] But it went without saying that navvies occupied the bottom rung among the manual laborers at the construction site and, therefore, stood at the farthest reach from the intellectual labor of the foremen, whose separation from manual laborers was not simply discursive or a matter of degree.[28] As Alfred Sohn-Rethel explicates it, the separation of manual from mental labor is constitutive of the capitalist mode of production because by relegating the organizational and technical aspects of the workplace to a specific cadre of individuals (the foremen), capital deprives manual laborers of the cohesive knowledge required to take production back into their own hands, thereby rendering them dependent on capital.[29] Moreover, the wage is integral to sustaining this division. For by conferring value on their labor, the individualizing wage reincorporates manual laborers back into sociality, only to sever them from one another, making it appear as if the power to produce belongs not to them as a social unit but to capital, whose property they have become and in whose interest they are made to produce surplus value by the foremen.[30] In this way, the division of mental from manual labor is constitutive of the wage laborer, whose reproduction Marx regarded as constitutive of capitalist production.[31] Lest head and hand unify against the shareholders and upper management of the Seichō Corporation, it was for this reason that the separation between overseers and manual laborers at the construction site was enforced so stringently. But it was perhaps also to maintain his indispensable place in the group that Kentarō never taught others how to use the vibrator or the electronic depth gauge. It went without saying that there was indeed a certain amount of know-how (as opposed to theoretical knowledge) that belonged almost exclusively to the manual laborers at the construction site.

Nevertheless, it was precisely its menial character that qualified navvy work as the end of the line. With the exception of the twenty-eight-year-old Wakami, almost everyone who worked as a navvy appeared older and less fit than workers in the other professions. While the scaffolder required the agility, balance, and fearlessness to work high along scaffolding, the ironworker needed the sheer upper-body strength to bend and carry metal reinforcements. But the navvy had to be able to use the shovel, carry things, clean, and sometimes operate equipment like a chainsaw, concrete vibrator, or electronic depth gauge. Very little specialization was required of bottom-rung navvies, and unlike older scaffolders, the navvy never commented on becoming unable to keep up with younger workers. In a typical reversal of hierarchies, Akira accounted for the ranking system between various workers at the construction site: the most important part in a building, or anything for that matter, was the "foundation," and in this sense, navvies did the most important work. As if he were speaking of San'ya itself, he added that, as a navvy, Kentarō did not take crap from anyone on the construction site.

Work as a navvy did, however, involve a range of tasks that varied in physical intensity, danger, and technical expertise. Maybe the simplest task was "digging holes" (ana hori), for which no instruction whatsoever seemed necessary, except for knowing how to pace oneself and pause. But this task was also considered one of the most demanding and entailed digging in places that the excavator could not reach. In this case, human labor power filled in for the machine, meaning that even at this most menial level of labor, the manual laborer was expected to match his actions to the pace of machinery such that, as Marx once observed, the conditions of work determined the speed and content of the laborer's motions, rather than the other way around.[32] By determining the pace and substance of labor, machinery superseded the disciplinary role of foremen, whose role it was to maximize productivity. Given the physical strain of digging holes, this task was usually given to younger members of the group, like Wakami or myself. It was work, like all the other tasks, in which the earth was destroyed, and human labor was expended to lay the foundations of a new building. At the age of fifty-six, Saruma thus explained that, to get through the day, especially when doing demanding physical labor, he needed to pace himself in accordance with the break periods held from ten to ten thirty, twelve to one (lunch), and three to three thirty. It was only the thought and certainty of an upcoming break that enabled him to continue, a little more, until the next break. Thus, time passed and constituted the abstract measure of bodily expenditure. Yet, unconcerned with the material contingencies of the workplace, this was a specific form of time, one oriented toward the future in a future-anterior mode in which the workday, like the portions of the day, *will have* ended.[33] At least one person had to bring either a wristwatch or phone out to the construction site, so the guys could ask each other, sometimes every five minutes, if the time for a break had arrived yet. The alternative was to wait endlessly for the other workers to head lazily back to the changing rooms. If a watch was on hand, it was possible to get a head start. In the summer, when workers were regularly hospitalized for heatstroke, the stretch between one and three o'clock felt especially long. At those times, it was better not to look at the watch, to stick it out, and be relieved that time had passed when one finally dared a glance.

Direct exposure to the sun and heat and seemingly endless swathes of time were most intense when cement work was scheduled. This was a task, moreover, that involved the highest degree of technical expertise and, hence, the clearest hierarchy in the division of labor among the navvies. Six navvies were required to lay the concrete floors of the high-rise apartment blocks built by Seichō. Two of these took turns operating the vibrator that released the cement, a heavy, plug-like object that had to be lugged about and dipped into the cement along the crevices of the walls and the slabs of the floors, to even it all out. There were only three or four in the group who knew how to do this work, which involved reading the texture and height of the cement, matching the movements of the man holding the cement pump, and anticipating how everything would even out when they came back from the other side. When dumping the vibrators inside the walls, this navvy had to gauge from the sound and feel of the vibrator how long it had to be held in place, releasing just enough. Meanwhile, another navvy brushed the protruding steel reinforcements of the walls with water so that excess concrete would not stick to them. And yet another navvy did two tasks, holding the wires of the vibrator so the navvy operating it did not have to haul them about (or the generator attached to them) and, as the concrete approached the margins of the floor, shoveling cement to even out the edges. The remaining two navvies stayed on the floor below, in the belly of the building. As cement poured into the walls—bolts and screws shaking from the vibrators and making a racket, as if a drill had been plugged inside, joined by the spout of the cement tube reaching up alongside the outside of the building like the neck of a beast—these two navvies hammered away on the bottom of the walls to make sure the concrete made it all the way down and, while the floor slabs were completed, cleaned up any excess cement that had spilled through the fissures in the walls and ceiling above. This latter job could be dangerous, because it could happen that the carpenters had not sufficiently secured the wooden frames of the walls. The sheer weight of the raw cement filling the walls could then cause the wooden mold to break and collapse on the navvy. This was not a big issue when there was space behind the navvy, but if work was in the cellar, the navvy had to crawl into a crevice between the wall and the soil, and if the navvy was in the crevice when the wall collapsed, he would be buried in a deluge of raw cement, wood, steel reinforcements, wires, and bolts. The navvy thus had to know from the sound of the hammer on the walls when the concrete had risen above the waist and climb out immediately. The navvies on the bottom floor were covered with cement by the end of the day, a prospect that the navvies holding the vibrators could prevent, depending on their ability to establish a rhythm with the man holding the pump. On days when cement was scheduled, every single movement of the worker was, in effect, matched to the rate at which the machine on the ground floor spouted out cement. If the concrete mixers did not arrive on time, work was stalled. This allowed everyone to take a break and "escape" to the shade in the summer, but it was also vexing as workers wanted to be finished. On the other hand, when the mixers were lined up downstairs, work continued nonstop, save for lunch, because breaks were not given on days when cement was slated. Forced upon them by the machinery, workers marched to the rhythm of capital. By this same token, the navvy had to keep up with the man lugging about the concrete spout, who, in accordance with the bulky weight of the spout, did not shy from showering an inexperienced or slow navvy with an unsparing string of invectives. In turn, the man who operated the spout connected to the concrete truck below had to match his movements to the pulse of the machine that pummeled concrete with beastly force, reining in the end of the spout and directing it with ropes. But the machine and tube had a life of their own.

The force of the concrete pump and the superhuman tube extending from it harbored the specter of accidents that overhung the working day. To begin with, the concrete itself contained chemicals that could burn straight through bare skin, leaving gaping sores. Sure enough, prolonged exposure to concrete wore down any working gloves and clothes, and although workers protected themselves against direct exposure with proper work gear, accidents could not be predicted. One day, the elevated tube connecting the concrete in the truck to the workers split in half right above our heads, writhing and spewing cement like a broken exhaust pipe. Everyone fled from the sight to clean themselves up, but it did not require much of an imagination to know that the tube, filled with cement, would have broken somebody's neck if it had fallen on their head. Contact with the force of the machinery would have been deadly. Indeed, during work, senior laborers would give brief but deadly serious instructions regarding dangers of the tasks at hand, the neglect of which could have real consequences. The cement pebbles in the air, for instance, petrified in the lungs: it was best not to breathe in too much. And if you started to feel dizzy during the summer—symptoms of heatstroke—you should go inside regardless of work and sit under the air conditioner. When accidents occurred, it became the subject of awed gossip, prompting workers in the changing rooms or San'ya to recount a series of other, similar experiences. The former scaffolder, Iwasawa, who was as frail as a stick in his early fifties and could hardly walk, had once fallen from a height of several stories, puncturing his ribs and breaking all sorts of other bones. Other younger scaffolders, too, had been paralyzed from the neck down. The long and short of it was that if you got into an accident, "no one is going to look after you," and this dictum of the workplace, where men were made to assume almost complete "self-responsibility" (jikosekinin), was carried over into the everyday life of San'ya, where physical confrontations and illnesses were regarded as self-incurred. San'ya constituted proof that no one would look after you, except, finally, the state, into whose hands the deteriorating health of laborers was handed over, forfeiting their masculinity. It was said that "you protect your own body by yourself" (jibun no mi wa jibun de mamoru). But the days only alternated between the self-destruction of drink and that of work, and in the changing rooms, workers would puff away in breaks, inundating the room with smoke.

Following on cement work, negiri (excavating the foundation) required most coordination between the navvies and machinery. In fact, excavation was what a navvy specialized in, and for this reason, they were in highest demand when the foundations of buildings were being laid. During such times, there was work for navvies every day, as the construction site had to be excavated before any other work could proceed. The guys were thus busiest at the beginning of the financial year—April 1 in Japan—when construction companies invested capital in new buildings. Navvies would then come to the construction site in the absence of scaffolders, steelworkers, carpenters, or electricians and transform the soil beside an excavator. Working side by side with the excavator entailed that the navvy had to be constantly aware of the location of the excavator up above, moving ceaselessly back and forth, humming and circling without rest as it dug

farther and farther along the floor plan of the building. It was said that machinists could operate the excavator for hours without rest, and navvies had to match
its speed, just as digging holes involved digging where its square beak could not
reach. Down below in the holes, navvies kept up by leveling out the height of
the ground with a shovel, cleaning the margins, and securing the walls of the hole
with wooden boards that were said to have come from Fukushima Prefecture
(thus, to be irradiated) and pipes, plunged into the ground so that the walls would
not crumble. Using an electronic depth indicator, one navvy—usually Riku or
Kentarō—read the floor plan and, with a spray can, indicated the places that required more digging and those that were all right, while two other navvies followed up with other work. Sometimes, the depth of the hole dug by the excavator
required one of the navvies to take a spade to correct the depth. Otherwise, the
remaining two navvies cleaned the insides of the excavation dug by the excavator, evening out the surfaces, and carried wooden boards and steel pipes to secure the sides of the excavation, which required several trips to the storage area,
due to the weight of the pipes and boards. Once the depth had been established
and the pipes and boards collected, the navvies signaled to the machinist that
they could go ahead and secure the walls. This last work required speed and nim-
ble fingers on the part of the navvy, who had to work with, keep up with, and
stay out of the way of the excavator. First, the navvy placed the wooden boards up
against the sides of the hole, nailing the edges together so they reached across
both vertically and horizontally. Second, the navvy signaled the machinist and
began putting the pipes in place. This required that the navvy place the pipe so
that it leaned against the wooden boards, placing pressure against them to hold
the soil behind in place. Depending on the size of the hole, there were usually
eight pipes per side. Because the machinist above could not gauge the distance to
these pipes, the navvy held the pipe in place with one hand and, with the other,
instructed the operator to move the beak of the excavator forward and down so
that it clasped the tip. At this point, the navvy had to "run out of the way," because
once the beak pushed down, the pipe was plunged into the earth. It went without saying that, if a finger was caught between the beak and the pipe, or if a foot
was stuck under the pipe, the force of the excavator would take it off. And sometimes, just when the excavator released its hold, the pipe bounced back toward
the face of the navvy, shredded across its tip.

The prevention of accidents required attending to dangerous contingencies,
yet, at the same time, it also demanded a deadening to the possibility of these
contingencies ever coming to deadly fruition. Thinking too much about the ever-
present possibility of accidents would have made work impossible, so energy
had to be invested in maintaining a certain "shield," as Freud once wrote, to block
out this possibility.[34] Confronted with the specter and penetrating shock of an

accident bound to happen at some point, manual workers at the construction site had to block out direct exposure to material contingencies. It was as if they labored in an abstract temporality imposed on them by capital, in which the time of production had been emptied out of the interruptive (yet inevitable) force of accidents and other hindrances.[35] At the end of the workday, the worker was drained to the point of fatigue since the tasks imposed on him required that he expend his energy as efficiently as possible but also because these tasks demanded that he deaden himself to the physical environment of the construction site—a deadening that resulted in an etiolation of material stimuli, for it deprived the manual laborer and man of a sensorial experience of the world that he could call his own. When dust particles flew in the air, he either turned his face or wrapped a towel around his mouth. If he stepped on a nail, he ignored the injury until lunch break, when he could run by a pharmacy. Even downright exhaustion left no choice but to carry on. Likewise, scaffolders knew what would happen if they fell from a height of thirty stories, since it had happened to others. One man related what passed through his mind when looking down from such a height: "If I fall from here, I will die." Nevertheless, he continued to work without the encumbrance of his safety gear. In this way, the possibility of accidents had to be bracketed and repressed as if it did not exist. During my first week at the construction site, before I myself had become desensitized, I wrote as follows of the excavation work:

> What the machines cannot do, we fill in. I remember being scared of the crane on the first day. Of working so close to it, having to align pipes to the boarded walls of craters, down in the bottom . . . holding the pipes in place while the crane put its snout to the top of the bar, and pushed it down. Incredible power. Super-human. Pushing that bar into the ground, two or three meters with no effort at all. Kentarō always saying immediately after the snout was placed and ready to push down: "run away." Yesterday, I realized why. The crane pushed down and because the pipe got stuck momentarily . . . the snout ripped straight through the metal. Put a huge gash in the top of the pipe. The day before, the crane was carrying one of those metal boards placed on the ground, across which vehicles drive. Kentarō said they weigh 1.5 tons. He added that if the driver is good, he can stack up to two boards at once, and carry them thus. Yesterday, Kentarō said, "look": the big crane was carrying the small crane up to a different level. When we put metal bars in place, for "stopping the mountain" (*yamadome*), we move to match the progress of the crane. We don't move at our own pace. We move so that the crane can move quickly on to other work.[36]

The work of excavation also involved the task of inserting wooden walls between giant H-shaped bars that had been driven into the ground beforehand to align with the future floor plan, separating the walls and supporting the building from its corners. The excavator began by digging along the edges of the building, uncovering the H-shaped bars that were separated by 100–150 centimeters. When two meters had been dug up, the navvies would step into the pit, armed with spades and crowbars, take away a layer of earth from behind the H-shaped bars, and insert wooden boards behind the H shape. The H shape of the bars prevented the boards from falling out, as the navvies worked from the bottom up, filling in soil behind the boards. Once 2 meters had been completed, the excavator would come back and dig another two meters, and thus the task was repeated until the wall was as deep as 10–20 meters. This was demanding work, especially when the earth was rock-hard clay or if it had been raining and work was done in knee-deep water. Sometimes, a water pump had to be dumped into the water to facilitate work, but regardless, soil and dust particles flew everywhere as the navvies cleared the walls of soil, and at least one span had to be kept open between the navvies, because sometimes the crowbars would slip when they struck out to the sides. Two navvies would thus remain down in the pit. There they would also measure the distance between bars and call up to a third navvy—usually Kentarō, who shirked work in the pit—who cut the wooden boards to the right length with a chainsaw and threw them down as they were concluded. These boards were heavy, especially when wet, and the navvies had to communicate so that they were thrown safely. Once the boards were all down in the pit, the navvies wedged them behind the H shape and moved along the side of the wall to start another span as the excavator came in to dig farther from where they had left off. But the earth behind the navvy was not held in place by anything. Once, after it had rained, this part of the excavation caved in on Takeda-san, leaving him knee-deep in soil. Alarmed and immediately to the rescue, Kentarō and the others laughed about the incident afterward, noting that one cannot move once the soil gets to knee level.

Finally, the most demanding of all tasks was to work as *tobi no temoto* (at the scaffolder's side), or as a helper to the scaffolder. After merely one day working at the scaffolder's side, Saruma swore to Kentarō that he would never do it again. Akira also complained endlessly of the one day he had worked with Saruma as a helper to the scaffolder. Keeping up had forced him to flee from work and to throw up from the exertion. After this incident, it was decided in the group that work with scaffolders would only be given to the younger crew, like Wakami or myself. Much like digging holes, this task was straightforward: the navvy had to assist scaffolders when the scaffolding came down, forming the last link in the human chain of scaffolders that extended up alongside the scaffolding, receiving and handing pieces on as they were dismantled. Standing at ground level, the navvies had to work faster than scaffolders since they had to carry off the pieces, which were heavy, and be ready to receive the next one. It was pure stamina work for navvies, who had to match the youth and speed of scaffolders with their electronic screwdrivers, and it was nonstop, as the pipes, bolts, and metal walking boards kept coming.

On a typical day, the group prepared to leave the construction site at around four thirty. If Kentarō was on-site, this last stretch of time was preceded by his looking at the clock every few minutes or his asking repeatedly what time it was of the person who had the watch. Hence, as everyone knew, getting ready to leave with Kentarō started around four fifteen, with a pretense to working while waiting for four thirty, when it was actually considered legitimate to start packing up.[37]

As if it were part of work itself, Kentarō did almost anything possible to end the working day early. He was always in a hurry to return: the first out of the changing room, rushing to make the earliest train and practically jogging to transfer trains. For a few months, he even got into the habit of buying confectionary at a cake store on the way home for the mama-san (proprietor) of his favorite eatery (*izakaya*). Laughing at the novelty of this practice, Kentarō said he had never done anything like it before and that it was "fun." Kentarō even had his laundry done by the proprietor of this eatery, who folded his clothes and presumably also charged him for the services. Of course, the dynamic of this relationship shifted whenever Kentarō fell into debt at the eatery, as it was his privilege and habit to drink on credit, and his mama-san would begin charging interest on this debt, calling his phone every day to come and drink or to pay up. Then, Kentarō would no longer come by with cakes after work but, begrudgingly, with increments of cash. But a month later, the debt was forgotten about, and Kentarō would be back drinking and trying to fondle the mama-san. Until Kentarō fired Suzuki and took over tehai, there existed a clear break for him between work at the construction site and the world of San'ya.

It was a distinctive feature of the day laborer's working day that the minute it was over at five o'clock, it was well and truly over. Work could not be taken home; nor were the hierarchical relations of the workplace reproduced in social relations among the guys in San'ya, albeit an elevated status did attach to the tehaishi or Kentarō. For in Yama, it was the unfailingly graceful and humble Takeda-san, paragon of a vanishing world of mobster values, who emerged as the mythic source of authority: a figure who looked out for everyone and treated everyone as equals.

The return to this world of San'ya was thus marked with a drink after work. After leaving the site and changing at four forty-five, all the guys invariably stopped by a convenience store before getting on the train. No matter the time of year, Riku would buy a One Cup Ozeki sake and sometimes something sweet, sharing at first. A lean figure in his late fifties with unshaven chin or a rough beard, Riku cut the figure of a lone wolf at the train station, sitting removed from the rest of the group, leaning against a pillar on his heels as he sipped from his sake and looked out in front of himself. On days when Riku did not work, the number of One Cups he drank grew to ten, he said, or sometimes fifteen. He laughed as he described his fondness for "liquor" and confessed he would start drinking at five in the morning, black out toward noon, and fall asleep either in his room or somewhere under the overhang of the Iroha arcade, where he could often be seen sleeping on the side of the street, a thin blanket spread over him, his traditional Japanese clogs (*geta*) sticking out from the bottom.[38] Days off were, unequivocally, days off, and this separation of work from the world of Yama began with the consumption of a drink on the train home. By the time everyone arrived in Minami-Senjū, they would each have a buzz. Hence, Takeda-san always bought a 500 ml Nodokoshi Kirin Happōshū beer and with it his trademark snack, *kaki no tane* (soy-flavored rice crisps and peanuts). Unless it was summer, when he would get a beer, as well, Kentarō always bought a cup of straight shochu that he tucked into the inside of his jacket or in his back pocket.

This consumption of alcohol on the train and cigarettes on the train platform separated the guys from regular commuters. While smoking on the platform was not permitted, drinking in the train was not prohibited, but it was certainly frowned on. It created an atmosphere of unease around the group when they openly flaunted the "rules" like this, especially on less crowded trains, where they were in plain sight. Of course, as Akira put it, some guys acted more like "gentlemen" on their way back than others. Takeda-san, for instance, never smoked in public, while Kentarō and the others would stand off to the side somewhere, behind a pillar, and smoke on the platform before the train arrived. To Akira's horror, Saruma simply smoked in the open. One time, when another commuter reminded Saruma that smoking was not allowed, Saruma proceeded to cuss the person out: "What's it got to do with you?" But all and sundry drank in the train, cutting a sharp contrast to other commuters. In addition, many of the guys were still in work clothes: Takeda-san sported a baseball cap backward with Nike sneakers after work, but he kept his baggy workpants, carrying a cell phone with *One-Piece* anime stickers, since he was an avid fan. The others similarly carried bulky bags and wore clothes stained with paint or cement, oftentimes ripped at the bottom. There was, indeed, a sense in which the guys consciously flaunted "manners" in the public space of the train compartment, although this was a far reach from the deliberate and threatening display of mobster affiliation that Yamamori took pleasure in enacting on every occasion he came face to face with general society. Nor did Yamamori ever go to work. It was only that, being tired after a day at work, having a drink took precedence over etiquette, and so the guys would help themselves—without exception—to a beer, sake, or shochu. Every once in a while, a prim, elder housewife would glare at us, and Takeda-san would react abashed, but such incidents were brushed off with a laugh as the guys settled into the loosening effects of alcohol. It was just as likely that the guys would give their seats away to a couple with a baby and play with the child for the remainder of the ride back. At Minami-Senjū Station, everyone each went his own way—some to meet Suzuki, Kentarō to deliver his confectionary, and Takeda-san to the local bathhouse—although there was a strong likelihood that many would end up drinking together later that evening, be it at Mutō's hole-in-the-wall, Sakura, Chūfukuro, Iseya, or Gen, on whose proprietor Kentarō had a crush.

The separation of the construction site from the world of San'ya fostered self-awareness of the social position the group occupied within general society and, in seeing the fruits of their labor externalized and dispossessed, of themselves as objects of labor. In fact, every time the train passed an apartment block or building the guys had worked on, they were reminded of the time they had spent constructing it. In this manner, there was a mutually constitutive dichotomy at play between the construction site and San'ya, reflected in the difference between the "disposable" laborer and the "skilled artisan" (*ude ga yoi shokunin*) or in the respect accorded to someone like the frail Iwasawa, who had "worked his butt off" when he was young and was experiencing the deadly effects of his labor for others, which had ultimately been for naught. It must be asked elsewhere whether this separation placed the manual worker in a different category from the salaryman— Georg Lukács once argued that intellectual labor must be differentiated from manual labor, since the latter does not consume the interiority of the mind and ends at five o'clock.[39] But it was nevertheless this antinomy between subject and object that gave rise to self-consciousness among San'ya's laborers and that necessitated mutual recognition among members of the group. Otherwise, the men of San'ya would have been nothing but the dying and disposed of.[40]

Regardless of what the laborer was aware of, however, economic necessity compelled the exchange of labor for wages. In this respect, the counterdiscourse of San'ya accommodated itself to and attenuated the cruelty of the workplace, for an artisan worked with dignity, and reversed the social arbitrariness and negativity of the wage—for which laborers exchanged their lives—with a narrative detour that installed an alternative modality of shame, honor, and sociality. To uphold the values of an upstanding otoko, who did good by his buddies and sacrificed himself for the group, it was necessary to maintain a poignant sensibility of failure and shame, because it was only in contradistinction to shame that honor and, therefore, dignity could be sustained, over against the shamelessness that the exclusive pursuit for money would engender. Taking precedence even over life itself, it was on the disavowed margins of Japan Inc., where the truth of labor was disclosed to consist in expendability and death, that the order of a singular master signifier was repeated over and over again. It was precisely there where nothing but equivalence seemed to reign and the commodity form of labor was materialized in its most spectral guise that a social signifier of honor was reiterated, for which many of the guys were willing to sacrifice themselves.[41] Coming back from the construction site exhausted was what an otoko did, but in San'ya, it was Takeda-san who occupied the singular place of an otoko who gave credence to the irreplaceable value of buddies, and it was his word that expressed everyone's desire. If something were to happen to Takeda-san, as Akira put it, everyone would "go running" to the rescue.

As the final effects of labor, however, bodily exhaustion and death were inescapable for capital rationalized the body to maximize productivity, and for capital, the name of the game was to minimize costs. In short, the fewer the workers needed to complete a job, the better, and while this strategy substituted for an endless working day, it also predicated premature exhaustion and death for workers.[42] Together with excessive alcohol consumption, the repetition of this work was deadly, and the guys had all witnessed the signs of imminent death before, and they recognized them. Thus, when Suzuki collapsed, Akira said, "This is how Okinawans die," and when Akira was carted out of his bunkhouse on a stretcher one night, Yamazawa from Sanyukai approached to watch in the crowd, remarking: "He's gonna die, isn't he."

In the spirit of surplus extraction, it was common practice for Seichō to assign a younger, workaholic member of its permanent navvies to sites doing excavation. Wakami clearly explained the reasoning for this when he said that Itō does the equivalent of three workers, simply by being on-site. At the age of forty-nine, Itō took the opposite approach from Kentarō, who was at work more than anyone else and explicitly avoided excessive physical exertion because he anticipated its long-term effects. Rather than merely instruct, Itō took it upon himself to do a vast part of the work, and he was, in fact, quicker at finishing tasks than anyone else; also, he preferred to work by himself as he moved ahead. As "head worker" (shokuchō) of the navvies, indicated by the red (rather than white) helmet he wore, Itō was directly employed by the subcontractor, Tenjima, and it was his responsibility that work progressed on schedule. Itō would thus pick up slack by investing his own extra labor. Often, he would work in the breaks, after hours, and even on Sundays. Because he was an employee of the subcontractor on a monthly salary, he was reputedly not paid overtime but had to work every day. It was also said that his salary was lower than that of the day laborers, if the monthly sum was divided by the number of days he worked. Riku said that, while Itō might not have been intending to guilt-trip the rest of the crew—which took its duly awarded breaks and went home at five—the effect was the same. There was something distinctly wrong with watching Itō's slender body slave away, back bent over a shovel in a water-filled ditch, while everyone took their break. As well as they got along, Kentarō remarked flat out of Itō's exertions that "the man is stupid." At some point, Itō's body was going to shut down beyond repair. He ought to have known how to conserve his energies.

But much as the guys had made an artform of preserving their energies, slacking whenever possible, there was an adulation among them of raw, physical "power" (*pawā*). These tendencies naturally formed two sides of one coin, insofar as they expressed desire for inexhaustibility at work. In San'ya, however, this praise of power took the form of banter, as many had longstanding reputations for their strength at the workplace, which translated into a prowess for fighting in San'ya. Perhaps Rikiishi was most well-known for his power, and unsurprisingly so when one came face-to-face with him. The guys had nicknamed him the "gorilla" on account of his tremendous upper body, swelling forearms, and hands with stubbly fingers the size of salt shakers. Kentarō, who also possessed a hefty upper body and hands worn, swollen, and heavy from decades of work, would hold up Rikiishi's hands for display, saying to everyone: "Have you seen these hands? Are these the hands of a human being!" True to his nickname, Rikiishi could often be found passed out on the benches lining the wall of Sakura. Upon waking, he would growl like an animal on the prowl and most often attack Shōkawa (one of his favorite prey), who, giggling away with an ice drink swaying in his hands, would beg him to stop as Rikiishi hugged him close, grunting intimately while he rubbed the stubble of his unshaven cheeks against Shōkawa's, and bit his scalp in loving imitation of a gorilla. And when he was especially drunk, Rikiishi would begin kissing and crying. The latter was, in fact, a penchant which many of the guys shared, including Kentarō—the white-haired "silver-back"—when they had drunk a drop too much.[43]

At the construction site, the praise of strength occurred in concrete scenarios, such as when someone dug a hole indefatigably, lifted an especially heavy rock, or carried lots of steel pipes at once, as if it required no effort. Then somebody might comment, "Nice power," and this machinic strength would become the subject of conversations over drinks, as one man lauded another (who might be absent) for his feats at work. Suzuki, in particular, liked to boast of his own physical prowess, telling the "youngsters" (*wakashū*) in the group that he would one day show them how to lift thirty-kilogram bags of rice; similarly, it was not uncommon upon meeting workers that someone remarked of them that they "have strength." Specific body "types" were also lauded as being especially "able to work," and contrary to expectation, these were not always hefty-bodied types but lean and agile. Kentarō, however, repeatedly warned against overexertion at the construction site, insisting that work take place at the worker's "own pace." Suzuki naturally hoped for the opposite because hard workers reflected well on himself, but it was an accepted dictum that "hurrying" or "pushing oneself" could lead to "accidents." In morning assemblies, the foremen pointed out that accidents occurred most frequently in the first hour or two of work. It was most important that workers pace themselves: a practice that entailed ceaseless attention to the possibility of accidents, for the construction site was a "horrific place" (*osoroshī tokoro*), but which also entailed a blocking out of this ever-present threat. Posters hanging here and there at construction sites detailed endless iterations of accidents: from tripping to getting caught under a machine or passing out from heatstroke. In effect, pacing entailed the sacrifice of direct exposure to the material contingencies of the construction site in an emptying out of time. When the end of the workday finally arrived, the worker wondered where the day had gone.

A capitalist conception of value inhered to the adulation of "power" and its regimentation, since it is the commodity form, or rather, the wage, that precipitates the abstraction of "labor power" into units of time. Although in diametrically opposed ways, the laborer and employer recognized labor power as a source of value, for the employer sought to maximize productivity, while the laborer sought to minimize his efforts so that he could last a little longer, earn his living for a few more years, and live a longer life. From the tehaishi's *pinhane* all the way up the pyramid of subcontractors, it was the quantification of labor power in units of time that facilitated the extraction of surplus on the basis of exchange.[44] Moreover, this extraction of surplus value through the payment of wages imposed a regime of labor on the construction worker, which required that material contingencies be emptied out of the workday, because the abstraction of the exchange relation demands that laborers work within a time and space conceived in the most abstract of terms, as if a machine in the absence of material impediments, dangers, or exhaustion.[45] But it should not be forgotten that the value of labor power is historically and socially determined, and it is for this reason that the appellation "unskilled labor" says more about the social circumstances that stipulate its value than it does about the content of the labor itself. In another place and time, Kentarō's labor could have been recognized as labor that few people could perform, and it was precisely such a reversal of values that the counterdiscourse of the otoko put into effect, although only within San'ya.

Even in San'ya, the *form* of value of the commodity and the laws of the market remained unquestioned, since the act of exchange had always already produced the value of labor power, measured in units of time, and this meant that day laborers acceded to the death-inducing effects of the wage. The quantification of "labor power" is immanent to the exchange of the subsistence wage for manual labor, in which the quantification of labor entails the conversion of labor power into a socially useful object, and it is only in its complete expenditure that labor power emerges as "labor power" proper, that is, in its complete exhaustion: maximization of productivity is implicit to its definition.[46] When wages were exchanged for "labor power" at the construction site, overseers expected that laborers exhaust themselves in maximum productivity. Rather than expressing a social metabolism, labor power thereby entails an utter deprivation of energy in which laborers consisted of nothing but a means toward the extraction of value. It is the violence of this rationalization that constituted the hierarchical relationship between overseers and workers at construction sites, where the conditions of exchange dictated that manual laborers be worked to the point of exhaustion and, finally, death. The group had no choice but to endure death-inducing fatigue, and thus, it was partly the inescapability of the market that was expressed in the fact that day laborers preferred money over health. Yet it was precisely their reduction to a point of utter deprivation that compelled the emergence of a dignifying counterdiscourse to the death-inducing discipline of the worksite. The exigency of this counterdiscourse instigated the conversion of leftover wages into the daily excesses of liquor and gambling, the latter of which involved an altogether different experience of time and contingency.

At the construction site, the working day was subdivided into dockets of time (eight thirty to ten, ten thirty to noon, one to three, three thirty to five) that fused the expenditure of bodily energy with the duration of time. Reflecting a nineteenth-century imperative to understand motion in terms of space and time, the workday was divided into sections whose passage was experienced in anticipation of a safe ending, across which energy was spent.[47] Like chronophotographic images of the late nineteenth century, time was compartmentalized, with the body occupying the centerpiece of this compartmentalization, because the laborer had to know that, by the time it was three o'clock—or by the time he was fifty or sixty years old—he still had enough energy left to make it till the end of the day.[48] It was precisely through such self-management, which necessitated working at "my pace" and slacking, that the top-down management of overseers was subverted. The best kind of working day was the "easy" one, one less demanding or that ended early, but the only type of work that occasionally ended early was cement work, and this was determined by the pace of the machinery. If the mixers arrived on time, the day could end as early as three o'clock. If not, it could extend past five. And it was for this reason that, during cement work, the spaces of the floor came to represent the passage of time. Since Seichō constructed apartment blocks, every floor was divided into equal-sized apartment blocks called "slabs," and each uncemented slab signified a compartment of time. Given that the mixers arrived on time, the guys counted the number of remaining slabs to calculate the remains of the day. If more than half the slabs were finished before noon, things were looking positive, but it was never certain that the mixers would continue to arrive on time.

No doubt, compartmentalizing the working day to manage its duration is not specific to the construction worker. But while the salaryman and convenience store person wait for breaks as much as anyone, biopolitics had been dispensed with in San'ya, and its laborers were discarded without consideration for their reproduction. The day laborer and construction worker thereby render explicit how the violence of absolute surplus extraction exhausts the body, bringing about death-inducing fatigue, and they disclose how the smooth performance of capital accumulation demands the blocking out of possible contingencies and accidents. Yet the risk of accidents is inescapable, and somebody must shoulder the possibility of their outbreak. Moreover, that someone is conveniently disposed of by construction companies at five o'clock every day.

The vanishing figure of the day laborer (*hiyatoi rōdōsha*) restores what Ernst Bloch once called a noncontemporaneity to a nation that was long misrepresented as all middle-class and that has now become about the "working poor," as if precarity were new. San'ya's remaining day laborers show that, in Japan today, not everyone lives in the same present.[49] The postwar is alive in San'ya, where its residents conjure the injustices that underpinned the stability and social securities of "Japanese society" in the 1980s. If anything, the face-to-face sociality that can still be found in San'ya testifies to the sheer difficulty with which mutual recognition and dignity are secured under labor conditions that predicate an anonymous, premature death, presaging the future for workers for whom the maintenance of sociality itself has become well-nigh impossible. Its day laborers are a vanishing breed, whose passing is joined with a fading hope for recognition from society at large and a wish for luck.

When the mood was right in the dive, Sakura, Takeda-san and Akira would occasionally sing the 1970s hit song by Okabayashi Nobuyasu, "San'ya Blues." As a resident of San'ya, Okabayashi gives plaintive voice to the plight of day laborers, the strain of manual labor, the pointlessness of life in a bunkhouse, and the palliative effects of liquor. Noting the stigma of San'ya, his song calls to mind that Japan's infrastructure would not exist without places like San'ya: "Will no one understand?". Almost mournfully, Okabayashi observes that crying and resenting are to no purpose. For when the working day is over, San'ya's day laborers become the discarded. That is, just when they had been restored to the generally recognized sociality of working men, that support is torn away. In its place, San'ya has become their "hometown," and there they wait for the deferred recognition that will "certainly, certainly come in time."[50]

GAMBLING

Every Sunday, a steady flow of men can be seen heading in the direction of Asakusa from San'ya. As if they had taken on the musty complexion of the newspapers they carry tucked under their arms or in their back pockets, they can be recognized by their monochromatic, frayed clothing and their ghostly outer appearance. Be it on foot or by bus (the Tōei bus is free for welfare recipients), everyone has one destination: WINS, the horse-race gambling hall in the Rokku area of Asakusa.[1] Just like pachinko gamblers, who queue every morning to secure their lucky seat, aficionados arrive early, even before opening, standing impatiently in a small crowd waiting for the shutters to open and for the gambling to commence. By noon, especially on Sundays, when the high-profile races are screened, the six-story WINS building is buzzing with crowds clumped around TV screens hanging from the ceiling. Most of the crowd is composed of middle-aged men, yet young gamblers and women are mixed in as well.

Many also sit on the staircases and in the few open spaces or by the walls and the corners of the hall, peering at the small print of the newspaper statistics spread on the floor before them. With a pen in one hand and a stack of blank betting cards by their side, they write on top of the statistics. Once they reach a decision, they fill in the numbers of their bet in the small circles on their betting card, using the signature green plastic pencil provided by WINS. The circles must be filled in completely; otherwise, the machine will not read them. Except for the liquor, chaos, and hubbub of the gambling floors, it is as if the gamblers are filling in responses to a standardized exam with predetermined answers. Some gamblers fill in their betting cards by standing-room tables at the back of the hall. Others come armed with picnic chairs and reading glasses. Yet others are lined up to buy their gambling tickets at the machines against the front wall, before time expires, and still others are queued to collect their returns.[2] All the while, multiple screens on every floor rotate to show horse races from one corner of Japan to the other, and a ceaseless PA system announces the closure of betting periods, the start of new races, and the final winnings.

The fanaticism and effervescence inside WINS spill out of its gambling halls and into the surrounding area of Asakusa, where, amid the merriment of eateries, dive bars, and kitsch street performances, blank betting cards lie within hand's reach and indoor TV screens show the races. In the back alleys of WINS can be found eateries that specialize in the clientele of WINS, offering cheap snacks, be it the regular fare that accompanies drinking, such as *gyōza* (pan-fried dumplings), *hiyayakko* (chilled tofu with ginger, bonito flakes, and scallion toppings), *yakizakana* (fried fish), and *tori no agemono* (deep-fried chicken nuggets), or eateries that grill *yakitori* (skewered chicken, meats, and veggies) alongside the street. Smoke rises from their stalls as their intoxicated customers, bunched up and boisterous, standing inside by high tables in front of a giant TV screen, smoke, talk, scream, and laugh, creating an atmosphere of exuberance. In each eatery of these backstreets, blank betting cards are placed on, if not spread across, the tables, so the clientele can fill in these betting cards as the day progresses, walk over to WINS to buy their gambling tickets, and settle back in front of the TV with a drink and food. Thus, on many Sundays, the guys in the Okinawa-gang would start their day early at an eatery in Asakusa or maybe even at the Okinawan restaurant Gajū-Maru, before liquor had gotten the better of them. Only toward two or three o'clock would they head back to Sakura with their tickets and watch the main races there. By this point they would either be trashed or at the peak of conviviality: singing karaoke, watching races, drinking shochu with ice and water or beer, and eating with a pile of shared cash lumped in the center of the table.

But betting on horse races begins at WINS, and it is there that each of the tools the gambler requires can be acquired. These include a ¥100 ($1) sports newspaper, since the regular newspaper does not list gambling statistics. Everyone has a favorite, as Akira noted, for the "newspaper has something to do with it," that is, with winning, his preference being *Nikkan Sports*. Also on sale are pamphlets that specialize in statistics relating to races that day, offering gamblers the added advantage of information tracking back the performances of each horse by ten or more races than the normal sports paper. Sold for an extra ¥400–¥500 ($4–$5), these pamphlets only provide statistics on horse races. The stalls on the ground floor of WINS also sell thick color pens in red, blue, and black for ¥100—the minimum bet is also ¥100—designed for the gambler to write atop the statistics in the newspapers with their own divination. And free of charge, WINS provides the gambler with flimsy, green plastic pencils with pointed lead and blank betting cards, both of which can be found in plastic receptacles hanging off the walls on each floor. It only remains for the gambler to bring cash, fill in the circles, and purchase the ticket. As if to make the point clear, the machines upstairs do not even accept betting cards before cash has been put in.

While gamblers prepare, races are in constant progression such that only a fifteen-minute interval separates race from race. Different screens, divided across the hall, screen different races: while a race is in live progress on one screen, another screen shows the odds of an upcoming race, and another announces the returns of a past race.[3] Depending on the season, horse races take place simultaneously in different parts of Japan, be it Tokyo, Sapporo, Kawasaki, Okayama, Fukushima, Yokohama, and so on. Hence, if three locations are active on a specific Saturday or Sunday, races are announced by location and number, so that Tokyo race #2 is followed by Fukushima race #2, then Sapporo race #2, after which Tokyo race #3 takes place. The main races take place toward the end of the day, and similarly, especially high-profile races are held on Sundays. In this way, the tension in the gambling hall rises as it gets later in the day, as it does from Saturday to Sunday. Likewise, high-profile races, like the Emperor's Cup (Tennōshō) or Japanese Derby (Tokyo Yūshun), which involve well-known horses and jockeys and a large stake, punctuate the calendar, so there is always something to anticipate. Naturally, the hardened gambler can go to Korakuen to gamble on horse races every day of the week—in most locations, WINS only opens for the weekends—but Saturdays and Sundays constitute the main attractions and, for the most part, were the only two days the Okinawa-gang gambled on horses.[4]

The rotation of races ensures that if a race the gambler had bet on was not in progression, it was anticipated later in the day, much like particularly high-profile races—like the Emperor's Cup—were anticipated through the year. Gamblers were thus kept in a constant state of expectation not for the races to be over, like the working day, but rather for the event of the race to occur. It was in the immediacy of the race and the contingency of the winning horse numbers that horse races held gamblers in its grip. Unlike boat races, in which the order of winning numbers was often decided in the first turn and the inside boat had the advantage, in horse races this moment of utter intoxication arrived in the final five to ten seconds of the race, when the horses broke into a sprint, and the configuration of numbers was thrown helter-skelter. Gambling on horses focused on that experience of coming close to winning and on the repetition thereof, as much as winning.

But the trick was to turn a surplus from one's bet. The guys would say, "It's OK as long as you win." Yet winning ¥100 for ¥100 was a joke—less even than the "hourly wage!"—and for this reason, the guys gambled on unlikely number configurations. At WINS, all the stages involved in turning a profit thus were condensed at once, as people could be seen studying the statistics, filling in their betting cards, purchasing their tickets, standing glued to the TV screen, and ripping up their ticket or collecting their returns from the machine. When an especially unlikely configuration of numbers came in and the screen announced a preposterous sum of returns, someone in the crowd might remark: "Making a fool of us?" It was the common experience of gamblers that they lost more than they gained or that they lost regularly. There were "waves" to winning and losing in gambling so that gamblers in a slump—which the guys were most of the time— waited for their time to come, and it would "certainly, certainly come in time." Hence, Takeda-san would say that "recently the horse races aren't coming" and forthwith reassure himself that "it will come." But at WINS, obsolete gambling tickets littered the entirety of the gambling floor, alongside a newspaper here and there and partially filled betting cards. It was a common habit for gamblers to tear or toss their losing tickets immediately after the race, such that a cleaner made the rounds occasionally, sweeping between the feet of the standing crowds.

Scavengers collected these tickets, in the hope of picking up a winning ticket that had been discarded. When the gambling hall was busy, such scavengers caused the ire of other gamblers by lining up at the machines with a stack of tickets picked from the floor. Inserting tickets one by one, they stalled the queue of gamblers anxious to place bets, and it was clear the tickets were not their own, because no money emerged from the machines. Only scavengers would put valueless tickets into the machine, hoping that a winning ticket had been mistakenly discarded by its owner. The gambling halls of WINS were hunting ground for value in whatever form it could be found. But ultimately, the profits of the endlessly squandered lost tickets went to the Japanese state. For the state owns JRA (Japan Racing Association), which manages WINS.[5]

On the streets flanking WINS could also be found old-fashioned tipsters (*yosōya*) selling their forecasts spread out face down on waist-high tables. Though their numbers had dwindled over the years, undoubtedly since their business had moved online, on weekends the tipster could be found surrounded by a small crowd of onlookers that was either listening intently to the tipster or craning over upturned past prophecies that proved the tipster's skill for getting the numbers right. Sometimes the tipster sat silently behind his wares and occasionally muttered something, but he generally allowed onlookers to take their look. At other times, he could be seen expostulating and putting on a performance. By using his predictions of past races, the tipster had to convince the crowd before him that he possessed the knowledge to predict what the gambler should have known all along or, rather, what the gambler knew from looking at the statistics but had not bet on. He was a magician of sorts, because where the newspaper provides an excess of information in numbers—starting with the numbers of the horses, their weight, age, placement in past races, their shifting placement in the course of past races (did the horse begin in ninth place and move into first?), the distance of past races, the average ranking of every horse, the time it took, the jockey, and so on—which the gambler has to decipher, the tipster puts on a performance to convince the crowd that the face down prediction *is* the unknown combination of winning numbers.[6] With expert knowledge, the tipster does for the gambler what they would, in any case, have had to do on their own. But as yet another technique the gambler could employ, like choosing a specific newspaper, it was only when someone decided to buy this knowledge from the tipster that their performance was consummated. There had to be something about the tipster that compelled a purchase, of which the size of the onlooking crowd constituted the first indication. Under the assumption that a large crowd drew more people, the tipster was said to work with a few others, called *sakura* (decoys), standing about to give the impression of a crowd. While the tipster performed before a rapt crowd, someone might thus be seen nodding along, as yet another person pointed at the upturned cards, exclaiming: "This is basic, this is basic!" Of course, if they already knew the winning numbers, one might also wonder why the tipster themselves did not gamble.

The guys in the Okinawa-gang literally gambled all the time: if not on horse races (*keiba*), then on boat races (*kyōtei*), bicycle races (*keirin*), flower cards (*hanafuda*), or the lottery (*takara kuji*).[7] If not on these, the guys were thinking of gambling. Kentarō, the consummate construction worker, whom Akira had dubbed the "Paul Newman of Japan," carried a card for the lottery called "NUMBERS" in his wallet 24/7, and like a talisman this wallet never left his body. Whether it was a day off or on the way to work, Kentarō bought a new lottery card every morning, stuck it in his wallet, and kept it on him.

The group veritably lived according to two distinct calendars. One was the regular, endless workday schedule; the other, that of gambling, supplemented the first with the ever-present possibility of incommensurable winnings. Sunday was the main gambling day of the week and started the minute someone woke up. Usually, Shōkawa was the first to wake, as early as seven or eight, when he would call Kentarō or Akira, who never did master the art of not picking up the phone, saying that he "valued his friends," and then they would begin drinking. Nothing was open at this time, however, so the guys might kill a few hours sipping shochu with a newspaper at the open-air sushi bar (figure 3.1) by Mutō's hole-in-the-wall or perhaps even buy some Jinro or Kurokirishima shochu at a convenience store, along with ice, plastic glasses, and water, and sit in an empty parking lot. By around nine thirty, they could start heading toward Asakusa or to Sakura inside the Iroha arcade, if Asakusa had become too far. In the latter case, someone in the group with a bicycle would be given cash and numbers and asked

FIGURE 3.1.   An informal affair: San'ya's early morning sushi stall.

to buy tickets for everyone at WINS. Seven hours later, by four thirty, the main races would be over. Rikiishi would have woken from the bench in Sakura, making ready to escort Takeda-san home. Shōkawa would be staggering bow-legged out the sliding door, heading for the "next" place, and Akira—lamenting that he had been "called out" at seven—would slip back to his bunkhouse unnoticed. Next day, on Monday, at work, some of the guys might confess they had no recollection of what had happened the day before. But if someone in the group or San'ya had won big the day before, the conversations in the train and changing rooms were infused with this news or rumor. For news tended to spread quickly so that the winnings of an acquaintance across town reached one within a day. Thus, the working week started on the back of a Sunday.

Whether in a state of immediate readiness to gamble or having lost so much money that they had decided *not* to gamble, the group was in continuous contact with gambling in one form or another. On the train rides to work or during breaks in the changing rooms, the statistics and predictions (*yosō*) for races— be it horses, boats, or bicycles—were always in someone's hands. This would spur occasional conversation, as one person might peer over the shoulders of another and remark: "Number seven is real likely to win, eh?" Even if someone had for the time being decided to stop gambling, they always seemed able to recount the circumstances of upcoming races: the odds, the stakes, which horse and jockey was strong, and what combinations would give the highest yield. And if it was a less well-known race, a mere glance at the statistics seemed to give them instant insight into the intricacies of the race in question. Gambling, especially betting on horses, formed such a locus of social knowledge that the guys could communicate in a string of ciphers (#7, #3, #13, #1) and in combination (#7 #3, #7 #1) and in triplets (#13 #7 #1, #3 #13 #7) that were instantly recognizable to the other speaker since they, too, had looked at the race in question and knew what horses the numbers stood for. During breaks, lunch, and sometimes even before work, Kentarō would gamble with other workers in the changing rooms with flower cards—albeit for smaller sums of ¥10, ¥100, or ¥1,000 (which it was rare to win)—and if it was Saturday and a main horse race was scheduled during break time, from three to three thirty, one of the other workers might pull out their smartphone, which functioned as a TV, and set it upright on the table for all to see. After Suzuki had woken for *tehai*, Kentarō might even call from the changing room to tell Suzuki to place bets on boats for himself and the others. If he won, Kentarō returned to Mutō's with his palm stretched out, demanding his money first thing.

In fact, when Kentarō had been staying in a bunkhouse, he kept track of the winning lottery numbers from day to day. He would record the numbers in columns on the back of a calendar hanging in his room, enabling him to track number patterns and anticipate future numbers. If the number three had not appeared for a long time, the likelihood of it appearing went up. By the same token, if the number three had appeared on consecutive days, the likelihood of this pattern continuing went down. Within limits, gamblers could rely on mathematical laws of probability to predict future numbers, but there were any number of ways to play the lottery, each of which was considered equally legitimate. One way was to doggedly pursue or "chase" (*oikakeru*) the same number—like a lucky horse—over and over, and there were any number of reasons why someone might prefer a specific number. It might be a number the person had won with numerous times before, or the number might have a special meaning—a calendrical date, for instance—that prompted them to repeat it. Such numbers were individualized and had that special air of being lucky, although there were some numbers that were generally known to be unlucky, like *shi* (four), which also signified "death" (*shi*). Finally, like seeking out online predictions or the tipster, the gambler of the lottery could have a computer assign a number on the basis of a calculation of probability. Each of these techniques constituted a legitimate means of gambling, of which the gambler could avail themselves as it felt right. Regardless of the technique, a win was credited not to chance but to the acumen of the gambler who placed the bet. As a daily investment, the monotony of the working day was doubled by a no less repetitive, long-term gambling habit, in which the abstraction of the subsistence wage assumed a life of its own. Kentarō had yet to win big at the lottery called "NUMBERS," but when he was strapped for cash, he would say: "It's OK, NUMBERS will come."

What every one of the guys hoped for, like every gambler undoubtedly, was a big win. Everyone, moreover, had a story of how they had won a considerable amount of money in the past. Akira would recount how he had won ¥150,000 ($1,500) on an off-chance bet he had hardly thought about. Kentarō recalled the time he had won ¥500,000 ($5,000) and how incredibly good the noise of the machine had sounded as it counted his money—pure sound of excess—before he flicked the cash into his pocket. And Saruma and Norihisa won big sums in the two years I was there—the latter, repeatedly. Such experiences were said to be formative of the inveterate gambler because that was how one became "hooked" (hamaru).[8] Then there were stories of people who had bought cars or houses with profits from gambling, yet everyone knew it was impossible to make a "living" from gambling. Overall, they lost more than they won. But still, every time the screen at WINS or Sakura broadcast the returns on main races, it confirmed that someone out there had taken the jackpot. Kentarō had actually worked with someone who had won so much at the lottery that he did not have to work anymore, and the mass media, too, was complicit in producing the myth that it was possible to make a living from gambling on horses. In fact, while I was in Japan, everyone spoke excitedly of an incident in which the state had charged someone with tax evasion for not declaring the ¥3 billion ($30 million) they had earned from horse racing.[9] Everyone in the Okinawa-gang had their theory of how this had been possible—the person had started betting low and then spread their bets—but it all began with ¥100 ($1).

Sums like ¥3 billion signified an impossible, incommensurable amount of money that the guys could only dream of winning. Indeed, the magnitude of such sums recalls Immanuel Kant's writing on the mathematical sublime, and it was no coincidence that laborers, already so alienated in the commodity form, were held in thrall by this mythic magnitude of money.[10] Gambling, moreover, appeared to reverse the position of the worker vis-à-vis the commodity: no longer selling but buying and squandering with the aim of turning an excess from their tickets. Their losses went to the state, like their wages spent on alcohol in San'ya fed the economy. But the thrill and intoxication of gambling, the high of skirting so close to the real of coincidence, rejuvenated the body and implied an aptitude for seeking out the contingent precisely where the shock factor would be greatest.[11] Contrary to the construction worker, the gambler in the crowd sought the encounter with the penetrating shock of the accidental, which, as every manual worker knew but repressed, was bound to reoccur at some point.

The Artistry of Gambling as Motor Connectivity to Fate

It was common to compliment victorious gamblers, because gambling was not regarded as a mere game of chance but, rather, as one that required a certain skill and knowledge. But this aptitude was differentiated from skills at the construction site. For as an occupation that was freely entered into, gambling was not labor but appeared as expenditure in the absence of production, as the squander of time, money, and an embodied acumen.[12] Whether it was on horses, boats, bicycles, the lottery, an array of flower card games, or, on rare occasions, dice games, the winner always received congratulations and applause. When Norihisa won ¥100,000 ($1,000) several times in a row on horses, Akira looked at his numbers only to remark: "And to think that he wins with this." Someone might say to a winner, "All the credit to you," and on the floors of WINS, gamblers would commend one another, while the winner stood tall. Yet the skill and knowledge of the gambler was of a very specific type and seemed to involve "instinct" (*kan*) far more than rational forethought or calculation. This instinct could lead the gambler to seek out the tipsters as much as it could lead the lottery gambler to purchase a computer-generated ticket or to fill out their own divinations. Walter Benjamin thus observed that the trick for the gambler was for the nerves of the body or inspiration to remain in touch with "fate."[13] But to exercise this faculty, it did not suffice that the gambler divine an outcome. He also had to place an actual bet, meaning that he had to render himself vulnerable to the fateful passage of time, activating his nerves in anticipation of the results.[14] And it was for this reason that horse gamblers stood rooted to their spot during the initial stage of a race, silently reining in their energies, only to release them in an unruly flood of excitement, jubilation, or dejection, as losers turned their backs and winners raised their hands in victory. Simply predicting an outcome, as every gambler knew, did not have the slightest significance if a bet was not placed. It was one thing to predict and quite another to gamble. The artistry of gambling was only disclosed through the practice of risk, in an embodied battle with fate: of staking one's money. This also gave the lie to the tipster, for the failure of the tipster to bet only indicated that contact between the nervous instincts and fate or coincidence had been severed.[15]

Hence, the key to gambling, Akira would say, was "not to think about it too much." Although on a monotonous day of gambling, Akira showed me how to place bets early on in our acquaintanceship:

> Headed into WINS, bought the newspaper, and up to the 3rd floor. Had the strangest feeling I would see Akira and lo and behold, as I turned to

the screen, there he was. We stayed and gambled for around two hours. There were fewer people in the hall today, it being Saturday, Akira said. Nothing much actually happened on the gambling side of things. Akira seemingly hasn't had much luck this month. Nor today. He said he'd gotten into a fight with the staff at Sanyukai—Guy-san, Bonobe, etc.—and that he felt like he'd been cast down from the Skytree. To feel better, he'd been gambling every day at Kōrakuen, while he wasn't at Sanyukai. Every day. Spent quite a bit of money, he said. I noticed that he doesn't write in the papers. He said he tries not to think about it too much. Nor write. He just uses the green WINS pen to circle on the paper every once in a while. But he can look at the papers in an instant and read, evaluate the horses. Whereas for me, it's like I can only read the basics. He merely glances. And he places the bet only a few minutes before each race begins.[16]

The guys would laugh at the bets I placed, sometimes even passing my numbers around, slanting their heads with a wry grin, as if there was little chance the horses would come in as I had bet on them. Even if they did, it would not make any money, since I had simply mixed up the highest-ranked horses and thrown in a wild card. But every gambler knew that the horses rarely came in as the predictions in the paper had forecast. Only an amateur would have bet as I did. Admittedly, when I won three consecutive races, each garnering me ¥100 for the ¥100 I had staked, it elicited the laughter of the guys once again. Yet when I placed bets on horses that seemed highly unlikely but not guaranteed *not* to win, the guys would laugh, only to retract by saying: "I don't know, it might come with that." For they were all believers in "beginner's luck," as if gambling necessitated a faculty in short supply for the seasoned gambler. In thinking or knowing too much, the connectivity of nervous instincts to the futurity of numbers was sacrificed.

There did, however, exist a corpus of knowledge requisite to success at gambling without which the gambler would have been ill-equipped to embark on "battle" (*shōbu*). For horses, boats, and bicycles, the gambler had to know how to read the statistics in the newspaper and the rules, and the same went for the various flower card games. This was enough: the gambler needed to know no more. Naturally, long experience brought knowledge of a profusion of further facts and honed techniques. The guys, for instance, were able to read the statistics of the newspaper with but a glance, as if the surfeit of miniscule numbers registered with them in a photographic instant. They also knew the names and career profiles of famous horses and jockeys and even their breed and offspring, though horses were without exception referred to by number. In horse racing, it was said, "The horse is 70 percent, the jockey is 30 percent," but such knowledge shifted with boat and bicycle races, although the guys were as acquainted with the names of strong racers in both. In boat racing, the boat on the inside lane—#1—had a decided advantage, so much so that it was not unusual for #1 to place first for an entire day, and in boat races, the female racers were said to be strong. Bicycle races constituted a whole other ballgame, in which racers, who competed in teams, would pair up and strategize to take the lead. Gamblers on bicycle races were said to be particularly fanatic, as the race did not involve animals or machines but humans who did not hesitate to knock shoulders against one another or even to bump another racer down. There was one such individual living in Akira's bunkhouse, who went to bicycle races every day and traveled around Japan, chasing his favorite racer. And then, there was flower cards, which functioned as numbered cards for the game Oicho-Kabu, which Gin sponsored illegally by the entry to Iroha, and as sets in Koi-Koi, which workers played most frequently in the changing rooms. The latter especially required knowledge of the deck and lucid memory, because the gambler had to keep track of the other player's cards. There was also Don-Don—a bluffing game—that the guys would play in Takeda-san's apartment after hours and hours of eating, because Nē-san liked it. And at Hasegawa's apartment, located on the second floor above Mutō's hole-in-the-wall, the guys would get together once every week to play mahjong, of which Riku explained that it was about "sticking it out" or "holding one's ground" (tsupparu) with the suits you had chosen, adding that "people are the same way" and that it was "finished" otherwise, if you dilly-dallied or failed to stick to your guns. Finally, there were dice games, like Chinchirorin, which a Kanamachi-ikka man sponsored every morning one alley down from Sanyukai, until he was jailed for murder, and that especially had to do with speed, instantaneity, and lack of hesitation.[17]

In addition to knowing this multifarious array of games, there was also a less rational factor to knowledge of gambling. Kentarō, for instance, observed that after decades of playing flower cards, "for some unknown reason," cards from the pine suit tended to appear toward the bottom of the deck. But there were as many pine cards in the deck as cards in the other suits, and there was no reason why cards of the pine suit should stick to the bottom of the shuffled deck. Similarly, Kentarō noted that sometimes in gambling, the same number kept repeating for some inexplicable reason. In horse races, in which the starting lanes of horses had nothing to do with their likelihood of winning, such repetition occurred when the same numbers kept winning, regardless of the race.[18] When this happened, someone might note: "Oh, it's number seven again." Or, fed up with missing the mark, someone might shout: "What, it's number seven again!" Such patterns were "strange" (okashī), since they defied rational expectation and made it seem as if the numbers led a life of their own, intimating other forces at work.[19] To induce an embodied accord with the numbers, there was a distinct sense in which "thinking," "studying," and predicting number configurations yielded nothing—yet had to be done to be set aside and forgotten.[20]

Once a gambler started winning, it might happen that he went on a veritable winning streak, winning one race after the other until their fortune could no longer be dismissed as a mere "fluke" (*magure*). Their aptitude, rather, demonstrated an escalating audacity that was grounded neither in rational knowledge nor intelligent prediction, but in the dangerous certainty of an abiding motor connectivity with fate.[21] When saying that it was best in gambling "not to think about it too much," Akira therefore mimicked the gesture of quickly sketching in a card, as if responding instantaneously to a spur-of-the-moment instinct and "feeling," because keeping in touch with the numbers necessitated a blind gesture of the body, "beginner's luck," that responded automatically to infinitesimal shifts in the nervous instincts.[22] Writing the numbers with a heavy hand would have involved too much consciousness. The trick in gambling, rather, was for the nerves of the body to remain in touch with "fate."[23]

The first bout of any winning streak therefore arrived unexpectedly, before the confidence and certainty of repetition hit in. Akira would recall how, just as he was about to leave WINS one day, he decided to place one last bet, for the hell of it. Hardly looking at the newspaper statistics, skimming and sketching what felt right, he placed a ¥100 ($1) bet on a trifecta: the hardest configuration to win, meaning that three horses have to finish precisely in first, second, and third place. And just as he was about to leave, he moved his eyes back and forth from his ticket to the screen, squinting to see whether the last numbers on the screen matched his own, still in disbelief when he withdrew ¥150,000 from the machine! This very same Akira would go through slumps in gambling, so much so that he would quit, cursing: "There is never enough money." But when he won, he won repeatedly, as he did one day in San'ya. First at boats at Mutō's hole-in-the-wall, then at bicycles at the open-air sushi stall. Akira walked back and forth between the two vendors, placing bets, collecting money, scanning the statistics as if seeing through them, and commenting on races as if he had seen them before. The crowd of marveling regulars turned to him, basking in the summer sun, and called him "sensei."[24]

Everyone knew of an incident in which someone had won several million yen at Mutō's hole-in-the-wall. Not knowing quite what to do, Mutō had gone to his guarantor, the local yakuza organization, the Kanamachi-ikka, to collect the money. Otherwise, the guys said, "no one will gamble there." The next day, this same person gambled at the open-air sushi bar next to Mutō's hole-in-the-wall, also backed by the Kanamachi-ikka, and won the same amount again. Once again, the Kanamachi-ikka backed the loss, only this time, the person was told never to return, as if his victories bespoke a sustainable acumen. Everyone could recount the incident, as if they shared in these victories. It is this motor connectivity with contingency that inscribes itself on consciousness as a memory, folding the past into the present in a narrative form as evident in the stories of victory told by day laborers as in the preeminent story of gambling: Dostoyevsky's "The Gambler."

The consummate gambler thus wins by betting on *unexpected* number combinations. To a certain extent, the decision to bet on unlikely combinations formed part of the repertoire of skills the gambler employed to make more money. The gambler had to know both which races had a large stake (the main ones) and which races the horses, boats, or bicyclists were most likely to come in contrary to the official predictions. The horse races held during the week at Kōrakuen, for instance, were unlikely to yield large returns, both because the stakes were small and the horses tended to arrive according to expectation. These races were unexciting. The trick was to bet against the odds and to win big. In short, the horse gambler was on the lookout for a breakout that went against the odds, without being altogether unthinkable. With boat racing, in which the inside boat had the decided advantage, it was thus common to include #1 in bets but to pair it (since betting on #1 and #2 would yield no returns) with a less likely number, like #6. Nothing felt as good as winning at boat races on #6, the boat in the outer lane. It was also common for Kentarō to place boat bets with others. Because only six boats competed in boat races, there were fewer possible boat combinations than horses in *keiba*—30 for "two in a row," 120 for "three in a row"—and he would try to cover all the likely bases. Pulling ¥500 from people left and right (the minimum bet at Sakura and Mutō's was ¥500), with the promise of sharing the winnings, Kentarō placed bets on a variety of combinations, but this, too, was usually to no avail. At the instant of the first turn, something unaccounted for invariably happened, only to be confirmed at the second turn, by which point the result of the race was as good as done. Kentarō would then sigh, shake his head, leave the immediacy of the TV screen, and sit back down with his shochu. In such instances, there was a sense in which the gambler felt duped by the game, which, at WINS, might elicit comments like not "to push it" or "make a fool of" the gambler.

Knowing from experience that winning occurred when it was least expected, the guys would try to replicate the circumstances preceding the original bet that was won. Everyone could recount the story of having won big and, more significantly, could clearly remember the details leading up to the event. Like Akira's experience of winning ¥150,000, the circumstances preceding the event were inscribed on consciousness like the lucid afterimage of shock. It might be that the person had stood in a particular spot at WINS, had eaten ramen noodles beforehand, or had bet on a particular horse or jockey or on a specific lucky number. In pachinko, there were likewise lucky machines and especially prosperous times of the month and not so prosperous ones, when Kawaii, the chronic pachinko gambler at Sanyukai, would bitterly mutter that the machines were "bullying" him. Pachinko gamblers would thus queue in the early morning to secure their lucky seat, before someone else took it, and would try to keep their winning streak by maintaining the patterns that had surrounded it from the beginning. The singular, winning quality of the pachinko machine gamblers chose was, in effect, besmirched when someone else sat at them. Not only this, but the cash the machine "put out" was no longer theirs. By the same token, the guys never shared their horse numbers with one another, unless they were placing bets to cover bases, until the final moment of purchasing their ticket. Leading up to this, comments exchanged remained within the sphere of noting that a certain horse was "likely to win." Gambling and winning with "someone else's numbers" was not considered a legitimate means of winning, for the work invested in the numbers had to be one's own, and the quality of the ticket was compromised in being identical to another. Singular winnings required singular, personalized combinations. Clearly this was not sufficient to secure a win. Yet, these practices disclosed a recognition of the less rational, embodied facet of gambling.

Alas, motor connectivity to the winning numbers could only be confirmed in the final instant of danger when the winning numbers were revealed. It was also this concentration of risk in a suspended, revelatory moment of time out of time that entailed a transformation of the abstract time of the working day into an experience of contingency and that caused the gambler to repeat the act. Akira placed that bet of ¥150,000 barely a minute before it was too late.[25] Likewise, with quick dice games, it was the very moment and gesture of throwing the dice that decided the outcome. So too, when teaching me games in which the aim was to pull an identical pair of flower cards, Rikiishi would half jokingly, half seriously insist that I hold the pair of cards together "real tight, real tight," before slowly sliding the one card down to reveal the other, as if holding them tight and leaning one's body into them could make the cards bleed into each other. In other card games, in which it helped to pull identical flower cards from the deck, it was common practice to throw the cards down fervently, with "spirit" (*kiai*). In fact, a soft mat had been placed on the table for this purpose. Kentarō would comment at how "unskilled" (*heta*) I was at pulling lottery cards and half seriously, half jokingly showed me how to pull a winning card out the box. In dice games, as in most flower card games, the moment of motor connectivity to the winning numbers almost coincided with their materialization. Different games had different rhythms and various displacements of the intoxicating instant of truth. Dice was instantaneous. With most flower card games, the moment arrived when all cards were finally revealed. With horses, boats, and bicycles, the last possible moment to place one's bet was separated from the race by a period of five minutes.[26] Yet as gambling races proper, they demonstrated the qualities of precipitation and jeopardy—of missing the mark—that Benjamin discerns in gambling.[27] With boats, this moment came at the beginning of the race, because the order of winning boats was usually established on the first turn (if not, on the second), when the leading boat put distance between itself and others. With horses and bicycles, however, this moment did not arrive until the end of the race, when the horses and bicycles accelerated into a sprint, and at WINS, the final seconds of a race were therefore accompanied by shouting and exultation. Sometimes, a computer image was needed to determine the order of horses, so narrow was the margin. In those moments, time was condensed into an immediate experience of contingency, mediated by the instantaneity of the TV screen.

As much as the pleasure of winning, just missing the mark propelled the gambler to repeat the act. Everyone would talk of coming close to winning. Maybe the same two horses on whose victory they had bet would win but in the opposite order from their bets! Watching the last fifteen seconds of any horse race left one enthralled with horses sprinting toward the finish line and with the possibility that anything could happen. Another way to achieve the singularity of an incommensurable win, however, came in the sheer negativity of loss—a propensity toward self-destruction that proved most compatible with the group's liquor intake. But it was first and foremost the *form* of the transformation of time that proved addictive. Regardless of the outcome, every single race (especially high-profile ones with vast sums at stake) exposed gamblers to the possibility of overturning the objective conditions of their lives, a possibility proffered to them in the form of compressed time. For as Anatole France once wrote, gambling is "the art of producing in a second the changes that Destiny ordinarily effects only in the course of many hours or even many years."[28] Contrary to the seemingly endless time of the working day, in which time was emptied out in anticipation for it to have been done, and the nerves of the body exhausted in an unrelenting necessity of registering, blocking, and protecting against contingency, time in gambling deceptively suggested the possibility of making infinite gains in an instant. In appearance, too, gambling seemed to reverse the conditions of surplus production, insofar as, in the moment of gambling that preceded victory or loss, the gambler was now owner of the ticket, the horse, the stocks, or the commodity (of time) from which surplus was extracted, in no time at all! In reality, the gambler had become the avid consumer of a commodity with no use value, except for the intrinsic thrill of the experience, and whose obsolescence was as instantaneous and cruel as the day laborer drained of labor power.

After a week of labor, liquor thus loosened the nerves, and gambling seemed to redeem time. The experience of having once won haunted the gambler so that he sought to repeat it, and the gambler was "hooked" (*hamatteru*) by that lucid first experience of winning, as if the contingency of the event had pierced his consciousness. Contrary to the construction site, where consciousness had to register and buffer all sorts of dangers, gambling therefore involved a desire to repeat the original coincidence of winning. Yet, like losing, winning too was never sufficient. In their conversion into money, winning combinations invariably produced a remainder of the real—just as losers witnessed how close they had come—for it was always possible to have bet more. Thus, winners would take their winnings and either augment their next bet or strategize by spreading out their next bets. It was one thing to win, say, ¥10,000 from a bet of ¥100. But the art of gambling resided in taking that ¥10,000 and, like the mythic individual who had won ¥3 billion, transforming it to a hundred times or a thousand times that figure—that is, until the winning-streak waned and the unpleasurable side of enjoyment emerged to the fore.

The compulsive gambler desired the experience of shock and coincidence that replicated the first encounter. Erected so relentlessly at the construction site, it was the "shield against stimuli" that the worker sought to penetrate, and to enable this penetration, the statistics in the newspaper took the place of consciousness at the workplace.[29] Where consciousness otherwise would have exhausted itself in outlining and weighing an endless list of details, the newspaper provided this information ready-made (figure 3.2). By doing the work of intellect for the gambler, the statistics facilitated the experience of gambling by liberating it from the drudgery of distilling the endless minutiae of prerequisite information.[30] The newspapers thereby functioned as a mere means of holding a surfeit of information in check, without acting on it. This allowed the gambler to apprehend upcoming races in broad strokes, releasing the instincts to do the work of scanning, sketching, and reacting to the minutest shifts in patterns to divine a winning code.[31] The sheer excess of statistics, already abstracted into a readily digestible form, made evident that the gambler could not aggregate their entirety. Instead, the gambler wrote on top of the statistics with a marker, circling here and there, and in their own shoddy handwriting numbered the horses. Likewise, the specialty pamphlets for ¥500 aided gamblers. The point was not to "study" but to shut out information.

Fingers crossed, the ticket bought on the back of this surfeit of numbered signifiers *is* the winning combination. For the surfeit of statistics foregrounded the absence of the only three significant numbers—the first three horses—that the gambler, like a soothsayer, had to provide. Gamblers knew all too well that their chances of winning were slim and that any winning streak would end. Nevertheless, they persisted in betting and, at times, to the point of ruin. Purchased at the last moment in an impatient queue, the ticket took on the value of a mate-

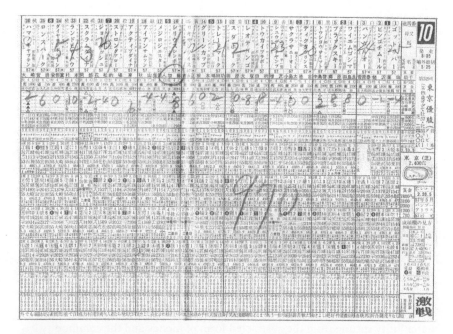

FIGURE 3.2. Newspaper statistics overwritten by the gambler's divining hand. This image originally appeared in Hammering, "Gambling, Dignity, and the Narcotic."

rial fetish, which, like Kentarō's lottery card, had to be renewed with the wish for success. The express purpose of the ticket was not to protect against but to stand in for, to be exchanged for a singular sum of money.

The sheer abstraction of the gambling ticket and the statistics in the papers recall Marx's elaboration of the dual character of the commodity form.[32] When gamblers spoke of horses, it was purely in numbers, as if the material qualities of the horse or jockey simply did not exist. Sure, there were famous jockeys and horses, such as Yutaka Take, who rode Deep Impact, or Secretariat in the United States, whose tickets at the famous 1973 Belmont race many gamblers kept rather than exchange for money.[33] Yet when it came to filling in the betting card, horses were indicated in numbers, and rows on rows of odds determined the final wins. Like financial stocks, the horse numbers took on a life of their own to be finally exchanged into a monetary figure. With the exception of the names of the horse and jockey, and a particular characteristic of the horse—maybe it was strong toward the end of the race or good at "breaking out" (*nukedasu*)—every other piece of information was written in numbers. But while the language of gambling was thoroughly abstracted into numbers, in its secrecy, the gambling ticket bore the signature of the gambler from the moment of its inscription.[34] Ticket numbers had to be kept secret so that they could not stand apart from the person who had written it, preempting an awkward situation in which one's numbers were the same as "someone else's."

Of baseball, on which everyone also bet, Riku spoke of the Hiroshima Toyo Carp as a team owned by Mazda, a car company that was not in the same league as major manufacturers, such as Honda or Toyota, and of its players who were also underdogs. But they played with their "might and main!" Nor did they use many foreigners. In fact, the one foreigner on the team was underpaid, and he was "doing his best!" In short, the Hiroshima Toyo Carp relied on their strength, without purchasing outside help, and "everyone knows of them." Alongside his observation that mahjong, like "humans," is about "sticking it out," Riku disclosed his life philosophy in the bets he placed on underdogs.[35] So too, Akira would speak of being an otoko and of the importance of "sticking to one's principles" (suji o tōsu). Oftentimes, their ticket numbers reflected their favorites, as well, and it was this quality that personalized the ticket, set it on its way to a singular value, and that rendered its final monetary value their very own.

In this way, the necessity of making a claim to one's gambles in the name of masculinity sprung from the abstracted form of money and the commodity itself. The act of gambling must be considered over against the wage of the working day. For it was the wage that determined the value and the abstract form of time through which value was conferred on San'ya's day laborers, whose bodies were emptied out until, finally, they were deemed altogether unusable.

Working from Freud's writings on repetition and trauma, Benjamin recognized a formal congruence between the automatic motions of the gambler and the factory worker. By describing a similitude of form in the repetition of bodily motions, he proposed that, at least on the surface of things, the drudgery of menial factory work constitutes an analog to the repeated act of throwing dice at craps or placing a bet at roulette.[36] At the end of my first day working in ditches, with an excavator circling above, Kentarō said: "You see, there's nothing much to it. Work is merely the repetition of this." And, indeed, in repeatedly anticipating the contingency of shock or accidents and screening out their possibility (at work), the drudgery of the construction worker forms a counterpart to that of the gambler on a losing streak, who, on the other hand, seeks out the shock of the accidental but fails repeatedly to experience it. With the notable exceptions of victories, near coincidences, or gamblers deliberately bent on self-destruction, in both gambling and manual labor, consciousness winds up operating as a "screen against stimuli," consigning the possibility of experience—of contacting stimuli such that they affect and inform the entirety of one's life—to a mere "hour in one's life."[37]

Yet social conditions in San'ya caused gambling to emerge as part of a counterdiscourse to the propriety of economic productivity, not merely as an analog to the repetition of labor. Everyone shared the necessity of elaborating alternate forms of sociality, for they had failed in the eyes of their families and general society. And while their arrival in San'ya marked the end point of a trajectory of failed masculinity, its space of face-to-face relations offered the possibility to reverse the abject conditions of labor to which they had been reduced. Everyone knew that workers from San'ya were mostly called on to complete dirty, dangerous, and demeaning labor, and unlike gambling, such labor conditions rarely received comment and certainly not with glee. Working days consisted in lifting heavy rocks while wearing steel-reinforced boots, if you had them; shoveling in a ditch, next to a thirty-ton excavator; or hammering away at walls to ensure that cement, which burned through bare skin, flowed into them properly. Yet the deadening effects of this draining monotony were overturned when an accident occurred, that is, when a body was pierced or wounded. Then, after work, firsthand witnesses would relate in detail how the floorboards had been loose, how so-and-so had plunged to the floor below, and how the white bones had protruded through the wound. When accidents occurred, the instinctual nerves of the body were activated to their utmost, and through narration, the event was transformed into a story, replete with suspicions that so-and-so had faked the fall to get insurance, as well as work-related safety lessons. Otherwise, the shield of consciousness or intellect sacrificed the content of sensory impressions by intercepting and registering stimuli at disconnected moments in time. The intellect thereby foreclosed experience by bracketing off and containing the event within the past of linear time, as yet another moment within a homogeneous succession of occurrences.[38]

But clearly a difference remains between the necessary repetition of labor, which the worker would not do without remuneration, and gambling, which the gambler engages in even if he incurs debt. As with any narcotic, in gambling there is the initiating thrill, followed usually by diminishing returns of excitement and the occasional "near miss," until gambling finally reverts to the drudgery of labor. Much as they strategized about how to begin with one hundred yen, spread their bets, and augment their stakes, gamblers in San'ya sought, above all, to draw out the high of near misses as they calibrated their gambles and punctuated their day with races of their choosing. Moreover, when it came to horses, bicycles, or boats, the order of the races was structured to reverse the law of diminishing returns, because the main races were scheduled at the end of the day and at the end of the week, on Sundays. The order of the races predisposed day laborers in San'ya to prolong the initiating thrill of victories, near misses, and self-destructive conduct, and when they stopped—which they did, saying, "I quit!"—it was when the excitement had turned to drudgery, when they had reached a thoroughly excessive financial limit, or, quite simply, when the last race had finished. Gambling in San'ya therefore assumed the form of concentrated sessions of inebriated social activity, which lasted half a day at most, since these sessions were quite possibly as extractive of energy and as self-destructive as manual labor itself, and for most individuals, they concluded naturally when the exhilaration calmed down. These concentrated sessions constituted a form of gambling, moreover, whose temporality was composed of punctuated bursts of intensity in an intensely social scene.[39] But for the San'ya day laborer to establish his recognition as an otoko, the energies of his depleted body operated as a vehicle that transformed the instrumental regimentation of time into an event of excessive expenditure that allowed for the past to be folded into the present. Through gambling, the lost time of manual labor remained to be actualized as a durative and curative experience, because construction work commits time to seriality without hope. Only "experience," Benjamin wrote, "rids man's soul of obsession with time."[40]

This obsession with time recalls its compartmentalization and the day laborer's obsession with the workday to *have been done*. While the material content of the workday was emptied out in attention to the contingencies of accidents—dust, soil, mud, heat, humidity, cold, rain, snow, chemical fumes, and danger of that steel bar bouncing back, with machinic force, in the face of the excavating laborer—the time of this working day had been abstracted in the assignation of a monetary value to the labor of the construction worker. In commodification, the commensurable form of the subsistence wage was thereby constitutive of work as a passage of empty time and of the day laborer from San'ya as an object of capital. Contrary to the salaryman, it was the distinction of construction work that the content of work resided in the fending off of material stimuli, resulting in physical fatigue, and the predisposition of the construction worker to gamble consisted in the combination of these two characteristics: the crystallization of the laborer in empty time and the etiolation of material stimuli.[41] At the end of a day at the construction site, the day laborer stood emptied out on the train platform, numbed in the body and wondering where the day had gone. Robbed of experience, this fatigued body was reinvigorated through the act of gambling, in which the form of money was proffered to the day laborer with the possibility of winning an incommensurable value. The very form that robbed work of content was transformed into the promise or wish of attaining singular value.

The seduction of gambling thus resides elsewhere than in the prospect of victory. Indeed, the gambler seeks the catastrophic and, hence, the *risk* of gambling and the excess of expenditure it requires in repeated losses or wins. Except for the rare occasions of winning streaks, in San'ya, it was the near coincidences that were excitedly announced over drinks, propelling the gamblers. How close the horses had come to arriving in the correct order! Only a hair's breadth separated gamblers from coincidence, and losers repeatedly complained how many times their horses had arrived in inverted order. Inevitable shortcomings triggered repetition unto exhaustion. In the absence of a victory (which often went unannounced so that winners could dispense of their money discreetly), the reality of gambling oneself into debt constituted the social fact of the scene. Nonetheless, these were eminently boisterous, effervescent gatherings, at seedy dives, in which liquor and snacks were accompanied by arm wrestling or the occasional knife fight and in which San'ya's gamblers repeatedly lived for the intoxicating moment of seeing their horses turn the corner. At the peak of their conviviality, everyone in the group was in debt by a few thousand dollars. This was a considerable amount, given the precarious availability of work and daily earnings of only ¥12,500 ($125). But they imbibed and gambled away their wages, holding one another accountable for their debts, because it was the reputation of the entire group that allowed its members to borrow from bars and eateries. After gambling, it was the condition of one's losses and indebtedness that was commented on and enacted through regular repayments, as a burden born with dignity. And it was in this way that, while each race promised incommensurable wins in the form of time, compressed into a "narcotic," there existed a reversibility to this promise: the narcotic could be experienced in loss, and the incommensurable could be achieved with certainty in the negativity of debt.[42] It was when Akira got into a verbal fight at Sanyukai that he decided to blow ¥200,000 ($2,000) in one fell swoop. By squandering such large sums of money, he created as memorable an event as victory. And although such moments of expenditure were rarely as decisively wasteful as Akira's, the day laborers made it common practice to dial up the stakes of their gambles, constantly placing their reputation on the line, keeping the thrill of gambling with them. In this way, in gambling as in life, a losing streak was never simply a losing streak. It was one that the day laborer had taken charge of and exacerbated in transgression of conventional propriety, to claim his worth in the negative excesses of liquor, gambling, and his accountability in debt.

It was not just victory that would actualize the value of time, transform the contingent into experience, and inscribe the circumstances of the gamble on memory. Rather, the repeated exposure to self-destructive loss allowed day laborers to carry these losses into the present to constitute a socially recognized self. On Monday mornings, on the train to work, the previous day had not simply been consigned to the dustbin of history: as if the embers were still aglow, the group conversed about the near misses, and if someone had declared a big win, news had traveled across town. Perhaps not everyone told the story of their losses, but they did not have to, since everyone shared in this indebtedness, and each of their bodies had been reactivated in an exhaustive exposure to the self-incurred shock of losses. Consigned to seriality without hope, the day-laborer-turned-gambler emerges as a poet of modernity and shock. As Benjamin wrote of Baudelaire: "Baudelaire battled the crowd—with the impotent rage of someone fighting the rain or the wind. This is the nature of something lived through (*Erlebnis*) to which Baudelaire has given the weight of an experience (*Erhfarung*). He indicated the price for which the sensation of the modern age may be had: the disintegration of the aura in the experience of shock."[43] In a "rage" of powerlessness, of having been robbed of experience, Baudelaire sought to raise the shock sensation of modernity to the level of experience. Yet, precisely when this experience would have been attained, the "price" of the experience of shock is disclosed in the evacuation of "aura," that is, of singularity.[44] So too, in the victory of coincidence, the gambler's aim is sacrificed, thereby producing the ground for repetition. For the commensurable form of money can never give enough, and it was the conversion of the ticket into money that effaced the dream of an incommensurable win.[45] Conversely, losing precipitated an enduring negativity of debt that tested and testified to the character of an otoko, because unlike a solitary victory, debts forced him into relations with others in which he had to uphold his obligations.

Masculinity, Credit, and Recognition in Indebtedness

It was not simply money but their social reputations and accountability as men that the guys risked in gambling, for incurred debts raised the question of whether a person was good for their word/money. Everyone in the group was in debt to an eatery or bar, which they would also frequent on credit, and some would even lend them money on request. Just inside the Iroha arcade, Sakura hosted illegal boat betting, like Mutō, and would lend people money on request. The small-statured, aging mama-san of Sakura sometimes sat tired out at the counter and recounted with her deep Kansai accent that, over the decades Sakura had been in business, she could not count the number of men who had run off without paying their debts. Still, if they knew you, Sakura would "dish out ¥200,000 [$2,000] without hesitation." Akira was in debt for this amount, and so were Kentarō and Shōkawa. The guys would jokingly refer to Sakura as the "Sakura bank," since everyone, at some point or other, availed themselves of its services. If not, the thought that they could do so afforded security, and not everyone ran off with Sakura's money. Akira seemed to bear the burden of his debt gracefully, complaining that he was "deep in debt" but typically turning a negative into a positive by noting that not everyone can borrow money: it required a good reputation. Yet debts and black-market interest rates did, indeed, prove burdensome. Kentarō even remarked that he was "up to his neck" (*kubi ga mawaranai*) in debt. But this burden also served as an indicator of a man's social prowess, even when he wound up returning double the original debt.

At the beginning of every month, Akira, Kentarō, and the others would make trips to pay their monthly installments, which never seemed to diminish—it took Akira two years to reduce his debt of ¥200,000 ($2,000) to a more manageable figure of ¥60,000. But Akira did not pull money from others and only borrowed from Sakura. Moreover, he was fastidious in his monthly installments, transforming the negative displeasure of his endless debt into a positive sign of his accountability, word, and reputation as an otoko. Of course, for Akira, it helped that he was not just on welfare but received more than other welfare recipients on account of his medical status.[46] Everyone seemed to know about this and his generosity, which often left him with only a few hundred yen in his bank account and more than a few days left in the month. The guys in the Okinawa-gang all knew where to go toward the end of the month, be it to Akira or a dive bar where they could put it on a tab, when the money ran out. Yet, in one respect, borrowing from Sakura involved a risk that was greater than borrowing from other members, because by borrowing from Sakura, the borrower put the reputation of the entire group at stake and, with it, the future possibility of taking money out from "Sakura bank." When Tetsu, another member of the Okinawa-gang, accrued a debt of several hundred thousand yen to Sakura and not only failed to make consistent payments but ceased to show at the dive, the burden of his debt redounded on the other members of the group. This was not simply a matter of the mama-san at Sakura putting pressure on the others to make Tetsu pay, asking them where he was or whether they had seen him. More importantly, Tetsu emerged as a source of consternation because he threatened the financial viability of everyone. In fact, Tetsu had a prior history of "running away" from debts—of disappearing—that earned him the reputation of someone not to be trusted. Kentarō had told Suzuki "not to use" him for work, and when Tetsu had an accident at work, he was suspected of having simulated the fall. It was finally decided that Suzuki would "talk" to Tetsu, yet this was also a risky strategy. When, more than one year later, Suzuki informed Sakura of Shōkawa's and Akira's phone numbers (as they were both still in debt), Suzuki received such a verbal thrashing from Akira that they had a prolonged falling-out. Pulling Suzuki aside in front of Mutō's—"Suzuki, come here a sec!"—Akira confronted Suzuki, who replied, "OK, sorry, I understand." But it was "too late to apologize," Akira said. "What's done is done!"

By incurring excessive debts, the stakes and significance of gambling became amplified, for by gambling beyond their means, men staked their very social existence. Staking one's self was also what an otoko did: in gambling, as in fights, an otoko was good for his word.[47] Hence, Riku said of mahjong: "Once you give

in, it's finished" (*magetara owari*). With credit giving testimony to a man's accountability, the question was how much negative value or debt an otoko could
accrue without letting others down. And while such debts were incurred in specific relations with others, they were made known to everyone through passing
remarks, so that indebtedness constituted a condition of being an otoko, one that
countered a statist discourse of productivity, much as illegal gambling did.[48] In
this way, the experience of gambling gave rise to an economy of gifting, in which
the credibility of an otoko was established across a temporality of deferral, in accordance with the timeliness with which he returned debts, loaned to others, or
paid for a meal or drinks. Unless someone had won big, it was always through a
state of indebtedness that an otoko established his reputation. Life itself was at
stake in this gamble.

More than anyone, Matsuda represented someone who was "finished," as
Akira or Riku phrased it, or "out," as Kentarō said. While Matsuda might not
have gambled away at games the ¥30,000,000 (about $300,000) borrowed from
the yakuza, he did invest it in unsuccessful business ventures and shamelessly
mixed business with pleasure as he traveled around Japan. Gradually, the photos
of Matsuda disappeared from around San'ya. Rumor had it that the Kanamachi-
ikka, a branch of the Yamaguchi-gumi, would kill him when they found him,
that he would be "buried somewhere," if he did not wind up in jail first. But no
one embodied the vulgarized form of the precept that an otoko was "finished"
when he "broke" as much as Yamamori, who gambled daily on flower cards
with Gīn, in plain sight of passing police cars. Yamamori was loath to let winners
leave the gambling table, and when his social position permitted him, he would
pull them back by the sleeve for them to stay at the table. Then, he would up the
stakes and keep going until the tide turned, if it did. When he had had a drop too
much to drink, moreover, he was as fervent for a bout of cards as an addict for
his fix.

Kentarō thus remarked that, if there were one or two people like Yamamori
gambling, things could easily get out of hand. It was one thing to gamble on
horses, boats, or bicycles and quite another to gamble among buddies. In fact,
when the guys gambled on flower cards, it was for low stakes. When they did so at
Takeda-san's apartment after eating, because Nē-san liked it, Takeda-san himself
never participated but sat off to the side by the TV, drinking beer, chatting, or
sleeping, and the winnings themselves had a roundabout way of making their
way into Nē-san's hands as the guys left, one by one giving their profits to her at
the doorway. Indeed, Kentarō would say of gambling among acquaintances that
one "should really not do it" because it sowed resentment. Gambling among
friends threatened the sociality of the group and its discourse of the otoko. On
the few occasions that the Okinawa-gang itself broke this precept, Akira would

say that it was really common practice, when gambling among buddies, to return 80 percent of the winnings once the session was over. He was against "taking money among buddies" (*nakama aida no kane tori*). But there was always a small amount of cash involved when the guys played mahjong or flower cards, the excess of which never remained long with the winner, because word spread rapidly of who had won, and a modicum of generosity was expected from them. When someone had won big at horses, announcing their victory to the world and taking an advance from Sakura (before returning to WINS for their winnings), even Yamamori could be seen slinking along the Sakura counter to collect his share.

There was a shamelessness to such actions, albeit one that was constrained by the trope of the otoko and the importance of buddies. In the absence of a reciprocating gaze, there was neither shame nor honor in front of the TV screen, and on the surface of things, the form of value sought in gambling—money—rendered all things commensurable.[49] Even a man's dignity had a price, as Akira experienced when his assailants demanded money in return for backing down from a fight. But it was exactly this commensurability of all things, epitomized by the individualizing labor market, that precipitated repetition of the otoko trope, which, in its excesses, required reference to a social third—Takeda-san—for its discourse to maintain integrity. In front of the TV screen, gamblers experienced no shaming gaze of propriety, and to a limited degree, this shamelessness was brazenly carried into the streets of San'ya. Every day, Gin, Yamamori, and others gambled illegally in the open and, on occasion, were joined by members of the Okinawa-gang, like Rikiishi or Akira. Everyone knew from experience that the regular police would not conduct arrests on account of gambling, because a special department of the police dealt with such cases. Yet everyone anticipated the arrest of Gin, who conducted his flower card operations in the open but was circumspect about selling meth. Insofar as danger was suspected, Gin and the others restrained from exhibiting the illegal elements of their conduct, which functioned as a marker of their territory, as a sign of irreverence for the legal, proper conformity of general society. Precisely on account of the negative excesses of their actions, signification had to remain in place: San'ya was "our town," in which one gambled on the sidewalks.[50]

Gin contemptuously reminded me of this constitutive difference between himself and me, when he learned I was teaching Akira "the computer" (*pasakon*). Left to ourselves in Sakura for an awkward moment, Gin hardly even looked at me when he said: "Well, good luck with the computer. But just remember our world is illegal." The necessity was for this sign of difference and counterdiscourse—of Yama as a "lawless zone"—to stay in force without being arrested or fleeing like Matsuda. Everyone thus knew what Gin did, that is, aside from running an illegal gambling business, but those other transactions were conducted behind closed doors. It was general social knowledge. Moreover, illegal *bakuchi* (gambling) had long been the domain of the yakuza of old in Japan. Its practice signified "another world" that, as Takeda-san put it, even "normal Japanese would not set foot in."[51]

Akira, who had risen to the rank of lieutenant (*kashira*) while working ten years as a yakuza, would say that he "still thinks like an outlaw." Sometimes, he would tack back to his days in the mob, when he had worked in extortion, and say, as if he was quoting a phrase, that "nothing is as dirty as general society." Nearly all his customers in Shinjuku had been members of general society who had lent money to another member of general society, who refused to return the funds. Consequently, the former sought help from the yakuza, where it had been Akira's job to find the latter's weakness and "threaten" (*kyōkatsu*) them into returning the money, a percentage of which was pocketed by his yakuza organization, the Nibikikai. Noting similarly how "general society" was structured so that it was those at the bottom who did all the work while those on top took the profits, Akira would observe: "The more respectable you become, the dirtier you become. That is why the yakuza is better." Notably, such views were difficult to reconcile with the avowed right-wing stance of most of the Okinawa-gang, except Saruma, who voted for the Japanese Communist Party (Nihon Kyōsantō), but they functioned as markers of difference that empowered the guys vis-à-vis society. Boasting was not necessary to prove that the guys did not care a wink about the police, for their conduct already demonstrated this. Kentarō's occasional comment that so-and-so was "stupid" for ending up back in jail meant nothing more: the notion they had done something ethically reprehensible was absent from such statements. On the contrary, the bravado of being an otoko more often entailed transgression despite or because of police presence.

Yet no one in the group wanted to be arrested or jailed. After a ten-day stint in detention for aiding Shōkawa in a fight, Akira grumbled he was too old for that sort of thing. It had been OK while he had been in the mob. But at the age of fifty-six, with physical illnesses, being jailed in a cell that hardly fit his body was not worth it. As for Shōkawa, he bawled his eyes out when Nē-san came to see him in detention.

Everyone knew that San'ya and many of their usual haunts were under surveillance by the police. It was said that the local police at the Mammoth police box had a good "grasp" of who hung out in front of Mutō's hole-in-the-wall. In fact, one day when Riku instigated a fight, the police from the Mammoth appeared in Sakura with a photo of his face, asking if anyone had seen "this man." Kentarō assumed that a camera had been placed high on the apartment building facing down on Mutō's, where no one could see it. Henceforth, they would have to be careful, he said, and do it in the back alleyway if they were going to fight. Members of the Matsuda-group, too, were thought to be followed around by undercover cops, as they had been arrested previously for possession of meth. Kon-chan had been arrested thus a second time and was awaiting a two-year jail sentence. Yamamori, too, would disappear from the entryway to Iroha for extended periods, ostensibly because he knew it was best to lie low awhile: "because he knows it's risky." And while the gambling at Mutō's and inside Sakura continued in brazen fashion, there were moments of paranoia when members of the Okinawa-gang talked suspiciously of new faces at Mutō's, wondering if they might be undercover police. When Suzuki's girlfriend received an anonymous call one evening from a man asking if "the tehaishi, Suzuki," was there, he became convinced that the "cops" (*satsu*)—indicated by the silent gesture of raising a fist to the forehead—were tracking his movements. How else would they know her phone number?

As it turned out, some of these fears were well-grounded, because one day the undercover police stormed Mutō's hole-in-the-wall en masse. Suzuki made his getaway in the nick of time, as he witnessed the police descend just as he was walking toward Mutō's from the end of the alley. From the second-floor window, Hasegawa looked down, horror-stricken, as events unfolded, at the arrests, the no-entry yellow tape, and the TV crews gathering with cameras. News of the event spread like wildfire in the Okinawa-gang, for it had been poor Shōkawa—whom, everyone knew, had started betting seriously on boats only a few weeks earlier, when his mother passed away—who was caught red-handed in the act of placing a bet. An undercover cop had been standing by his side and just as Shōkawa told Mutō (writing in his ledger) his numbers and was handing over the ¥500, the undercover police shouted: "Hold it!" With this, the remaining police charged from the wings, detaining Shōkawa, Mutō, and two of the other drunkards lounging about on the rickety stools, no doubt too drunk to stand.

To Akira's embarrassment, news of the arrest made it onto the NHK news the following day at noon, when everyone at Sanyukai happened to be eating lunch with the TV on. Since the cops had invited the media along for the scoop, the incident was also reported in newspapers, and as was the wont of mass media at the time, the reportage focused less on the illegality of unlicensed gambling and more on the self-evident scandal of welfare recipients seeping state-acquired funds away into the Yamaguchi-gumi. The *Sankei News* reported as follows:

Boat Gambling with Welfare? Yamaguchi-gumi Members Arrested under Suspicion of Illegal Bookmaking, Tokyo, San'ya

On account of illegal bookmaking on motorboat races with welfare recipients in the San'ya district of Tokyo, the Metropolitan Police Department Office of Security has arrested Uga Kaho (42), a leader in the designated organized crime syndicate Yamaguchi-gumi in Tokyo,

Arakawa-ku, Minami-Senjū, and Mutō Isami (73), manager of an eatery in Sumida-ku, Zutsumi-dōri, as well as three bookkeepers and three customers, on suspicion of breaking the motorboat racing law (illegal bookmaking). According to the police, the suspect, Uga Kaho, is keeping silent.

The arrest took place on the 20th around 3:00 p.m., at the yakitori eatery managed by the suspect, Mutō, with a TV streaming motorboat races, where he paid back winners made to bet on an estimate of ¥10,500 per ¥100.

According to the police, Ugo Kaho and suspects have profited upwards of ¥100 million since 2008, half of which is thought to have become funds for the organized crime syndicate. Half the customers were welfare recipients, and the upper limit of bets was set at ¥10,000 per person.[52]

While this article in the *Sankei News* pays some degree of homage to San'ya, localizing the events in San'ya, another article in the NHK news does not even mention San'ya, stating merely that the arrests took place in the Taitō Ward of Tokyo.[53] But it is the missing term in both articles that gives them the normative force of self-evidence, namely, the "state" (*kuni*) or "nation" (*kuni*), two terms between which there is slippage in Japanese, for it is only in relation to the state that the central terms in the articles fall into place: "welfare recipients," "illegal bookmaking," and the "designated organized crime syndicate Yamaguchi-gumi."[54] Not only was Mutō running an unlicensed boat racing operation at his hole-in-the-wall, but the odds of the bets themselves were being calibrated illegally, such that gamblers did not win as much as the official odds would have given them. The guys were aware of this, expressing surprise, if anything, at how much the police actually knew about the intricacies of Mutō's operation, because in addition to Mutō, the cops had also arrested Uga Kaho, an unknown organizer behind the scenes, as well as a lower-level member of the Kanamachi-ikka, who used to bicycle past Mutō's hole-in-the-wall to pick up the profits and hand them on to the Kanamachi-ikka. Moreover, the police also appeared to know everything about the profits that this Uga figure had reaped over the years and the guys surmised that the cops had been staking the place out for a long time; in fact, when Shōkawa was held in detention, he seemed to notice familiar faces among the police. After his release a few days later, Shōkawa recounted what the police had asked him and how he had concocted some cock-and-bull story about never having gambled there before. For a brief period, it even seemed that the Kanamachi-ikka wanted to speak with Shōkawa in person, to debrief him. Ultimately, the police did not indict Mutō, although he remained in detention for close to a month, and when he restarted business, the little TV screen had disappeared from its place on the wall across from the bamboo *kumade* (rake) from Ōtori Shrine, hung to bring good fortune in business. For good reason, the staff at Sakura grew wary after this incident. The group, too, began to circulate rumors that unknown individuals had been seen outside Sakura, taking photos of the entrance. A police siege was imminent, Saruma said, but still, Akira and others kept going undeterred. Naturally, all this changed when Sakura decided to acquire a license for boat racing, thereby legalizing the gambling, but the mama-san still grumbled when guys would pull out a bowl with dice, handing over a couple thousand yen as a token of gratitude for letting them play.

Wariness and avoidance of arrest differed from "ratting" (*chinkoro*) on buddies. An otoko would have dishonored himself by informing on friends or enemies, and therein resided his code of conduct. In effect, the occasion of arrest for what the mass media depicted as the most shameless of acts—flushing away welfare into the black market of a mob organization—emerged as a pretext to affirm dignity as an otoko. Whereas the state would have affixed insufficiency and shame in the punishment of confinement, reference to the counterdiscourse of the otoko and buddies counteracted and nullified this shame. It was in solidarity that dignity was upheld by protecting the social entity of the group. Anticipating Shōkawa's release, the guys shared knowledge of police procedures to predict when he would be released and how the arrest itself had taken place. Norihisa expressed concern that Shōkawa (formerly in the Japan Self-Defense Forces) had an air gun stowed away in his room and for what might happen if the cops searched his bunkhouse. When his phone finally connected at five o'clock in the afternoon, someone called Shōkawa, told him to forget the train, and to take a taxi that everyone would chip in for. Akira noted it was "normal" (*futsū*) to do as much, and thirty minutes later, Shōkawa pulled in at the Iroha entry in a taxi, where some fifteen people were waiting for him on a blue sheet spread on the ground, partly because they had been called and partly by chance, as Matsuda was doing his *tehai*, ambling about with the wad of ¥10,000 bills in his hand. High on meth, Yamamori declared that he had been the one to think of paying for the taxi and kept insisting that an *itchō* (single) block of tofu be passed around the group, starting and ending with Shōkawa, who had to finish the tofu but did not, a ceremony that most of the guys clearly found tiresome but went through with anyway.[55] Kentarō laughed at the sober-faced Shōkawa, who recounted tales from detention once the alcohol started coursing through him. Less than a year later, Shōkawa was back in detention for fighting with an opponent who refused to drop charges.

Kentarō described such compulsively repetitive and transgressive conduct as characteristic of San'ya. Referring to the well-known 1986 novel by the former mobster Abe Jōji—*Incarcerated and Incorrigible*—Kentarō identified San'ya as a space of incarceration and likened the transgressive conduct one witnesses in San'ya to that in a jail.[56] No one ever learns. Yet, within the confinement of San'ya, it was only by repeatedly transgressing the social norms of upstanding society that the trope of masculinity was materialized in its mode of conduct and enjoyment, as a solicitation for recognition. Insofar as the enactment of masculinity in San'ya organized enjoyment through an array of practices that could never be entirely one's own and that was therefore always threatened, performing the values of an otoko constituted an obsessive object of identification. The claim to masculinity could never be consummated, and for this reason, it mandated repetition.[57]

Notably, there were other modes of enjoyment than those of transgression through fighting or gambling, one of which was ubiquitous in San'ya's dive bars: karaoke. Shōkawa's favorite song, which he sang every Sunday, was the hugely popular song by the Okinawan band, *BEGIN*, "The Treasure of Islanders." Saturated with nostalgia, its lyrics give life to the vanishing natural beauties of Okinawa by asking how well the singer knows its evanescent corrals, skies, and dialects that cannot be captured on TV, radio, or in textbooks. "Surely," the lyrics resound, "there is something precious here," as if this "something" does not consist in Okinawa's stars or local traditions, but is somehow disclosed through them.[58] When Shōkawa sang the lyrics—"surely, there is something precious here"—they emerged as a reference to the people present at the table on each occasion he sang the song. This was indicated by Shōkawa pointing at the table in rhythm to the lyrics, while everyone else joined in for the refrain, depending on each their state of inebriation. Displaced into the lyrics of the song, the sociality of the group did not consist in the vanishing stars, skies, ocean, festivals, or dialects of Okinawa, as if the essence of this sociality did not entirely belong to them. Rather, it was revealed through these fugitive entities, and in karaoke, it was created through the practice of singing of the song. Of course, karaoke occurred alongside gambling, and the spirit of collective effervescence easily spilled into violence. As an obsessive object of identification, this masculine sociality gave itself to be recognized as excessive to general society, the gaze of which it both required and was threatened by and the propriety of which it threatened, in turn, in its excesses. The only alternative would have been to be fixed in shame without end or reprieve, aspiring to normativity and productivity. But the otoko of San'ya had his "dignity" (*iji*). Takeda-san and others would compare dyed-in-the-wool workers from San'ya with laborers from elsewhere, noting that San'ya's workers were "skilled" and "exceptional" at their trade. Laughing, Shōkawa added: "For the rest, they're just drinking." Defiant, the thoroughbred worker of San'ya knew their work better than anyone but threw propriety to the wind. If, like Kentarō, they did not feel like going to work, they "opened a hole, on purpose."

The ultimate price of decades of excessive working and drinking could be seen in the feeble fifty-year-old Iwasawa, who had "become increasingly incoherent" and of whom it was said that he only had a few years left. Akira was not much different, in and out of hospitals, and Kentarō himself would react indifferently whenever someone told him to drink less or to use a condom in the neighboring red-light district, Yoshiwara. In the imminent specter of the end, it was better to gamble now than to wait until it was too late. "When you die, you die," Kentarō said. Disregard for health, for the productive life, the biopolitical, and for death itself emerged as the negativity of life as an otoko: a trope that opposed the generalized social propriety propagated by the state and, in so doing, recovered a modicum of dignity for the otoko. Naturally, the guys were much less sanguine about death when it really faced them, but nevertheless, they persisted in their lifestyles undeterred, back to sipping shochu with ice and water at Mutō's hours after they had been let out of hospital, having just been ordered by doctors to lay off liquor. Kentarō worried about his blood pressure because it rose above 170 whenever he checked it, but he still drank shochu at all times of the day; nor did he ever consult a doctor, knowing full well that he should, preferring to say: "There's nothing wrong with me." Taking all sorts of medication, including painkillers and sleeping pills that did not mix well with alcohol, Akira would claim that doctors had not told him not to combine—although they clearly had!—and though he occasionally went sober for a few days, he would drink days on end, vomiting up the food he had eaten during the day. Shōkawa, too, would spend days drinking nonstop, starting when he woke up. Kentarō observed that everyone's liver hurt but that they continued drinking, hoping that "somehow it would turn out all right." Likewise, some of the guys might go on a fighting spree, repeatedly getting themselves into altercations and ending up in the local Mammoth. Be it with the cops or the doctors, the activities of the guys earned them a reputation so that Rikiishi was known with the police, and doctors knew that Akira was not, in any case, intent on getting any better. In fact, being recognized by the police was something that some of them fantasized and bragged about. Thus, when it came time for the yearly Obon festival held in Tamahime Park, Makoto and Akira would both comment on how the public order police (kōan keisatsu) eyed them as they entered the park, looking at their callused hands.[59] Akira would say that, given his record, the police "kept an eye on" him.

The day laborer, welfare recipient, and sometimes convicted criminal, if not active member of the yakuza, only validated himself as an otoko by doing what he did despite the disciplinary, punitive gaze of the state. It would have been "embarrassing" (hazukashī) if authorities kept someone from acting as he desired. Thus, Akira would say that he had "no shame" (haji wa nai).[60] He was not simply reacting but was quite conscious of the obvious: that the conduct of an otoko required that "weakness not be shown." Likewise, Kentarō asserted that "there is no way" he would spend the money of others, which he had been put in charge of keeping. There existed an explicit code of conduct that an otoko would have been ashamed to fall short of, and in Shōkawa's case, this involved not informing on one's buddies. By positing their own articulation of shame, the reference to buddies enabled the shaming gaze of the state to be repulsed. Yet, as with gambling, this solicitation for recognition was driven by a constitutive insufficiency that threatened to spiral out of control.

On the few occasions the guys won at gambling, it was never sufficient. Even when the returns were considerable, the form of money never conferred satisfaction. Rather, as the stand-in for an impossible presence, money assumed the force of a fetish that was repeatedly gambled or expended but never saved or used toward everyday expenses or the payment of debts. Returns from gambling were inevitably spent on activities as excessive as gambling itself, such as prostitutes in Yoshiwara, hostess clubs, or restaurants. Both gambling and the multifarious activities that followed a victory would have achieved mastery, but the aim of gambling was impossible to begin with: to restore the individual to plenitude.[61] Thus, the object cause of desire appeared retroactively, when it occurred to the gambler just how close they had come to victory. Most guys let up on gambling only when they had gotten so sick of losing that gambling, albeit temporarily, did not prick them.

For others, gambling assumed a self-destructive character that collapsed into a negativity without limit, especially when gambling was exacerbated by other external failures. Hence, Akira explained that he turned to gambling after getting into a verbal fight at Sanyukai. Feeling hurt, he decided to blow a couple hundred thousand yen at Kōrakuen, transforming the commensurable form of money into a singular negativity that was hard for him to return. Yet Akira did stop gambling when he lost several hundred thousand yen. His original conduct had thrown caution to the wind, but Akira was reckless in a manner that enabled him to assert his self-possession and to successfully impose himself on his fellows in San'ya, who recognized his character. By setting a limit, albeit a thoroughly excessive limit, to their gambling debts, not to mention their drinking and fighting habits, the group harnessed negativity in their favor.[62] Yet, slowly but surely, the excesses of their activities accelerated the demise of the guys, unraveling the social fabric that bound them together and undermining the sociality that shielded them against the normative gaze of "general society." Within the group, it was the disappearance of the meth-driven Matsuda that exemplified the sheer plunge into negativity, not to mention the obliteration of accountability and social existence.[63] It was only by referencing the group that expenditure was constrained.

By a strange inversion, therefore, singular debts incurred through gambling coincided with incommensurable winnings, and it was by sticking it out in this negativity that the day laborers and gamblers of San'ya laid claim to a life otherwise consigned to that of the anonymous manual laborer, worked to death. As a solicitation for recognition from other men in the area, gambling sought to master the abjection of San'ya by countering the death-inducing form of the subsistence wage and by transforming the modern passage of empty time into an experience of contingency that created debt and sociality. This was a negativity achieved through the repetitive and embodied exposure to the contingencies of gambling, the risks of which were often compounded by the unlicensed, illegal character of the local gambling venues at which men staked their reputations. But it was also precisely this transgressive aspect of gambling that allowed men in San'ya to repulse the normative gaze of upstanding society and that allowed them to comport themselves with a dignity recognized by their fellows, insofar as they made good on their debts. Credit, thus, emerged as the foremost sign of their accountability and of their singular value as an otoko. Like boxers on the ropes, however, the men had a limit to the amount of damage they could endure without collapsing, and the excessive lifestyles of individuals in San'ya foreshadowed their death, if not that of the day-laborer district itself. Ultimately, as it was said of construction work, gambling, fights, and liquor: "The bill catches up with you" (*tsuke ga mawatte kuru*).

Gamblers thereby sacrificed and paid for their failures with their social reputation as men, if not with their lives, and for this reason, gambling emerged as a metaphor for life in San'ya. Only a few, like Kentarō or Rikiishi, possessed the physique necessary to survive the excessive lifestyle predicated in Yama, but even these two were ticking time bombs, waiting to collapse. Akira would say of Kentarō's "type" that their bodies crashed suddenly, and he was right. Of himself, Akira would say that his failing health was a direct consequence of the excessive lifestyle he had led.

At Sanyukai, one did not speak of gambling: an activity that was obviously regarded as an "addiction" (*izonshō*).[64] Although everyone did gamble, such talk undermined Sanyukai as a space grounded on the denegation of unproductive forms of life, because at Sanyukai, even the long-lost alcoholic father with a gambling addiction and criminal record could be redeemed to take part in forms of sociality that did not revolve around excess. He could be trained both into docility and to shamelessly accept charity that sought to rescue him from himself and his environment, for he was, in their eyes, "pitiable" (*kawaisō*).[65] Individuals who came from outside San'ya and volunteered at Sanyukai spoke thus of the homeless people who lived in tents along the river, to whom the institution handed out food parcels once per week. The rest of San'ya, however, such as the entryway to the Iroha arcade, where the drunks gathered, or even Mutō's hole-in-the-wall, remained strangely beside the grid of Sanyukai's activities: at once immediately adjacent to Sanyukai yet nonexistent. Nor did staff or volunteers from outside San'ya ever make a stop at San'ya's dive bars on their way home from work, preferring to make a beeline for Minami-Senjū Station. Likewise, Sanyukai never reserved venues within San'ya for events like the end-of-the-year party, opting instead for Asakusa.

In a disquieting display of obsequiousness, one charity organization in San'ya even required that recipients of food sing Christian hymns before receiving their weekly ration. On every Sunday, a strangely pliable, straggly crowd of men could be seen lining up in a long row along Tamahime Park, holding white sheets of music, facing the opposite side of the street, where loudspeakers had been positioned and staff members faced them in turn. Like the divide between the inside and outside of the Sanyukai entryway, an imaginary line had been drawn that established charity givers vis-à-vis the Other, on whose recognition the institution was dependent.[66]

Institutions like Sanyukai could not enforce sociality among its members without expelling the excessive elements that threatened the institution at its core. Indeed, it was founded on negating the negativity of these excesses. By ousting disobedient men from its territory, however, Sanyukai repeated the originary gesture that had landed individuals in San'ya in the first place, confined and cut off from family and society. But it was not only institutions, families, and general society that could not tolerate and survive the excessive, repetitive lifestyle of the guys. Money and alcohol spelled the eventual dissolution of the Okinawa-gang itself.

The self-destruction of social reputations oftentimes began from borrowing meager sums of money. Especially at the end of the month, the group would have spent their out-of-work aid or welfare allowance and turned to one another for small sums of cash, lest they retreat to their rooms. It was equally common, however, for the guys to lose track of how much they had borrowed and lent, and from or to whom. This was no surprise, given that the guys were most often inebriated when they pulled money from one another, that is, when they asked for the bill. Akira would grumble at the end of every month that Shōkawa had demanded that he return ¥10,000 ($100) when he had not borrowed anything to begin with. To avoid a confrontation, Akira would dish the money out and disappear into his room for the last week of the month, living off instant noodles and water since he only had a couple hundred yen (a couple dollars) left in his account. Others, however, would get themselves into fights on account of paltry sums, having raised the anger of the lender either by failing, repeatedly, to return the debt or by feigning forgetfulness. What pricked lenders most was when they found borrowers spending cash on liquor or gambling which clearly indicated that they were in possession of money they chose not to return. Ironically, lenders thereby replicated the very infuriation expressed by upstanding members of general society who paid their taxes and did not forgive welfare recipients who wasted tax money. After Suzuki's fall from grace as tehaishi, Akira would therefore caution him "not to borrow from anyone!" Because instead of returning money or, even worse, failing to give individuals their wages and promising to do so the next day, Suzuki set money aside to drink, raising the ire of Matsuda, whose underlings he had decided not to pay, muttering under his breath: "How come only I can't drink?" Matsuda, in turn, would make a fuss with other members of the Okinawa-gang, insisting that Kentarō do something about his brother or that Akira talk to him. It was to no avail, however, as even Kentarō acted as if Suzuki's doings had nothing to do with himself, thereby seeming to give others the freedom to act as they wished. But everyone assumed that Kentarō would retaliate if Suzuki was harmed. Thus, it was said, Suzuki was safe and protected by the presence of his older brother.

Holding his forefinger and thumb millimeters apart, Akira explained that over only one hundred yen, the personal slight experienced by a lender could prompt them to kill. It was not the money itself but the affront to the person and reputation of the individual that caused them to assert themselves as men. Thus, the trope of the otoko could spill into irrecoverable excess, for which the individual had to take responsibility, or it could shore up this negativity by placing limits on excess. In this sense, Akira, who received more welfare than others and was also more generous with his money, had made a rule of not asking people to return money when the amount was less than three thousand yen (thirty dollars). Any other conduct would have been unbecoming. But when it came to fights, Akira asserted that nothing could hold him back, neither the police nor the danger of physical injury, and that he had no problem wielding a broken bottle. When it came down to it, he said, the other party backed down.

In San'ya, "no one but me," Akira would boast, can take things "to the limit" thus. But it was usually someone else who committed the deed, like the slightly crazed, very short-tempered Izami, who had previously been jailed for murder and this time had stabbed an "old man" in his seventies. News of such murders spread like wildfire, as if everyone knew that, at some point or other, it was bound to happen again.

FORBEARANCE

Akira's life shattered at the age of twenty-five. At the time, he was living in Tokyo and working in the demolition business, heading up his own group of laborers. Fortune had favored him up until then. His bosses had liked him, and thus, he found himself on the cusp of establishing his own company at a very early age. Like so many of the guys, Akira had dropped out of high school and traveled from Okinawa to the mainland to find work as a teenage manual laborer, conscripted by poverty into Japan's postwar labor force.[1] At twenty-five, he had almost made it in the construction world.

As leader of his crew, Akira's daily routine involved picking up everyone in the morning, driving them to the site in a minivan, and leading work itself. Decades later, he would reflect on the health consequences of having done his share of demolition work at a time when hardly any health measures were observed. Workers merely wrapped a towel around their mouths to keep out toxic fumes and dust. Thirty years after, when Akira was ailing from multiple illnesses, including a brain tumor and the so-called it-hurts-it-hurts disease (*itai-itai byō*), he wondered whether demolition work had caused his condition.[2]

But when he was twenty-five, it was a fight that spelled the turning point in his life. When he and his crew arrived on-site, it turned out another group of workers had been hired to do the same work. This double booking transformed into a confrontation between the leaders of the two groups, as both refused to give the day's work to the other. Hungover and bellicose, Akira reacted instantly when the leader of the other group put a hand on him. Before anyone could separate them,

Akira had flipped the man to the ground and kicked him in the chest when he tried to get back up. The kick had been just a light nudge, Akira would say.

Life continued as usual for a few weeks after the incident, until one day, Akira arrived home to a line of police cars parked out front. Charged with manslaughter, he was incarcerated, and in his first trial, he was found guilty of involuntarily killing his adversary. On looking back years later, however, Akira would bitterly recount that it was not until his lawyers contested this verdict that the case was to alter his life permanently. When his lawyers succeeded in receiving a retrial on the grounds of medical malpractice, the case caught the attention of the mass media, and Akira's name was made known to the public. Akira was finally given a three-year sentence. Yet it was not the prison term but the publicization of the court case that redirected the course of his life. For Akira, who would go to jail several times again, twice for over a year and once as a "substitute" (*miga-wari*) for someone higher in the mob echelons, jail could be endured, but the stain to his person could not be repaired.[3]

When he was released, Akira was, in fact, offered his old job back, but he declined. Shortly thereafter, he was approached by the yakuza through an acquaintance and offered a place in the organization if he should desire it. Akira was to spend ten years of his life in the Kantō-based Nibikikai. Before the Nibikikai dissolved, Akira would rise from driver to bodyguard to lieutenant of his own group, until infighting put him on disciplinary probation, having to eke out a living in San'ya. When this finally happened, Akira paid the ward office a visit and, in the exhibitionist mobster style of Yamamori, threatened the state into giving him welfare. Working the system constituted a righteous technique of survival, the successful outcome of which redounded to his credit.[4]

Sociality, Honor, and the Circulation of Violence

A week rarely passed without one of the guys getting into a confrontation or fight. Even Saruma, who might have appeared the least hotheaded of the bunch, had a history of winding up in detention centers. The graduate of an elite Okinawan high school and of Meiji University, Saruma had been president of his own small company that specialized in the installation of LAN lines. Yet he would also recall breaking bottles and "half killing" opponents in bar brawls. What was the point of breaking bottles, he asked, if not to half kill your adversary?

But the most well-known fighter was Rikiishi, "bodyguard," "junior," confidant, and friend to the lean and elegant Takeda-san. Indeed, once he was set off in a fight, Kentarō remarked, "there is no stopping" Rikiishi. By this same token, however, Rikiishi could be counted on to come to one's aid, unlike anyone else, Akira would say. He would "come running" without giving it a second thought. Notwithstanding his unstoppable character, the steadfast Rikiishi thereby upheld a principle of consideration for buddies that Akira explained with reference to one of his favorite ideograms, namely, "forbearance" (*nin*).[5] By either deciding to fight solo, that is, without involving others, or by always coming to the rescue, even the formidable Rikiishi restrained and sacrificed himself for his buddies, at least in fights. He thus embodied what Akira would elaborate as his philosophy of forbearance, with reference to its ideogram, which consists in the combination of a protective "heart" (*kokoro*) or "shield" (*tate*) and a "sword" (*katana*) that was only wielded at the very limit of endurance.[6] If it got to that point, Akira, like Rikiishi, might strike and unleash violence in all its excess, but unless that moment arrived, he would control himself in the interest of others.

Though alcohol blurred judgment, the expression of an idealized code of honor could be discerned in fighting. As Shōkawa emphatically explained upon first meeting me—an outsider—the fundamental principle of fighting resided in protecting one's buddies. He asked me if it was not "normal" (*futsū*) that one "look out for" the members of one's group and, if any member was threatened or beaten up, that one strike back.[7] As such, the compulsion to fight invoked the necessity of protecting sociality itself, and reference was therefore made beyond the dyadic relation: to buddies. And as Shōkawa continued to explain, these rules of conduct also functioned to maintain order, hierarchy, and formality within the group. As Okinawans, he said, it was not allowed to "lay a hand on" anyone senior in age to oneself. Juniors could talk back at seniors, but to physically strike them was not accepted. On the contrary, violence might be employed by seniors to reinstate the proper order of things. Or an apology could be accepted from the offending party. The reciprocity of violence could thereby give rise to alliance, much as Marcel Mauss once observed that the exchange of gifts may replace warfare, paving the way for indebtedness, sociality, and a temporality of deferral within which reputations were either created or destroyed.[8] An apology and its acceptance created social obligation and demanded the remembrance thereof, such that obligations would be fulfilled over time and, in this case, either by sacrificing oneself for or restraining oneself from entangling a buddy in one's brawls.[9] In fact, this was how Shōkawa and Akira's friendship was forged. Akira had started off their relationship with a faux pas, offending when he should have been deferential to Shōkawa, who was four years senior to Akira. But Akira had set himself aside and apologized. Camaraderie had been established by acceding to a social system of seniority that both individuals recognized, and by the time Akira ended up in detention at Asakusa police headquarters for aiding

Shōkawa in a brawl, the latter was introducing Akira to others as his "younger brother" (*otōto*).

Still, the failure to observe proper deference was rare for core members, and its enforcement was primarily reserved for individuals within the periphery of the group, as Akira had been when he had offended Shōkawa. In this way, a younger man in his midthirties was given a battering after work one day, for he had a bad habit of becoming offensive when he was drinking, and Suzuki, Kentarō, and Rikiishi had had enough. Since it would have been awkward for Suzuki—his tehaishi caretaker—to put the man in place, Rikiishi did it. A week later, the man's face was still swollen, and one eye was bloodred. It had been "much worse," Kentarō said, right after the beating. But everyone continued work as before, save for a brief urging from Kentarō to fix the habit. Nonetheless, Kentarō acknowledged, it was difficult to alter habits.

The enforcement of deference transpired similarly one day outside Mutō's hole-in-the-wall, where Kentarō witnessed a slightly younger man lambasting the senior Hasegawa for his condescending attitude. Notably, Kentarō and others in the Okinawa-gang had not been very fond of Hasegawa at the time, likely for the very same reason the man was shouting at him. Kentarō himself had moved out of Hasegawa's apartment because he was being asked to pay a monthly shower fee of ¥5,000 ($50). Nonetheless, in this instance, the flagrant disregard of deference prompted Kentarō to take the younger man to task. Demanding what kind of behavior it was to speak thus to a "senior" (*meue*)—"he's your senior, right?"— Kentarō challenged the man to a fight when the latter persisted in justifying himself. As Kentarō broke into a shadowboxing stance, flinging his fists about, he beckoned the other man to join him around the corner. Sure enough, the younger man apologized shortly after, first to Kentarō and then to Hasegawa, and as the man lowered his head and shook hands, Kentarō went about introducing him to everyone as if he were a new recruit.[10]

Where talk was endlessly unproductive, the threat of violence facilitated instant resolution, and in so doing, it extended the influence of the group. It was not just the prospect of fighting but of losing to a person as intimidating as Kentarō that enforced submission to a certain social order. After all, Kentarō had a reputation, and he himself professed to beating the hell out of adversaries. But as Kentarō declared one day, he was also well aware that no one in the group stood a chance against someone twenty years younger. Perhaps for this reason, he had a knack for establishing his authority before fights had even begun, and it was in one such instance that I found myself in a snack bar with Kentarō, sitting next to a hoodlum (*chinpira*). Dressed in baggy sports clothes, the youth was clearly sizing us up. Yet, at the slightest hint of an attitude from our neighbor, Kentarō ended the situation by simply saying: "I don't know if you're part of some organization, but it's irrelevant." His words sent a quick ripple through the man, and in an instant, the tension had been diffused, because Kentarō had made it clear that it did not matter whether he was yakuza affiliated or not. If they were going to fight, they might as well skip the posturing and have it out right away. Or they could get along drinking. It was one or the other. Kentarō thereby called the man's bluff, and the next day he was laughing about the hoodlum cheerily toasting with us by the end of the night.[11]

In most cases, however, fighting caused a tiresome inconvenience to other members of the group. Unlike Kentarō's no-nonsense confrontations, most brawls involved situations in which other members either had to prevent the fight or provide aid when things got out of hand. In fact, the sixty-year-old Shōkawa was regarded as the most troublesome drunk of the lot, because he constantly embroiled others in his confrontations. But it was not just Shōkawa. One evening, the guys had to chase down Hayashi when he insisted on antagonizing his opponent, driving him down the street until they ended up in front of the Mammoth. So too, Akira repeatedly had to step in to prevent Riku, Saruma, and countless other acquaintances from fighting. It was a weekly, if not a daily, occurrence that somebody got themselves into a confrontation, such that the rest of the crew would sigh, lower their heads, and moan: "Not again." And in addition to the trouble of preventing or aiding, there were other inconveniences to brawls. At times, the furniture in bars was broken so that everyone involved either had to pay for repairs or someone had to fix things with a drill and hammer. Naturally, the individual who had instigated the fight justified his conduct, throwing blame on the other party. He insisted that there had been no choice but to fight, and in this way, everyone had to live with the self-righteous machismo of the others. Indeed, brawls could give occasion for the group to come together.

Looking after and indulging one another fostered bonds of indebtedness that strengthened the group, but such indebtedness could also accrue to the point at which someone destroyed their own reputation. It was especially burdensome when someone ended up in detention or jail because the others had to visit. Personages like Takeda-san and Nē-san would also go by with magazines and clothing, while Matsuda deployed his police connections, at least to give the appearance of securing an early release. The strongest bond ought to have arisen on the occasion that someone was detained on account of someone else. Yet such an outcome was contingent on the remembrance of debt and reciprocal conduct over time, with a slight difference, as the return of the gift demands.

On the other hand, coming to the rescue enhanced the reputation of the rescuing individual. When Matsuda was beaten down in front of Mutō's place, Akira stepped in since it looked like Matsuda "would take a beating." After they had been hauled into the Mammoth, Akira proceeded to kick the other man in the stomach when he accused Akira of having started the affair. This incident earned Akira the reputation of someone who would not side with the police to play to his advantage and, with it, a nickname coined by Matsuda, for having kicked the other man inside the police box, in front of the cops. Reminiscent of Miyazaki Manabu's "devil-may-care type," Matsuda would henceforth refer to Akira as "the devil's man." As Akira himself would say, he looked to the "actions" of others to evaluate them, and in this case, his actions had established his worth.[12]

Matters unfolded similarly when Akira wound up in detention on account of Shōkawa. But it was from a third person, Riku, that Shōkawa inherited the fight. Riku had abruptly abandoned a confrontation in the hands of Shōkawa, who called Akira. Faced with a crazed opponent who was about to throw a bicycle at Shōkawa when Akira arrived, the two of them retaliated by pummeling the man to the ground with an aluminum trash can. Once the police had detained the three of them, the other man insisted on pressing charges, causing Shōkawa and Akira to spend two weeks in detention. As a consequence, the only person whose reputation remained unscathed after this incident was Akira since he had played no part in starting the fight. He had only gone running when Shōkawa phoned, as his code of ethics dictated and despite others advising him it was "better not to go." As luck would have it, Akira also wound up in a two-by-one-meter cell, while Shōkawa lounged in an empty six-person cell. Their release gave occasion for everyone to get together, including a remorseful Riku and Matsuda, the facilitator of their early release, and in this way, sociality was sustained. Yet Akira's self-sacrifice called for return, and Shōkawa's failure to be mindful of this left their relationship fraught. Only by protecting Akira or someone else could Shōkawa return or pass onward the gift of self-sacrifice.[13] Violence was thus made to circulate in San'ya and to take on an incremental character, because it was expected that buddies go the extra mile. But this logic constituted a double-edged sword. Although violence in the name of solidarity sealed buddies as buddies, it also sowed vengeance in outsiders, and the violence that was inflicted was the violence that would be (or had been) returned, originating in an impossible, inexhaustible source that exceeded the limits that forbearance would have placed on it.[14]

As if the damage inflicted could never be enough, there was an excess to the violence with which the guys engaged their adversaries. An indelible mark had to be left behind, either on their opponents or themselves. One day, Rikiishi took on the man reputed to "have been the strongest" in San'ya, giving him injuries that required several months of hospitalization. Fortunately for Rikiishi, this man did not press charges but did give him an elbow injury that would stay with him "for life." Shōkawa likewise laughed at the "footprint" left by Akira's slipper on someone's face when he kicked them outside Sakura. Only a week later, Shōkawa recounted how he had "pride" (*puraido*) and had therefore held on tightly to the aluminum can as he beat his opponent, even as the aluminum sliced through his finger. In effect, the offense that precipitated the confrontation had triggered a violence whose source could not be located or extinguished. The drive to violence circulated an excess for which reciprocity could not suffice.

Fights had to be repeated because they sought to reestablish masculinity, and in doing this, they invariably referenced the degenerate social status of San'ya. It was never enough, and lest the individual in question could restrain himself, fights threatened to unleash an excess that undercut their self-assertions. The important thing was that everyone recognize them as an otoko. Rather than cause a "burden" (meiwaku) to the group, therefore, it happened that some of the guys embroiled themselves in solo confrontations and that they went on veritable fighting sprees alone. In fact, Rikiishi never involved anyone else, and when he got injured, he had been getting himself into fights for months. Having just turned fifty, this fighting spree notably coincided with a period in his life when he was suffering from something akin to panic attacks. Unable to make a fist, Rikiishi grasped a plastic bottle at all times and exhibited all sorts of strange behavior, like bolting in and out of Sakura or calling Akira in the early mornings to go for calming walks. And when he drank, he drank to the point of becoming so "hammered" that, one evening, he could be found swaying and bracing himself against the electric pole right in front of the Mammoth, grunting and barely able to keep his eyes open. Thus, he would drink and sleep in Sakura, only to wake and drink. Having turned fifty, Rikiishi would later explain that, up until that point, he had "risen and risen" at work, imagining that he would reach the top. But the moment seemed to have passed without his being aware of it, and now he was on the way down. He could keep up with younger scaffolders for a day or so. But otherwise, he fell behind. As the result of age and decades of construction work, this insufficiency was transposed through fighting into a reaffirmation of masculinity.

In fact, Akira was constantly attuned to actualizing his principle of fighting, which he would illustrate with the proverb: "Side with the weak, and crush the strong" (yowaki o tasuke tsuyoki o kujiku). Being good at karaoke, traditional enka songs, and proverbs, Akira had more than a dozen sayings memorized to suit various occasions. In this instance, the proverb referenced yakuza ideals of old, and by cloaking its world with an aura of virtue, it reversed the assignation of guilt that had constituted Akira's life as an "outlaw."[15] By refiguring the act that landed him in jail, fighting would reverse the order of justice, guilt, and punishment. It would install Akira as an otoko in his own right, and he staked himself to this end. Hence, when Akira's older sister died, and he was unable to attend the funeral in Okinawa for lack of cash, his powerlessness caused him to "go amok" (abareru). Taking on three opponents in the Iroha arcade, he woke in the hospital with broken ribs. The excess of violence could, in effect, be directed at the self as much as another. It could be exteriorized and passed onward, or it could be internalized in the form of self-loathing and the consequent infliction of self-harm. Just as Akira's "anger" at Sanyukai was "eternal," this violence was inexhaustible in its transposition, and its excess triggered repetition while giving rise to pleasure in pain. As if his ribs would never heal, Akira repeatedly refractured them and never seemed to get rid of his bandages. The mark of the altercation functioned as a badge of masculinity but compelled repetition in its insufficiency.

It was not only the excess of violence that impelled physical altercations, but a desire for these acts to signify in their excess and to do so exhaustively. Even though no one might have seen the spectacle, it was in the interest of making it intelligible that there was so much talk about what had happened, both by participants and others. Above and beyond the sociality of the group, there was a dramatic aspect to fighting that recalls Barthes's work "The World of Wrestling." Be it a slur, blow, wound, or the manner in which the event was recounted, there was an excess to the characterization of personalities involved, and every detail of the altercation seemed to carry a meaning. Not unlike "the forearm smash" or "hold" in wrestling, there was the "chokehold," "beating the hell out of" adversaries, or the finishing kick in the face.[16] Whether it was enforcement of submission by someone merciful enough to grant second chances, ruthless violence to eliminate a wrongdoer by someone prepared to go the whole nine yards, or the crowning blow of incontestable supremacy by someone who threw repercussions to the wind, there was a personal extravagance to acts of violence that was equally evident in the suffering incurred through brawls. Only the uncontrollable Rikiishi received elbow damage for life, whereas Akira suffered broken ribs in silent interiority, and Kentarō always returned intact, if with a nick on the knuckle. Where Rikiishi was simply unstoppable in his rage, Akira waited for the odds to be stacked against him, and Kentarō read his opponents before challenging them to an altercation that they would prefer to avoid: be it in gambling or fights, Kentarō was the "Paul Newman of Japan." Everyone had a role to play and, in the exuberance of that performance, a mask to wear. As Akira observed of pro wrestling one day, it is enjoyable to watch precisely because it is an "act!"[17]

Staking themselves in physical altercations allowed for the guys to follow their convictions through and to display this accomplishment. Much as fighting could miscarry, its violence did not consist in a plunge into the sheer excess of negativity, as proponents of Bataille might have it, for there was a signification at stake in the act, if only to rest content with oneself. In the enactment of an idealized code of honor, it was not only suffering, retribution, and justice that were rendered intelligible—an eye for an eye, as Barthes himself says, plus a little more—but an ennobled model of how righteous men should conduct themselves in an ideal world. Of course, the assertion of these ideals could only occur in contradistinction to the underhanded, cunning, and devious ways of the likes of Yamamori, who performed his role of the hoodlum fiend to perfection. Either way, the efficacy of the enactment consisted of the extent to which individuals expressed an excess of interiority in the legible exteriority of signs.[18] Thus, when Akira offered himself up to a battering by three men or Riku pulled a knife in Sakura, there was an aspiration for their actions to meet a standard of conduct, and this was so even when they were inebriated. Being drunk obviously tended to exacerbate difficult situations and to blur righteous distinctions. Yet the true problem was that confrontations in San'ya revived wounds whose source was always located elsewhere, and for this reason, the violence deployed in everyday spats could be well-nigh inexhaustible. The enactment of justice missed the common plight of men in San'ya, whose sufferings first and foremost derived from the state. Although it was by transgressing against the rules of general society that the group attained their self-empowering form of justice, they could not but succumb to the state power that rendered them a means within the overriding economy. The loose entity of the group filled the lacuna left by state authority, determining according to its forgiving and impromptu standards whether so-and-so had acted with consideration for its members.

Ultimately, it was failure to account for repercussions on other members of the group that caused the assertion of masculinity to backfire, and this entailed that individuals place limits on their conduct. While everyone was usually supportive of members who got the others involved in confrontations, there was a limit to such indulgence. Like Suzuki, Shōkawa had brought about one too many inconveniences, and their bragging had grown hollow and tiresome for lack of group recognition. But it was the laconic Riku who was made to bear the brunt of the blame for the two-week incarceration of Akira and Shōkawa. Kentarō, who rarely went out of his way to lecture anyone, had to sit down with Riku to talk over what had happened. The problem or violence had to be addressed and quelled at what appeared to be its source, namely, an individual who repeatedly embroiled others in his own brawls. Behind his back, Riku was now called a "troublemaker," and even Shōkawa would mutter that Riku was "finished." After detention, Akira, too, said that he had already intervened for Riku several times and that he would no longer get involved. From then on, he would take a "no touch" policy, claiming: "The real winner is the one who walks away." With a few exceptions, however, almost everyone had been in Riku's position before.

Indeed, save for Takeda-san, it seemed that almost anyone could occupy the place of the individual who was causing a burden to everyone else. In fact, only months before the fight, Kentarō and Akira were lauding Riku precisely for being the kind of person who did not entangle others in his affairs. Riku was known for taking care of things by himself, and on this note, he refused to seek or accept financial support from the state. To the exasperation of Kentarō, who was adamantly of the stance that "you take what you can get," Riku had even severed the support he received while being treated for an illness, thought to be cancer. Years earlier, Kentarō had likewise found Riku injured in Asakusa after a fight, but despite several broken ribs, Riku insisted on returning by himself. Thus, Riku would come to be known for his warped sense of honor and for his drunken fits, when it was not unusual for him to pull a knife. But this time, Riku had broken his own mahjong dictum—people are "finished if they compromise" (*magetara owari*)— and he had fallen into the category of being "out," as Kentarō called those who could not uphold their own standards. The fall and rise of individuals came swiftly, such that at one point in the year, Hayashi might have fallen out of favor, while, half a year later, Hayashi himself joined the others in complaining about someone else. The guys fell consistently short of their own standards, precisely in instantiating them, and this failure prompted repetition. It was never enough.

In this way, there was simmering tension, if not antipathy between some members, and the seemingly arbitrary choice of someone to be "out" appeared to consolidate group sentiment. This logic of exclusion is similar to the more widespread one of "bullying" (*ijime*) in Japan, in which a mark of difference singles out an individual target for social violence, and one is reminded of the supposedly functional operations of violence in creating unanimity.[19] The designation of a sacrificial victim would deflect the reciprocal character of violence onto an external object, and in so doing, it would regenerate the unity of the social, such that the expulsion finally assumes a ritual form in which a mimetic object comes to replace the original sacrifice. Threatened on all sides, a "lawless zone" like San'ya would lend itself to the conditions under which an originary crisis necessitates the founding of the social in sacrifice, and there was, indeed, a conventional character to the manner in which everyone grumbled about so-and-so. But the violence circulating in San'ya owed its cause to the market that rendered the San'ya man disposable: there was an anterior agency that justified that good-for-nothings be disposed of, and this limitless source of violence, which had been lived daily for decades, was therefore far from immanent to relations within San'ya.[20] It was state recognition that contained violence within San'ya and against statist norms that the group sought justice through transgression. Violence was normally deflected onto outsiders to the group, powerless as they were before the state itself, but the tension between its members could just as well unravel its own social fabric. Notwithstanding the choice of an individual to be "out," it was only forbearance that secured the mutual respect of buddies.

In its transgressive mode, the trope of the otoko referenced an ideal that was embodied by Takeda-san as the emblem of solidarity, hierarchy, and hospitality. In a poignant rendition of the importance of the group, Takeda-san recalled how he had first arrived in San'ya decades earlier and wondered whether he would "be able to make it in this town." At the time, he knew no one. Hence, years later, Takeda-san would say that buddies are "everything." If he were to go to another town, he would have to start from scratch. But in "this town"—Yama—Takeda-san had his buddies and his partner, Nē-san. For lack of any other markers of social status—college degree, résumé—recognition by others in one's immediate vicinity took on paramount significance. Such social recognition was "everything": it marked the difference between the violence of disposability—death—that the labor market predicated for San'ya and the dignity conferred by recognition as an otoko.[21] In face of the objective, individualizing conditions of capitalist dispossession, the proximity of buddies in San'ya enabled a sociality of mutual recognition that stood in contrast to more advanced, fully alienated formations of sociality and discipline that exist at, say, a white-collar company or among workers for a temp agency.[22]

Contrary to expulsion and confinement to San'ya, Takeda-san and Nē-san made a practice of inviting everyone home for meals and alcohol. Once or twice every month, particularly on holidays, long weekends, and breaks like the New Year or Obon, Takeda-san and Nē-san hosted gatherings for the Okinawa-gang and an endless range of friends and acquaintances. Their tiny living room was no more than five by two meters, opening up through sliding doors (*fusuma*) onto an even smaller tatami bedroom, a narrow kitchen with barely enough space for one person, and an entryway that fed directly into the kitchen, and beside which was located a basic Japanese-style toilet. The apartment had no shower or bath, meaning that Takeda-san and Nē-san frequented the nearby public bathhouse. During these get-togethers, the living room would get so crowded that people had to squeeze between each other at the table or sit behind one another to fit. Takeda-san would sit at the far end of the table, beside the small TV, chatting with someone and occasionally directing Nē-san to get this or that. As for Nē-san, she would sit in *seiza* (knees bent underneath her) in the bedroom adjacent to the living room, occasionally making food, adding it to a table already decked out with all kinds of dishes, drinks, and ashtrays. But she would overturn this image of docility with a sarcastic, quick-witted humor that knew nothing of decency in parrying comments from the guys. Nē-san also would not drink, as she could not take alcohol, and it was only much later in the night, usually after midnight, when the food had been consumed and everyone had settled into a drinking-only mode, that she relaxed and took part in gambling with flower cards. As I was instructed by Kentarō, at Takeda-san's apartment one had to eat "without hesitation" (*enryō naku*) to make the hosts "happy." Indeed, this hospitality was extended to all and sundry, some of whom came empty-handed—which was welcomed—but most often laden with large bags of ice or bottles of shochu, if not a box of Takeda-san's Nodokoshi Kirin Happōshū beer. And when the New Year arrived, the guys would plan what to get for Takeda-san and Nē-san in advance, knowing they would spend several evenings, if not days, in their apartment, occasionally sleeping over.

The New Year left everyone penniless, but the feasts at Takeda-san and Nē-san's apartment displayed the extravagance and largesse of a modern-day pot-latch. After all, Georges Bataille once observed that it is in poverty, in the disdain for riches, and in the disregard for the value of upright labor that the modern potlatch can be rediscovered, marking the restoration of exuberance to life.[23] Indeed, feasts at Takeda-san and Nē-san's apartment were quintessential events of nonproductive expenditure, wherein rank was established precisely through its effacement. It simply was not done to hesitate or carry on with formalities, and if gratitude was to be expressed, it was to be done without ceremony or in the form of a contribution to the potlatch. For the magic of Takeda-san's influence resided in the absence of self-interest and calculation to his largesse.[24] True generosity and hospitality were to be encountered under conditions of poverty and utter social marginalization. Thus, Kentarō marveled at Robin Hood as a figure who "scatters" riches to the poor. Of New Year's Eve at Takeda-san and Nē-san's apartment, I wrote as follows:

> Nē-san was sitting a little off to the side all the while. Not joining us at the actual table. Earlier in the evening, she'd been dealing with the food, moving back and forth. Later, she took a seat beside us in the adjacent room. When I'd offered to help in the kitchen, Rikiishi had come forth with a Japanese saying to the effect that the kitchen is the domain of women, not to be stepped into by a man. At my side, Kentarō noted that it was an old saying . . . but that young people today don't care either way. Anyway, when Nē-san took a seat next to us later in the evening, she was looking on all the while to make sure we had everything needed. On occasion, Takeda-san would ask her to do this or that. The otoko of the house. And how cutely Nē-san was dressed, in baggy brown cotton pants and large-buttoned sweater with designs seamed into the pockets. Like a figure out of a Miyazaki anime. But always looking at you intently, like Takeda-san, straight in the eye. I can't even begin to list the food that was put on the table . . . from the regular osechi ryōri (traditional New Year dishes) to sashimi, tuna, fish eggs, grilled shrimp, crab legs, homemade potato salad, fried spam, pork/meat stew, rice . . . and toshikoshi soba (year-crossing soba)—which, Takeda-san noted, had to be eaten before midnight, like they did as children, before being put to sleep. The whole table was stacked with food. Akira dealing out the ice

and Jinro, and a box of beer outside the window. I think Mijime brought
the crab, and Norihisa later came along with around 15 cans of the Nodokoshi Kirin Happoshu which Takeda-san drinks. It was an incredible meal . . . and the food just kept coming. They must have spent quite a
lot of money on it all, but this wasn't mentioned.[25]

But the ultimate, irrevocable mark of the importance Takeda-san placed on buddies consisted in his three severed fingers, cut five times. To the uninitiated of
general society, the missing fingers signified that Takeda-san was a past or present member of the mob. Like fighting and the otoko trope, their transgressive
character might elicit wariness, revulsion, and fear in the outside world, but this
compelled respect and deference in San'ya. The fact of Takeda-san's sacrifice had
been established in San'ya and had assumed mythical proportions. Kentarō
rarely praised anyone and never adulated anyone, but he would emphatically
state of Takeda-san's missing fingers that this was "extremely rare." In like fashion, Akira would declare that Takeda-san was a "man's man" or even a "man of
legend." As self-sacrifice, the missing fingers indicated the amount of "suffering"
Takeda-san had undergone for those under him. Kentarō added that there was "a
stupid aspect to" Takeda-san, insofar as he might not have had to sever his fingers
but had insisted upon it. As Akira explained, severing one's fingers could become
a "habit." Still, Kentarō said that Takeda-san was "an incredible person" on account of his past in the yakuza, where had been part of the "top of the yakuza."
He was said to be "famous in Fukuoka." Looking to Akira for confirmation, who
nodded affirmatively, Kentarō admitted that he "only knew half" the story but
that—speaking to me—"it's clear from Nē-san's manner" that Takeda-san is a
person of considerable influence. For this reason, "because such a person is being
used," Kentarō would not call Takeda-san directly if work was available. Instead,
he "put in a call to Nē-san." Takeda-san might then "be sitting next to" Nē-san
and nod, "yes, I'll go," which Nē-san would then convey to Kentarō.

In this manner, Kentarō made sure "to be attentive and cautious" in his dealings with Takeda-san, since, he said, "things slip out of place if Takeda-san gets
angry." Akira would also attribute an almost supernatural power to Takeda-san,
claiming that if Takeda-san ordered it, or if Takeda-san was in trouble, everyone would go running. As Kentarō put it, one "cannot live up to" (*atama ga aga-
ranai*) Takeda-san. Or as Akira would say, it is "not possible to imitate"
Takeda-san. So too, Saruma would note that "everyone is indebted to" Takeda-
san and Nē-san. The two were located at the very source of hospitality in San'ya,
of all places, where most men had all but been expelled from general society, and
as such, they acted as guarantors of a sociality and counterdiscourse, grounded in
the otoko trope. Takeda-san was an emperor without a ¥10 billion endowment,

who hoped to blow his gambling winnings on others. In this way, all talk of being an upstanding otoko started and ended with Takeda-san. But despite his elegance, often sporting a long scarf and knit sweater in the winter or a patterned collared shirt and baseball cap in the summer, Takeda-san revealed not a hint of self-importance or egotism in his demeanor, which, if anything, was self-deprecating to an excessive degree. He was at once the regular guy—who liked the children's anime series *One Piece*, stayed at home to watch it, and had his phone covered in *One Piece* stickers—and the former mafia don. Takeda-san could have been arrogant and conceited on account of his mythic past, and yet, Kentarō said, Takeda-san would sit down at a table next to someone like me, smile, and have a drink. For this, Kentarō gave Takeda-san a thumbs-up. At once at the pinnacle of hierarchy among the guys and in San'ya itself, Takeda-san did not distinguish between people on the basis of reputation but liked them based on his experience with them. The disarming quality of his person and manner was evident everywhere, and his reputation appeared to precede and follow him about like some kind of "aura" (*ōra*)—a word that the younger Wakami used to describe him—only to be confirmed upon interacting with him. Takeda-san would leave an eatery, returning the already profuse bows of the owner by bowing even lower, and Kentarō might say, as if to himself, that Takeda-san was, "after all, incredible." It was normal for the Kanamachi-ikka to put out a bottle for Takeda-san when they happened to be in the same eatery. But, likewise, Akira would remark that an otoko must have gone through an incredible amount of suffering to treat anyone with the same humility, be it the homeless man lying at the entrance to the Iroha arcade or the Kanamachi-ikka.[26] Takeda-san was as familiar as anyone with the drunks hanging about the entrance to Iroha, in front of Sōgidan, and would lower his head as he passed by. As such, he embodied a vanishing set of yakuza values in which the "top" looked out for "the weak."[27]

At work, Takeda-san was as polite and deferential as anyone could be. Indeed, if anything, he was more assiduous than the others, as he was well aware that his physical strength was not on par with other workers. When I first worked with Takeda-san, we attended the induction meeting for new workers together, and at this meeting, the twenty-eight-year-old foreman snickered because Takeda-san had written part of his paperwork in syllabic alphabet (katakana), but he did not ask Takeda-san to rewrite it.[28] Unphased by this condescension, Takeda-san went right to work. Only once, after years of working with Kentarō, did Takeda-san in any way object to work conditions. He had met with Kentarō for drinks, and—while looking at his fingers and noting that he had, in fact, gone to such lengths—he said he would "never again do" cement work. Apparently, he had ended up with the job of shoveling concrete on the upper story, which found others—from different companies—telling him over and over what to do, and not in the nicest manner. "You get told things" was how Kentarō put it, meaning that someone brusquely told you to shovel here and then there and to take a little off the top. In fact, Kentarō never did this task, as he always operated the vibrator. But thereafter, Kentarō refrained from sending Takeda-san to do concrete work, and in a sense, Kentarō was giving Takeda-san preferential treatment because he was unforgiving of complaints from others. Yet, unlike many others, Takeda-san had put in his time and had chosen the moment to address the issue. Kentarō's protectiveness of Takeda-san thus emerged in barely noticeable ways, as when one day, Suzuki failed to inform Kentarō that a new worker in the group had been bad-mouthing Takeda-san on the train home. Kentarō flipped at Suzuki in front of everyone, shouting how "fucked up" it was that everyone knew but himself. The worker in question quit of his own accord, and it was not necessary for Suzuki to take further action. But the incident led Akira to instruct Suzuki that the "harmony" (wa) of the group was more important than anything else. The slur to Takeda-san had threatened the integrity and balance of the entire group.

As rarely as it was deployed, Takeda-san's word imposed a law of order on the group. This was most evident when there was strife between individuals or among mutual acquaintances whom he wanted to get along amicably. Unity was thus restored under the figure of Takeda-san when he asked Kentarō to make up with Mijime, although Kentarō and others in the Okinawa-gang had never cared for Mijime. Kentarō went drinking with Mijime and, afterward, informed Takeda-san that there was "no more" awkwardness between them. The peace was an uneasy one, not least since it was Mijime and two accomplices who had put Akira in the hospital with broken ribs a year earlier, when Akira had apologized and then gone amok in the Iroha arcade. Yet even Akira held his peace after Takeda-san requested that Kentarō make up with Mijime. At gatherings at which Akira and Mijime were present—be it at Takeda-san's apartment, Sakura, or Fukuhachi, Mijime's dive bar, where the guys started drinking—Akira held his tongue, even when Mijime commented snidely: "What's with your face color? It's kind of blue. Are you gonna die soon?" No doubt, Mijime knew that Akira had been diagnosed with a tumor. Still, even in the absence of Mijime, Akira did not utter a single word bad-mouthing him, save in the company of those closest to him. For all the simmering tension, Takeda-san's request had imposed a functional peace and the appearance of amity. Indeed, like the "men of influence" of whom Miyazaki writes in Toppamono, Takeda-san used to receive a fee from the Kanamachi-ikka to arbitrate and settle disputes between rival factions in San'ya. Now that San'ya had settled down, Takeda-san said, he did this for free.[29]

It was not as if Takeda-san and Nē-san themselves had not partaken in their fair share of violence. The social fact that Takeda-san "knows everything about" the intricate hierarchies of the yakuza not only authorized him to impose order in what he described as the "lawless zone" of San'ya. As the constitutive form in which order was enforced, this fact attributed a knowledge of violence to Takeda-san that was inaccessible to others. For in San'ya, it was the strongest who survived. It was as if Takeda-san's past, shrouded in the stuff of myth, empowered him to speak of things that the others passed over in silence. Thus, Takeda-san would lower his head and say to Nē-san, "We did some terrible things, yeah." It had not just been a matter of striking back, Nē-san said, but of preempting: of striking before the other party did. Only in recent years—five, ten years back—had things calmed down in San'ya. But on one chance occasion, Takeda-san and Nē-san had encountered an old nemesis on the streets. Takeda-san had ended up in a scuffle with the man, rolling around on the sidewalk, while Nē-san threw rocks from the side. There had also been friends who had been killed, they said. Kentarō likewise recounted how it used to be that people disappeared, and no one would know what had happened until someone said: "Did you know?" Back then, "gangs" had likewise been active in San'ya.[30] Such gangs were known to keep track of the work schedules of individuals who had gone away to construction sites for days in a row, and they would lie in wait for these individuals outside Minami-Senjū Station, assault them, and strip them of their money. It had likewise been unsafe to sleep outside, especially in the Iroha arcade, since it was not uncommon for groups to beat the sleeping individual and rob them. Mijime had been the leader of such a gang, Akira said, which preyed on "the weak." Everyone ostensibly knew of this. Yet Takeda-san would describe Mijime as a natural leader with a knack for attracting followers: a figure one could rely on to come to one's aid, in force.[31]

Takeda-san, moreover, was attuned to the marginal social status of San'ya in a manner that, unlike the others, allowed him to comment on this fact. When everyone was drinking and Rikiishi asked me where Germany and France were, Takeda-san raised an attentive eye, which was not so much concerned as thoroughly aware that this was a situation in which Rikiishi could be made to look foolish. As if he had overcome certain wounds, Takeda-san could speak with Kentarō about being poor. Or when my partner had become visibly concerned by the rowdy crowd in his living room, he could read her concern and assure her that we would be looked after. Everyone was aware of the outcast status San'ya was accorded in the imaginary of proper Japanese society. Yet, except for the rare occasions when Akira would say to me in private that San'ya's workers were "human garbage," the fact of its marginalization was either passed over in silence or only referred to obliquely in passing. Akira, for instance, said that there were two reasons why he could not be with a woman. The first was his conviction for manslaughter. The second was the fact that he lived in San'ya. Because he did not explain, it only occurred to me later that Akira was implicitly referring to the stigma of San'ya. Still, Suzuki was always flirting with someone, and Ikuchi had stopped doing meth, pulled his act together, and found a girlfriend within a year of his release from prison. Finally, Takeda-san was with Nē-san, and he was most faithful to her, noting how much they had been through in the years and that it would be unthinkable to betray her. Though Takeda-san certainly drank to excess, it was even said that he was doing "all right" because of Nē-san, who reined in his consumption. More importantly, however, Nē-san validated Takeda-san as an otoko. Without Nē-san, it never would have been possible for the group to come over. Nē-san enabled the feasts and homeliness of Takeda-san's place, and in so doing, she gave everyone the closest experience they would have to eating in a family setting.[32]

Takeda-san and Nē-san were not married. Nē-san was older than Takeda-san by a few years, had been married with children earlier, and had at least half a dozen grandchildren. As for Takeda-san, he, too, had been with someone else earlier in his life. This earlier life, however, was passed over with a pause and the comment that there was "no point" dwelling on the "past." But aside from references to past women, particularly in the presence of Nē-san, Takeda-san commented on the status of San'ya as if he had mastered the shame that separated the guys from general society. Where Akira and the others desired to be in a relationship with a woman, a prospect that Kentarō deemed "impossible," Takeda-san and Nē-san had each other. Where everyone remained silent regarding the constitutive failures that confined San'ya to San'ya, Takeda-san discoursed freely, noting, for instance, that I was venturing into a place that even Japanese people would not come to: a "lawless zone." Whether on account of his past, the amount of suffering he had endured, or the presence of Nē-san, something authorized Takeda-san to speak of the unspeakable: the failures that constituted San'ya.

With the exception of Takeda-san, almost everyone had run out of luck in both their family lives and romantic pursuits. Akira and Rikiishi had never had a relationship, and their only sexual experiences had been with prostitutes. Nearly everyone else had been married with kids. Saruma had been married three times and had one daughter from each marriage. He spoke to two of them once every year, and the third, whom he had never met and wished most to meet, lived somewhere in Kagoshima. Kentarō, who had been married to a nurse, had two sons in Okinawa, about the age of thirty. Hayashi had children here and there in the world, as he was an incorrigible womanizer (like Suzuki), but he also had a daughter with a Japanese woman. That this daughter was Japanese seemed to distinguish her from the other children, because this was the only child with whom Hayashi was in touch, and she had forgiven him when he had apologized for the father he had been, telling him that "things happen." Still, Hayashi spoke frequently of his plans to return to the Philippines since he was only in San'ya temporarily, and there was a distinct sense in which his discarded women and children confirmed his identity as a Japanese man. Similarly, Hasegawa had kids in Thailand, but he could not return because he had been banned for engaging in illegal activities. Suzuki had raised his two daughters with his wife until they were self-sufficient and had only left his wife in recent years. His daughters now had kids. But he also had another child on the side, whom he had never met—but that everyone, including his wife and daughters, knew all about—and he was incorrigible in his efforts to "sow his wild oats" (*tane o maku*), as the others described it. Even as he planned to get back together with his wife, Suzuki was flirting with other women, and while he had been dating Ai (in the San'ya neighborhood), he had actively been trying to get her pregnant. He had told her that he would pay for the birth, and the prospect seemed to make him happy, but that was it. Sometimes, Ai would have to call Kentarō because Suzuki had become drunk and violent, and shortly after their plans to have a child, the couple broke up. But Shōkawa was the most vociferous in lamenting the loss of his boy and girl in Okinawa. His wife, whom he still lauded as being "beautiful," had snuck into his house during their breakup and taken his son. As if it indicated his masculinity, Shōkawa recalled how the fight to keep his children had been an "incredible" affair. Yet he would lower his head when he expressed how much he regretted giving them up.

At some point, everyone expressed nostalgia for their past lives, if not regret and desire to see their children and family. These admissions rarely took place, however, and when they did, it was late in the evening, under the considerable influence of alcohol. They likewise ended quickly, observing the pattern of one man mentioning his children in passing, another suggesting it might be possible to contact them, and the first man shaking his lowered head. Naturally, Akira's reaction to my suggestion that Kentarō wanted to see his children was to deny this fact, since, Akira claimed, Kentarō "is not that type of otoko." Perhaps Kentarō would not have been an otoko at all had he wanted to see his kids. Yet, he had, in fact, wished for this, and Akira had been present. Nevertheless, Akira insisted Kentarō had neither regrets nor weaknesses: a trait he projected on Kentarō, as if regret reflected badly on the latter. It was not done to speak of failure. But it was precisely this failure that constituted the ground of possibility for the counterdiscourse of the otoko and that gave it its force.

On the other hand, the guys invested considerable energy and money in compensating for the absence of a spousal relation. It was common knowledge that Kentarō had a favorite "soapland" or "soap" in Yoshiwara, so called because the services provided at these brothels include a full body wash with soap, after which intercourse takes place. He knew all the women there, mostly Chinese, and for ¥10,000 ($100), it was possible to have intercourse without protection. Rumor had it that Kentarō went at least twice per month and, no doubt, more than this after he assumed the role of tehaishi. When others started saying that Kentarō had become "stingy" with cash and that Kentarō was not the Kentarō of old, it was likewise said that the cash was going to soaps. Matsuda, too, was rumored to be supporting a woman in Yoshiwara, and Akira could regale any listener with tales from back in the day when he had been in the Nibikikai: of the girls he had saved from prostitution and debt and of how he had given money left and right to hostesses, without, he said, asking for anything in return. It was out of character for Akira to mix such gifts with an expectation of return, as he took pride in the selflessness of his actions. Instead, Akira went to Yoshiwara when he had to "take care of things." Indeed, Yoshiwara was just about the only place where the guys had intimate experiences with the other gender (Suzuki excepted). Medication even circulated to ensure that they could perform. On one such night, during his days as tehaishi, Suzuki was said to have blown upward of ¥50,000 ($500) in Yoshiwara.

Apart from Yoshiwara, the only contact anyone had with the other gender was either with Nē-san or the older mama-sans and younger waitresses at eateries, snack bars, and hostess clubs. Kentarō took daily pleasure in drinking and eating in the presence of these women, who were often from China or Korea, and he exchanged phone numbers with them so that his phone would begin ringing in the middle of the afternoon, when the eateries were empty. Or else they would call to remind him of his debt. These affairs never went beyond the confines of the eatery, even when the mama-san of Gen started doing laundry for Kentarō, presumably for a fee. So too, Saruma's affair with a woman in Chōfu fizzled out. Suzuki expectedly broke up with Ai, whom he had threatened with violence one too many times, and dumped the next woman, a graduate of Tōdai (Tokyo University), as he started planning a reunion with his wife in Okinawa. This was a prospect that everyone thought was doomed to failure, since there was no way Suzuki could bring her to Tokyo, as they planned. As it turned out, everyone was wrong, and eleven years later, in 2023, Suzuki was still living with his wife in Tokyo. Otherwise, the only person who maintained relations with his child was the "mild-mannered" and "earnest" Norihisa. Yet Norihisa, too, had fallen out of wedlock.

But the most poignant story of broken family relations belonged to Matsuda. Born into a Buraku, or so-called outcaste, family and village in northern Japan, Matsuda recounted how the fact of being an outcaste was only made real to him when his first child was born.[33] Matsuda had been aware of his social status growing up in a secluded hamlet, exclusively for Buraku people. As a child, it was difficult to enter the neighboring hamlet because men were on guard outside the train station, to prohibit the entry of undesirable persons from his Buraku town. Such was the policed boundary dividing and separating regular folk from the outcastes. And when he got married, Matsuda's mother-in-law objected to the marriage on account of his being Buraku. While recounting this story, Matsuda held up his right hand with the palm forwards and two middle fingers bent in towards the palm, so that only the forefinger and pinkie were protruding. He asked rhetorically if Akira "knew" what this meant—Akira nodded—and explained that it designated outcastes. The missing fingers were meant to signify that Buraku passed on physical deformities through their genes. Hence, when Matsuda's child was born, his mother-in-law immediately inspected the fingers, giving out a sigh of relief to find them all present. Only then, Matsuda said, did he understand what it entailed to be a Buraku. When I asked Matsuda whether he was in touch with his kids and wife, he shook his head resentfully and said he had long lost touch with them.

It was this failure as economic providers, family, and father figures that prompted men in San'ya to assert themselves as otoko. Where normative society judged them to be failures as upstanding, productive, and reproductive fathers, San'ya offered reference to a counterdiscourse that functioned as an ideology of work (an otoko labored) but that also conferred a modicum of dignity through transgression. There was, in fact, a fundamental ambivalence to this discourse of the otoko, because in many aspects, it dovetailed with the statist discourse on upstanding masculinity. An otoko made a virtue of that which could not be escaped, manual labor, but flipped its stigmatization into an assertion of worth: Just look at all those salarymen in their cheap suits! Our gear costs more than their suits, and they have never labored by the sweat of their brow! Thus, the gaze of the state attained to a certain primacy, for the silencing of wounds conceded that there was shame and pain. Only Takeda-san discoursed freely on such matters and, in so doing, liberated the guys from the chains of their past.

In fact, the silence to which constitutive wounds were relegated could work most favorably for the state, for it could translate into a refusal to accept welfare. Riku refused any kind of support simply since he did not want to be dependent on anything. But others decided not to seek welfare because they did not wish for their families to know their situation or whereabouts. If someone applied for welfare, the ward office contacted their spouse or next of kin to investigate if the family could take financial responsibility for the person, thereby disclosing their whereabouts and, worse, their financial situation. By seeking welfare, the men inadvertently placed a burden on their families, many of whom had not seen them for decades, and they risked being made to feel, once again, like good-for-nothings. Rather than have the welfare office contact their family, many men went without welfare and therefore also without medical care. Naturally, some of the guys just wanted to stay under the radar of the state. Yet, as an extension of the state, it was the unit and institution of the family that caused shame. By contacting family, the state made the individual man beholden to others with whom he had either cut contact or from whom he had been cut off. In this way, the state threatened to open wounds that undercut the idealized "freedom" (*jiyū*) of the otoko, and the family did, indeed, exert a normative force sufficient to deter men from seeking the aid they clearly needed. In short, if the state could not do it, the family retrojected responsibility on the individual man. At one extreme, this could result in someone choosing to live in a tent along the Sumida River. Or, as with Riku, it could result in someone destroying their body, working to survive, and refusing any assistance. Despite repeated insistence from Sanyukai staff, there was one man who refused medical attention until he was on his last legs, dying a few weeks later from terminal cancer.

Manifest in the family, there was a constitutive aspect to the state's gaze and that of general society, the stain of which was difficult to overcome, and something inevitably and unexpectedly undercut assertions of masculinity within San'ya, opening old wounds. One day, a sibling or parent might pass away, or for whatever reason, one was reminded of the past. Akira said he thought each and every day about the "guilt" (*zaiakukan*) of having killed someone. The instant of that fatal kick to the chest was frozen in time. But, so too, Akira said that he thought every night of all the buddies who had passed away over the years. Ultimately, it was the specter of an early death that drove the truth of disposability home, at once undoing and precipitating San'ya's discourse of the otoko, and as we shall see, at the end of the day, it was the state that exercised this power of death over people in San'ya. Only the sociality of the group provided respite from the individualizing violence of the market, requiring that reference be made to the figure of Takeda-san: someone for whom everyone would ideally sacrifice themselves, should the sociality he embodied be threatened.

By this reasoning, the ideal otoko was someone who set themselves aside as day laborers and sacrificed themselves as otoko for everyone else. Much as there were chronic troublemakers in the group, everyone seemed to reference the same code of conduct, and when members refrained from involving others in their altercations, the response from the group was consistent with their conduct. In such instances, it was more common for others to express concern, even if this meant calling someone "stupid." No one grumbled when Rikiishi went on his fighting spree, but Takeda-san and others worried that someone might take "revenge" (*fukushū*). One day, when a crowd had gathered in front of Mutō's hole-in-the-wall (figure 4.1), Kentarō likewise went out of his way to avoid police involvement. A man holding a grudge against Kentarō suddenly exploded at him and swore to summon the police. But Kentarō slapped him across the head and told him to "get out of here," and everyone laughed as the infuriated figure darted down the street to tell on Kentarō. Still, the imminent arrival of policemen would disrupt proceed-

FIGURE 4.1.   Mutō-san's hole-in-the-wall, shortly after dusk.

ings at Mutō's, and after a brief pause, Kentarō went running after the man to confront him by the Mammoth itself. Everyone laughed again, and Akira noted that "it's like a manga": Kentarō did not even care about the police! Riku, too, had gone running after Kentarō to halt the police. By shifting the nuisance to the Mammoth, they ensured that no one else was affected by Kentarō's actions.

If there was one thing that triggered the anger of Rikiishi or Kentarō, however, it was a past or present yakuza exhibiting his tattoos to intimidate. There was a "reason," Akira said, that they got into fights with such men. Rikiishi, in particular, was known to take on yakuza from outside San'ya, swaggering through town in sharp-cuffed suits, shiny black shoes, crew cuts, tattoos, and gold jewelry visible through the openings in their shirts. These men were asking for it. Kentarō, too, was known to lose it if it turned out that an opponent had traditional tattoos. The person's attitude might have been bad to begin with, but if they also had tattoos—as Kentarō might notice upon grabbing them—it triggered rage. Just as Rikiishi was "unstoppable" in these instances, Kentarō would beat the hell out of these men. Not enough could be done to eliminate the abuse of yakuza iconography. For if San'ya constituted a stain in relation to general society, the abuse of vanishing mobster ideals disclosed a constitutive stain in the discourse of the otoko. Embodied in a self-effacing figure who protected the weak against the strong, it was by referencing idealized yakuza conduct that the group protected against the intrusion of shame. The adversary who abused this ideal therefore had to be battered. But battering triggered repetition, as if the disgrace could not be contained. In San'ya, it was individuals like Yamamori, of Matsuda's group, who personified this abuse of yakuza iconography.[34]

Accordingly, there existed two polarized modes of being an otoko. Takeda-san represented the first mode of conduct, in which an otoko assumed responsibility for his own actions and observed deference, yet dissimulated his own authority in a hospitality that extended horizontally to include everybody. In this idealized mode of the Okinawa-gang, the leader of the group sacrificed himself to look after other members. The Matsuda-group represented the second mode, in which a man dissimulated money-grubbing egotism by pretending to selfless authority and made use of yakuza iconography for personal gain. Ultimately driven by pecuniary profit, the latter was a sham of the former and replicated the market logic that the former looked down upon.

This difference between the Okinawa-gang and the Matsuda-group was clearly evident in their respective hierarchies and wage systems. When I arrived in San'ya, Matsuda still had not founded his construction company, Sanja Kensetsu, and neither the Okinawa-gang nor the Matsuda-group constituted formal institutions per se. But the groups could be differentiated on the basis of their informal membership. Although Takeda-san came from Fukuoka, the members of the Okinawa-gang were primarily from Okinawa, whereas members of the Matsuda-group came from a variety of places, and Matsuda used anyone as laborers who could be "used." His seemingly limitless pool of workers included homeless people, which made it even more difficult to make out who made up the Matsuda-group. By instantiating a hierarchy of unequal and vertical relations, Matsuda's system of remuneration reflected this complexity, because everyone fell differently on the pay grade. On the other hand, Suzuki and Kentarō paid every worker a flat amount of ¥12,500, from which they deducted ¥500 ($5) per head. In the Okinawa-gang, the tehaishi took only what was considered his fair due for providing work, and the remainder of his income came directly from subcontractors. The ¥500 of *pinhane* could earn Suzuki a maximum of ¥10,000 ($100) in one day. But this was the exception since Suzuki rarely sent out more than ten workers. In the Matsuda-group, however, it was normal for Matsuda to rake in a total of ¥20,000 ($200) in *pinhane* from his workers every day. At the top of his empire, Matsuda ripped his workers off, whereas the ultimate authority of the Okinawa-gang—Takeda-san—worked in the trenches alongside everyone else.

There was one final, definitive difference between members of the Okinawa-gang and the Matsuda-group, namely, that everybody in the Okinawa-gang frowned on the use of recreational drugs. Kentarō instantly described anyone who shot meth as "out." Naturally, this was not said of Matsuda, on whom Kentarō depended for workers, nor of Yamamori. On the contrary, Kentarō castigated Wakami for joking about Matsuda's habit. But when it came to younger members of the Matsuda-group, like Kon-chan, the Okinawa-gang did not hesitate in pointing out that he shot meth. With this, any talk of the likeability of the person was "finished with a single stroke." Thus, no one said anything when Matsuda would disappear for several days, although everyone attributed it to meth, and the final downfall of Matsuda was, in fact, attributed to meth, since he had lost touch with reality and overextended his resources. Unlike alcohol, it was said that meth made a person unaccountable for his or her own actions.[35] It ruined their accountability as men. In Matsuda's case, meth had even bankrupted him. In this way, Akira would recall an incident from his youth when he had been made to do meth. Not knowing what it was, he had demolished an outdoor stall (*tekiya*) and was consequently beaten by a gang of yakuza. Takeda-san, too, said that, among his underlings, there had been those he had warned of going down that road. No matter how much one said, it was to no avail.

Yet, despite their differences, both groups gathered under the roof of Takeda-san and Nē-san, for Takeda-san—who was at once of the Okinawa-gang and beyond it—functioned as a point of unity between the two groups. In his home, Takeda-san might take the liberty to warn Suzuki not to do meth and that he would have nothing to do with Suzuki if this occurred. In fact, when Takeda-san said this, Suzuki was sitting beside Yamamori, who was poring over his needle marks as he ran a finger up and down the veins of his arm. It went without saying that Yamamori would never have said anything in front of Takeda-san. There was no disputing who the senior figure was, and Matsuda, too, deferred to Takeda-san upon the slightest prompt.

As far as outsiders to the groups were concerned, both the Okinawa-gang and the Matsuda-group justified their conduct as an eye for an eye. Condensed in an adage that everyone in San'ya seemed to quote—*yararetara yarikaese* (an eye for an eye)—it was not simply that an otoko was established through reciprocity but that survival necessitated violence, and an otoko designated someone who could hold their own in San'ya.[36] If someone did not strike back, they could expect to be taken advantage of. It was only respectability or seniority that earned someone the luxury of refraining from retribution, but such a social reputation also implied a prior deployment of violence. Only thus could indulgence be transformed into benevolence and emerge as a sign of magnanimity.

Directed toward outsiders, the imperative of giving an eye for an eye made the guys wary of others seeking revenge. Matsuda, for one, explained that one had to develop eyes in the back of one's head to survive in San'ya. In fact, much as Matsuda would disappear for days doing *shabu*, he never became excessively drunk, for fear of sleeping outside where he might be found by someone with a grudge: "Wait, isn't that Matsuda lying there?" Indeed, one day Matsuda was beaten down in front of Mutō's, and this was when Akira stepped in. A year later, Matsuda was to return this favor by negotiating Shōkawa and Akira's early release from detention. Yet, just as Matsuda's actions had returned in the form of revenge, Akira and Shōkawa would have to look out for another person holding a grudge. Shōkawa warned that it was summer and that people "get strange." Sure enough, a few weeks later, the man dropped by Sanyukai with two buddies in tow, an appearance that Akira interpreted as an intimidation and threat. Like gambling debts, the guys would thus accrue vengeance. If they got themselves into one too many fruitless confrontations, the inevitable was bound to happen. Shōkawa, in particular, seemed to have it coming, and this was no laughing matter, as it was not merely violence but death that circulated in San'ya.

In fact, everyone could remember an incident in which the death of a buddy had occurred on account of someone else. They might not have been 100 percent certain, but it was likely their friend had been murdered. One old-timer and colleague of Takeda-san observed that it was "especially the case" in San'ya that "the bill catches up with you" (*tsuke ga mawatte kuru*). This stocky man with traditional tattoos, a missing pinky, and a bad knee that caused him to limp still carried his knife about, noting that there was no changing the way of "an old yakuza." He recounted the story of someone called "Champion," the only other individual of equal rank to himself and Takeda-san. Everyone else had been underlings, he said, drawing a line in the air between himself and those under him. Originally a boxer from the Kansai region, Champion had been so strong that he could grab someone by the throat and kill them by squeezing. Hence, Takeda-san's colleague had intervened in countless fights to restrain Champion. But nowadays, Champion had become so weak in the knees that he had to wear braces. This was beside the point, however, for Takeda-san's colleague said of Champion that he "cannot return" to San'ya on account of enemies. In fact, Akira had encountered Champion in a previous lifetime, more than a decade earlier, when Akira had just come to San'ya. He attributed the death of his friend to this Champion, who had driven his friend into debt and, finally, to suicide. Akira's body would perk up at the slightest mention that Champion had made a rare appearance in San'ya. Yet, at Takeda-san's place, when Rikiishi had hushed the room for an important phone call between Takeda-san and Champion, Akira sat with his head lowered and never mentioned Champion after Takeda-san's friendship had become apparent. In this way, deference quelled the outbreak of violence within the group, while outsiders were fair game.

It was as if the history of the adage had been forgotten, and consequently, an eye for an eye missed the originary violence that consigned San'ya to death and oblivion. Led by militant unions, riots in the early 1980s had, in fact, embraced the slogan as a justification for insurrection against the state and yakuza, but San'ya had long been quiet, and the guys themselves had conceded defeat where the overriding forces of the state and market were concerned. This was partly due to the fact that they were powerless and perhaps partly due to the fact that powerlessness predisposed them to identify with the abstraction of a status quo that appeared to harmonize with their values: one sacrificed oneself for the greater good of the nation.[37] As a result, the individualizing violence of the market was introjected onto relations between neighbors in San'ya, who were misrecognized as its source. The economic principle that confined a conglomerate of useless men to San'ya was passed over, and what remained of anger at the state assumed the form of resentment against concrete manifestations of its authority: the local police. Of course, the local cops had had enough of petty fights and preferred to "turn a blind eye." Winding up in the Mammoth was therefore not as bad as ending up in the Asakusa police station, where police actively punished fighting. At the Mammoth, the guys could be sure of release within hours, but if they were taken to another police station, it meant serious trouble. The Mammoth functioned merely to contain violence, and the guys were familiar with its policemen, often treating them as objects of ridicule. Like Kentarō, Akira enjoyed taunting the cops in front of the Mammoth, greeting them causally as he passed by or walking straight up to them to start a conversation. Kentarō said it was OK to "poke fun at" the police.

When it came to national politics, however, Akira was as right-wing as possible. If he had a "nuclear bomb," he said, he would bomb North Korea and China off the map. After all, it used to be that warring clans in Japan had exterminated their enemies. Moreover, if he had been in good health, Akira would be driving around a black-and-white right-wing truck with loudspeakers up top. Had I heard of the Nikkyōsō (Japan Teachers' Union)? He would "threaten" them and stick the cash in his pocket. To Akira, Japan was a "nation of the gods" (kami no kuni) and "etiquette" (reigi sahō), as symbolized by its "emperor" (tennō). The "Rape of Nanjing" had been exaggerated, and Japan had merely been "deceived" into World War II by the United States. Notably, Akira never mentioned "comfort women." But his stance on these issues was implicit in his support of right-wing politicians like Ishihara Shintaro, if not in his denial of the "Rape of Nanjing." So too, when Akira recounted past encounters with Philippine hostesses and prostitutes, it was with a mixture of self-aggrandizing benevolence and racism. When

Akira had been released from his stint in jail as a "substitute," his underworld bosses had presented him with a pick of three Philippine prostitutes. But Akira had not taken up the offer, preferring to chat with the woman he picked because she was "a Philippine" and because one "should not do women that easily." Maybe his conduct was laudable, yet his rhetoric had imperialist overtones and evokes Spivak's observation that men justify war in the name of liberating women.[38]

While everyone in the Okinawa-gang frequented eateries and dives where Chinese, Philippine, or Thai women worked, the conviviality of these gatherings was contradicted by racist comments. At one eatery, there was laughter, fondling, and even a fining system for every occasion the guys inappropriately touched the bodies of younger waitresses (one of whom was deported, escorted out by the cops, in cuffs). And when a female proprietor called Kentarō to remind him of his debt, someone would invariably say something like: "Their way of thinking is different." These were attentions, however, that Kentarō at once disparaged and thrived on, because it was primarily in the presence of foreign waitresses, proprietors, and hostesses that his identity as a Japanese man was affirmed. On occasion, the guys did frequent bars run by Japanese hostesses, but such hostess bars were expensive. They not only burdened the guys with hefty bills that had to be paid that same night but confronted the guys with salarymen or yakuza affiliates whose income clearly surpassed their own. It was in the local eateries and dives that the guys felt at home drinking, singing, fighting, gossiping, fondling women, or talking about the news.

In accordance with the political leanings of the group, Akira voted for the LDP (Liberal Democratic Party)—the only party that pitched "strong" leaders and, despite the name, is Japan's conservative, nationalist part—and political conversations, which I avoided, started and ended on the note that Japan needed more leaders like Ishihara Shintaro. Only once did Akira express concern that some conservative politicians would end welfare if they had their way. Still, when welfare was cut in early 2014, Akira did not complain. Like a good subject, he acceded to the policies of the elite, adding that someone like himself had no place contesting such decisions. On the other hand, Akira claimed that the terms with which the Far Left waged politics—*proletariat, capitalists, the state*—were arcane and incomprehensible. Where it might have been supposed that Akira would espouse leftist politics, the opposite was the case. In omitting the fact that rightwing interests conflicted with his own, Akira transposed his vision of the ideal world onto national politics. The political elite worked for the good of the nation, and citizens sacrificed themselves for this good. Thus, Akira's espousal of yakuza ethics dovetailed with out-and-out fascism.[39]

The political inclinations of other members of the Okinawa-gang did not differ much from Akira, although he was by far the most vociferous advocate of emperor worship. Shōkawa had volunteered for the Jieitai (Japan Self-Defense Forces), kept an air gun in his apartment as a memento, and would expatiate on Japan's military power. Only Kentarō expressed something like hatred for the US military bases that had all but overrun Okinawa, noting, however, that there was "nothing to do about it" (shōganai). History had run its course. Okinawans had put up the strongest front and sacrificed more than other Japanese, and if there was to be war, he would volunteer and take down at least one enemy. What manifested itself as bravado in daily life translated into a naive misrecognition of interests when it came to national politics. With the exception of Saruma, every one of the guys espoused a rhetoric of right-wing nationalism, which resonated with their everyday ideals and appeared to represent their interests but whose conservative bent was violently opposed to sustaining individuals through welfare payments. The concrete actions that actualized Takeda-san's authority could not have been further from the hypocrisy of right-wing politicians, but the discourse of the nation (and emperor) resonated with the discourse of the otoko. Above and beyond the discrimination the guys experienced in their daily encounters with the state or police, the nation restored them to an inclusiveness that they were deprived of in these encounters. It was on account of their distance from the powers that be that the discourse of the nation successfully interpellated them.

For those receiving welfare, their state case worker was an authority to be wary and careful of, because unlike the local police, this individual possessed the power either to put them on the street or to limit their livelihoods exclusively to construction work. Appointments therefore had to be kept punctiliously, not to mention in a sober state, and the guys were surprisingly observant of this. Welfare recipients were even prohibited from drinking on welfare, and as a result, the guys were constantly conscious of the state's gaze. If the case worker called while one was away from the phone (at work), or worse, if they paid an unannounced visit to one's bunkhouse while one was out, it gave rise to endless speculation. More than anything, the guys were nervous they were in trouble, which, at the extreme, could cause them to lose their welfare. Most often, however, it was a trivial matter or even good news. A new insurance card might have arrived, or the ward might have given permission to move into an apartment. Hence, when the guys spoke on the phone with their officer, they adopted a tone and formality of address that was most polite and obsequious. There could be dire consequences to failing to live up to the expectations of the ward officer, and thus, anything to do with the ward office became the subject of anxiety. Especially worrisome were instances in which the guys were put in police detention and, therefore, could not keep their appointments. At such times, they could only hope that their absence had gone unnoticed and that the cops had not contacted the ward.

Indeed, given their transgressive lifestyle and their failure to declare income, the prospect of being "cut off" threatened them constantly. After delirium tremens caused his hospitalization in a mental hospital, Suzuki was particularly worrisome. The hospitalization had enabled his welfare application, but if this happened again, he would be cut off, and the state was unforgiving in this sense. One and a half years after his hospitalization, Suzuki was drinking again, and he was seeing and hearing things. To keep the ghosts away, his floor was covered in salt. He had to be weaned off the alcohol, yet if he was hospitalized (as he had been before), Suzuki would lose his welfare. Unable to work, he would wind up on the street.

Over time, San'ya had thus become a "welfare town." The conditions of the market had dealt their blow, and being a welfare recipient was no longer frowned upon, at least not entirely. It had become "normal" (*futsū*).[40] San'ya's aging population now lived and passed away behind the doors of its bunkhouses, which were at full occupancy, and with a handful of exceptions, everyone in the group had to remain in the good graces of the state. Their lives hung in the balance. Consequently, the notion of confronting the state was invested with a futility that underscored everyone's dependence. Adding insult to injury, the onus of indebtedness had been pushed on the San'ya man. At the ward office, he had to be submissive. In San'ya, he could not but act the part of an otoko.

So too, left-wing institutions like Sōgidan had lost any appeal that they once held for people like Akira, namely, their power. In the past, Akira would say, Sōgidan "was incredible." Anyone with but a rudimentary knowledge of San'ya could recall the riots that rocked San'ya in the early 1980s, not to mention the title of the 1985 documentary sponsored by Sōgidan and directed by Saitō Mitsuo, who was killed by the Kanamachi-ikka while filming the documentary: *Yama: Yararetara Yarikaese* (*Yama—Attack to Attack*).[41] Likewise, in another well-known murder, a policeman was stabbed to death by a laborer who had had enough.[42] But while the legacies of these events persisted in San'ya, they had largely been relegated to the past. On June 9, the day on which the San'ya policeman was killed, an annual symposium was held apropos the event and culprit, who was serving a life sentence. Portraits of Saitō Mitsuo could similarly be found in the Sōgidan office, and when it came time for Sōgidan to host its biannual events in Tamahime Park—during Obon in summer and for the New Year's wake in winter—the labor union erected a shrine in the park with portraits of Saitō Mitsuo and others murdered by the mob. As a carryover from the past, the blue vans of riot police then lined Namidabashi, and the public order police gathered in throngs outside the park, distinctly recognizable in civilian clothes: shoulder bags or dated waist packs, plain pants, shirts, vests, caps, sharp-looking glasses, and peering black eyes. Only on these few occasions did residents of

San'ya gather for Sōgidan events, which otherwise consisted of a paltry gathering of five to six members marching through the empty streets on Friday mornings. With a red and white union flag billowing above them, these members would expostulate over loudspeakers against the state, standing about with political flyers in their hands, ready to hand out to an absent crowd.

The Beneficence of Charity

In tandem with its transformation into a "welfare town," San'ya had seen a mushrooming of nonprofits for the needy, and with a history of more than three decades operating in San'ya, the oldest of these was Sanyukai. With its longstanding director, Guy-san, this missionary institution had witnessed the rise and fall of San'ya, and it was as much an intrinsic part of San'ya's postwar history as it set itself apart from it, working with the municipality while bowing to its commands. In fact, Sanyukai was loath to call an ambulance for rambunctious workers unlikely to receive care from the state.

Sanyukai opened its doors at ten o'clock in the morning on weekdays and every third and fourth Saturday of the month. Together with a handful of volunteers, the staff prepared benches and ashtrays in the alleyway outside, setting up every day for the generic crew of men who began gathering for their free meal around ten and who left by one in the afternoon. Without exception, the few hangers-on after lunch were either intimate with the staff or waiting for an appointment in the clinic. Everyone else—and so the regular volunteers said, often with disdain—left without putting in any work.

Every day, the process of calling the men outside up to eat occurred in the same way. Guy-san stood outside from the moment Sanyukai opened its shutters and appeared to keep track of the order in which everyone arrived so that those who arrived first got to eat first. Most often, however, this process was offhand and casual. Especially when there was a crowd of thirty or forty—toward the end of the month, when welfare payments had run out—Guy-san lost track of who had been called up to eat and who had not. Nevertheless, he knew almost everyone outside and demonstrated this knowledge when he indicated that so-and-so could go up to eat by addressing them with their name and flicking his forefinger upward, a gesture that was often accompanied by a more or less humble bowing or bobbing up and down of the head and shoulders. The scene made a spectacle of intimacy between the head of the NPO and the men outside, who often displayed an unconcealed pleasure in having Guy-san call them by their nickname, be it Kubota "the Fake," Akira "the Okinawa-dude," Kawamiya "Kawaii," and Tanbo "Tanbo-chan."[43] Yet this display of familiarity only belied the hierarchy of the relationship between the staff and those outside, and that was its appeal. For a moment, it dispelled the shame of having had to wait two hours for a free meal.

This daily enactment of intimacy dissimulated the gaze of social authority and replaced it with what Akira liked to call "the structure of *amae*."[44] By referring to the famous book of the same title, Akira's sarcasm indicated what should have been obvious, namely, that the power to shame remained with Sanyukai. When it so wished, Sanyukai could discard its beneficent posturing and remind the men outside that they were beneficiaries of services bestowed upon them. There was a constitutive hierarchy inscribed in Sanyukai's charity that could not be divested from its relationship with the men outside. Even Kubota, a former post-office worker made to retire during Koizumi's privatization of the postal system, noted that there was "something distinctly wrong" with the scenario of grown otoko sitting two hours with lowered heads to receive a meal, only to have a finger flicked at them—"something distinctly wrong," as if Kubota could not say what that "something" was, because the concealment of shame carried a normative power. By mandating that the men wait two hours and by passing over the shame inherent in having to do so, Sanyukai designated the shame of waiting as shameful. It reinforced shame and, by holding the men in its thrall, demanded a certain conduct, the negligence of which could have serious consequences. For intimacy with the staff could mean the difference between receiving and not receiving medical care in their clinic.

But it was difficult for an uninitiated passerby to decipher what was happening in the alley outside. Except when Guy-san and other staff went around to liven up the atmosphere, most often by poking fun, the alleyway was crowded and silent. One time, a stranger asked Kawaii why there were so many people gathered in the alley, and Kawaii, who was clearly embarrassed, had to lie. He told me later that he "could not possibly say" that free meals were given upstairs. Kawaii's reluctance to confess bespoke both a consideration for Sanyukai, since it would burden the institution if random people started lining up—brought about, no less, than through Kawaii's indiscretion!—and a bashfulness regarding the fact that he himself was waiting for such a meal. What occurred at Sanyukai was not to be prattled about, to strangers least of all.

Many of the men who came to Sanyukai, especially those close to the staff, would complain that others came to eat but left without lifting a finger. Indeed, there were a few freeloaders even among the men close to the staff, including someone who had lived with Guy-san. Most, however, had risen through the ranks by volunteering, that is, by providing services that were indispensable to Sanyukai but that anyone else could also do. In this way, even volunteering was treated as an opportunity provided by Sanyukai: the mimesis of a job for which there were plenty of reserves and the remuneration for which came solely in the form of recognition. Thus, Akira, who had risen to the top of the volunteers, would say of freeloaders that they "know no shame" (*haji shirazu*). At his most derisive, he would refer to Sanyukai as a "dining hall" and to those outside as "pigs." Albeit in less harsh terms, Kubota repeated this description when he said that none of Sanyukai's activities "connect" to the recovery of independence. By handing out food along the Sumida River and giving meals, Sanyukai gave respite for the stomach and wallet, and thereby, it kept people coming back for more. It was, indeed, entirely possible to feed oneself every day of the year by shifting from one food handout to the next. For those lacking in requisite knowledge, Sōgidan published and circulated a calendar that listed where and when free food was on offer each day of the week.

In fact, according to one staff member, 80 percent of those who came to Sanyukai were already receiving welfare, and Sanyukai made it rather clear that this was the type of person to whom they catered. For when a truly dirty homeless person came along, they were handed a lunchbox on the pretext that it was not sanitary to let them inside. There was, of course, some truth to this hygiene claim. Still, Akira would note, there was also something obviously wrong with a setup that turned away individuals with access to neither welfare nor medical care and embraced welfare recipients who could use a little more aid: to ease the burden of their gambling habit, to balance their drinking budget, or just to find a place away from the solitude of their rooms. Every once in a while, Guy-san could thus be seen turning the corner of the alley with someone in tow. Beyond the corner, he would hand them the ¥1,000 or so they had requested. As these transactions occurred more or less out of sight, it was never clear how much someone was able to acquire from Guy-san. But it went without saying that the latter felt obliged to give and that prospective recipients calculated when Guy-san was most likely to grant their request.

The most notorious and helpless borrower at Sanyukai was Kawaii, who, once upon a time, had accrued such an astronomical gambling debt that he had been forced to flee from loan sharks. Alas, even after Kawaii had lived for a decade in a tent by the river, a dogged loan shark tracked him down when he went on welfare and his name entered the records. A lawyer at Sanyukai finally resolved the matter by having the claim declared illegal and by having Kawaii's name eliminated from the accounts. On meeting him, however, it was difficult to believe that the soft-spoken and diminutive Kawaii had amassed a debt that sent loan sharks chasing him for more than a decade, forcing him to disappear. At Sanyukai, Kawaii was known for his colored pencil drawings of children's anime characters—Crayon Shin-chan, Doraemon, Sazae-san, Chibi Maruko-chan— which decorated the fridge upstairs, as for his ability to sew and fix the hems of his clothing. He worked six days every week cleaning a pachinko parlor in Shinjuku. The job started at five in the morning and lasted a few hours, after which Kawaii would bicycle to Sanyukai on a pink fold-up bicycle (a gift from Akira, who had found it too feminine), arriving in time for lunch. On Thursdays, when Kawaii was supposed to make rice balls, he would peep around the door to the second floor—hoping to find the room full so that he could head back to the alley to stand around and chat only to be hailed as "late" and told to come in and help! But Kawaii, who dutifully reported his earnings to the ward office, had money trouble. Kubota described Kawaii as "ill." After all: "What fifty-year-old asks to borrow a hundred yen?" Hooked on pachinko, Kawaii invariably ran out of money at the end of the month, when he would be asking if so-and-so could not spare a hundred yen. It was one person one day, another the next, and everyone knew that these coins were destined for the one-yen pachinko, for Kawaii complained helplessly of the headache it caused that ATMs only dispensed bills. This prevented Kawaii from withdrawing the coins that would take him through the month. But there was a way to circumvent this problem, and that was by commuting to the bank's central branch, where money, including coins, was dispensed over the counter.

Everyone at Sanyukai knew of Kawaii's secret habits, as of everyone else's and of Guy-san's lending. Yet, like the structuring events that had precipitated the arrival of Sanyukai regulars in San'ya, these topics were not spoken of. Lending and borrowing thus formed an informal economy that constituted the silent substructure of Sanyukai. Unless one was standing at the margins of the Sanyukai alley—where requests and lending took place—no one spoke of drinking, gambling, going to Yoshiwara, or borrowing from Guy-san. The staff, too, was complicit in this silencing of topics that touched on the core existence of men who came to Sanyukai. There was a proactive attempt on their behalf to transform the atmosphere into a jolly one in which jokes were bantered and conversation was limited to the recent weather and news. Certain conversations were even shut down by staff maneuvering away from subjects like soaplands, upcoming or past races, and pachinko. Otherwise, staff members sat with their heads lowered, unable to stop or participate in an increasingly indecent discourse. Nonetheless, talking about soaplands or gambling in front of the staff required a unique strain of shamelessness. Indeed, such topics went against the mission of Sanyukai— aiding those in need and, if possible, rehabilitating them for work—an institution that ostensibly did not wish to facilitate gambling or drinking by lowering the over-all cost of life. But it was through such indulgence that Sanyukai sustained the spectacle of need that justified its existence, not to mention the donations that ensured staff salaries. Hence, the habitual handouts that kept everybody coming back were swept under the rug.

For the men outside, the cost of institutional indulgence required that they accede to shame by silencing activities that involved excessive expenditures. But the paradox of the scene outside consisted in the fact that it was easier to assume the shameful place of waiting if one was shameless. Either way, it did not matter whether Sanyukai was faced with shame or the shameless pretension to shame, because whether or not the men were pretending, Sanyukai appeared as their benefactor, and their conduct adhered to the institution's demands. They behaved themselves, and this entailed the silencing not only of gambling, drinking, or red-light districts but of how they had first come to San'ya. It was best not to speak of being fired or of debilitating illnesses, and once again, it was at the far end of the alley that Kawaii, Sawada, Kubota, and Akira might recount their life stories. Before his troubles at Sanyukai began, it was there that Akira recounted how, after his years with the Nibikikai, he had been laid off from construction work because his illness had caused him to miss too many days. Observing that San'ya constituted a "problem of disposability" (tsukaisute no mondai), he uncharacteristically lowered his head, as if to make an admission, and confessed that his health had rendered him redundant. There was nothing more "shameful" (hazukashī), Akira said, than living off "other people's money." He was therefore doing his "very best" by volunteering at Sanyukai.

Notwithstanding the enactment of intimacy, the staff at Sanyukai had instituted a strict line of division between Sanyukai and San'ya itself. Yamazawa, for example, worked nearly full-time at menial tasks to supplement his paltry pension, but his labor was segregated from the supervisory role that other staff assumed. Although Yamazawa had lived in San'ya for over a decade and knew more about San'ya than the staff, he was either setting up the entrance, serving tea at the top of the stairs, or helping with the preparation of rice balls and bread for distribution, while the remainder of the full-time staff held their private morning meetings. It was rumored that the case of every individual outside was discussed at these morning meetings by Guy-san, four administrators, two nurses, and one rotating kitchen member, but the contents of these meetings remained secret. When a decades-old veteran, volunteer, and worker at Sanyukai ceased coming to work, only to be found dead at home, Yamazawa was likewise excluded from the discussion of who would take his place, notwithstanding that it was Yamazawa who would have to work with this person. It was not his place to contribute to this decision. The power to decide which volunteer was qualified to rise to a paid part-time job was exclusively relegated to staff members who commuted to Sanyukai and had little experience of San'ya itself. Yet, as Kubota noted, so-and-so might be "docile and gentle" at Sanyukai while they were getting themselves into fights outside. It might be added that drunks were asked to leave and were promptly led out of the alley upon failure to do so. It was usually Yamori or Bonobe who took care of this by forcibly grabbing the drunk to see him off. But these send-offs often turned into rather comical affairs when the uncomprehending drunk returned to the reception on their heels. Drinking in the alley was thus frowned upon, except on Fridays and Saturdays after the day had finished, when select individuals were invited upstairs for snacks and drinks. Sure enough, there was justification for imposing a "no drinking" rule in San'ya, of all places. One head nurse could vividly recall a man beating another man's head against the wall, and in another instance, someone was getting ready to stab another man with the metal pole used to roll up the shutters. This nurse, who had worked in San'ya for decades, insisted that safety was her first concern and that a male staff member be on duty all the time. In this fashion, certain acts that were intrinsic to San'ya outside Sanyukai—drinking, fighting, and being an otoko—were disallowed in the confined space of Sanyukai. In yakuza style, Akira had set himself up as a protector of Sanyukai: holding hostile forces at bay from his strategic position at the end of the alley. He had monopolized the right to violence on behalf of Sanyukai, and given the amount of labor he invested, Akira felt justified in making requests on behalf of men who felt less comfortable doing so. By providing clothing, meals, or medical appointments, he operated as a pivot between Sanyukai and the unspoken desires of San'ya at large. But this was a tricky position to occupy, for even Yamazawa had consciously adopted a stance of "not saying anything" when it came time for administrative decisions, as if he was scared. One day, the seventy-year-old Hirai expressed an opinion to the effect that Sanyukai might compensate its volunteers financially, and Yamori broke into a rage. From up in the entryway, from behind the pedestal on which the tea was placed, Yamori dealt a tirade to Hirai, shouting that he "will not accept it a second time" if Hirai—head lowered at this point, raising his hand apologetically—were to bring this matter up again. Except for Akira, who remarked that the beast had finally reared its head, no one outside criticized Yamori for his actions afterward. The responsibility lay with Hirai, who was known to grumble and had stepped out of line. In this manner, there existed a latent fear among the men outside of breaching Sanyukai etiquette, lest they fall out of favor and lose their privileges.

The conduct necessitated by such fear was diametrically opposed to that of an otoko. Where an otoko was self-reliant, Sanyukai required that the men outside wait for their food or the end-of-the-week party. It even happened that Guy-san neglected to call someone upstairs. Whether he had forgotten or forgotten on purpose, such neglect resulted in leaving someone out in the cold, and it invariably reminded them of their vulnerability. The "self-respect" and "dignity" (iji) of an otoko had to be set aside at Sanyukai. To maintain privileges, a man had to be compliant. He had to forget about values like refusing to "bend" (mageru), walking one's "own way" (jibun no michi), "sticking to one's principles" (suji o tōsu), "protecting" and "taking care" of buddies, or protecting "the weak." It was precisely for this reason that some regular members of Sanyukai found it necessary to go amok away from Sanyukai. An island within San'ya, Sanyukai could only establish itself in contradistinction to the mores that it opposed, and thus, it required and fed itself off the world of San'ya outside it and of Akira within it.

The institution nevertheless substituted for the absence of familial and romantic relations, since nearly everyone had severed their relations with family. As one staff member noted, the men outside had no "connections" (*en*) with their kin. Even after the 3/11 tsunami and nuclear disasters, there had been no effort to contact their families, and like the Okinawa-gang, the men at Sanyukai would frequent prostitutes. Obviously, this was not spoken of in front of staff. It was only at the margin of the alley that Sawada would grin, baring his toothless mouth, when asked how he had spent his latest winnings and whether it had been on "this": the pinkie stuck out to indicate a woman. In the absence of the staff, people like Amai would talk unabashedly of how the best job in a "pink salon" was that of the manager, who got to teach girls how to give blowjobs. But alongside this covert practice of paying for sexual services with welfare, the men at Sanyukai also engaged in more overt competition for the attention of the kitchen staff, most of whom were women. Notably, there was little possibility of succeeding with any of these women, because they were almost all nuns, and if not, they were either married with kids or at least twenty years younger than the men. Nonetheless, the men would flirt when given the chance: exchanging comments and smiling when they returned their dirty plates. Some would even take flirtation to the next step, like Izumo, who gave feminine gifts and wrote letters on pink Barbie doll paper. He had made a practice, too, of giving back "massages" to the staff downstairs and sometimes to the kitchen staff, while everyone else was out doing food handouts by the Sumida River. It was said that he snuck upstairs when everyone was out. To the consternation of others, Amai would similarly situate himself strategically close to the kitchen when the Friday and Saturday afternoon "drinking parties" were held on the second floor, enabling him to chat with the women while everyone else remained seated in the adjacent room. Numaju likewise had a relationship going with one of the kitchen staff, whom he also knew from another NPO in San'ya, and seemed to flaunt his connection with conversations that were irrelevant to everyone else. Acquiring the private phone numbers of the women was considered quite a feat, giving rise to endless speculation as to whether so-and-so had gotten so-and-so's number. Lastly, going shopping for or, far better, *with* the kitchen staff was regarded as an enviable privilege: a duty that was assigned to a single individual until, by whim of the staff, another person was picked. Staff favoritism even determined the proximity with and the duration of time for which the men at Sanyukai could keep company with staff in the kitchen.

Not surprisingly, the volunteers at Sanyukai therefore vied with one another to become favorites of the male staff, who occupied the decision-making positions in the organization.

Though it was far from explicit, a hierarchy could be discerned among the men outside by their proximity to the entryway and by the ease with which they spoke to each other and the staff. The fifty-year-old Izumo, who had suffered a stroke, sat either on the steps leading up to the entry or on a chair immediately adjacent to it. Adorned with giant plastic, fluorescent Buddhist prayer beads around his neck, a black T-shirt with a white dragon design, baggy black pants, round eyeglasses, and sandals, Izumo had a bald round head with a stubble of a beard and a couple of front teeth that showed every time he talked or laughed, and his jaw hung open every time someone slapped him jokingly on the scalp. Too weak to partake in food handouts, Izumo could be found giving massages either at the bottom of the steps or inside the entryway to volunteers and staff alike.

One of the oldest and longest volunteers at Sanyukai, Tanbo, too, would sit right by the entry, often on a low, fold-up camping chair that fit his short, lean stature. Originally a fisherman, scarcity of work had forced Tanbo into unemployment and, eventually, to live in a blue tent by the Sumida River. Back in the day, Tanbo had been known for his traditional performances of dance and song, and he would dress up for festivals, but the years had gradually taken the energy from him, and a stroke had led him—with the aid of Sanyukai—to take a room in the bunkhouse just in front of Sanyukai. Nowadays, he could most often be found sitting quietly by the entryway, occasionally cracking a dry joke in response to some comment by the staff or heading up the rice-ball making on Thursdays. Tanbo never ate lunch upstairs. Instead, the kitchen staff prepared a lunchbox for him every day (his name was written on it), to be eaten, he said, in the evening as a snack with his "rice alcohol."

A relative newcomer to Sanyukai who had risen rapidly in favorability with the staff, Amai would step out of his conveniently located bunkhouse opposite Sanyukai at eleven, barely bothering to put on his shoes as he dragged them across the ground and arrived in time for lunch. Amai would sit or stand just about anywhere, and seemingly oblivious to the monumental silence that had been erected around specific topics, he conversed on everything from soaplands to gambling. Kubota, too, seemed to have mastered the art of arriving just in time for lunch. After helping to make rice balls in the morning, he would return to his room, catch an episode of a historical drama, and come back to Sanyukai for lunch. So too, Sawada, yet another incorrigible gambler in his seventies, would arrive half an hour before noon, and he would do this especially toward the end of the month. Laid off during the 1970s era of "high economic development," Sawada had been a salaryman and then security guard, and he would occasionally show photos of himself from his earlier days, when he had been to Hiroshima and Korea on business trips: in Hiroshima Peace Park, ringing the bell at Miyajima Shrine, with a Korean hostess in a snack bar, and as a uniformed security guard. One photo showed him dressed in a loincloth, shouldering a portable shrine (*omikoshi*) for the Kanda festival. He had lost touch with everyone in the photos. But he still looked the likeness of his younger self in the frayed, glossy images from another era, though his back was now slightly hunched, and he had lost most of his hair. Folded to the horse-gambling page, a newspaper was invariably tucked in his back pants pocket, alongside a pack of cigarettes. Like the generic gambler, Sawada wore thick cotton pants, a button-up shirt, black plastic shoes, and, to add a bit of drama, a black cap with a white dragon design. He had the most lovable smile and was an incessant talker, hardly listening as he moved relentlessly from topic to topic, shuffling about on his feet. On the few occasions that he won at horse races, Sawada would embarrassedly admit that he had spent the money on food and soaplands.

Indeed, behind its facade of silence, Sanyukai was composed of a plethora of truly singular characters. There was Tamura, who bicycled to Sanyukai from afar and, alongside Yamazawa, received a salary for helping a few days per week at Sanyukai's partner bunkhouse, Sanyūsō. Still in his early fifties, Tamura had a penchant for flashy dressing. He would sometimes come in yellow-black tiger design leggings strapped above his shoes, but he was most well-known for his pink G-string underwear that showed from behind whenever he sat. Years ago, Tamura—who went by an alias—had gotten into a bicycle accident and, having been laid off in the aftermath, sought help from Sanyukai. He spoke fondly of his daughters and might even tell of the life and wife he had "fled" from, but it was unclear whether he was in touch with them, and his use of an alias attracted suspicion. Tamura would tell tales of Pantagruelian proportions, of dining and drinking and staying awake for days on end. But one week he failed to show and was found dead, surrounded by bottles, in his room. Yamamoto likewise died from terminal cancer during the course of my two years in San'ya. A lean, silent, and elderly man who passed his time sitting on a fold-up stool outside his bunkhouse, Yamamoto observed life as it moved by. The quiet and ever-polite Shibasawa was always underdressed in winter, wearing nothing but a plain collared shirt and green workers' pants. He helped every day to set up and could be found sitting on the benches, muttering inaudibly to himself while everyone else chatted. At six in the morning, Shibasawa could also be standing on Namidabashi, hoping for one of the vans that still picked up laborers for miscellaneous jobs. At the extreme periphery of Sanyukai's social sphere, there was also Tamori, a man in his forties who was so withdrawn that it was difficult to sustain a conversation with him or, rather, to do so without becoming distracted and forgetting about him. For Tamori shied away from personal topics as if it were the plague, endlessly commenting instead on the weather for which he, too, was remarkably underdressed in winter. Despite repeated comments by the staff to dress warmly, Tamori would shiver on the benches with neither jacket nor scarf. Over time, his few clothes had become worn and grubby, and as it became increasingly apparent that Tamori was losing control over the most basic aspects of self-care, the staff repeatedly asked him where he lived, only to be told evasively that it was somewhere beyond Minami-Senjū Station. Gonkun likewise lived in his own world. At a height of 180 cm, with a protruding tummy and an equally pudgy face, Gonkun was the biggest man at Sanyukai, but he was also the spitting image of an elementary schoolboy, trapped in the body of an adult. He was always wearing the same blue shorts, the same faded and yellow button-up shirt, and the same flat-sole shoes with socks stretched up his legs. He never went anywhere without his portable radio and backpack, stuffed to the brim, and when he came to Sanyukai, he would always be sitting with a Japan road map unfolded no more than 10 cm from his face. Peering endlessly into the map, he would wait for lunch, eat, leave, and spend the remainder of his day walking about San'ya and its parks, where he slept.

Then there was Akira, who was often misrecognized as a Sanyukai employee from the way in which he worked side by side with Yamazawa, running menial tasks from opening to closing. Unless he was helping in the kitchen or preparing for food handouts on Wednesdays and Thursdays, he would stand at the far corner and end of the alley flanking Sanyukai, from where he could survey both the alley itself and all the men sitting on the benches, as well as greet and speak to the steady stream of men coming down the street forming a T with the Sanyukai alley. Akira thus functioned as a counterweight to the Sanyukai entryway, as he greeted and chatted with an endless number of passersby, including—to the discomfort of Sanyukai staff—members of the Kanamachi-ikka. From his position, greeting everyone even before they reached the entryway, it was as if Akira were the informal front man of the organization. If it were not for Sanyukai's limited finances, it might have been assumed that Akira was making a profit from racketeering.

Having worked his way up through the ranks of volunteers from San'ya, Akira helped with the distribution of secondhand clothes from a storage house by Tamahime Park, and it was in this capacity that he could provide goods upon demand. He was approachable in his status as a fellow resident of San'ya, and it was for this reason that men would bypass the staff and queues to ask him whether he could not get this or that: a pair of shorts, a vest, underwear, a toothbrush, soap. Asking Akira did not entail the trouble of having to face the staff. It could be done informally, without fear of rebuff or of being indirectly told that they had asked for one too many favors. Akira would pull his weight with staff in place of others, making sure they got their due. When he was not working, Akira would there-fore situate himself at the far margins of Sanyukai, where he could take requests and chat freely. It was as if he had set up an underground, subsidiary booth to Sanyukai, at which his leverage with the staff ensured the provision of goods. And Akira was not afraid to ask the staff for this and that for so-and-so, since, in his mind, he had worked his way into a position from which he was entitled to make requests.

Akira even pushed the balance of indebtedness in his own interest. Not only did he take care of all the menial tasks—cleaning, taking out the garbage, load-ing and unloading packages—which none of the administrative staff did. He also treated volunteers to beer when the day was over, and for the weekly Saturday mahjong sessions at Guy-san's apartment, he would come with food and liquor and pay for everyone's taxi ride there. It was therefore difficult for the staff to re-fuse Akira, which he was well aware of and took advantage of. In fact, Akira would ask for favors even if there was a likelihood of refusal. "I don't care if they say no," he said, and this pushed the onus of refusal on the staff. Rather than oc-cupy the position of the party that hesitated to ask for fear of rejection, Akira outdid himself as a volunteer and, thereby, placed the staff in a position from which it was difficult to refuse his requests. Still, Akira used his discretion in granting favors, giving preference to some individuals over others. For Akira had foes and friends at Sanyukai, both among the other volunteers and the staff.

There was growing concern among the staff, as Guy-san said, that Akira was "standing out" (*medatsu*). Reminiscent of that all-too-often quoted adage, "the nail that stands up gets hammered down" (*deru kui wa utareru*), it was said that another volunteer should be given the opportunity to take the position Akira had carved out for himself. Tension had gradually arisen between Akira and the staff because he was increasingly acting as a broker between Sanyukai and the people outside, and from this place, he stirred the envy and discomfort of others. At the end of the alley, Akira was often surrounded by his own group of acquaintances, a congregation that was twice the size of the circle formed around Guy-san and other staff in the immediate vicinity of the stairway leading into the reception and further into the inner sanctum of the clinic. In fact, while Akira's health was still good enough, he would get up and stand outside on the corner starting at eight o'clock in the morning, before the staff arrived. Unless one took a detour south around the block to enter from the other end of the alley, it was impossi-ble to avoid Akira, who greeted everyone as they came and left. And Akira's cir-cle of acquaintances in Yama was wide, such that by standing on the corner, he pulled all sorts of other characters into the periphery of Sanyukai. After a couple of decades in San'ya, Akira knew folks from past work, from living in various bunkhouses, and now from Sanyukai, where newcomers to San'ya tended to gravitate. He had a knack for talking to anyone, be it the homeless people along the Sumida River and in Tamahime Park or the yakuza down the street, all of whom knew him by name. By standing thus on the corner, Akira was at once living his philosophy of looking out for "the weak" and aggrandizing his own sphere of benevolent influence.

Akira's previous job in Kotobukichō had been comparable to his tasks at Sanyukai. He had made it apparent to the mob in Kotobukichō that he was "usable" as a lookout for the illegal gambling dens they operated, and as part of his work, he would stand on the street and scout for trouble, be it uniformed or undercover police or troublemakers in general. At Sanyukai, Akira was merely deploying knowledge he had acquired in other places, and this entailed working as a "bodyguard" who inserted his body between Sanyukai and trouble. Indeed, after Akira quit, the staff had no choice but to make an embarrassing call to the police when someone hit Yamori, one of the staff members. By whatever means necessary, Akira would have escorted such trouble out of the alley or spotted it before it arrived. "Nothing escapes my eye," he would say.

Yet, as Akira's influence expanded at Sanyukai, he was slowly but ineluctably headed on a collision course with the staff. The denouement was to occur over a member of the kitchen staff. For, in addition to being the most conspicuous and hardworking of the volunteers outside, in whose presence the atmosphere could transform instantaneously from somber to exuberant, Akira was also the favorite among the kitchen staff. When there was a lack of kitchen workers, Akira would enter the kitchen to help, and on Wednesdays, when preparations had to be made for curry the following day, Akira would stay after everyone else had left, peeling and cutting potatoes, carrots, and onions, because on Thursdays, a Christian nun in her early forties was in charge of the kitchen, and Akira was in love.

A concatenation of events snowballed into Akira's ousting from Sanyukai. First, there was the problem of Akira's excessive visibility. It was unfair, and the organization needed to make way for "new faces." Akira had responded that he understood. He said that he "knew" his presence at Sanyukai had become too much. Moreover, he noted that he had become "too deeply involved." With wariness, he watched the rise into favorability of new characters, like Amai, whom he personally vowed to keep in place, and one day, when Akira went upstairs to prepare for curry, who should be sitting there, ready to offer his services, but Izumo. It had been decided at a Sanyukai staff meeting that certain work was to be rotated among volunteers. Sure enough, Izumo's presence was enough to drive Akira away, who increasingly took to disrupting his rhythm of volunteering every day. He might spend several days in a row drinking by Mutō's only to appear at Sanyukai, where some staff members had started asking questions and even saying that there might be problems with Akira continuing to volunteer if his appearances were so sporadic. He had ceased to be accountable, saying in private that it "did not matter" whether he was at Sanyukai or not. Without bothering to call, he would spend a couple days working with the guys in the Okinawa-gang and then reappear at Sanyukai to volunteer. Akira had also taken to noting the instances when he and others had been slighted by staff or their affiliates. There had been the time when an employee from a partner organization had refused to give Akira her phone number, saying: "Why do I have to give you my phone number?" Akira had also taken up Christianity during his time at Sanyukai, but when Akira went to church in Asakusa, he was given the cold shoulder by members of the Sanyukai staff, who belonged to the congregation. He had found himself sitting off to the side, by himself, during the Sunday sermon. Later he would caustically remark that "this is not Christianity." It had likewise irked him when the Christian caretaker at Sanyūsō had commented on the death of a mutual acquaintance: "That's OK, isn't it, since he lived as he wanted." Taken aback by this offhand remark, Akira retorted in private: "You don't say that. No matter what, you don't say that." Where Akira had wanted to reminisce, he had been rebuffed by "indifference." Then there was the time when Akira was drinking by Mutō's, and a Sanyukai staff member walked right by him without saying a word. When asked the next day why they had not said anything, the staff member simply replied that he did not frequent "such places" (sō iu toko). Sure enough, Mutō's place appeared on the NHK news a few months later, during lunch no less, when the TV was on upstairs. Finally, there was that earlier occasion when Akira had flipped out at Guy-san, shouting angrily at him in front of everyone in the alley only to burst away. In retrospect, Akira would recount that he had been justified in his anger, adding that no one, especially not the paid staff, which was composed of "yes-men," could call Guy-san into line like that. "Only I can do it." Akira would explain that it had not been a big issue that had triggered his anger. Guy-san had only passed a snide remark at Akira, but Akira would not let it go. It would have been all right if it had come from someone else, but when it came from a man of authority, he would not let it pass.

No doubt, Akira was aware that the staff thought that he had issues. One day Akira had been shouting at Guy-san, who was considered irreproachable, and then he had been spotted drinking at the open-air dive, hiding his drink behind his back. At least at Sanyukai, it was said, Guy-san and others kept a tab on how much he drank. But by then he was drinking by himself. Things were getting out of hand. On the first occasion of his outburst at Guy-san, Akira stopped going to Sanyukai for a few weeks until some of the staff finally relented and asked Akira to come back. When things went awry the second time, they were not as indulgent.

One day, Akira was drinking by Mutō's, and lo and behold, Amai was on his way back from shopping with Akira's crush. As they turned the corner, Akira noticed that his crush had taken hold of Amai's arm, to nudge him along. This "smallest detail" triggered a fit of rage. Putting his drink aside and telling Suzuki that he would be right back, Akira bolted around the corner, up the Sanyukai staircase, and pounced on Amai, flinging him to the floor.[45]

Shortly thereafter, Akira stopped going to Sanyukai. He had worked with its staff for three years. Yet the final break was not reached in the form of a dialogue or verbal disagreement but as a gradual fizzling out. For Sanyukai never expressed their explicit disapproval of Akira's conduct. Rather, some staff members took to simply ignoring Akira when he visited the Sanyukai alley, not even saying hello (which Akira did not do either), and others avoided him (so Akira thought) when they spotted him down the street, only to veer into an alley. The sad truth was that Akira did not have anything else to do. He could not work with the Okinawa-gang, since his body would not keep up, and the only alternative was to drink. Thus, Akira tried to return. Believing that Guy-san had given him permission, Akira showed up weeks later on the second floor, only to have a staff member tell him that they had "heard of no such thing." With this, he was sent back downstairs. This was to be the last humiliation.

Contrary to anger against other individuals in San'ya, which ended with a fight, the anger against Sanyukai, Akira said, was "eternal." The wound revived wounds that would not heal, and the silence to which the staff consigned Akira enclosed him in guilt, questioning what he had done wrong. Confined to a shameful silence before others, Akira had come to occupy a place analogous to that of Foucault's "madman," such that the resumption of his social existence at Sanyukai was conditional on Akira's acknowledgment of guilt.[46]

It would be another eight years before it became clear that what Akira referred to as the "it-hurts-it-hurts disease" had been misdiagnosed as "schizophrenia" one year prior to his falling out with Sanyukai, when Akira was fifty-four—a suspiciously late age to be diagnosed with schizophrenia, the symptoms of which tend to appear in the late teens or early twenties. No doubt, some of the staff at Sanyukai knew of this diagnosis, because they had accompanied Akira to the hospital innumerable times, as he went in search of treatment for his pain, and unlike Akira, they probably understood the social significance of this judgment. But whether they knew of the diagnosis or not, their elimination of Akira from Sanyukai echoed a diagnosis in which the social judgment of a person's value had taken precedence over proper medical treatment. Akira's pain had as little claim to reality as his righteous conduct deserved to be addressed and recognized. Perhaps it was precisely because he had been diagnosed with schizophrenia that the staff presumed that there was nothing to do about his "case." It might be asked why Akira himself did not object to the diagnosis, and looking back, there was a moment when Akira trashed his medications because he realized that they were meant to treat the symptoms of Parkinson's disease (antipsychotic drugs like chlorpromazine can cause Parkinson's disease and are therefore often paired with medication to treat Parkinson's disease). But the fact of the matter was that Akira, like most of the guys around him, did not know what schizophrenia was, and he did not have access to the internet to check what this word signified or, for that matter, to read what staff at Sanyukai had written about him online. Be it by the psychiatrist or staff, his exclusion from and inability to access such educated discourse had been assumed, and to a certain degree, they were correct. As a result, Akira remained unaware for eight years that he had been taking a daily cocktail of sleeping pills, sedatives, antipsychotic drugs, and drugs to alleviate the symptoms of Parkinson's—including chlorpromazine, blonanserin, promethazine, quazepam, brotizolam, and etizolam—to cope with physical pain. One day, shortly before I asked him what medication he was taking, Akira remarked that the paracetamol—a regular painkiller, prescribed by a physician—eased the pain but that the medication prescribed by the psychiatrist did not.[47] Moreover, many of the symptoms that everyone interpreted as proof of Akira's deteriorating condition could be identified as the effects of antipsychotic drugs, such as weight gain and extremely slow, if not impaired, and repetitive bodily movements suggestive of Parkinson's disease, akathisia, or tardive dyskinesia.

After eight years, in 2019, this was how Akira's condition was explained when I arranged for him to meet at a café with the Sanyukai psychiatrist, who had volunteered with Akira for three years. Remarking on the arbitrariness of the diagnosis, the psychiatrist noted that many of the side effects would slowly subside if Akira weaned himself off the chlorpromazine, blonanserin, and promethazine, which Akira proceeded to do. But this leaves the original question of Akira's physical pain unaddressed, not to mention the psychic pain of having been expelled from Sanyukai, and I return therefore to the moment of his humiliating departure from the institution, because this was also the moment in which he was handed over completely to the medical establishment. Akira might not have been considered "mad" per se by staff members at Sanyukai, but the force of this diagnosis was allowed to hold sway, much like a burdensome family member or troublesome child may be consigned to the care of the state or, indeed, to a psychiatrist.

There was only one place for Akira to turn for recognition after this: back to the Okinawa-gang, where Takeda-san giggled at the tale of Akira's "expulsion." This was a giggle that disclosed fondness of Akira's ways, and though it could not heal, the giggle restored Akira to his errant self.

DISINTEGRATION

The Okinawa-gang had been in a steady state of decline in the summer of 2014, three years after I first met them. Both Akira and Shōkawa had received approval from the ward to move into apartments, and they only came to San'ya intermittently, as it suited them. Suzuki had long been deposed as tehaishi. Saruma was caught in a bitter argument with his cousin Kentarō, and Akira and Shōkawa were barely speaking. There was increasing resentment within the group, whose members were going each their solitary way, retreating into their rooms, and drinking alone. In the absence of solidarity, each of its members was emerging as an isolated individual.

But the champion of individualism, Kentarō, had rented a dilapidated two-story dive bar off the Iroha arcade, complete with a counter and tatami alcove. The money he made from *tehai* was now said to exceed ¥400,000 ($4,000) per month, and he was "all right" paying the monthly rent of ¥90,000. Kentarō's place had become the new hangout spot for a motley crew of new workers that included members of the old Okinawa-gang. Hayashi rented a space on the floor upstairs for ¥10,000 every month, together with another man who worked for Kentarō. A hose had been attached to the faucet of a sink outside, functioning as a shower, and a stove and fridge could be found on the ground floor behind the counter. The necessities of life had been gathered, and it was now common for meetings to take place at Kentarō's dive bar rather than at Sakura or other dives. This reduced costs considerably, since people could bring their own liquor, stash it in the fridge, and even cook. Kentarō especially seemed to thrive on the steady availability of complimentary drinks and food, and sometimes strangers would peek through the sliding doors and ask: "Are you open?" Yet, except for Kentarō, the guys were suffering more than ever from lack of work and money, as well as ill health. Akira and Shōkawa still had debts at Sakura, as did Tetsu, who had been diagnosed with cancer, like Barasawa. Nevertheless, Kentarō gambled daily on boats, and people noted that he had changed: "He's different from the old Kentarō, no?" In fact, everyone had changed. Saruma no longer answered the phone, ostensibly because he had gone crazy with pachinko. Suzuki had taken to dragging strangers around as if they were his entourage, borrowing left and right, and Shōkawa spent weeks away from San'ya, prompting Akira to say that he was not a buddy.

Every Man for Himself

Of these sporadic presences and absences, Kentarō noted gleefully that "this is really a fun town." Preferring that everyone came and went "as they liked" (*jibun katte*), the veteran construction worker disliked the group affiliation that Suzuki had cultivated among the workers. He had long wanted to restore the individualizing law of the market in which the "free worker," as Marx put it, is compelled to sell their living labor power, and much as Kentarō himself tried to destroy the notion that individual workers belonged to any group, what he was witnessing in the gradual disintegration of the group owed to market forces.[1] Work had gone scarce, and this scarcity not only splintered the group but interrupted the largesse that had sustained its sociality. There had always been borrowing, but now there was also intense bitterness. Only one person embodied the selflessness necessary to counter the individualizing violence of the market, but Takeda-san's place within the Okinawa-gang had been grounded in work, and the group itself had lost its cohesiveness. Takeda-san now worked elsewhere, as did Saruma and Riku. Suzuki had also kept the subcontractors with whom he had established connections on his own, and more importantly, there simply was not much work.

While Kentarō celebrated the fact that everyone was going their own way, the sociality of the group had been sacrificed, and this disempowered the guys. It meant that they had to fend for themselves and that they would no longer be sustained by the recognition of their buddies. Even people outside the Okinawa-gang were saying that the group was not its former self. It used to be that the group had a reputation in San'ya, be it with the police or general acquaintances, and it was the self-assurance that derived from this knowledge that enabled the guys to reverse the shaming gaze of general society. But the group no longer presented a united front of solidarity. Gatherings at Takeda-san's apartment had become infrequent, and the guys no longer convened to drink and gamble on Sundays. Everyone, as Akira put it, had "split up."

Implicit in the market violence of "every man for himself," the final outcome of such social atomization was everywhere evident in San'ya. While its bunkhouses enjoyed full occupancy, its streets were empty, because the aging denizens of San'ya had retreated into their rooms.[2] They thus constituted what Marx described as "an immense mass" of serialized, now-defunct productive units, between whom lateral recognition had been obstructed.[3] Moreover, they had exchanged their lives in return for wages. Nearly every day, an ambulance could be seen in front of a bunkhouse, carting someone away, and one day, a man was found dead on the street beside Sanyukai. Social atomization heralded a solitary death.

To be sure, for many welfare recipients in San'ya, social connectivity had become limited to contact with state representatives. Having no recourse but to welfare, they were dependent on the state for their livelihood and consequently gave themselves to be recognized as such. Manifested in encounters with doctors or ward officers, state power was therefore intimately intertwined with death. In having no choice but to submit to its gaze, the state emerged as the preeminent institution before which the men of San'ya were made to experience failure and insufficiency. It possessed the power to reduce individuals to a condition of abjection, predisposing them to be incorporated into the fold of its docile subjects. Indeed, it was only in moments of complete helplessness that fiercely independent individuals, like Riku or Suzuki, submitted themselves to the care of the state. On the one hand, their lives were at stake in these moments. On the other, the state exploited the opportunity to ensure that they remained in its thrall, which had become indistinguishable from death itself.

As I was to learn, certain regulations ensured that, for many welfare recipients, even death would remain a solitary one, administered by the state. When Akira's health had deteriorated to the point at which anything could happen, the two of us asked his ward officer to register the contact information of a friend in San'ya. We were rebuffed. In the event of death, we were told, the ward would send a letter to an address listed in Akira's family registry. They could put a phone number on record, too, but this phone number had to belong to a family member whose name was recorded in the family registry.[4] Instead of lying, we said that Akira had severed his relationship with these family members decades ago, but it was to no avail.

While such powerlessness reinvigorated assertions of masculinity in San'ya, it also entailed that the guys had to master the art of shamelessness. At some point, everyone would need welfare, and the shame of this had to be rendered palatable by displacing it with the shameless performance of helplessness. The initial shame had to be quenched, pushed aside, and replaced by an enactment that secured welfare. Thus, if Akira said an otoko had to know "shame" (haji), this statement meant something altogether different from having to know shame before the state or society at large. In fact, what it meant was that an otoko determined the conditions under which he experienced shame and that he rebuffed unsolicited shame. For this was a statement of allegiance. Famously explicated by Ruth Benedict, Akira was using a traditionalist term for shame—*haji*—which invoked the entire set of values espoused by the group within San'ya.[5] It resonated with the yakuza terminology that the guys used to express relations of seniority, be it "blood brother" (*kyōdaibun*) or "underling" (*shatei*), and with the virtues of having a sense of "indebtedness" (*on*) or *giri-ninjō*, a combination of *giri* and *ninjō*, the former of which loosely translates as "duty" or "obligation" and the latter as "human feeling" or "human sympathy."[6] In this fashion, Akira carried about a traditional Japanese *sensu* (fan), Riku wore *geta* (clogs), and Takeda-san was described as a "man of legend," as if this portrayal made no reference to the 1983 yakuza movie.[7] Bamboozling the state was forgiven by this transgressive code of conduct, which ultimately sought to reference a social entity that transcended individual life, enabling the laborer to sacrifice himself for the longevity of the group. It was in accordance with these values that a real otoko aspired out of a sense of "shame" (*haji*), for they staved off the stigma of failure and ensured that his life would not have been in vain, but still, the shaming gaze of the state was well-nigh inescapable. Indeed, it was because there was shame that it had to be negated with shamelessness, and as the guys aged, this dialectic shifted definitively in favor of the state. In the final analysis, they would be dependent on the state for their livelihood, and much as they differentiated themselves from the men outside Sanyukai, they were caught in a relationship to the state that was analogous to that shameful place of sitting. The very prospect of waiting for a meal might have appeared so shameful to them that one would have to be shameless to do so, but everyone in the group knew and exchanged information on how to become a welfare recipient: what to say, what not to say, and how to act.[8] It had become a veritable technique of survival, and for this reason, there was no mistaking that the guys became truly submissive when they were desperate. Alongside death, the state was always on the horizon, limiting their references to the vanishing virtues of a criminal underworld.

But much as the state gaze threatened masculinity, it was also constitutive of it. The group required an external entity that acknowledged their transgressive character, and at least at first, this was also the capacity in which I was incorporated into the group, with wariness and a standoffish desire to be recognized on their own terms. There was an obsessive object of identification at stake in the enactment of vanishing mobster values, caught up in the state and foreign researcher to whom it gave itself to be seen.[9] One late night, I found myself with Kentarō at a snack bar where, with a senior hostess nodding solemnly by his side, he asserted that it was "impossible" for me to "understand" the intricacies of being Japanese. Knowledge thereof belonged exclusively to insiders and, in this case, to insiders to San'ya. I nodded along, but then Kentarō told me to send him my writing and to ask him if I had any questions. I responded honestly that I did not, and this was true, because I had decided earlier that I would not compromise my relationship with the guys in the name of "research." Besides, if I had questions, I would ask Akira, whom everyone accepted as my confidant. With this, Kentarō smiled briefly, and the matter was never mentioned again. In any case, it would have been impossible for me to send him my writings, which were in English, but it was also precisely this foreign, teratological quality of writing that manifested a gaze that was at once threatening—"understanding," not to mention translation, was impossible, as I would get it all wrong—and constitutive, because it was only in the gaze of the Other that the transgressive (in relation to state norms) and Japanese (in relation to the West) quality of *giri-ninjō* derived its value. It was in the gaze of such Others that the group's disintegration had caused it to lose social currency, disempowering its old members. Under Kentarō's leadership, even work had ceased to operate as a unifying force.

After deposing Suzuki as tehaishi, Kentarō had successfully disbanded the core workers of the Okinawa-gang. Saying that he was tired of people who "cannot uphold obligations," he had gotten rid of workers that Suzuki had cherished. After all their complaints and, worst of all, failures to show for work, Kentarō declared that he didn't need them! In this way, the twenty-eight-year-old Wakami had to find alternative sources of work, despite being the most versatile and energetic worker. After a verbal fight, Kentarō had even vowed never to send Saruma (his cousin) to work, prompting Takeda-san to mediate and ask that they "get along." Takeda-san had himself decided to seek work as a scaffolder through another acquaintance, although Kentarō still called Nē-san with work, and Takeda-san did sometimes go. Over time, the number of workers Kentarō could count on had dwindled, and while work continued to trickle in, the quota of workers from the subcontractor company Tenjima had also diminished. In midsummer, Kentarō had difficulty filling a quota of five. Even worse, he himself would fail to show for work, which he justified by saying that he was "purposely leaving a hole." Supposedly, it was his "strong point" to "do it to perfection" the next day, giving no one an excuse to complain.

Another sign of social disintegration lay in the near failure of the monthly meetings of the *mujin kō*, otherwise known in English as a rotating savings and credit association (ROSCA), or as a pooling club.[10] This club consisted of once-per-month gatherings in which members contributed ¥10,000 ($100) toward a sum that one individual took home. It ideally consisted of twelve members so that meetings could continue for twelve months and so that one person pocketed ¥120,000 on each occasion.[11] Everyone used this money for expenses that their regular income did not permit. Akira, Kentarō, and Shōkawa would use the money to end their debts at Sakura. Saruma and Suzuki would travel to Okinawa. Such expenditures were luxurious, and the pooling club posited the group as the source of this largesse. Just as Takeda-san and Nē-san transformed the money form into hospitality, the club produced the illusion of surplus in the absence of labor, and it was the solidarity of buddies that produced this excess.[12] The club functioned at once as an affirmation and test of group solidarity. On the one hand, it took the form of a celebration. Everyone met to wine and dine at a certain venue, and speeches and toasts were even given. On the other hand, the club never worked as it was intended to. There might be logistical hiccups, like agreeing on a time, date, and place. But the real problems began when its social obligations strained personal relations. Rather than establishing the sociality of the group as the source of wealth, the pooling club then caused money to come between everyone. If one person failed to contribute, it could lead the group to fracture. In this sense, the pooling club was akin to the shared pile of money that could be found on the table at Sakura on Sundays, except that the rules of the club were formalized. On Sundays, one did not necessarily have to give, but this was not an option in the club.

The first time the Okinawa-gang undertook a pooling club, it lasted a month. After a sumptuous feast at Hikari-sushi, Saruma pocketed the first installment of money and flew to Okinawa. But Saruma himself would later object to the composition of the club, because back in the heyday of the Okinawa-gang, this club had expanded to include characters like Yamamori and Matsuda, with whom Saruma did not want to take part. Finally, the frustrated organizer of the club, Suzuki, had to end it, exclaiming that Saruma and others "should have said so to begin with."[13]

Two years later, similar conflicts arose when Saruma insisted on doing the pooling club at a venue like Hikari-sushi, while others said this was too extravagant (indeed, dinner for one cost ¥3,000) and that it was better to meet somewhere informal. But Saruma objected to this setup and refused to take part. Thus, the club was "messed up" from the get-go. The solidarity of its members had been compromised and, to make matters worse, by someone who, it was rumored, had not returned the cash he had received two years earlier. Moreover, whereas two years earlier, it had been the sheer excess of participants that had caused failure, the 2014 club was plagued by a shortage of members. Having difficulty coming up with ¥10,000, some individuals dropped out along the way. As Shōkawa put it, such individuals were not buddies, for it should have been altogether possible to come up with ¥10,000. Moreover, realizing that the club was "in trouble" (*yabai*), Nē-san had even asked to take her turn as soon as possible, that is, before others jumped boat. Because returns would diminish as the year progressed, the unreliability of members jeopardized investments that everyone had already made.

In its inevitable shortcomings, the pooling club formalized the unspoken con-tractual relationships that sustained the viability of the working group, and in so doing, it replaced labor with the mutual generosity of its members. But where Su-zuki had been forgiving, Kentarō's intransigence had caused the number of work-ing individuals to dwindle to five. Core members of the Okinawa-gang, like Rikiishi or Norihisa, were also not participating, and Saruma had cursed the en-tire venture. In addition, two members had already dropped out. As if of gam-bling, it was said that those who remained were "certain" to stick it out. But to avert further contingencies, it was decided that the money be collected at the be-ginning of every month when everyone had come into funds. Moreover, there was to be no celebration, as the money was to be dropped off at Kentarō's and handed on. As a result, the club had been stripped of its social aspect. It had devolved into a pecuniary function in which participants did not meet face-to-face.

In the spirit of this fractured club, the petty disagreements that divided for-mer members of the Okinawa-gang invariably involved money. Akira resented Shōkawa because, when Akira had been asked to write an emergency phone number at the hospital, he had used Shōkawa's. Upon learning this, Shōkawa gave Akira a verbal thrashing, saying that Akira should have discussed the matter with him beforehand. If they had been in the yakuza together, Shōkawa's re-sponse would have been quite unforgivable, Akira said, for the two of them had done time in the joint together, and Akira had come to Shōkawa's rescue. Yet the fact of the matter was that they were not in the yakuza. There were no formal obligations between buddies, which at once endowed their relations with a gen-uine character but also meant that things could easily fall apart. In this instance, referencing yakuza tropes was moot. If Shōkawa was afraid of shouldering a fu-neral bill, nothing could be done. Indeed, money was causing everyone to de-fault on their social obligations and reputations. Saruma was repeatedly criticized for failing to return the money from the last club. Suzuki was said to be stealing money when no one was looking, and gambling was now taking place in which individuals would "take money from each other," that is, "among buddies."

It was only in Takeda-san and Nē-san's home that money was distilled into hospitality for everyone, including those who had fallen into disrepute. At Kentarō's place, on the other hand, it was a market logic that prevailed, in which bad performers were disinvited. Individuals brought their own goods, and par-ticipation was conditional upon the observance of a standard of conduct. This was contractual, and those who failed were "out." Yet, as Kentarō himself would experience when he almost died, Takeda-san and Nē-san's hospitality compen-sated for the failures that nearly every San'ya resident would undergo. In all its self-destructive force, the transgressive lifestyle of San'ya invariably led individuals to ruin themselves, and this was particularly the case when the individualizing logic of the market caused egotism to rear its head.

Just as everyone could remember when San'ya had been a booming town of day laborers, it was possible to witness the rapid boom and bust of its denizens. Although this rise and fall of workers was grounded in manual labor as a process of surplus extraction, there appeared to be two ways in which men ruined their accountability. One was to resent their lot and grumble, which was brought about by penury. The other was to become bloated with money and to bankrupt oneself. The first of these led the guys to borrow without returning or to complain about work. Saruma, for one, had fallen into disfavor because he was too fastidious in his demands and criticized too much. The insistent ways of the former company boss did "not agree with" San'ya, and much as Saruma complained with good intentions, his voice assumed a self-righteous tone that did not sit well with Kentarō or the rest of the group. In short, he was "a pain." Then there was Hayashi, who complained left and right about the quality of work Matsuda sent his way and repeatedly failed to show up. Rumor of Hayashi's inconstancy spread like a virus, and he quickly became a person to be shunned. But Hayashi eventually made up with Matsuda. After a final spat in a dive, Hayashi took his glasses off and raised his head for Matsuda to slap him across the face. With this, the two were said to have "made up," and one year later, Hayashi was living with his most severe critic, Kentarō.

Another year later, Hayashi was found dead in his room. If anything, his death testified to the utterly self-destructive violence with which the group imbibed, as if they had internalized the negative social evaluation of them by society. In fact, Hayashi had been shooting meth throughout my time in San'ya and had even been carted off in an ambulance after fainting in his room. As for Akira, he too was in and out of the hospital, carried off in an ambulance twice or thrice per year, and took to drinking suicidal amounts of alcohol after I left. But his self-destructive lifestyle never seemed to cause disrepute.

It was when excessive consumption combined with egotism that self-destruction engulfed a person in the entirety of their bodily and social aspects. Sufficient funds were necessary for such self-destruction to take place, and unless the person started borrowing, it was therefore the tehaishi who bankrupted himself in this manner. Matsuda had fled San'ya thus, and only one year after his takeover, Kentarō was showing signs of waning as tehaishi. Despite his income, the role of holding workers accountable had grown tiresome for Kentarō, the veteran worker, and he spoke of quitting. But the truth was that, like Suzuki before him, Kentarō had ceased going to work and was living (or drinking) solely off his income as tehaishi. Saruma criticized Kentarō for this, as he had Suzuki, insisting that no one would "follow" (tsuiteiku) Kentarō the way he was carrying on.

Drinking too much to go to work, Kentarō risked holding others accountable to standards that he himself would not observe. Meanwhile, Suzuki was waiting in the wings for Kentarō's subcontractors to return, although this was unlikely to happen, since Suzuki was also in a bad state, drinking more than ever. But if it did happen, all the subcontractors would once again be united under one tehaishi. So given to expanding his domain, it was when Suzuki was deposed as tehaishi that the unity of the group had begun to fracture. Without an excess of work, there could be no generosity among members.

Delirium Tremens

Things unraveled slowly but definitively for the tehaishi, Suzuki. It all started when he stopped going to work. At first, he had worked while doing the *tehai*, but as demands intensified, this became impossible. He dedicated himself solely to doing the *tehai*, which was a daunting task especially in the first year, but he continued to see everyone in the mornings. After this first year, however, Suzuki stopped getting up unless it was necessary. His day started at three or four in the afternoon with a shochu with ice and water at Mutō's, and as time progressed, Suzuki gradually acquired a negative reputation. Saruma cautioned him that he was "drinking too much." Suzuki never once made the effort to go to work, even when his presence would have completed the quota. No doubt, Suzuki knew that his deteriorating physical condition would have made a fool of him at work. Yet the effort would surely have been recognized, since it increasingly seemed like Suzuki was making others work *for* him. By the time Suzuki started his *tehai*, he was now already drunk, and undeniably so by the time workers trickled back to Sakura or Mutō's. Worst of all, workers peripheral to the Okinawa-gang were complaining of Suzuki's conduct. They would say that, having been sent consecutive days to sites more than an hour and half away, they had asked Suzuki where work would be the following day, expressly stating that they did not wish to go far (a reasonable request). Their livelihood hinged on time to rest after work and on the reduction of transportation costs. But Suzuki only responded that it would be "OK" and to be at the station at six o'clock. When they got to the station next morning, their fears were confirmed, for Suzuki had ignored their requests. In this manner, Suzuki's attitude became impudent—"Just go to work!"—as he expected individuals to work, no questions asked. Suzuki had grown "arrogant" and worse. Witnessing the turn of events, the no-nonsense Riku had altogether stopped working for Suzuki. Even Takeda-san expressed consternation over Suzuki's unbecoming conduct as the boss (*oyabun*) of twenty-five workers, showing up for the New Year's party with a hickey on his neck and doodles on his forehead, drawn by his girlfriend. "It doesn't look good," Shōkawa said, turning to Kentarō to ask why he did not act: "It's your younger brother, right?" But matters were worse than they seemed, for Suzuki was failing to pay workers. It had happened repeatedly that, on exiting Sakura with an envelope, workers had been cut short by a couple thousand yen. Every day, Suzuki was slipping himself some more drinking money from less influential workers, and he had become a terrible spendthrift, bandying about his money. Cash had become the sign of his power.

Suzuki's denouement came one day when everyone, back from work, was calling him about work the following day. Suzuki was not picking up. Nor had he picked up when Barasawa, the Tenjima company's middleman, had called him to convey the quota. Instead, Kentarō had received a call from Barasawa, and it was swiftly decided that the *tehai* would be completed in Suzuki's absence. Half an hour after the *tehai* had been settled, Suzuki burst through the doors of Sakura, his face as white as a sheet. Discomfited by comments—"Your face is white, are you OK?"—it took him a moment to realize that the *tehai* had been concluded. Within a week of this occurrence, Kentarō had spoken to Barasawa and fired Suzuki.

Fallen from his high horse and shunned by the majority of the group, this was not yet Suzuki's lowest point. He still did *tehai* for his own subcontractors, although this was insufficient to cover his expenses, and he hung out with the equally unpopular Hayashi. But he had realized that he had a drinking problem and had started going for walks in the early afternoons. Thus, he could be seen walking alone along the Sumida River.

One day, Suzuki was discovered passed out on the street:

> The first thing Akira said was that Suzuki had been taken to the hospital in an ambulance. Apparently, he had gone to Sanyukai by himself in the morning but had been turned back because there was no doctor there that morning. Abe-san and Hasegawa later found Suzuki on the street by Mutō's place and called an ambulance. Kentarō had also called Akira to ask whether Sanyukai could not do something. At the time, it still was not clear what had happened to Suzuki at the hospital, but I do distinctly remember Akira saying: "This is how people from Okinawa die."
>
> After lunch, Akira and I headed out to Iroha because Kentarō said he'd be there. Kentarō himself was playing Oicho-Kabu on the cardboard by the entrance to Iroha arcade. Inside Sakura, Shōkawa was drunk and Hasegawa was talking about the morning. Kentarō was outside. . . . I had to head off to an interview, but before I went, I spoke to Kentarō. At first, when I said I'd go to see Suzuki, he said it'd be "better not to go," but when I insisted that this had to be the chance to have

Suzuki hospitalized and well, he put his hands together and said "please" and, if possible, to have Suzuki hospitalized for a month or two. He did also say that "when this kind of thing happens, I get worried too."

When I got back from the interview, and in spite of the fact that Abe-san and Hasegawa had gone to the hospital—ostensibly to ensure Suzuki was hospitalized, Suzuki had been turned away and had to walk home from the hospital by himself . . . he had gotten back and was upstairs on the second floor of Mutō's. Everyone was downstairs drinking out front—quite a crowd, because it was one of the first sunny days of the year: Kentarō, Shōkawa, Norihisa, Norihisa's "junior" Naota, and the list just continued. The first thing Kentarō said to me when I got there was to go upstairs and talk to Suzuki. Well, as usual, when Kentarō says "talk," he means to go and "give him a real talking to."

When I got upstairs, Suzuki was lying there sweating and shaking all over. He even had trouble talking, with his lips shaking. He was half-awake, half-asleep. . . . I tried to convince him that we should call an ambulance again, but Suzuki just kept saying that he was tired and wanted to sleep. People were coming in and out of the room . . . Rikiishi and others. Downstairs, outside, it was chaos with the guys drinking. Hasegawa, indecisive and full of himself as usual, saying that they were thinking of various schemes to take care of Suzuki.

I went to Sanyukai—Guy-san giving me a weird look like: "What the hell are you doing here?"—to ask if they'd see Suzuki the next morning. I explained the situation. Guy-san said that the only way Suzuki could get hospitalized would be if he were unconscious. He also said that they could see Suzuki in the morning, but that they would not call an ambulance.[14]

I went back to Mutō's. Kentarō was actually quite emotional, turning away from everyone and crying. He'd say, "Thank you, thank you," and shaking our/my hands. Shifting in and out of crying, turning away, his face puffed up and red. Then, he'd turn back and drink. . . . At one point, this new nerdy-looking guy with glasses started talking shit to Hasegawa, who was sitting right across from Kentarō. (There must have been around fifteen people sitting outside at this point.) The guy with glasses shouted: "You, you've been arrogant from way back" (*Omae, mukashi kara erasō ni!*) Then Kentarō stepped in between saying not to address Hasegawa as: "'You,' don't say 'you'! He's your senior, right?!" ('*Omae*,' '*omae*' *wa nai daro! Meue desho?!*).[15] Since the guy wouldn't back down, Kentarō said, "Fine, let's take it around the corner." Kentarō then got up, took practicing swings at people, and moved around like he was in a boxing ring. Laughing and saying: "Here we go, it's been a while since I really fought." I remarked that Kentarō always defuses situations by challenging to a fight, and Kentarō responded, laughingly saying that "it's because I beat the hell out of them." Sure enough, Kentarō went around the corner to wait for the guy . . . and while he was there, the younger guy changed his mind and said he was just going to go over and shake Kentarō's hand. All of a sudden, he was docile, like clay in Kentarō's hands. And Kentarō started to introduce him to everyone. The younger man bowed his head to us all and clinked glasses.

While this whole show was going down, Saruma arrived. We'd been trying to get in touch with Saruma all day, but he'd forgotten his cell phone at Hasegawa's place the night before. I told him what had happened—with him saying "no way"—and we headed upstairs. Mijime was there with Abe-san in the room adjoining Suzuki's. It turned out that Shirahige hospital, where Suzuki was sent that morning, was the worst. In fact, Akira had said it's the hospital where you are a living "human experiment," and "I told you so," when Suzuki had been turned away in the morning. Mijime was actually quite knowledgeable about things, saying that from his experience it'd be best if Suzuki drank weak *mizuwari* throughout the night, rather than stop/cut liquor completely. While he spoke, Saruma and I decided that we should take Suzuki to the hospital right away. We called an ambulance and told Suzuki to keep his eyes closed as if he were unconscious. Suzuki told us that he wouldn't be able to "act." When the ambulance folks came upstairs, Shōkawa was just getting in the way, drunk on the second floor, as if he'd just come upstairs to have a look. Saruma got pissed at him. In fact, there were so many people, especially downstairs, hanging around and approaching me, Saruma, and Suzuki. As for us, we were trying to clear space for Suzuki and to get rid of the "smell of alcohol." It was like everyone was approaching us. Or me. We'd decided in a matter-of-fact way that it would be Saruma and me who would take Suzuki to the hospital. So Akira was like "please" to me, and Norihisa came up repeatedly, bowing, worried, and saying, "Please take care of Suzuki." I felt pressure, with others, too, bequeathing Suzuki into my hands. Even Riku, sitting solitary at a short distance, waved me over to say it was OK that Saruma was going with me to the hospital, but that if Kentarō came back in time, to go with Kentarō instead. I.e., to go with the real brother instead; it somehow being implicit that I go instead of Saruma. Notably, Kentarō disappeared somewhere the moment Suzuki was being carried downstairs. I only saw him when Saruma and I—discussing how to keep it a secret that Suzuki had been taken to hospital in the morning and how to avoid Shirahige hospital—were waiting for the ambulance staff to get in touch with a hospital, while checking Suzuki's vital signs. Riku almost forcibly dragged Kentarō to the ambulance, where Kentarō pulled away. Two policemen had come over at this time to check on what was going on, taking a peek in the ambulance to see who was there. When they'd crossed the street, on the way back to the Mammoth, I saw Kentarō running across the street and accosting the policemen from across the rails, as if shouting at them.

Saruma and I tried to convince the ambulance staff not to take us to Shirahige hospital, but because Suzuki was unconscious—i.e., not opening his eyes—they were scared it could have been something with his brain, and Shirahige was the only place that could treat that. We decided that there was nothing to do about it and headed back to the hospital where Suzuki had been turned away in the morning. It was around five o'clock at this time. It would take us another six hours to get Suzuki hospitalized.

We arrived at Shirahige hospital and Suzuki was taken through the regular tests. We were shut out of the room Suzuki was in. (Later, when we went to see Suzuki at the mental hospital, he told us he'd been lying there visibly with pain in his chest, breathing real hard, and the nurses had acted like they hadn't noticed; how it scared him.) At one point, though, I saw him through the open door, and I went inside. Suzuki was there sweating—pretty much abandoned by the nurses and doctor, who were elsewhere—with pain in his chest. He smelled, because he hadn't washed. Getting the chills. Breaking out in sweat. He was in a panic, though, saying to me: "Not here. Here is impossible." Also putting his fingers together to say that he'd been told to pay ¥60,000, to get the money now. He wanted to go home and I got worried. I asked the nurse if someone had told him to pay, and she immediately said no. I didn't realize at the time how scared Suzuki had gotten by the way they ignored him. I also did not know that Suzuki was hallucinating at the time. He had, in fact, been hallucinating from the beginning of this year. On the way to the hospital, Saruma had held Suzuki's hand, and Suzuki had refused to let go. (In the hospital itself, the doctor recorded that Suzuki had been seeing things and saying that "there's a cockroach on the wall" when there was none).

Saruma came inside, too, and told Suzuki not to worry about ridiculous things like money. The doctor came over. I flipped out and said it was ridiculous that someone in this state would be turned away. The doctor got angry at me, in turn, saying there was no right for me to speak to him like that. He said he'd stop the examination of Suzuki if I didn't leave the room. (By this time, it had leaked that Suzuki had been at the hospital in the morning. "Did you know he was here this morning?" the nurse said, to which Saruma and I said, "No, we didn't," concocting a story, pushing responsibility onto the establishment for having turned away Suzuki in the first place.) At least, this is what I presume Saruma continued to do, because I got kicked out of the room. For a short while, I could hear Saruma talking to the doctor inside. When Saruma came back, he told me that it had been decided that the doctor/ambulance staff contact a psychiatric hospital because Shirahige hospital was not able to treat the issues that Suzuki was dealing with, i.e., the hallucinations and coming off alcohol. It took us at least another two hours before the next hospital was decided: the crazy long wait, of which the ambulance staff had warned us, before we actually headed out with Suzuki in the back. Crazy long wait. When they finally did find a hospital, the ambulance staff came back to us and suggested that, perhaps—with Suzuki himself hinting that he wanted to go home—it would be better to take Suzuki home, watch over him for the night, and go to a mental clinic. My interpretation of the ambulance staff saying this was that the mental hospital itself had suggested this. Indeed, the ambulance staff themselves said that this was the case. But Saruma started to flip out, saying: "It's all about money!!"—holding his thumb to forefinger to signify money. Before that, the ambulance staff had asked him repeatedly if Suzuki had his insurance card. Saruma had also been on the phone with the mental hospital and had been asked— as the cousin—to bring ¥100,000 that very evening. Another big issue was whether or not the older brother could come along.

Finally, it was decided that we go. Much to Saruma's consternation, however, it was not a given that Suzuki be hospitalized at the other end. But they had agreed to at least see Suzuki. So Saruma headed back to San'ya, to get Suzuki's insurance card and to get Kentarō, who had agreed to come but was passed out, sleeping in Sakura when Saruma got there. They drove from San'ya to the mental hospital in Nishi-Arai. I stayed with Suzuki in the ambulance.

After the ride to the mental hospital in Nishi-Arai, we finally arrived. We entered the hospital through the back entrance. . . . Everything was dark and it took a while before the staff on the inside opened the door. It was an intimidating building, from the inside too, with imposing walls and locks on every door. You definitely got the feel that you were locked in and couldn't get out unless someone brought a key along. We were introduced into a small room, and I was told that I could sit next to Suzuki. I went about assuring the nurse on duty that we were bringing along the insurance card and that the older brother was also coming.

The doctor finally came. Young man, in his mid-thirties. I immediately got a bad vibe/feeling from this person. . . . He wasn't making eye contact with either Suzuki or myself. Looking down and to the side, as if to say we weren't even worthy of his attention—that he was condescending to speak to us: a pain—he asked standard questions like when the last time Suzuki had had any alcohol. I think he asked questions for about three minutes max. He was real hesitant about writing, as well—half-assed—scribbling and crossing his letters out, looking down at the paper as if it was a distraction from us, something to keep from looking at us. He kept doing this even after I shouted at / criticized him . . . because after three minutes of asking questions and muttering condescendingly to me—"What, you're just a friend"—he suggested that we go home with medication. I flipped out, saying that he'd only spoken to Suzuki for three minutes when we'd spent twelve hours arriving—there was a wince in the room when I said this, from the nurse and the ambulance staff member—and to please wait until the older brother came. The doctor said he could wait ten minutes. It was ridiculous. I said it was "ridiculous" that the doctor would decide based on three minutes. That he was "responsible" for Suzuki—who, one in a million, could die if he didn't receive care from going off the liquor—and that it was "ridiculous" to say that they would send Suzuki home with medication "so that would not happen." I.e., so he would not die from withdrawal. There was another wince from the people in the room. (In fact, Suzuki's intravenous therapy was changed three times that night.)[16]

I have to say, though, that I've never seen Suzuki as docile as he was that night. The doctor also had the audacity to say early on that even if Suzuki was hospitalized, he didn't know if Suzuki would stop drinking anyway (so what was the point of hospitalization?). I asked the doctor whether it wasn't proper to ask—normal, as a psychologist—about Suzuki's family situation etc., and he returned arrogantly, addressing me with a supercilious "you" (*anata*) and insisting that I was asking this and that to no purpose.[17] I responded by saying that I was just asking and that, surely, they would inquire about such family matters henceforth, and: "Please." For an instant, the doctor seemed ashamed, to be conscious of himself . . . and while we waited, a ridiculous situation ensued in which there was just silence, the doctor scribbling and crossing out to avoid dialogue . . . when he could have used the fifteen minutes we waited for Kentarō to arrive to talk to Suzuki. So I asked Suzuki questions instead and whether he himself wanted to say something. He said, "Not particularly." As for the doctor, he said he already knew all that stuff, i.e., because he had read the report from the other hospital. He also asked Suzuki "himself" what he wanted, and Suzuki said he "wanted to be hospitalized."

Finally, the doctor seemed to break, noting that Suzuki's liver readings were quite high and that it might be an idea to have him stay one night, have the family come in next morning, and have the doctor the next day make the decision. I felt relief at this, because it meant it'd be OK if Kentarō didn't show up in time. I kept calling Saruma and Kentarō, telling them to come right away, rather than buy stuff at the convenience store. They finally arrived, Kentarō smelling heavily of liquor, going straight to the table beside Suzuki—telling me to shut up because he wanted to hear what the doctor had to say!—and answering questions. The main question being whether there were other siblings, family members. And finally, the verdict: given that Suzuki's been drinking a little—"for three years!" I interjected, only to be shut up by Kentarō!—the plan was to have Suzuki hospitalized a week (the amount of time it would take for the symptoms to go away).

Hard as it was for him, Kentarō massaged Suzuki's shoulders and sent him off.

After they took Suzuki away, Kentarō started to flirt with the two nurses in the room. One was real big . . . but she smiled and said, "Ugh, it really stinks of liquor," when Kentarō asked, "Whoa, how do you get so big?!" and jokingly butted stomachs with her. And to the other petite nurse, Kentarō said—while she smiled and laughed—"What are you doing here with the body of an elementary school kid?"

We drove back, stopping off at a convenience store to get beer—Kentarō getting a Smirnoff Ice—and finished off the night drinking on the second floor of Hasegawa's place, above Mutō's. Kentarō even tried to convince me to go to work the next day instead of him. I declined.[18]

Suzuki was discharged from the hospital ten days later. His hallucinations had ceased, as they turned out to have been alcohol induced, and he had been altogether weaned off alcohol. Saruma and Kentarō had assumed responsibility for collecting money for the hospital bill, which exceeded ¥100,000 ($1,000). Everyone Suzuki had once sent to work was approached, and if they provided funds, their names were written down next to the amount they had given. The plan was to force Suzuki to face up to his conduct and the fact of having been a burden to so many. As expected, Takeda-san had Suzuki home after his discharge, simply to check in and see how he was doing, noting in his absence that it might take him one or two years to become his old self. But others were more skeptical. Akira, for one, said that the "environment" in San'ya was "too bad"; there was no way for Suzuki to break free from it. Sure enough, after a couple months of medication, sobriety, and welfare, Suzuki was back to his old self, drinking from dawn till dusk. One day, when Suzuki insisted that his word carried weight in San'ya, Kentarō flat out retorted that someone on welfare had "no trust."

A year after the fact, Akira would comment on Suzuki's "all too self-righteous" (*jibun katte sugiru*) behavior that he had no sense of "indebtedness" (*on*). Suzuki had been saved by the group, and yet his actions demonstrated that he was unashamed and had no consideration for the others. But what was Suzuki to do? It was not just Suzuki but everyone, according to Akira, that was being self-righteous. This was how everyone got along, complaining about one another in private: so-and-so had not returned money, Shōkawa was fighting, or Saruma was being a loudmouth. Everyone, Kentarō said, "gets along, while grumbling under their breath." While Suzuki could have apologized for taking things too far, his conduct replicated that of everyone else, and he was understandably loath to get down on his knees. Rather than give in to shame, he rebuffed it, and thus, he became shameless in the eyes of the group.

When masculinity was asserted in moments of evident weakness, however, in the absence of group recognition, it assumed a hollow air, devoid of self-assurance. In such moments, Hayashi, Suzuki, or Saruma became isolated and pathetic figures, having no choice but to insist on their ways. Shunned by everyone, Suzuki's boasting took on an abject, pitiful air, as did Akira, when he insisted that his suicide attempt would have succeeded if the knife had been sharp. In fact, Akira was living with serious health issues that not only alienated him from the others, who had not been diagnosed with life-threatening illnesses, but that gradually robbed him of the mental and physical certitude necessary to earn the respectability of an intimidating individual. Incessant physical pain, invisible on the outside, led him to drink and to combine crazy amounts of alcohol with painkillers, sleeping pills, and other medication. Eventually, the painkillers would take over.

One day, Akira was informed by doctors that he should expect a brain hemorrhage and that the eventuality of this hemorrhage could not be prevented because his tumor could not be excised. He could only wait for the inevitable rupture that would be recognizable by "incredible pain" and take himself to the hospital when it happened. Chances were that Akira would survive, he was told, but that he would be paralyzed from the waist down. Having learned this earlier in the day, Akira puttered around Mutō's hole-in-the-wall, drunk, occasionally saying, "I don't want to live." He threw up as he rounded the corner to go to his bunkhouse and, later in the evening, stabbed himself in the stomach with a kitchen knife borrowed from a neighbor across the hallway. But the knife was dull. It caught in the fat as Akira tried to slice across his stomach, and then he changed his mind, walked down the stairs, and called an ambulance. Thirty-six hours later, he had been discharged from the hospital. Akira's suicide attempt was to have been a "pure" (*isagiyoi*) gesture of slicing his bowels open in traditional style. Rather than reflect that its failure had been fortunate, Akira insisted afterward that the knife had been dull. So too, he kept on drinking, as if the specter of disaster did not exist. "Rather than bend my convictions" (*shinnen o mageru yori*), Akira said, he preferred to "die early."

The truth was that everyone was terrified in their weakest moments, and this vulnerability exposed multifarious, humbling wounds. Fearing for his life, Suzuki held tightly to Saruma's arm in the ambulance and, during his hospitalization, expressed regret at the way he had treated his girlfriend, Ai. For all his talk that he had nothing to do with his brother, Kentarō repeatedly broke into tears while Suzuki was lying helpless upstairs, and while Akira always conveniently forgot about the times when he had been carted off by an ambulance in the throes of death, in the hospital afterward he would admit remorse regarding his severed family relations, his deteriorating health, or his strained interactions with Sanyukai. Immobilized in the hospital, Akira would say that there were "other things" that bothered him. In these moments, the guys were utterly in the hands of the state, and one is therefore reminded of Hegel's master-slave dialectic, in which the possibility of self-consciousness resides with the slave because they have experienced and lived in the totalizing fear of death. In their helplessness, the guys had been reduced to a condition of pure negativity in which they had to recognize the state, which exercised the power of death over them, but were not recognized in turn. These were moments in which the guys—shuddering and paranoid in the ambulance or having just stabbed himself in the stomach— underwent what Kojève has described as the complete liquidation of support within the subjugated person. It was the apotheosis of the structural condition of existence of "San'ya," in which it was not only contained in the interest of affirming state authority but negated in this very containment, negated in its negativity so as eradicate every vestige of potentially disruptive insubordination. Yet, as the dialectic entails, the master or state is stuck in a deadlock because they are recognized by an entity that they do not recognize, and hence, the satisfaction of mutual recognition is foreclosed. In his self-identity, the master can only insist on his authority, whereas the laboring slave, who has nothing, has an incentive to overcome his condition from within and, in the process, establishes a novel relationship to himself.[19] He thereby sees himself for what he is, and within

FIGURE 5.1.   An everyday occurrence.

the group, the possibility for mutual recognition was indeed present. It goes without saying that, while the guys occasionally reversed the dialectic by imposing
themselves on state representatives (figure 5.1), the revolutionary potential of
San'ya had passed. San'ya, forced into docility and written out of history, had become a negative legacy of Japan's "miraculous" postwar economic recovery.
Still, as with the fleeting late-night dialogues when the guys expressed desire to
see their children, there were confessional moments that were consigned to silence after the fact, as if history had not run its course.

If a strangely silent defeatism descended on the group while Suzuki was lying
supine on the floor, it was not simply the specter of death but powerlessness before
the state that elicited this reaction. As it turned out, Suzuki would never have been
hospitalized at the mental hospital without an insurance card (*hokensho*). For lack
of cash—¥100,000 up front—Suzuki was entirely dependent on state recognition,
and it would have been nearly impossible to collect such money in time. Faced
with the medical establishment, masculine bravado gave way to resignation before
fate, and it was better for a foreign graduate student to take Suzuki to the hospital
than it was for the guys. The objective was not even that Suzuki receive good care.
It was only that he be admitted to a hospital, and any hospital at that. This was a
problem of old in San'ya. It used to be that Sanyukai would call ambulances, only

to have the patient dropped off around the corner. Thus, one way of ensuring hospitalization was to act unconscious at a train station in a wealthier ward, like Setagaya-ku, in which persons requiring hospitalization were more likely to be treated. By the same token, it used to be that patients from San'ya were housed in old wooden extensions of hospitals, before these were demolished. It was from prior experience that the guys knew that Suzuki was in serious trouble and that his earlier dismissal from Shirahige Hospital could have resulted in death. They might not have understood the specifics of Suzuki's condition—alcohol withdrawal syndrome—but they recognized the situation. Akira, in particular, could list endless abuses by the medical establishment, starting with flagrantly wrong prescriptions and the seeming failure by doctors to acknowledge bone fractures that other doctors recognized right away. Without money or state recognition—an insurance card—the group could make no claims on the medical establishment.

It was at the hospital or ward that the guys were reduced to a condition of abjection that rendered them malleable and ready to conform to expectations. There was simply nothing to hang on to when Suzuki was down with delirium tremens or when Akira attempted suicide, and while such moments facilitated admissions of loss and weakness, they also left the guys with no choice but to be recognized in accordance with state demands. Having lost their social moorings, the guys hardly expressed any compunctions about secondary elaborations of subjectivity, such as acting like an otoko or being submissive to the point of humiliation.[20] In moments of emergency, the bottom line was that the suffering individual be located within a social discourse that spared them from death, and the only institution that could provide this security was the state. It was thus in their weakest moments that the guys were predisposed to interpellation, and though they knew that their salvation hinged on a gut-wrenching split and sham, this self-presentation had real effects for both the state and its new subject. In giving himself to be recognized as dependent, the suffering individual recognized state authority in turn, and it was this power of state recognition that forestalled backtalk and forced the circulation of violence to remain within San'ya.

But it cannot be emphasized enough that the power and violence of state recognition had always-already been at work in the all-encompassing labor market, whose strictures could not be escaped. It was also for this reason that, from the get-go, the discourse of the otoko manifested an ambivalence that rendered it complicit with statist norms. Indeed, it fervently espoused the foremost demand that the state placed on the laborer—namely, that he labored. Of course, an otoko not only worked but reserved the right to ditch work, and the type of work he did—manual labor—set him apart from other men. It was the "pride" (*puraido*) and "dignity" (*iji*) of every San'ya man to survive within the strictures of this labor market, and when someone like Riku lost it, shouting, "You fucking with a

Yama person?"—he was making implicit reference to such self-sufficiency. But in embracing "self-responsibility" (*jikosekinin*), the counterdiscourse of the otoko complied with the demands of the state and replicated the guilt that general society attributed to the men of San'ya. Moreover, two decades had passed since Sōgidan mounted massive riots against the state, and the day laborers of San'ya had grown old. For lack of numbers—"power"—taking issue with the state had become pointless, and the discourse of the otoko had caved into a narrative of economic productivity.

There was an internal tension to this narrative, however, that compelled the reemergence of social forms that restored the qualitative. Whether this assumed the form of fascism or a counterdiscourse, it was precisely insofar as the economy individualized productive units that it produced the desire for a sociality akin to that manifest in buddies, which ultimately sought to reference a social third that overturned the pointlessness of a life exchanged for money and, finally, for death. It was the negativity to which exchange consigned the day laborer that gave the discourse of the otoko its force and his voice the value of truth. The wounds inflicted by the violence of the market were therefore constitutive and ever in danger of being reopened.

Because it stamped their lives with finality, it was most often when a family member passed away that the full force of these wounds was unleashed. For the guys who were remotely in touch with their kin, news of death reached them by phone. Akira learned thus of his older sister passing away, but for lack of money, he chose to remain in San'ya, and he advised Shōkawa to do the same when his mother passed away. The problem was twofold. Flying back to Okinawa required funds that the guys would have to borrow from Sakura, which would take at least one year to return. More significantly, in Akira's case it was unclear whether his family would welcome him. On the other hand, Shōkawa could muster enough money to pay the fare to Okinawa, but he would have to ask his family to help pay for the return. Rather than suffer the humiliation, not to mention the possibility of being stranded in Okinawa, Akira told Shōkawa not to go.

Shōkawa mourned the passing of his mother in a dive bar off Namidabashi:

> The guys, especially Hayashi and Shōkawa, were pretty drunk. Shōkawa and I walking shoulder to shoulder down the street. At some point after we'd gotten to Izumi, and after we'd tried to convince Akira to come to the construction site Friday—he said he was scared after so long, noting the ten-year gap while he had been an "outlaw"—Shōkawa said, "It's OK to tell him." At which point, Akira turned to me to say that "Shōkawa's mother has passed away." I'm not sure how long it took after that, but at some point briefly afterwards, I noticed Shōkawa tearing.

His eyes welling up. I can't quite describe the sight . . . this man, now in his late fifties, strongly built with jeans, leather belt, and collared, red short-sleeve shirt . . . graying, flowing hair with worn face but straight eyes . . . completely break down in tears. Soon, Hayashi had his arm around the back of Shōkawa, looking away and crying too, his baseball cap backwards on his head along with his glasses strung smartly from the back, the black stud of a plastic earring in his left ear. At some point, even Akira said, "I'm gonna start crying, too," and started tearing, albeit not like the other two. While Shōkawa was lamenting, mourning with Hayashi's arm around his back, Akira explained to me the trouble of collecting money for a ticket back to Okinawa. The costs, ¥100,000 or such one way. Apparently, they'd tried to collect . . . but even if Shōkawa were to go one way, he would have to make his own money in Okinawa to come back. Shōkawa had come to Akira to seek advice, saying that he'd take the one-way ticket, but Akira had advised him against it. Now, it was too late. The funeral ceremony was over. At that very moment. Crying out loud, Shōkawa kept saying things like: "I wanted to see her face and hug her before!" "She is gone from this world!" "Even if I go to Okinawa . . . there is nothing!" "There is nothing anymore!" "Forgive me, mother, for being such a pathetic son." "Mama . . . Mama . . ." Crying all the while . . . he asked which direction Okinawa was in, and Akira pointed south, towards the ventilator in the store. Then, Shōkawa got down on his knees, crying, and bowed repeatedly toward that direction, talking to his mother, asking for forgiveness for being such a bad son, and saying he would live "her part" from here on in. He said "it pains me"—not to be able to see and part from his mother in person. Apparently, Shōkawa had not slept for four nights before this . . . probably in anticipation of his mother's death. He said the one thing he would not do is "fight" because his mother wouldn't want him to. It'd be a bad thing to do. "That I won't do." He kept saying "thank you" and "sorry" to us, saying that now he'd stop crying. In response to him, the others—both four years younger—said things like: "That's an otoko's tears" (*otoko no namida*) . . . "from the soul" (*tamashī kara*), Akira said, of when an otoko really cries. . . . Hayashi described how he'd been able to meet his father on his deathbed before dying and that he could understand how hard it was for Shōkawa not to be able to meet or see his mother before the actual putting away of her. . . . Hayashi started crying again at this point, too. Akira saying, "That's it, cry it out, let him cry it out." Trying, too, to put a bit of a break on it after Shōkawa had done bowing to his mother, saying, "That's it, it's over." Akira noted how this would go on for a week, because the guys on the corner were being so "nice." Akira noted, too, how he'd "gone wild" (*abareta*) in Iroha arcade after his older sister had passed away this year. He told the story of how he hadn't been able to pay for the ticket, how he'd called his brother . . . and been told to "take care of his own stuff, as in, they would take care of things in Okinawa." There's "nothing you can do." Shōkawa said this today, too: "Nothing I can do."

Meanwhile, a phone call came from Suzuki because Rikiishi was seemingly going at it . . . in a fighting, trouble-making mood again. Akira said, "It's better not to go." . . . Shōkawa went and came back, saying Norihisa is getting angry with Rikiishi now.

Shōkawa told me not to fight. Looking at Akira, he said they came out of that generation. . . . Shōkawa's father (who had committed hara-kiri and died) had told him not to fight, even if you came back crying. But if they hit you, then you can come back at them with all you've got—it's alright, OK.

Akira said he "doesn't like trouble, but that he will protect his buddies," regardless of his own cost. Regardless of what might happen to him. There was some disagreement here . . . because Shōkawa said that some of the guys, even if they are buddies, are wrong and he will tell them so on such occasions . . . to which Hayashi said that the point of being "buddies" is that you will stand with your buddies even if they are wrong.

Akira said, "It's important for an otoko to live every day with a sense of his 'guilt' (*zaiakukan*)." Hayashi said, in response: "You say some good things."[21]

Everyone knew that death was awaiting them in San'ya. When cautioned about his sexual, drinking, or gambling habits, even Kentarō, who still appeared to be a functional worker, would say: "I don't have long to go anyways." It was not just that the group had reached an age in which their parents, if not older siblings, were likely to pass away. The guys lived with the prospect of their own death, because Tetsu, Barasawa, Ikuchi, and Ishikawa-san had already been diagnosed with cancer, and Akira was waiting for his blood vessel to rupture. Takeda-san was said to have taken on in years, since he would get drunk quickly, and Kentarō said he could not fight and win against a younger worker. Everyone, too, had witnessed friends pass away in the past. Whether they had died of natural causes, been murdered, committed suicide, or passed away as early as in their forties, Akira said, he would think of them every evening, and he could count them using all fingers. Kentarō likewise observed that it was a "good thing" to talk about the dead. For there was guilt involved in remembrance of the deceased. Akira, for instance, would recall reading the suicide note of a friend and chasing after him before he flung himself off Sakura-bashi in Asakusa. When Akira had later been living in Kotobukichō, Yokohama, two other friends committed suicide, one after the other. Discovering the body of the latter hanging from the ceiling, Akira decided to return to San'ya. There was "nothing to do," he said. As if he was directing the violence at himself, it was similarly guilt over powerlessness that led Akira to fight three opponents in the Iroha arcade, and Shōkawa's failure to attend his mother's funeral led him to gamble, after which he was put in detention, only to go straight back to brawling. Nor was it a coincidence that Kentarō decided to assert the values of deference and hierarchy while Suzuki lay prostrate upstairs or that he was taunting the cops right when the ambulance arrived. State recognition had confined the guys to San'ya in an impotence that prompted them to introject the loss of family in guilt, and while their powerlessness was deflected into self-assertion, the originary cause of their predicament could only be misrecognized in neighboring men or the local police. If a slur from a neighbor or the attitude of local cops permitted reciprocity, state power otherwise kept them in their place. Despite their efforts, nothing could be done, and an early death was an inescapable fact in San'ya. With few other cultural references at their disposal, the guys could only stake their bodies, although in a gamble against death that would be lost.

That San'ya constituted a space of accelerated obsolescence and death went unremarked in society at large. In fact, if they occurred in San'ya, almost any kind of death remained beneath the threshold of general visibility. Even the twenty-nine-year-old Wakami noticed that crimes (*jiken*) and homicides (*satsujin*) in San'ya went unreported in the daily news, whereas issues that touched on politically relevant issues of the day, like gambling on welfare, made it on the nationally televised NHK. By this same token, there was never mention on the news of the many men who died from heatstroke, several every day, on the streets of San'ya in the summer.

As one Sanyukai regular said, it was ideal for the Japanese state that welfare recipients in San'ya died and, if this could not be brought about swiftly, that every last bit of surplus be extracted from them. Unlike the suicide rate of productive middle-aged salarymen, the men of San'ya were dead weight. Costs had to be cut, and while the state did give welfare, it provided a minimal amount that predisposed individuals to undertake work that no one else would want to do—that is, to put themselves to use on the black market. Naturally, such income had to be reported, but there was a systematic disincentive to declaring these earnings, since it resulted in an overall drop of income. Many men in San'ya therefore chose to live with the danger of having their welfare severed, thereby empowering the state while providing a labor force for work that was unregulated, underpaid, and unsafe. It was an economic imperative that demanded the death of San'ya, and the unabating gaze of the state prevented such death from spilling into back-talk: these men had brought it upon themselves. If welfare recipients were considered fit enough to earn their living, they were constantly reminded that they should find a proper job. Welfare officers also informed them that infractions like gambling or drinking would not be tolerated. Hardly any different, the non-welfare recipient lived in the constant precarity of never having a secure income and of being arrested for gambling, drugs, or fighting. In effect, every aspect of life in San'ya was conditioned by the threatening gaze of the state, which was nearly ubiquitous. It could materialize in anything from the look of a stranger, who might be an undercover cop or ward officer, or in the surreptitious security cameras, said to have been placed by the police.

The guys had so internalized the notion of self-responsibility that when a stranger in San'ya was murdered or died, the event did not concern them. The structural conditions that placed them in the same predicament as the victim were sidelined and deflected into rumors, which spread like quickfire. So-and-so had seen legs sticking out of a garbage can. Riku knew the suspects: they had brought it upon themselves. Someone might even comment on how surprising it was that the murder "had made it on the news," but it might as well have been one of them. In this way, self-responsibility obstructed solidarity, and the vanishing mass of workers in San'ya were each on their own. At the end of the day, it was powerlessness before the economic order that caused the self-evidence of survival and self-responsibility, granting it the force of ideology. Either dead men had met their natural end, or they had failed to adapt to the strictures of the game.

It was a different story when everyone knew the person who had died, and this was the case regardless of how popular he had been. The flamboyant Tamura at Sanyukai had been disliked by Akira and Kubota, but news of his death was received by them as a shock. Akira broke into a sob and instantly cut the phone. Equally unnerved, Kubota said that "liking or disliking did not matter": Tamura had been a buddy. For a few days, Tamura's death created camaraderie among foes, for his death in his early fifties constituted a commentary on the plight of every San'ya man: repeatedly repressed yet triggered by proximity to death. Everyone knew what lay in store for them, but they nevertheless repeated the fetishized trope of the otoko. San'ya, as Akira put it, was located "next to hell." Its aging population had already degenerated into alienated ghosts, and its suicides were said to have no social connections: no job, no friends, no family. The one future link the guys could be assured of was to the state, in death, no less.

For many aging workers, this transition from independence to welfare dependence began at Sanyukai, which helped with applications for welfare. Sanyukai itself did not receive state funding, but it enjoyed an amicable and symbiotic relationship with the state that enabled it to facilitate applications. If the ward offices relinquished troublesome cases to Sanyukai, they also returned favors, thereby allowing the NPO to broaden the circle of its dependents and to create an indebtedness that dissimulated staff dependence on donations, not to mention on the men outside. Strictly speaking, it acted as an intermediary, yet it placed itself at the very source of beneficence, personalizing its gifts in the form of cash handouts. And in demanding proper behavior, Sanyukai replicated the state discourse that threatened to sever privileges extended in the indulgent embrace of *amae*. The staff decided who qualified for its attentions, and those who did not give themselves to be recognized remained outside their purview. Homage had to be paid, and the price of attention was precisely the "dignity" (*iji*) of the "person of Yama" (*yama no ningen*). In this way, Sanyukai "turned a blind eye" to the excesses of San'ya, much as the local police preferred not to see the circulation of violence. It at once revived wounds and banished them to the containment of San'ya, as if these wounds did not exist, and there was nothing the men outside could do. Their acceptance by Sanyukai was conditional on silencing the injustice of their lives and conceding guilt for their misfortunes. Displaced by Sanyukai, it would be as if San'ya had never existed.

One of the less mentioned services that Sanyukai provided was, in fact, for the deceased to be included in a so-called potter's field (*muenbochi*). Designed for persons without family, the potter's field responded to a veritable problem in San'ya, because whenever someone passed away, there was the question of whether or how to contact their family, if they had any. Even before this, however, there was the question of whether a proper cremation could be afforded, not to mention whether the deceased would have wanted his family contacted or where he wanted to be entombed. Certainly, none of the guys had money for a proper cremation. They would have to scrape together, as they had for Suzuki's hospital bill. More than likely, they would have to relinquish the body to the ward, which would manage the rest. Yet, even if a cremation could be afforded, who would take home the ashes of the departed? Akira was never in contact with his family but was confident that "someone" would retrieve his remains; however, the others were less confident, and Akira himself refused to tell his relatives that he wanted to be included in his mother's tomb. This wish was instead bequeathed to those around him. Everyone's family relations had fractured to the point at which the state might have to dispense of the body unless a third party intervened. When Suzuki had presented Kentarō with the money for a flight to Okinawa, the latter had refused to attend their father's cremation. Nor had they been able to locate their other brother, who had gone missing for years. Contrary to custom, in which "the oldest son" (*chōnan*)—Kentarō—directed the funeral, it had therefore been Suzuki, the youngest son, who flew back to Okinawa (with money borrowed from Sakura) and pressed the incinerator button. Nor was Kentarō the only one to have traumatic paternal relations: Shōkawa's father had committed suicide by disembowelment, and Akira had never met his father.[22] He had been raised by his mother, who had carried him while she did construction work in Okinawa, raising four other children. Born of poverty, shattered and inoperative relationships had been passed on from generation to generation. Thus, when Tamura was found dead in his room, Sanyukai could not contact his family, wife, or daughters because no phone numbers were listed on his phone. Tamura had volunteered and worked at Sanyukai for more than two decades, but the only contact number that could be found was of a barmaid from the local eatery, who was the only person to attend Tamura's funeral, aside from Sanyukai affiliates. Still, Tamura and the guys were among the fortunate, for they knew that their deaths would be noticed.

In the absence of relatives, Sanyukai organized Tamura's funeral, and their preparations went awry from the beginning. It was not just that Tamura's family could not be contacted. Sanyukai itself neglected to send out notices stating that Tamura had passed away and that a funeral would take place at a certain time and place, even to volunteers who had worked with him for years. Hence, on the day of the cremation, it was only a straggling crowd of Sanyukai regulars that could be seen trailing toward the station. Some of them barely able to make the trip, this was one of the few occasions when they boarded a train. But when they finally arrived at the funeral parlor, there was no cremation scheduled. Sanyukai had gotten the date wrong, and so the next day, when the funeral had actually been scheduled, only half the crowd went along.

When the group heard this story from Akira, Kentarō said it was "unthinkable" to mistake the day of a funeral. Sanyukai had not just slipped up. The missed funeral was indicative of an ethos in which the death of Sanyukai regulars was swept under the carpet. Most offensive of all, Akira said, was the fact that staff members, who had worked decades with Tamura, did not attend. In not-so-subtle ways, the line separating the staff from the men outside had been reiterated. The living, who would be memorialized, had been separated from the dying, whose deaths were administered and committed to oblivion.

Tamura's death foreshadowed the final passing of the ways of San'ya's day laborer. Time was running out rapidly for the guys, whose bodies were increasingly failing them. In 2015, Kentarō was hospitalized for two months and was told by doctors that he would die if he continued to drink. He looked like a "mummy" when he was discharged, Akira said, and Akira himself was drinking every day to the point at which the mixture of medication and alcohol caused him to lose mobility in his body. At this rate, it was said, Akira "does not have long to go." It was "scary."

It was the nearly complete absence of young men in San'ya that signaled an end to the lifestyles embodied by its aging residents. In 2013, the old postwar gathering place for day laborers, the *yoseba*, had long since been superseded by another flexible labor pool, dispersed across Tokyo and connected only by cell phone. Yet I recall moments from the construction site when I seemed to glimpse similarities between our older group and a younger generation of construction workers. During lunch, I could only peer across the tables of the changing room at a bunched-up group of able-bodied ironworkers, many of whom looked younger than twenty, certainly no older than twenty-five, hunched over the table as they puffed away at cigarettes, cutting a distinct difference from our group with their earrings and their golden-dyed hair. Whether these workers lived with their families, in apartments dispersed across the city, or in a company dorm, there was a clear hierarchy inscribed in their relations, as their midtwenties leader shouted instructions from the end of the table while they smoked away the remainder of their time.

EPILOGUE

In the summer of 2015, I spent five days with Akira on the Okinawan island of his childhood and birthplace, Miyakojima. From San'ya to Haneda Airport, followed by a three-hour flight to the capital of Okinawa, Naha, and another one-hour flight to Miyakojima, the voyage would transport Akira beyond his comfort zone. Far removed from his haunts in the squalor of San'ya, the trip turned into an anxiety-stricken affair for Akira, who had not returned home in decades and for whom the stay involved visiting his mother's tomb for the first time. Our stay in Miyakojima would act as a painful reminder of the life he had lived and of the figure he cut against the backdrop of both his family and mainstream society.

Miyakojima

I only accompanied Akira on one of his family visits, for which he typically decided to show up unannounced, with an embarrassed, foreign friend in tow, no less. Unabashed, he had rung the bell of a three-story countryside mansion, and when he was asked inside by his cousin, he insisted to me—a "friend" waiting in the car—that it was all right to come in. In this way, while Akira and his cousin reminisced, I wound up sipping iced tea under a fan in the airy living room of a rural house, flanked through open windows by the blistering heat of farmlands. Nothing seemed amiss, save for a passing reference to that time, decades earlier, when Akira's cousins had seen him at a funeral in Yokohama, fearing that he might die because he had been so bandaged up. When I asked him about it afterward, he did not want to explain.

Akira's anxiety became increasingly evident as we drove our rental car along the sweeping vistas of Miyakojima's shorelines, past rows upon rows of sugarcane fields, and spent our evenings in restaurants catering to tourists with local food and Okinawan music shows. Saying that he was feeling "neurotic" and did not want to risk becoming a burden to his brother by being hospitalized, Akira refrained from drinking much in the evenings. One day, I had left him with the family of an old friend, only to return to find him scouring the countryside streets for me, panic-stricken and lost. More than anything, the prospect of visiting his mother's tomb prompted Akira's anxiety, and it was only when his older brother told him that it was not necessary to visit the tomb a second time that Akira seemed to calm down.

It was during one of the evening performances of Okinawan music that I noticed how Akira had grown sensitive to the gaze of others. As it happens during such tourist shows, halfway through our meal the lead singer decided it was time for everyone in the audience to introduce themselves, and thus, perched on a center-stage stool, he proceeded to address each of our tables, asking where customers were from, what had brought them to Miyakojima, and so forth, only to finish off each table with a comment for comic effect. There were no locals in the audience, which was composed almost exclusively of younger tourists and businessmen from the mainland, out for an evening of Indigenous music after snorkeling or work. But the clincher was delivered *not* when we had to account for our motley appearance in the midst of this uniform crowd—Akira was unmistakably dressed in a short-sleeve collared shirt with a floral Hawaiian design of fluorescent proportions—but when the lead singer neglected to address us, effectively skipping us by moving on to the next table. I was relieved, thinking that by some fortuitous fluke, we had been spared from public speaking. But for Akira, the purposeful neglect functioned as a confirmation of suspicions he had already been harboring. When I remarked how fortunate it was that we had not been called on, he merely muttered that it was because the man could not make sense of the oddball combination of "an old yakuza and foreigner." It was not simply that the bandleader could not place us that vexed Akira but that this had led him deliberately to omit any reference to our presence in the room, as if we might upset a certain equilibrium among his customers. Indeed, the bandleader and manager eyed us intently as we left the restaurant. And as if to confirm such apprehensions, Akira and I were to undergo a similar experience on the flight back to Tokyo (figure E.1), when the many questions from a garrulous neighboring passenger reached the point beyond which we no longer felt comfortable answering. Perhaps

FIGURE E.1.   Miyakojima from our airplane window.

we really did have something to hide. Was it not kind of Akira to have taken me with him to Okinawa? How had we met?

Within San'ya or at the construction site, it would never even have been necessary to parry such questions, which could be answered with carefree honesty or bluntly saying: "It's none of your business." But the social context had shifted, causing Akira to forfeit the fortitude he possessed in San'ya and at its interface with society. Much as Akira continued to sport a smile and flirt with the receptionists at our hotel in Miyakojima, there was a vulnerability about him in the evenings, when he would recount things he had learned during the day, such as how his mother had passed strapped to a bed with dementia or how the one friend he had hoped to see had committed suicide by disemboweling himself. Repeating how his siblings considered him a persona non grata on account of his former outlaw status, Akira fell to brooding and appeared to want nothing so much as to return safely to San'ya.

On the morning of our departure, Akira's phone rang nonstop with last-minute gift requests from the guys, and later that day, everyone gathered for the homecoming in San'ya. But the cheerful mood quickly turned sour when Shōkawa insisted on haranguing Akira regarding how little he knew Miyako-jima and how stupid he had been not to show me this or that. Akira eventually took it personally and, in a rare emotional outburst, told Shōkawa to "shut up" before he left for Mutō's place, where he could reminisce in peace.

It had, no doubt, occurred to Akira that he might not be returning to Miyakojima. His health had been rapidly deteriorating, and thus, what was to have been a celebratory homecoming brought a painful finality to bear on the trip. The return to San'ya called for a moment of reckoning that had otherwise been long deferred.

Even decades after the guys had left home to find work, there was a distinct sense in which family wounds retained a primacy that was difficult to overcome. For Akira, there was the disgrace and publicity of his manslaughter conviction. For Saruma, Kentarō, Matsuda, Suzuki, and Hayashi, there was the opprobrium of failed marriages and long-lost children, which redounded in the judgmental echo chamber of their next of kin, dead or alive. Parents lived on in the imagination, although a noticeable number of fathers had been absent during childhood. Shōkawa's father, for instance, had committed suicide by disembowelment.

It would be a mistake, however, to say that it was failure in the eyes of family that caused the conduct of an otoko, as if the trope was simply reactionary. There was a quite conscious and deliberate manner in which the conduct of an otoko was deployed to manage or contain inexpiable wounds or, rather, to make it clear that certain things ought to remain unspoken. Kentarō's mother was an old "hag" (babā), and up until his trip to Miyakojima, Akira had "left Okinawa behind for good." Moreover, when such comments were let slip, everyone recognized that it had better stay that way. There was not much that could be done, in any case, and drawing attention to impotence was to invite rage. Either there was no money to fly back, or the family members in question had died or gone missing. Like Akira, Rikiishi did return to Okinawa for a brief visit—his first ever—but otherwise, everyone could only wait for the ineluctable. Then, when news of someone passing reached San'ya, or when the guys were faced with the prospect of their own death, the full brunt of the San'ya man's low self-estimation was brought forth once again.

Faced with the finality of death, almost everything seemed to confirm the worthlessness of someone who had wound up in San'ya. As if by some fatalistic logic, a constellation of factors fell suddenly into place, reflecting just how much they had disappointed not only their loved ones, but themselves. From their welfare status to self-incurred ill health, the social stigmata piled one upon the other, and it was all somehow capped and condensed in the (often secret) fact of their living in San'ya. It was thus with the passing of Shōkawa's mother, and as we shall see, it was thus when Akira attempted suicide. Only the presence of comradeship could hold shame and destructive self-incrimination at bay.

What the pervasively negative judgment of San'ya shows, however, is that family wounds were determined by an institution anterior to the idiosyncrasies of personal relations, and this was the state. It was the normative power of state recognition that stigmatized failure as failure and, in so doing, prompted family members to dissociate themselves from potentially unruly, disreputable, and contagious elements.

But only a historical perspective can disclose how the state has been strategically invested in producing an expendable labor force. The nearly defunct system that provided out-of-work aid had been put into effect for precisely this purpose. More significant, however, is the immediate postwar era in which the destruction of rural economies not only facilitated their dispossession and subsumption by capitalism but availed capital of individuals with no choice but to submit to grievous conditions of labor. And while it might be objected that the Japanese state did not intend to lose World War II, it could likewise be pointed out that it did not plan the Fukushima nuclear catastrophes but that the destruction wrought by the 3/11 tsunami has nevertheless provided capital with the opportunity to penetrate less accessible economies. It is not a coincidence that "Fukushima" has joined the ranks of "Okinawa" as a locality that has been systematically exploited and sacrificed by the state. Nor is it a coincidence that, among other rural locations, there was a prevalence of men from Okinawa in San'ya. If only from the number of students attending Akira's old school in Miyakojima, the postwar years entailed a mass exodus either to the Okinawan "main island" (hontō), where jobs revolve around tourism and the US military industry, or to the Japanese mainland (naichi). When Akira grew up, in the 1960s, there had been hundreds of students in attendance. In 2015, there were fewer than twenty. So too, the blue lagoon where Akira swam as a child had been transformed into a tourist spot for snorkeling, flanked by rental stores and, behind them, dilapidated concrete homes for local residents. Magnificent hotels stood farther down the shoreline, towering above the ocean, sealed off from their surroundings. It was obvious that the profits made in these self-contained compounds were funneled off the island and that it was locals who provided the service industry with cut-rate labor. Any one of these high-rise compounds could have enclosed the downtown area of Miyakojima City, which was pretty much deserted. Hence, Kentarō said to me upon our return: "You get it, right? There's nothing!" The dearth of jobs in Okinawa had forced almost every one of the guys to relocate to mainland Japan, but this story of primitive accumulation followed by pauperism would not end there.[1] Only a few years after our return from Miyakojima, an utterly devastated and depressed Rikiishi would say the same of San'ya, in a broken voice: "There's nothing"—no future, no hope, nothing. From start to finish, destitution, depredation, and social and economic failure had conditioned the lives of the guys, leaving them no choice but to sell their labor on the black market, as part of Japan's postwar labor force.[2]

For this reason, the originary wounds of the subaltern day laborer and otoko were eminently more conscious than those of the upstanding son, husband, or father. These wounds were dissimulated because that is precisely what the oppositional character of the otoko was meant to achieve, and its sociality could assume a blinding and violent force. Yet, even behind statements like Kentarō's—it's "finished" once you have kids—there was lurking an acute awareness of loss and insufficiency. The truth was that Kentarō really did want to meet his two sons, although he rarely mentioned this. Moreover, meetings with welfare officers and everyday labor conditions not only operated as repetitive reminders of the day laborer's worth in general society but instilled an awareness of his relation to statist propriety. As with members of other marginalized social groups, the San'ya man was therefore conscious of that which "general society" (*ippan shakai*) was not, for while general society embodied the normative gaze of the state, its members were not privy to the doubling of perspective that social exclusion can afford. Everyone knew that docile interactions with welfare officials were an act, if not an outright farce. When Kentarō was asked to don a safety badge at the construction site, he did so with a glee and gusto that bordered on parody.[3] Then again, if obeisance to workplace discipline was an act, so too was masculinity in San'ya: only one Japanese character differentiates the yakuza (mobster) from the *yakusha* (actor). Be it inside or outside of San'ya, its residents were predisposed to give the lie to the myth of Japanese social conformity—a disclosure in which the very self-evidence of the ideological was at stake.[4]

Nothing, after all, facilitates critical reflection on convictions so much as their undoing in failure. A double reading is called for, because not only does the death knell of places like San'ya announce the failure and repressed truth of Japanese society today, but the self-evidence of the upstanding otoko must be interpreted where it, too, breaks down: be it in the face of gender differences that do not conform to the heteronormative patriarchy of San'ya (which it shared with Japanese society at large), in the hospital, at the welfare office, or at an eatery outside of San'ya, where a giggling group of customers might have remarked upon the non-Japanese appearance of the guys, asking, "Where are you from?" Such comments would either prompt a sharp rebuke or a confrontation, if the offenders were men. But they would also lead Kentarō to remark with spiteful humor in private, "I am not Japanese."[5]

I turn, therefore, to the journal entries of two incidents that occurred during my time in San'ya. While the second of these concerns Akira's suicide attempt and what was said in the hospital after, the first focuses on a blind outburst of transphobic violence.[6] This latter event was occasioned by the furtive appearances of a transgender person in the Iroha arcade, where they caught the eye of Yamamori. Treating his environs as his personal domain, Yamamori, who was supposedly on meth that evening, hailed the transgender person to sit beside him on the blue tarpaulin that had been pulled out by the arcade entryway. With all the swagger of a former mobster, Yamamori proceeded to

rip the top off the transgender person, displaying their upper body for everybody to see. It was an uncomfortable moment for me. Nobody intervened. What was almost weirder was that the person didn't seem to mind . . . being deprived of clothing in this way. Being displayed.

Later, inside Sakura, the transgender person happened to be sitting just across from me. Next to me was Suzuki, Akira, and Yamamori, who continuously acted brash and pushy. From across the table, Suzuki looked intently at the transgender person, and asked if they would give a blowjob: "Will you suck me?" Yamamori was meanwhile getting more and more rowdy. Going around the table to sit next to the transgender person, he again tore their top down. Threateningly asked if the breasts were real. Moving back and forth vigorously between his chair and the transgender person, standing and sitting, he proceeded to lift the transgender person's skirt, tearing their underwear off. Asked: "Do you have a dick?" Then he said something to the extent of: "If you're gonna work in this area, you gotta pay up to the Kanamachi-ikka, because that's the kind of place this is." Only Akira turned to the transgender person and said to just come back some day when this guy—Yamamori—wasn't there.

Since I had work the next day, I went home of everyone's urging around nine. Before that, though, there was an awkward moment when Yamamori was trying to give me ¥1,000. At first, I handed the money back, but he was insistent. Pushy. Inflated. I didn't want to accept money from this guy who had done such terrible things to the person across from me. So I put the money back on the table. But Yamamori kept insisting. My eyes moved back and forth between Akira and Suzuki to see what to do. Waving their hands indifferently, they said something to the effect of: "Yeah, sure, just take the money." So I took it, bowing out whilst saying "thank you," and that I would eat something good with it.

In my apartment, later that evening with Akira, Kentarō, and Shōkawa, Akira noted that he felt sorry for the transgender person. Yet no one really seemed to think the incident serious. If anything, it was laughable, and the conversation moved on.[7]

For obvious reasons, I never encountered the transgender person afterward, and this was the only incident in which phobia toward gender difference was expressed with such despicable, physical, and humiliating violence. But it would be wrong to relegate this assault to the category of an exception that would not have taken place if Yamamori had not been there, which Akira proceeded to do (it was just Yamamori going off the wire, he said) because that is precisely how patriarchy dismisses violence endemic to its social order.[8] Indeed, it should be noted that, in this instance, not only has the oppositional difference between Yamamori (as the vulgar hoodlum) and the Okinawa-gang collapsed, since nobody stepped in to "protect the weak." In the absence of restraints on outright physical violence, Yamamori's assault has become one with the "bullying" (*ijime*) that transgender people in Japan experience, be it in school or society at large, and his rabid insistence upon identifying the sex of the transgender person (as if this would somehow settle the matter) replicates a medical discourse in which the genitalia of an individual constitutes the final marker of their sexual identity as an "otoko" (man) or "onna" (woman).[9] Because I was not able to speak to the transgender person who was assaulted or to other transgender people in San'ya (I did not become close enough to any), I cannot write of their experiences in San'ya, but a Human Rights Watch report of 2016 spells out the sheer discrimination and social violence that the LGBTQ community in Japan lives with from the moment one begins to work out one's gender: "Hateful anti-LGBT rhetoric is nearly ubiquitous in Japanese schools, driving LGBT students into silence, self-loathing, and in some cases, self-harm."[10] If Takeda-san, Nē-san, or Rikiishi had been present, perhaps Yamamori would have been made to restrain himself, but the fact of the matter remains that it was no longer the San'ya man who was caught in a no-man's-land of abjection but the transgender person who was violated, violently banished and reduced to their sex and yet again made to occupy a no-place that Susan Stryker describes at once as abject and harboring potential for transformation.[11] So too, the violence that Yamamori deploys is no longer that of a man taking out his ire on another man (when there is dignity even in taking a beating) but of a macho order that is revolted because the conventional markers of gender have become muddled, threatening and troubling what Yamamori himself is in relation to the transgender person. Short of killing the transgender person, Yamomori would reestablish the conventional markers of masculinity and femininity by banishing anything inbetween. For, as Stryker says, to "encounter the transsexual body, to apprehend a transgendered consciousness articulating itself, is to risk a revelation of the constructedness of the natural order." It was precisely in being threatened in his masculinity that Yamamori carried out the assault and "cultural rape" of the transgender person, and no one at the table intervened, as if everyone had a vested interest in Yamamori's actions.[12] In all its vulgar crudity, the proper order of things had to be reasserted. Yet Yamamori's use of excessive violence, not to mention his use of money to buy allegiance and seniority where it was otherwise uncertain, undercut his assertions. Even the troupe commented on the pitiful air of

Yamamori's remonstrations, insofar as he "cannot make it in this town" without handing out money like that. Where there was to have been subordination, there was desperate exhibitionism, and where there was to have been singular masculinity, there was reference to the money form. It was only poetic justice that Yamamori was ousted from San'ya by the Kanamachi-ikka when he made the mistake of telling them that he had had previous dealings with the Sumiyoshi-kai, an adversary of the Yamaguchi-gumi, to which the Kanamachi-ikka was subordinate. Afterward, it was said that Yamamori had gone to work at the Fukushima Daiichi Nuclear Power Plant, but this news, too, was intercepted as boasting.[13]

The fact of the matter was that it was impossible to secure the figuration of a thoroughgoing masculine masculinity, and it was precisely this impossibility that triggered repetition and, in this instance, sexual assault. As if no one was entirely convinced of themselves, there was always something left to be desired, another assertion of masculinity to be made. The certainty of identity was necessarily interrupted by differences that were as exterior as they were intimately interior to those who negated them. God forbid that Yamamori should have felt inclined to cross-dress or, for that matter, that I should have felt compelled to inflict violence as Yamamori did, because the fact of the matter was that I could have intervened but that I chose to remain inconspicuous. If I had not had a stake in establishing relations with the troupe, perhaps that evening would have transpired differently, but I knew that the troupe respected my decision to keep my place—it was not for me, an outsider, to criticize—and so I kept my silence. Everyone had a reputation to uphold, to which certain actions were at least thought to be anathema.

As horrific and violent as Yamamori's actions were, however, it should be stated that they were not as straightforward as they might seem. It was not unusual to encounter people who cross-dressed in San'ya, and before Yamamori's assault, the transgender person above had been giving blowjobs to regulars in Sakura's toilet and in the back alleys adjacent to the dive. Resonating with stories from the past, when old-timers had witnessed everything from oral sex to outright intercourse on the streets, intimacy among men was intrinsic to San'ya. In fact, Yamamori's constant consort and gambling buddy was a so-called "o—" (f—), who cut an intimidating figure while he sported a handbag over a muscular forearm. The two were virtually inseparable in the Iroha arcade, where they could be seen gambling or sauntering along: Yamamori in a billowing jacket, and his counterpart in a tightly knit blouse that accentuated his robust chest. It was not just any gender difference that caused Yamomori to assault the transgender person but rather that, in this instance, he could not recognize this person as an otoko dressing as a woman.[14] It was one thing to pay for sex in the red-light district of Yoshiwara or for men to have intercourse with one another in San'ya—the conventional markers of gender and patriarchy were upheld. It was quite another matter when an individual could not be recognized either as a man or woman.

Indeed, while there was a modicum of hospitality toward gender differences in the troupe, the guys distanced themselves from such departures. Akira had worked for more than a decade in Tokyo's gay district, Shinjuku Ni-chōme, and the others never frowned when someone thought to be a "f—" (o—) joined us at Sakura or Mutō's hole-in-the-wall. Conversations then continued as usual, but when the person had gone home or to the bathroom, it would be asked whether they were not "this," followed by the gesture of raising one hand to the opposite cheek, palm outward. Sometimes these questions were posed simply, as a matter of fact. At others, they were accompanied by a smile that was disconcerting in its implications but that functioned to reiterate a line of distinction where it might have been obfuscated. Identity, thus, could only be established across differences that were constitutive precisely insofar as they were interruptive of masculinity. In this sense, Yamamori's partner was his perfect counterpart. For while they shared the menacing comportment of street gangsters, each accentuated the features of the other, throwing them into relief. The threatening property of gender difference resided in its capacity to undo the artifice of self-presentation.

But while differently gendered people could be avoided or expelled from San'ya, the reality of everyone's deteriorating physical condition could not be escaped. Above all, it was death that instigated assertions of masculinity and death that caused the hardened gambler to fold his hand in a final admission of defeat. Time was up. After a lifetime of repetitive detours, there could be a return to origins and the instauration of a masculinity imbued with humility. Miyazaki Manabu writes:

> I didn't only gamble in Kyoto, but in Osaka, too. It was there that I was once admonished by a veteran gambler belonging to a long-established gambling syndicate, the Sakaume-gumi. He was about seventy and had known my grandfather.
>
> That day, I kept losing and was starting to behave rashly. Young guy that I was, I just kept on betting, determined not to quit until I won. Then someone patted me on the shoulder.
>
> "Why not just die? Come on, walk away!"
>
> I turned around to see the old gambler from the Sakaume-gumi.
>
> Strangely enough, his words were all it took to calm me. The harder you gamble, the harder it is to get out of trouble if it's not your lucky day. What's important in gambling is to "die"—admit that you have lost. This is what the old man taught me. Afterward, he took me to a separate room.

"I'll tell you something," he said. "It's only when you lose that you prove yourself as a man. It's easy to be a winner. How you behave as a loser says everything."[15]

Walking Away

One night, I accompanied Akira in an ambulance after he had been carried out of his bunkhouse on a stretcher, altogether unable to move. But when we arrived at the hospital, we were told first by the nurse and then by the doctor that he was to return home because his pain was being caused by alcohol. In retrospect, I interpret this dismissal as a moral judgment deeming Akira ineligible for care. They knew where he had come from and were used to others like him, from San'ya: Akira was a good-for-nothing drunk on welfare. Social judgment had taken the place of medical diagnosis, not to mention care. What struck me in the moment was the absurdity of sending home someone who could hardly move, let alone speak, and as it turned out, Akira had fractured a disk in his spinal column. No doubt partly motivated by financial considerations, partly by the disrepute that individuals like Akira could bring upon the institution, the medical establishment had taken it upon itself to push responsibility and guilt onto the welfare recipient who could not cover his own costs, and this was an adjudication that structured just about every interaction between the San'ya man and representatives of the state, be it welfare officers or the police. Such treatment called for a glass of shochu upon returning to San'ya: a drink to patch up the injury of enforced servility.

Self-possession was recovered with more difficulty, however, when Akira attempted suicide by disembowelment and Suzuki suffered from delirium tremens. There was an excess to these hospitalizations that stoked guilt and ambivalence by reopening old wounds, casting doubt over a lifetime lived in adherence to a transgressive masculinity. To add, both Suzuki and Akira were ashamed before the troupe. While Suzuki had to go on welfare, Akira asked me not to tell them what had happened. Naturally, everyone was supportive when they were discharged, which is to say that the guys truly did have buddies in their stigmatized penury—a luxury of which the salaryman or part-time worker today has largely been stripped. But whereas Suzuki was not on welfare at the time of his hospitalization and therefore received one solid week of care, Akira, who had stabbed himself in the gut with a kitchen knife, was discharged thirty-six hours after he had arrived.

During those thirty-six hours, I visited Akira in the emergency ward:

The guards by the entry gate gave me a bit of a hard time because I was visiting outside of hours. I think they were even more weirded out because I was just a "friend" whom the patient himself had called. Neither a family member, nor someone the doctors had called. And Akira is not supposed to be able to call from inside the emergency ward. But he had. So they let me in outside of hours. They told me to wear a mask inside, but when the nurse came to collect me at the boundary point, it seemed like it wasn't necessary. (I have to admit, given the bureaucracy I was coming up against at the entrance, I was scared they wouldn't let me see Akira at all.) I walked in. Akira was in the far room of the hallway, in a bed in the closer, far side towards the hallway. (To be honest, I had been nervous about seeing him, not knowing how to approach such a situation, almost wanting to run away from it.) The first thing he said was probably sorry and thank you. What I remember is him talking in this weak voice, describing what he had done to himself and gesturing with his hands to enact. Stretching his forefingers some twenty centimeters apart, he said that it had looked like a fine knife. Then making as if to hold the knife by the hilt, pointing at the side of his stomach, he made a stabbing motion inward. Opening his mouth slowly and painfully and jabbing slowly—up and down—he had remembered that the knife wouldn't cut. He must have tried to cut himself a bunch of times. At some point, he said something like: "If that thing had been a real knife, I'd have flayed the stomach open in one stroke." Moving his arms vigorously across his stomach. But the knife had not cut. After a while, it had begun to hurt, to become painful. Bleeding, he had thought that maybe if he just took some sleeping pills like this, he'd "pass away." He didn't actually say "pass away"; silence there. Earlier that day, he said, he'd "been left all alone" by Bonobe and Yamori, both of whom want to get rid of Akira (so Akira said). So he'd gone drinking. As always, he talked about Wakako's slippers no longer being beside his own, perhaps even on a different shelf. He spoke of Izumo massaging Wakako and one not knowing where that might go. How he had even gotten down on his knees to apologize (*dogeza*) to Wakako when she had rebuffed him—saying that one doesn't do that kind of thing—by stating that everyone, even Orin, is getting massaged. Akira himself could give massages, Akira said, but "it's a clinic" so you don't do that kind of thing. He'd spoken of how tired the guys get, walking in the heat to do food handouts—spoke real passionately here—and how neither Bonobe nor Izumo get this. Meanwhile, Bonobe is actually sending Izumo upstairs to massage Wakako and Orin.

At some point, after he had done the deed of cutting his stomach, Akira had thought "what a ridiculous thing to throw one's life away over." Meaning the disagreement with Sanyukai staff. I guess that's when he got around to calling an ambulance. His eyes teared when I explained to him that I didn't know what had happened until after I'd spoken to his mama-san. (Why? As if it confirmed that . . . he had been alone through-out the experience.) He didn't remember that he had called me twice the night before. His eyes teared again, looking away, saying that there were "other things" bothering him than the staff at Sanyukai. The Saturday before, he had been told by the doctor upstairs that there had developed a blood-vessel swelling right next to the tumor. He pointed to his head, again explaining that the tumor is in a place where they don't want to operate, deep and in the center. Same as the blood-vessel swelling. He'd asked the doctor what to do if the clot swelled even more, and the doctor had said to come to the hospital. Asking how he would know whether the clot had swelled or not, the doctor had responded that he would experi-ence "incredible pain." Akira's response to this was like: "What the hell, there's nothing to do." Or rather, "What kind of response was that from the doctor?" If it swells, Akira effectively dies. And speaking of its loca-tion, drawing a line down the center of his body, Akira noted that this was something like his "lifeline." I interpret: his lifeline threatened. He also said that when he thinks of his illness . . . he can see the road ahead.

He also spoke of having been in the mob, again emphasizing that a lot of the guys in the mob are better than regular folk. (I realize, hy-pothesize, that he may have been fighting this bad image of the mob . . . internally . . . and that, perhaps, volunteering at Sanyukai has been a sort of compensation for the past.) Laughing a little to himself—because he looks thus—he explained how all of them on the corner had asked him what sort of yakuza he had been. He'd told Kentarō that he had re-lations with the yakuza, but not that he had been in it. He repeated the distinction he had made. And he'd told the guys to come to Sanyukai to see for themselves if they didn't believe (that he wasn't former mob). In the mob, Akira said straight-out, he had specialized in extortion. I.e., to collect the money that one civilian owed to another. He's described this to me before, saying that no one is as "dirty" as "regular folk." That and gambling he had done. Because—raising his thumb—his boss only en-gaged in those things. I.e., he didn't do drugs or women. He wasn't the latter kind of yakuza. (I wonder now why he was so straight-out about what he'd done in the mob, at that moment, lying in bed.) The nurse came by to ask him how he was doing and he responded that it hurts. The evening before, they'd used anesthetic, but he said it had hurt when they operated on him.[16]

In light of the references that Akira himself makes to his criminal past, it is possible to interpret this failed suicide attempt as a condensation of the social forces active throughout Akira's life. As an institution that exploits his labor, that will not understand the hardship that this labor involves, and that humiliates him before women, Sanyukai emerges as a stand-in for general society. Rather than speak to him about their concerns, moreover, the representatives of this respectable institution give him the cold shoulder, making it clear they want him gone. The act of suicide itself emerges as an internalization of worthlessness and of the violent social prescription that the worthless should be eliminated. But it also attempts to reverse this judgment through the reiteration of a transgressive masculinity that shifts guilt back on the institution. In the pure style of an otoko, slicing the stomach would have achieved recognition through revenge: the institution would have had to acknowledge Akira on his own terms. In this instance, however, the act of suicide is ambivalent and fails to meet the standards of an otoko. A real otoko would have completed the act with a single, fatal stroke.

It is the silences and ellipses in Akira's narrative that indicate constitutive wounds, metaphorized by Akira's "tumor." The physical threat that the tumor poses is clearly very real. Yet Akira himself interprets his affliction when he draws a finger down the center of his body, saying that the unextractable tumor threatens his "lifeline" (*seimeisen*). Like death, the bursting of the adjacent blood vessel is perhaps imminent and certainly inescapable. But it is the specter of "pain" that aligns this bursting with the resurgence of the "other things"—silenced—that he himself references and silences. Having had a close call with death, the thirty-six hours in the emergency ward take the form of an analog to that which Akira anticipates down the road.

Set into motion by the contingency of the displaced slippers, everything appears to take on the form of a repetition without difference. If Akira's brush with death anticipates the future, it also revisits his life trajectory from succeeding as an upstanding construction manager—Sanyukai was his opportunity to go legit—only to be convicted of manslaughter, be rejected by his family, and then to embrace life as an outlaw: mobsters are often better people than members of the general public. So too, there had been a sense of honor to his work in the mob: no prostitution or drugs. No one is as "dirty" (*kitanai*) as "ordinary folk" (*ippan no hito*).[17] Indeed, Akira already had scars on his wrist, where he had cut himself previously, and violent suicide was a fantasy that he continued to entertain afterward, remarking that, if it were not for fear, he would have sliced his throat open or thrown himself into traffic. Yet, despite Akira's insistence that he would have flayed his stomach open if the knife had been sharp, there is a difference in this instance from his convictions at other times. He walks away from the deadlock between the institution and his avowed values as an otoko. As Akira recalls, there is a moment when, in the very midst of the violence, he awakens to himself and realizes that showing up the institution is not worth killing this self for. What he wants resides neither in the recognition of what the upstanding institution deems as appropriate behavior nor in recognition as an otoko.

Beyond San'ya

Twelve years after the Fukushima nuclear catastrophes, it has become abundantly clear how swiftly anti-state sentiments can explode into a mass movement, only to lose their momentum and recede from public visibility. By short-circuiting memories of war, fascism, and sacrifices incurred to nuclear radiation, it was the force of coincidence that galvanized mass sentiments into the antinuclear movement. But what has happened to the tens of thousands of protesters who took to the streets in 2011? If the embers of a movement are still glowing, the flame has gone out.

While I cannot examine here the techniques deployed to shut down anti-state sentiment, it must be underscored that their logics are similar to those that have consigned San'ya to death and that they are anchored in the power of state recognition to set the limits of propriety, visibility, and sayability. Ultimately, such techniques of recognition concern the power of the state to achieve an ideological penetration, making it self-evident that individuals fend for themselves within an overpowering market. Conditions that have been discussed under the name of "neoliberalism" (shinjiyūshugi), be it in leftist circles or in the academy, have thus existed in San'ya for decades.

Places like San'ya disclose the class-oriented character not only of much anti-state rhetoric in Japan but of discourses that have popularized themselves through their focus on "Fukushima." It is curious how quickly activists and academics gravitated around "Fukushima" when segments of the Japanese population had long been laboring under deadly social conditions, as egregious as any in northeastern Japan today. Of course, the sheer scale of the nuclear disasters warranted this attention. Yet, twelve years after the nuclear meltdowns, it should be asked why the discourse of "Fukushima" was so self-contained and why it did not link radiation exposure to other forms of sordid labor, be it prostitution, leather tanning, or that of homeless people. After all, the same word is used in Japanese to describe how each of such topics remain unspoken: tabū (taboo).

In fact, during the two years I gathered materials for this book (2011–2013), the very same phrase was used to account for the predicament of San'ya and Fukushima: "nothing to do about it" (shikatanai). Meaning both that it was best not to agitate emotions by complaining and that there was, indeed, nothing to be done, such words blocked criticism and violence from being directed at the state and deflected them onto neighbors. Presaging the future, San'ya illustrates what happens when individuals are made to buck up, and violence is made to circulate within society itself rather than being rearticulated and returned to its source. Buttressed by the inescapable conditions of the labor market, the power of state recognition forecloses the potential for backtalk. Already alienated and disconnected by the economy, state recognition consigns potentially disruptive populations or individuals to an anonymous, early death, and such alienation has intensified with the dispersal of postwar labor pools like the *yoseba*, which has been replaced by the cell phone. In this way, places like San'ya have been thrust beneath the threshold of visibility, stricken from consciousness, and sanitized within history.

What the death of San'ya leaves us with, however, is also precisely that which the lackluster, uniform appearance of an increasingly alienated labor force of Japanese society has lost: the immemorable beauty of an obscene cast of characters, ever enacting the justice they would never have. Everybody in the troupe wore a mask—masks that could not be escaped, certainly, yet masks that could also be worn with an irony that opened a distance between themselves and their social personas. There was Rikiishi, the unstoppable and indomitably constant "gorilla"; Kentarō, the procurer of work and no-nonsense "silverback"; Akira, the former mobster, emperorist, and protector of the weak, also known as the "devil's man"; Takeda-san, the ineffably elegant, humble, and self-effacing source of authority and hospitality in San'ya, a "legendary man"; Matsuda, the crafty, burlesque, and driven subcontractor of many questionable connections; Saruma, the salaryman-gone-bankrupt cousin whom everyone relied on in times of need; Suzuki, the braggart of a younger brother, as given to fighting as to kindness; and Nē-san, the quick-witted, solicitous, yet equally truculent "older sister" to the entire gang; and the list of singular characters goes on and on. In San'ya, their singularities were amplified, and insofar as the sociality of the troupe prevailed, they were rewarded with mutual recognition.

It was as if everyone was waiting for something that would not arrive. The Olympics, they would say—we just want to make it to the 2020 Tokyo Olympics. After all, everyone in the troupe had been teenagers for the 1964 Tokyo Olympics—the crowning achievement of Japan's postwar recovery from World War II. Perhaps it was fitting that what had begun with the Olympics would end upon the occasion of another Olympics, whose stadiums had been constructed by able-bodied younger men. Still, when it had become late night and everyone had become especially nostalgic, it was throwbacks from childhood and adolescence they wanted to hear, like Okabayashi's "San'ya Blues," Tsuruta Kōji's "Otoko," or Narciso Yepes's wistful guitar theme from René Clément's 1952

World War II film, *Forbidden Games*. History was closing its pages on San'ya and its experience of Japan's postwar, but as long as the guys were alive, as some of them were in 2023, there would be time for another song and gamble.

Kentarō passed away on July 4, 2023. In his later years, he had become fortunate enough to find a partner in life, Chizuko, a.k.a. "razor blade Chizu" (*kamisori no Chizu*). Born and raised in Asakusa and formerly married to a member of the yakuza, Chizuko is a true native of Tokyo's *shitamachi* (low-city). She was by Kentarō's side when he died.

Acknowledgments

I cannot name the people to whom this book owes its primary debt, the people who let me into their world, who extended me hospitality, and who allowed me to write about them, knowing that I would get things wrong. My name may be on the cover of this book, but it does not belong to me. If Akira, Kentarō, Takeda-san, or Nē-san ever pick up a Japanese version of this book, I hope that they will recognize themselves in it and feel that it does a modicum of justice to their lives. The source of this ethnography resides in the poetry of their everyday conduct. In the academy, Marilyn Ivy has acted as an unstinting source of intellectual support for almost fifteen years. Through COVID-19, intolerable reviews, and my departure from the academy, she continued to rally for the publication of this manuscript. It would not have come into existence in her absence. I would have given up. I know that Christopher T. Nelson acted as an absolutely vital source of support for this manuscript, that he did so more than once, and that he did so with nothing to gain. Thank you. The manuscript also owes an impossible debt to my mentors: Harry Harootunian, Thomas LaMarre, Rosalind C. Morris, and John Pemberton—they inspired its substance and navigated its politics of publication. At Columbia University's Weatherhead East Asian Institute, I would like to thank Ariana King, who promoted the book and acted as a constant, reassuring presence through the entirety of an anxious, seemingly endless process. I would also like to thank Carol Gluck. At Sophia University, I would like to thank David H. Slater, who sparked my interest in cultural anthropology, and who pushed for me to study in the United States twenty years ago. At Cornell University Press, I would like to thank my editors, Jim Lance and Ellen Labbate, who pushed for publication within an astonishing timeline, and Mary Kate Murphy. I would also like to thank the Society for the Humanities at Cornell University and its fellows from 2018–2019. Beyond the academy, I would like to thank Oliver Alexander, Tommy Birkett, Jennifer D. Carlson, Familien Damgård, Marguerite France, Charles Jester, Dounyazade Joyce Jester, Kanemoto Sensei, Kiki (our pup), Nadia Latif, Andrew McKenzie-McHarg, Aslı Menevse, Harumi Osaki, Reviewer #1 for *CA*, David Rojas, Hector Ivan Saenz, Kerry Suzuki, Miyako Tanimoto, Monica Lorenzo Tejedor, and Cindy Truong. Finally, I would like to express my heartfelt gratitude to Anson Wigner, who created potential cover images for this book, knowing that discretion to use these images resided entirely with the press. In closing, it goes without saying that this book started with the many trips that my parents brought me on as a child, to impress upon me the importance and excitement of interpretation across cultural difference. But if there is one person who has acted as a lifeline of support through the entire arc of this book, from its beginnings on 149th Street in Washington Heights, to Takeda-san's apartment in San'ya, to Avenue des Érables in Montreal, and who had my back through the woes of publication, urging upon me the importance of life when my inability to publish had assumed a destructive force, it has been my partner in life and spouse, Nhu Truong.

Glossary of Key Characters

There are some fifty characters and therefore some fifty names in this book, many of whom only make one appearance, like the yakuza representative who was involved in nuclear decontamination work in Fukushima Prefecture or many of the men who either volunteered for or received services from a local nonprofit organization. Although I could have eliminated many of these characters or given them generic pseudonyms (A, B, C, D), I have decided to retain their proper, albeit fictitious, names throughout the text. The oftentimes bewildering number of characters is part of the social scene of San'ya, where up to forty men might be gathered at once in an alleyway. But more importantly, this book has been expressly written to restore a sense of singularity to an area of Tokyo that does not appear on maps and whose population has been consigned to an anonymous death. Repeating that which I write against would have been unconscionable. Instead, I offer this glossary of the main characters in the book so that the reader may revert to this section when in doubt.

Akira: A former demolition worker, right-wing emperorist, and professional extortionist for the now-defunct Nibikikai yakuza organization, Akira was my main interlocutor in San'ya. Long ago, Akira was convicted of manslaughter, and upon his release from jail, he joined the yakuza until his membership in the organization was suspended on account of infighting. After being diagnosed with a brain tumor, Akira was finally forced to go on welfare. I first met him at a local nonprofit organization in San'ya, where he spent his time volunteering. No one at the nonprofit knew of his past.

Kentarō: A burly no-nonsense worker who ensured the availability of work for everyone through his connections and presence at construction sites. Possessing a hefty upper body with hands worn, swollen, and heavy from decades of work, Kentarō had been dubbed the "silverback" of the group on account of his streak of white hair. But Kentarō was also one of the most hardened gamblers in the group, and for this reason, he had also been nicknamed the "Paul Newman of Japan."

Matsuda: The crafty, burlesque, and meth-driven street-level labor broker (tehaishi) for his own group of workers, the Matsuda-group, over the years, Matsuda had developed quite a reputation in San'ya, not only with other workers and the yakuza but with the police, for whom he did the occasional favor by resolving disputes. Matsuda was engaged in the decontamination of radiation in Fukushima Prefecture, among other semilegal, questionable pursuits, and he made a practice of slashing his worker's wages by a more than unfair amount.

Nē-san: Takeda-san's partner, whom everyone called "Nē-san" (lit., "older sister"), as one does in the yakuza world to refer to the caretaking partner of a senior male figure, during get-togethers at Takeda-san and Nē-san's apartment, Nē-san would sit in *seiza* (knees bent underneath her) in the tiny bedroom adjacent to the living room, occasionally making food, adding it to a table already decked out with all kinds of dishes, drinks, and ashtrays. She would overturn this image of docility with a sarcastic, quick-witted humor that knew nothing of decency.

Rikiishi: Nicknamed the "gorilla" (*gorira*) on account of his tremendous upper body, swelling forearms, and hands with stubbly fingers the size of salt shakers, Rikiishi was bodyguard, junior, and underling to the lean and elegant Takeda-san. Once Rikiishi was set off in a fight, there was no stopping him, but by this same token, Rikiishi could be counted on to come to one's aid, unlike anyone else.

Saruma: The salaryman-gone-insolvent cousin of Suzuki and Kentarō, unversed in the ways of San'ya, this former businessman and company boss's insistent manners did "not agree with" San'ya. Much as Saruma complained with good intentions, his voice assumed a self-righteous tone that did not sit well with many.

Shōkawa: A veteran ironworker, former member of the Japan Self-Defense Forces, and Kentarō's closest drinking buddy, Shōkawa had the strongest Miyakojima accent in the group. After mourning his mother's death, Shōkawa turned to gambling illegally on boats and was arrested. Less than a year later, Shōkawa was back in detention, having embroiled Akira in a fight against an adversary who would not drop suit.

Suzuki: A relative newcomer to San'ya, Suzuki had come to occupy the position of a street-level labor broker (tehaishi) through his affiliation with his older brother, Kentarō, who had worked in San'ya for decades. An inveterate drinker, successful womanizer, and braggart who spoke of how he had become "famous in this town" after rumors spread of his prowess at fighting, Suzuki had a genuinely kind side. Until his demise, he acted as broker for the group of workers known as the Okinawa-gang.

Takeda-san: Eminently graceful, self-effacing, and humble, Takeda-san occupied the place of authority and hospitality in San'ya. His personage had assumed mythical proportions in the district, both on account of his past in the upper echelons of the Fukuoka yakuza and because of his three missing fingers, which had been severed five times to take the blame for those below him. (Yakuza members often cut their fingers to compensate for infractions committed against the organization's rules.) Together with his partner, Nē-san, Takeda-san welcomed all and sundry home for endless meals and drinking.

Yamamori: A man who shows that he has been in the yakuza for years by allowing his traditional, elbow-length tattoos to emerge from below the sleeves of his shirt, Yamamori was an incorrigible gambler, oftentimes driven by meth, always upping the stakes, and a bad boy of intimidation and vulgar ostentation. The arrogance and threatening display of yakuza affiliation that Yamamori took such pleasure in enacting was precisely the kind of behavior that could land him in serious trouble with other prominent figures in San'ya, like Rikiishi or Kentarō.

abure teate (**or just** *abure*): A reference to the "out-of-work aid" or "unemployment pay" system that was designed specifically for old day-laborer districts, both to sustain the livelihood of laborers and to sustain them as an available pool of laborers. Thus, laborers had to work in order to receive this out-of-work aid, and workers approved by the ward were given a "pocket notebook" (*techō*) in which to receive stamps from their employers as proof of having worked.

ana hori: Digging holes.

ana o akeru: Literally "to open a hole" in the number of workers requested at a construction site, meaning that the crew will be one man down.

aniki: Usually simply means "older brother," but in the context of San'ya, *aniki* was also used to refer to someone senior to oneself—a caretaking figure to whom one was indebted, perhaps within the same organization. In a mobster context, it was common practice to become "sworn brothers" (*kyōdaibun*) with a senior figure within the organization, and this person was referred to as an *aniki*.

asa ichi: Literally the "morning market" of San'ya, also known as the "thieves' market" (*dorobō ichi*) because many of the objects on sale were said to have been stolen and because its stalls did not have permission from the city to operate. Stall owners therefore paid a fee to the local yakuza organization, the Kanamachi-ikka, which presumably handled the extralegal aspects of the market.

baken: Called a "gambling ticket" in English, meaning the ticket you purchase at a gambling hall to claim your winnings.

bentōya: Usually a simple counter opening onto the street or Iroha arcade, where Japanese-style lunchboxes (*bentō*) and rice balls could be purchased. Depending on the price, such lunchboxes would include rice with pickles, a stir-fry with vegetables and meat, deep-fried chicken, and some kind of salad. The rice balls were likewise flavored with fillings, be it of cod roe, dried kelp, dried bonito, salmon, or Japanese plum.

Buraku: A minority group of descendants from the outcaste group within the premodern, feudal order of Japan. As Joseph D. Hankins observes, discrimination against Buraku is now associated with specific neighborhoods, but I will nevertheless defer to the self-identification provided by the International Movement against All Forms of Discrimination and Racism (IMADR): "Buraku people are a Japanese social minority group, ethnically and linguistically indistinguishable from other Japanese people. They face discrimination in Japan because of an association with work once considered impure, such as butchering animals or tanning leather. In particular, they often have trouble finding marriage partners or employment" (cited in Hankins, *Working Skin*, 34).

Chinchirorin: Also known as Cee-lo in the United States, this is a simple dice game that requires dice and a bowl.

daiku: Carpenter.

dokata: Manual laborers at construction sites whose primary task consists in helping to excavate the foundation of buildings. It is therefore no coincidence that the Japanese ideograms for *dokata* contain the ideogram for "earth" or "soil" (*tsuchi*) and that a dictionary search for *dokata kotoba* (*dokata* language) will turn up "bad language" or "low language." In fact, the very word *dokata* carries pejorative connotations, and for this reason, I have translated it into the nineteenth-century English word "navvy." Like *dokata*, navvy does not merely invoke the literally lowest, most basic, menial, and brute form of labor but also a specific type of uncouth and unruly character.

Don-Don: A flower card game in which the stakes are raised by "bluffing" (*hattari*) other players.

dogeza: To prostrate oneself, or to kneel down and bow to the point of touching one's head to the ground.

dōkyūsei: Literally "classmates," but more commonly used to express social intimacy by referring to the fact that one is the same age as another man.

doya: Bunkhouses expressly built to house the day laborers of San'ya, many of which have been transformed into tourist hotels. With the exception of huge institutions like the Palace Hotel, which could house hundreds of laborers, the *doya* is usually two stories tall, oftentimes made out of wood or plain concrete, with a single corridor running along each floor. No larger than 1.5 by 2.5 meters, single rooms flank each side of the corridor, separated by thin wooden walls. Each is equipped with a mini-TV and air-conditioner. Toilets and a common bathing area are shared among residents, who must observe designated bathing hours. Depending on the *doya*, there may also be a gas stove available, but residents must pay for every minute of use. Electrical sockets are most often blocked, as residents are not allowed to use electrical appliances. So too, many old *doya* have a curfew. The daily price of a room ranges ¥1,800–3,000 ($18–30), the monthly total of which often exceeds rent for a reasonable apartment. But residents on welfare must have permission from their ward to relocate to an apartment, and individuals who work must have guarantors and be ready to deposit approximately four times the monthly rent (as real estate agents ask) to move into an apartment.

doyagai: The backstreets of San'ya, lined with *doya* and bicycles.

enka: While invoking traditional Japanese instrumentation, *enka* songs or ballads usually adopt a sentimental, nostalgic, or wistful theme and tone. Their place in Japanese society has often been compared to that of American country music.

Eta: Another term for the Buraku minority, the ideograms for which include *kegare*, meaning "impurity," "uncleanness," or "defilement."

geta: Traditional Japanese footwear, wooden and heavy like clogs but held fast like flip-flops.

giri-ninjō: One of those Japanese terms that (like *haji*) are said to resist translation and, in so doing, secure the inscrutability to outsiders of "Japanese culture." The term consists in a combination of *giri* and *ninjō*, the former of which translates loosely as the sentiment of "duty" or "obligation," and the latter as the "human feeling" or "human sympathy" that resides in the sentiment of wishing to do good by someone else.

gyōza: Pan-fried dumplings.

haji: A term that would secure the inscrutability of "Japanese culture," it is not surprising that *haji* was first interpreted through the eyes of an American anthropologist, Ruth

Benedict. Although the term has also emerged as a point of identification for Japanese culture more generally (albeit *haji* carries anachronistic connotations and is generally not used outside specific circles, be they right-wing or traditionalist), in San'ya, *haji* was described in virtually the same terms that Benedict used to explicate the normative force of shame among "the Japanese": "A failure to follow their explicit signposts of good behavior, a failure to balance obligations or to foresee contingencies is a shame (*haji*). Shame, they say, is the root of virtue. A man who is sensitive to it will carry out all the rules of good behavior. 'A man who knows shame' is sometimes translated as 'virtuous man,' sometimes 'man of honor'" (Benedict, *Chrysanthemum and the Sword*, 224).

hanafuda: Literally translates as "flower cards." Unlike the Western card deck, the flower card deck is composed of twelve suits of four, making a total of forty-eight cards. Each suit is represented by a traditional drawing of a flower or leaf that is known to sprout in a specific month of the year, which gives that card its value. Hence, cherry blossoms (*sakura*) signify March and "3," while pine (*matsu*) signifies January and "1." There are no number indications on the cards, save for the images, and the complexity of the deck allows for an array of games because some cards in specific suits are further marked with a red ribbon, a poetry ribbon, a purple ribbon, and animals—a crane, a bush warbler, a cuckoo, butterflies, a boar, geese, a deer, a swallow, and a Chinese phoenix—which can be combined. Then, of course, there is also the so-called Rainman (*Ono no Michikaze*) card, the Chrysanthemum Poetry Cup (*Kiku no Sakazuki*) card, and so on.

harakiri: Literally to "cut the stomach," meaning suicide by disembowelment.

Hinin: Another term for the Buraku minority, the ideograms of which translate as "nonhuman."

hiyatoi rōdōsha (**or simply** *hiyatoi*): A day laborer.

hiyayakko: Chilled tofu with ginger, bonito flakes, and scallion toppings, usually consumed as a starter or side dish accompanying drinks.

itai-itai byō: As it is also called in English, the itai-itai disease, or "it-hurts it-hurts disease," was discovered and named in early twentieth-century Toyama Prefecture, where cadmium poisoning had caused individuals to experience constant pain. As it turned out, Mitsui Mining and Smelting Co. had been releasing the chemical into a river that proceeded to poison local water and food.

jidaigeki: Historical drama, usually tacking back to the Edo period (1600–1868).

kado o otosu: To "take off the corners" or "edges"; in this case, a phrase that is used with reference to the ritual act of an individual eating the corners of a piece of tofu after their release from jail, so as to prepare for life in society.

kaki no tane: A snack composed of soy-flavored rice crisps and peanuts.

Kanamachi-ikka: The local yakuza organization in San'ya, which was a subsidiary of the famous Yamaguchi-gumi.

kashira: Mobster terminology for the head or lieutenant of a crew. In San'ya, the use of the term was rather loose and could invoke a range of seniority levels, from top to bottom.

keiba: Literally "horse racing," but more specifically, gambling on horse races.

keirin: Literally "bicycle racing," but more specifically, gambling on bicycle races.

kiritori: Yakuza terminology for extortion or intervening to ensure that a debt is returned.

Koi-Koi: A flower card game in which the winner can raise the stakes by challenging the losing party to another round. Hence, the name of the game literally translates as "Come on, Come on."

konkuri: Concrete work at the construction site, which either entailed filling walls or floors with concrete.

konjō: Courage, spirit, guts, staying power, or grit.

koseki: Criticized for providing the grounds for discrimination by preserving such information as Buraku background or parental marriage status, *koseki* refers to the state-endorsed family registry dating from premodern Japan.

kumade: A rake, but in this case a ritual rake purchased at the nearby Ōtori Shrine, decorated with colorful figures, animals, writings, golden coins, or traditional ropes. Inscribed with the name of the business establishment in which it was hung, this ritual rake was meant to rake in good fortune.

kyōdaibun: Buddies, mates, or, in this case, "sworn brothers," insofar as this term invoked the formal relationship established with someone inside a yakuza organization or between individual members tasked to look out for one another. Supposedly, this relationship was rendered official through the ritual act of making an incision in the forearms, joining these bleeding wounds by crossing arms, and drinking a glass of sake thus. Sworn brothers were expected to protect each other with their lives.

kyōtei: Literally "boat racing," but more specifically, gambling on boat races.

māku kādo: Called a "betting card" in English, meaning the card that you fill out at a gambling hall to purchase a gambling ticket. *Māku kādo* literally translates as "mark card."

mama-chari: A combination of *mama*, or "mom," and "*chari*," which is slang for "bicycle," thus, a *mama-chari*, or "mom-bike." Designed for practical purposes, the *mama-chari* is not exactly an aesthetically pleasing means of transportation, but with a low middle bar, a wide seat, a basket, and handles that bend back towards the arms, it is easily ridden.

mama-san: Usually an older female caretaker, manager, or perhaps even proprietor of an eating and drinking establishment or of a *doya* (bunkhouse).

matsu: Pine, but in this case, the pine card in the flower card deck, which signifies January or the value of "1," also referred to as *pin*, as in the *pin* or slice that is skimmed in the tehaishi's *pinhane* (finder's fee).

mizuwari: Shochu mixed with water and ice. Unless one was ordering a bottle or had one on hold, in which case the bottle was brought along with a bucket of ice and water, this was all that needed to be said to order a glass of house shochu mixed with water and ice. The other option was to have it with tea and ice or simply ice, if the shochu was good quality, but it was never consumed neat.

muenbochi: A so-called potter's field or, in this case, shrine where the ashes of the departed are gathered. *Muen* translates as "without connections," and *bochi* means "graveyard" or "cemetery."

mujin kō: Also known as a *tanomoshikō*, a rotating savings and credit association (ROSCA), or a pooling club, which, in this case, takes the specific form of once-per-month gatherings in which members contribute ¥10,000 ($100) toward a sum that one individual takes home. It ideally consists of twelve members so that meetings continue for twelve months and one person pockets ¥120,000 on each occasion. Notably, the *mujin kō* has premodern origins and has been considered a form of gambling because in some of its iterations, the lucky individual to take the pot home was decided by a draw. But the *mujin*, which literally translates as "inexhaustible," has also functioned as a financial aid for the poor—everyone contributes a little—or as a bank for those without credit. Moreover, as an underground institution, the *mujin* has historically been subject to regulation by the Japanese state and the Ministry of Finance.

nakama: Although *nakama* may be translated variously as "companions," "colleagues," "comrades," or "fellows," I translate *nakama* as "buddies" because "buddies" conveys a casual, loose character of social intimacy without invoking the cold formality of a "friend" (*tomodachi*). Of course, buddies were first and foremost drinking buddies; however, the term was also used to signal inclusion and exclusion, such that someone might note of an absent other that "he is a buddy" (*nakama da*) or, if they had had a falling out, that "he is not a buddy" (*nakama jya nai*), even if they were drinking together as part of the larger group. There were also times when individuals were shunned by the group or, rather, by "everyone" (*minna*), and at such times, it would be apt to translate *nakama* as "group," such that these individuals were "excluded from the group" (*nakama hazure*). In short, there was the buddy, and there were buddies, each of which referenced the social entity of the group but could be used variously to signal personal intimacy and trust or inclusion within the group at large. It was the *social* character of the group that was at stake in the use of this word: if someone was a buddy, he was one of us. But there was one exception to this terminology of exclusivity, and that was in death. Whether or not someone had been a buddy in life, when they died, they were reincorporated into the fold of the social, as a buddy (*nakama*).

naichi: Literally the "mainland" or "interior" as people in Okinawa refer to the four main Japanese islands of Honshu, Kyushu, Hokkaido, and Shikoku.

negiri: Excavating the foundations of a building block, meaning that a hole had to be dug by hand and excavators.

Nē-san: Literally means "older sister," but this term also draws upon the world of the yakuza and specifically references the caretaking figure and companion to a senior man in a place of authority.

Obon: Buddhist festival of ancestors held across Japan during three days in mid-August, celebrated with traditional dances, outdoor food stalls (*tekiya*), and such.

omikoshi: A portable shrine that is carried about town during such festivals as *Obon*.

on: Like *giri*, the sentiment of "duty" or "obligation" to return that which was given or done for oneself—hence, the phrase *on gaeshi*, which translates literally as "to return the debt" or "favor."

Oicho-Kabu: Similar to baccarat, this was a game that was played with flower cards in San'ya, in which the aim was to reach a total card value of nine. *Oicho* means "eight," while *kabu* means "nine."

osechi ryōri: Traditional foods eaten only during the New Year holiday. They consist of a variety of *osechi*, or small dishes, served in partitioned, *bentō*-like boxes, stacked one on top of the other.

otoko: Literally translated as "man." But in the context of San'ya, the word had assumed the force of a trope that referenced an older world of virtues among the downtrodden. An otoko, thus, was someone who upheld his obligations to others—who had a sensibility of *giri-ninjō*—and sacrificed himself for others rather than pursue his self-interest, as capitalist society would have us do. What allowed him to do so, moreover, was that he possessed a poignant sensibility for failure or for the shame—*haji*—entailed in letting others down. Self-reliant to the point of extremity, an otoko upheld his virtues and did not burden others, but he was also given to moments of weakness and sentimentality, and this was why it was important for him to sing the occasional *enka* song.

otsumami: Snacks to nibble on, usually with drinks.

pinhane: The "finder's fee" charged by the tehaishi, although it would perhaps be more correct to describe this extraction as the surplus value or excess obtained by skimming off someone else's labor and wages, usually at an unfair percentage. Though the signification of the term applies just as well to the state (consider taxes) and capitalism at large, *pinhane* is associated with sordid labor practices of corrupt companies or the mobster underworld. In gambling terminology, *pin* might refer to "1," and thus to a fraction or slice, and *hane* derives from the verb *haneru*, which, in this instance, means "to skim off."

pūtarō: An unemployed person, vagabond, floater, drifter, vagrant, or day laborer.

sakura: A decoy or simply someone who was undercover, be it a representative of the ward to spy on the activities of welfare recipients or a cop.

seiza: Formal sitting position in which you kneel and sit, such that your butt is resting on the soles of your feet.

sentō: Unlike an *onsen*, the *sentō* or local downtown bathhouse is an inexpensive and informal affair. They usually cost no more than ¥500, and the ward office distributes discount coupons to those on welfare, which can also be purchased at the morning market. The bathhouses themselves usually include baths of various kinds, be it at different temperatures, a jacuzzi-like area, or an electric bath (*denkiburo*). If their patrons are lucky, there may also be a sauna, a cold bath, and an outdoor bathing area. The locals who frequent these bathhouses know each other, converse, and gossip, and many of them have no choice but to frequent these institutions, because they have no shower or bath at home.

shabu (or formally, *kakuseizai*): Methamphetamines or meth, which was consumed by injection in San'ya, meaning that the high was more intense and that its consumers kept a kit hidden in their rooms.

shatei: Mobster lingo for an "underling" or "younger brother" within the same organization.

shussho: Release from jail.

sōpurando (or simply *sōpu*): A soapland, soap, or brothel, so called because the services provided at these brothels include a full-body wash with soap, after which intercourse takes place. Whether or not protection is required depends on the institution or on a negotiation that may take place with the prostitute herself.

suji o tōsu: To see things through to completion.

Sumiyoshi-kai: An adversary of the main yakuza organization in Japan, the Yamaguchi-gumi, the Sumiyoshi-kai is primarily located in the Kanto region of Tokyo.

takidashi: Food handouts, or more literally, the distribution of something that has been boiled or cooked, such as rice.

takobeya: Literally translated as an "octopus-room." Although the precise etymology of *takobeya* is not clear, the term derives historically from the inhuman conditions under which laborers were caught, like octopi perhaps, and sent to work on the far northern borders of Japan, in Hokkaido, as forced laborers. Dating back to the 1880s, the term is associated with early modernity, colonialism, and the forced labor of Koreans. But in San'ya, it referred to the conditions of virtual confinement in which individuals were made to work off their debt to the mob, while they were crammed like octopi into a single room, for which they also paid. Notably, there were numerous shady schemes operating in the underground world of San'ya and homeless people, who would be enticed to get off the streets by moving into a dormitory, which would be located in the hinterlands of Japan and was designed to divest them of their welfare funds.

tehaishi: The street-level labor broker of day laborers. The noun *tehai* refers to the daily work of brokering so that one might ask of a tehaishi: "Have you finished *tehai*?" (*tehai owatta?*). The ideograms used to write *tehai* combine "hand" (*te*) with "to distribute" (*kubaru*), suggesting the distribution of hands or labor.

tekiya: Outdoor, portable food stalls that set up shop for festivals and such, associated of old with the lower classes, the Buraku people, itinerancy, and the mob.

tekkinya: Ironworker.

tobi: Scaffolder. At the time of writing, there were hardly any hierarchical distinctions between men of different professions in San'ya, but Ōyama Shirō writes as follows of scaffolders back in the day: "Tobi are the aristocrats of San'ya. In the same way that it is possible, in Europe, to distinguish the aristocracy from the common folk by how they look, so it is possible to distinguish tobi from common day laborers by their appearance (their faces more than their physique). The training required to nurture their skills to a level worthy of their calling and the confidence gained through having those skills recognized by their peers give them a commanding presence and bestow on their countenance a certain poise. All in all they cut a very dashing figure. There is a certain crispness about their movements and indeed about their entire demeanor. I would imagine that their individual abilities vary considerably, but the best have a truly unmistakable aura about them. One can tell at a glance: yes, this man, without question, is a tobi.... Here, the word *shokunin*—skilled worker—means only one thing, and that is tobi" (Oyama, *Man with No Talents*, 61).

tobi no temoto: To work at the side or base of scaffolders, who formed a string of laborers up the side of a building, or more literally, "at the scaffolder's hand."

tonko suru: To skip or flake on work, thereby "opening a hole" (*ana o akeru*) in the number of workers requested.

toppamono: A "devil-may-care type" of character.

tori no agemono: Deep-fried chicken.

toshikoshi soba: Literally "year-crossing soba" or "seeing-the-old-year-out soba," referring to the traditional buckwheat noodles eaten on New Year's Eve.

yakitori: Grilled skewers of chicken, meats, or veggies.

yakizakana: Fried fish, usually flavored with salt or soy.

yakusha: Actor.

"Yama": Derives from an alternative reading of the ideograms that compose San'ya. The ideogram for "San" (mountain) can be read as "ya," while the ideogram for "-ya" (valley) can be read as "ma," to create "Yama." As "Yama," San'ya takes on a local connotation: a city of mountains and valleys, or of highs and lows.

Yamaguchi-gumi: The main yakuza organization in Japan, with origins on the docks of Kobe.

yoseba: A gathering place for day laborers, like San'ya. The word consists of a combination of the ideograms meaning "to set aside" (*yoseru*) and "place" (*ba*). In this way, it signifies a place where an excess of workers has been set aside.

yosōya: The street tipster who sells predictions for upcoming horse races, face down on pieces of paper spread across a table. Successful predictions are turned up when their races conclude.

Notes

INTRODUCTION

1. Japan officially handed Okinawa over to US control under the 1952 Treaty of San Francisco, only to be returned in 1972. The islands of Okinawa, however, continue to be overrun by US military bases (a concession that the Japanese government granted the United States as a condition of Okinawa's reversion, thereby betraying the people of Okinawa). For a critical take on this history and its implications for the present, see Nelson, *Dancing with the Dead*. While it was no coincidence that I encountered men from Okinawa in San'ya, it should be emphasized that theirs was by no means the predominant demographic in San'ya. I return briefly to the history of Okinawa as a site of capitalist, imperialist, and military expropriation in the epilogue.

2. It should be stated off the bat that the aim of this introduction and book is not to provide a historical or sociological account of San'ya but, rather, to give life to a contingent moment as it was lived by a number of individual men in the area. For English readers seeking a standard introduction to San'ya as a geographical location with specific landmarks, statistics, and a history that dates back before World War II, see Fowler, *San'ya Blues*; de Bary, "Sanya"; Tessei, "Street Labour Markets"; or Gill, "Sanya Street Life." For up-to-date Japanese sources on the area, see the annual "Jigyō Annai" (Summary of Activities) published by San'ya's Jōhoku Welfare Center or the annual report of the *Japan Association for the Study of* Yoseba (Nihon Yoseba Gakkai), though the latter ceased its publications in 2013. Publications on San'ya have notably diminished because the district has been in decline since Japan's economic bubble burst in 1991 and Fowler's "Suggested Readings" in *San'ya Blues* remains the most comprehensive list of writings on San'ya.

3. According to San'ya's Jōhoku Welfare Center's annual "Summary of Activities" (Jigyō Annai), San'ya's population of day laborers experienced its peak in 1963, when 15,000 men resided in its bunkhouses. By 1995, four years after Japan's economic bubble burst, there were only 6,123 men living in San'ya's bunkhouses, and in 2012, there were 4,765. While most men in San'ya's bunkhouses were actively working as day laborers in 1963, that is, during Japan's two decades of high economic growth (mid-1950s–mid-1970s), and thereafter, during Japan's bubble economy (which burst in 1991), by 2012, 87.1 percent of the men living in San'ya's bunkhouses were considered to be on welfare, and their average age was estimated at 64.7. I should add that a considerable number of the men living in San'ya's bunkhouses in 2012 were not and had not been day laborers and that the 4,765 men living in San'ya's bunkhouses in 2012 only composed a fraction of the 37,000 residents living in the area, which would include shop owners, white-collar workers, and any number of individuals and families who were not associated with day laborers. Jōhoku Welfare Center, "Jigyō Annai: Heisei 28."

4. Until 1991, when Japan's economic bubble burst, San'ya's population was regularly replenished through dislocations caused by the pursuit of economic growth. After 1945, the drive to industrialize caused farmers to lose their livelihoods and their breadwinners to go to San'ya. In the 1950s, the switch from domestic coal to foreign oil forced miners to go to San'ya. By the 1960s, when Japan's "miraculous" recovery from World War II was touted as a model for the world, men in San'ya had already paid the price of economic restructuring, and they would go on to build the infrastructure of Japan's crowning postwar

achievement—the 1964 Olympics—not to mention highways, subways, and Tokyo itself. So too, men moved to San'ya after the 1973 Oil Shock, which tanked Japan's shipbuilding industry, and again, in the 1980s, after metal industries moved production abroad. Acting as both an absorbing buffer against economic hardships and dispensable labor force, the *yoseba* was therefore instrumental to Japan's postwar period of high growth (1950s–1970s). During the 1980s, it underpinned the stability of middle-class "Japanese society," legendary today for its social securities and life-time employment system. I draw here on Fowler, *San'ya Blues*.

5. It is difficult to translate the sheer range of eating and drinking establishments that the men in San'ya frequented, and I therefore take some liberty in calling the more sordid establishments dive bars, or quite simply, dives, because these were truly seedy establishments where cheap drinks could be had, in addition to an array of (often insalubrious) dishes. Sometimes, there was a mouse inhabiting these dives (he or she had acquired a nickname), and regulars virtually lived in them during the day, where it was common to find them passed out or singing karaoke for hours on end. A sign on the outside of such dives might simply have categorized them as a "drinking and eating places" (*nomikuidokoro*), for they did not rise to the standards of what I translate as an "eatery" (*izakaya*), where food was served at a higher quality and the drinks were more expensive. While it was generally the case that the men I came to know would spend at least an hour or two at establishments they frequented, true dives were venues where they could literally spend the entirety of their day, drinking, eating, and singing karaoke.

6. San'ya is located north of the old entertainment district of Asakusa and is split between Tokyo's Taitō and Arakawa Wards, where it occupies parts of Kiyokawa, Nihonzutsumi, Hashiba, Higashi Asakusa, and Minami-Senjū. At least, that is how San'ya's Jōhoku Welfare Center continues to depict San'ya on its map of the district. But this is more of a historical representation of how large San'ya used to be, and while one may still get a whiff of the old San'ya while walking down a backstreet of Hashiba in Taitō Ward or Minami-Senjū in Arakawa Ward, it would be more accurate to say that the only place where the old townscape of San'ya can still be encountered is south of Meiji Street, in Kiyokawa and Nihonzutsumi, which is to say that my estimate of a one-kilometer-square area is generous.

7. The masculinity I describe hails from an older, vanishing generation that remains stigmatized in contemporary Japan, and its demographic must be distinguished from the demise of Japan's middle-class society and its masculinity. Patrick Galbraith and David H. Slater make passing reference to such stigmatized "margins," thrust beneath the threshold of public visibility: "Our analysis follows Tom Gill's work on day laborers and Roberson's analysis of blue-collar factory workers, both of which point out the important link between labor and masculinity, and how men's claims to legitimate alternatives are compromised when practiced outside of the corporate context. But our argument that links social class to masculinity . . . is less about compromise at the margins (those who almost never emerge into the popular media) than it is about the collapse of middle-class masculinity." Galbraith and Slater, "Re-Narrating Social Class." On the collapse of Japan's once-lauded middle class, see Allison, *Precarious Japan*.

8. Redolent with the sounds of traditional Japanese instrumentation, enka songs or ballads most frequently adopt a sentimental, nostalgic, or wistful theme and tone. Their place in Japanese society has often been compared to that of American country music. Notably, the careers of many famous enka singers (including those, for instance, of Tsuruta Kōji and Misora Hibari) were helped along by the yakuza. For an account of the performative aspect of enka in terms of gender and nationalism, see Yano, "Burning of Men."

9. Bataille, "Notion of Expenditure," 119.

10. See Miyazaki, *Toppamono*, 207, 216–18. When I invoke the word *sacrifice*, I do so insofar as sacrifice would create sociality, social recognition, and longevity for a group of

individuals consigned to San'ya. Of sacrifice, Hubert and Mauss write: "*This procedure consists in establishing a means of communication between the sacred and the profane worlds through the mediation of a victim, that is, of a thing that in the course of the ceremony is destroyed.* Now contrary to what Smith believed, the victim does not necessarily come to the sacrifice with a religious nature already perfected and clearly defined: it is the sacrifice that confers this upon it. Sacrifice can therefore impart to the victim most varied powers, either by different rites or during the same rite." Hubert and Mauss, *Sacrifice*, 97.

11. For the reader's convenience, I have included a glossary of key characters.

12. It is no coincidence that the classic, preeminent boxing character of Japanese anime hails from San'ya. As Valerie Walkerdine writes of the *Rocky* movies: "The fantasy of the fighter is the fantasy of a working-class male omnipotence over the forces of humiliating oppression which mutilate and break the body in manual labor." Walkerdine, "Video Replay," 173.

13. Marx, *Capital*, 643–54.

14. As Gill observes, "death is a subject of consuming significance to Japanese writers who study the *yoseba*. The short life expectancy mentioned above, and the fact that dead bodies are sometimes found in the street in the *yoseba*, are unavoidable facts of life: hence such books as Aoki Hideo's *Yoseba Rōdōsha no Sei to Shi* (*The Life and Death of the Yoseba Worker*), an academic work that sees the early death of day laborers as the ultimate form of capitalist exploitation, and Funamoto Shuji's collection of militant tracts, *Damatte Notarejinu-na* (*Do Not Be Silent and Die in the Gutter*), a call for day laborers to abandon quietism and take action against capitalist exploiters." Gill, "Wage Hunting," 127.

15. As if poverty and nuclear contamination were new to Japan, however, the discourse of insecurity in millennial and post-Fukushima Japan sidelines the fact that their object of nostalgia—the famous, secure life of the 1980s—was itself grounded in social unevenness, the victims of which are dead or dying untimely deaths. Likewise, nuclear labor has been around in Japan since the 1970s, when the state started its harebrained project of constructing fifty-four nuclear power plants on top of an earthquake fault line. Notwithstanding the overdue attention that the topic of nuclear labor received after Fukushima, this also means that nuclear labor has been around in Japan for a half century, and nuclear workers have long constituted part of the population of old day-laborer districts, where their profession crosses over into other dangerous forms of labor, as neglected as their own had been before Fukushima. In chapter 2, I return momentarily to the question of nuclear labor in San'ya and to its association with the underworld of the yakuza.

16. For an account of Japan's economic transformation into a land of neoliberal insecurity and of the effects that Japan's three decades of recession have had on the general population and, more specifically, on the youth, see, for instance, Amamiya, *Ikisasero!*, Arai, "Killing Kids," Allison, *Precarious Japan*, Genda, *Nagging Sense*, Iwata, *Gendai no Hinkon*, and Yuasa, *Hanhinkon*.

17. Nuclear laborers have been called "nuclear gypsies" (*genpatsu jipusī*) on account of their gypsy-like migration from nuclear plant to plant, in response to the demand for laborers to clean different plants as they shut down under rotating schedules every year. See Horie Kunio's 1979 classic, *Genpatsu Jipusī* (Nuclear Gypsy), as well as Horie and Mizuki Shigeru's 1979 *Fukushima Genpatsu no Yami* (The Darkness of Fukushima Nuclear Plant). For more on nuclear power and labor in Japan, see Hirose Takashi's books, especially *Genshiro Jigen Bakudan* (Nuclear Reactor Time Bomb), in which he predicts the nuclear catastrophe specifically at Fukushima Daiichi Nuclear Power Plant. Not surprisingly, Takashi is no longer dismissed as a writer with science fictional aspirations.

18. See Mutō, *From Fukushima to You*.

19. On the 1964 Olympics, see Edward Fowler's history of San'ya in *San'ya Blues*, 9–52. At the end of the day, there was never any outbreak of COVID-19 in San'ya, although

hospitals that service its residents emerged as hot spots in 2020, and individuals were diagnosed positive. As I describe in chapter 1, it is impossible to practice social distancing in the bunkhouses (*doya*) of San'ya, and during COVID, many of the characters in this book went about their lives, singing karaoke and gambling, as if nothing had changed. Finally, it should be said that unlike the years leading up to the 1964 Olympics, San'ya did not receive an influx of work prior to the 2020 Olympics. Its residents have long been considered too old and unfit for quality work.

20. Tsukuda, *Dakara San'ya ga Yamerarenē*.

21. Fowler, *San'ya Blues*, 14.

22. For an account of this transformation of day-laborer districts into "welfare towns," see Stevens, *Margins of Japanese Society*.

23. Gill concludes his 2001 book on day laborers in the Kotobukichō district of Yokohama as follows: "What we are seeing in Japan is a transformation in the pattern of casual labor: from heavy industry to the service sector, from the middle aged and elderly to the young, from men to women. A new vocabulary accompanies this transition: in place of the *hiyatoi rōdōsha*, or the more derogatory *ankō* or *pūta-rō*, we have the eminently respectable *rinji saiyōsha* (temporary employee), the pleasantly exotic *pāto* (a contraction of "part-timer"), or even the appealingly libertarian-sounding *furiitaa* (a contraction of "free arbeiter"; see p. 193). Recruitment is handled by large, legal companies which nevertheless take just as large a cut of the casual labor wage as the tehaishi standing on the street corner (cf p. 60). The people who do these jobs do not gather anywhere: they get their employment through the rapidly proliferating employment magazines, from the pages of sports newspapers, and even in some cases through the Internet." Gill, *Men of Uncertainty*, 198.

24. Derrida, "Rhetoric of Drugs."

25. Although Alcoholics Anonymous entered Japan in 1976 and has since produced local offshoots, like DARC (Drug Addiction Rehabilitation Center) or Danshukai (Alcohol Abstinence Society), the discourse of alcohol addiction was largely absent within San'ya itself. I myself only encountered it from physicians, psychologists, and Western college students who had come to volunteer in the district. For more on the discourse of alcoholism in Japan and its gendered configurations, see Borovoy, *Too-Good Wife*.

26. In this respect, Derrida writes: "It is the making proper of the proper itself (*propriation du propre même*), in as much as the proper is opposed to the heterogeneity of the im-proper, and to every mode of foreignness or alienation that might be recognized in someone's resorting to drugs." Derrida, "Rhetoric of Drugs," 241. For a similar elaboration of purity in relation to the contaminating effects of that which is considered dangerous, see Douglas, *Purity and Danger*.

27. See Derrida, "Restricted to General Economy," and chap. 3.

28. I draw here on poststructuralist texts that explore how a constitutive excess attends signification as its condition of possibility and, therefore, of impossibility, triggering repetition. See Derrida, "Signature Event Context," and Siegel, *Naming the Witch*. Siegel in particular focuses on historical conditions that trigger violence and repetition.

29. In San'ya, the discourse of the skilled construction worker echoed a discourse that Dorinne Kondo's has described as that of traditional artisans in the *shitamachi* (low-city) district of Tokyo. As in its association with a discourse of "shame" (*haji*), here the masculinity of day laborers in San'ya occupies the place of a postwar legacy rapidly heading for extinction. Kondo unpacks the mythology of the Japanese "artisan" (*shokunin*) in *Crafting Selves*. Offering some history, Kondo writes: "The industrialization of the Meiji period saw segments of the artisanal population becoming *shokkō*, factory operatives, rather than artisans. The status of these operatives slipped well below that of the merchant, and factory workers generally were considered part of lower-class society (cf. e.g., Gordon 1985; T. C.

Smith 1988). These parameters have changed in the postwar period; for the people I knew, the more salient divisions . . . are between *shokunin*, artisan, and *shain*, company employee. . . . In the ward of Tokyo where my informants lived, the term *shokunin* was used for virtually anyone who worked with his hands, even for people who seemed to be doing assembly-line work. Lathe operators, people who operated metal presses, painters of metal parts, makers of industrial-strength soap, as well as the makers of more obviously 'traditional' handicrafts, all considered themselves *shokunin*. And although middle-class executives are accorded a certain dominant social prestige, *shokunin* had their own special place as the bearers of a unique Japanese 'tradition.'" Kondo, *Crafting Selves*, 234–35.

30. Lest the colonial legacies of Okinawa be forgotten, I cite from Steve Rabson: "Interviewed in July 1999, a man who had migrated to Osaka in the mid-1960s said he had trouble at first because he was ashamed of his Okinawan accent. He explained that many newcomers from Okinawa were reluctant to express themselves because they remembered how, at school in Okinawa, they were made to wear wooden 'dialect tags' as a punishment if they happened to utter a word in an Okinawan dialect." Rabson, *Okinawan Diaspora*, 190.

31. On this note, I make little reference to *Precarious Japan* or Gill's writings on gambling in Kotobukichō. My reason is simple: neither Allison's nor Gill's work is grounded in a thorough engagement with the people they write about. As Gill himself professes, he never accompanied day laborers to their workplace. As for Anne Allison, *Precarious Japan* accords all due respect to contemporary theorizations of precarity and representatives of nonprofits in Japan, but there is no engagement with the so-called precariat beyond interviews (conducted at nonprofits—red flag) and interludes in which friends comment on the state of Japanese society. Suzuki Takayuki deserves honorable mention as someone who lived the life he represents, as a documentary producer. My point here is not about theory. Get to know the people you write about, and get to know them beyond formalized contexts between social scientist and subject. Both Allison and Gill have deep pockets, as tenured professors. So why no real effort? The answer, perhaps, resides in the violence that social scientists commit in order to abstract, theorize, and establish their reputation. Jacques Rancière has offered a scathing critique of such violence as a strategy of writing, with specific reference to Marx's representation of the so-called "lumpenproletariat." Lump it all together—*Precarious Japan*—imbue your writing with pathos, enclose your subjects in negativity, and repeat what "can be counted among the master logics of modernity: exclusion by homage." Rancière, *Philosopher and His Poor*, xxvi.

32. João Biehl puts it nicely: "A human form of life that is no longer worth living is not just bare life—language and desire continue." Biehl, *Vita*, 318.

33. Of the form of language and its relation to secondary elaborations of subjectivity, Lacan observes: "In the sense that it will also be the rootstock of secondary identifications . . . this form situates the agency known as the ego, prior to its social determination, in a fictional direction that will forever remain irreducible for any single individual or, rather, that will only asymptotically approach the subject's becoming, no matter how successful the dialectical syntheses by which he must resolve, as *I*, his discordance with his own reality." Lacan, "Mirror Stage," 76. For a psychoanalytic elaboration of the abjection I refer to, see Kristeva, *Powers of Horror*. Please note that all italicized quotations in this book are italics in the original.

34. Insofar as the state exercised the power of death over its subjects, I draw here on Hegel's master-slave dialectic and Alexandre Kojève's *Introduction to the Reading of Hegel*.

35. See Pine, *Art of Making Do*; Bourgois, *In Search of Respect*; and Liebow, *Tally's Corner*.

36. Starting with Ron P. Dore's classic, *City Life in Japan*, see Bestor, *Neighborhood Tokyo*; and Seidensticker, *Low City, High City*. On gender and labor, see Kondo, *Crafting*

Selves; Allison, *Nightwork*; or Roberson and Suzuki, *Men and Masculinities*. As these texts elucidate, one should be aware of the internal differences that compose masculinities in Japan today. Yet one should also note that, while San'ya has been thrust beneath the threshold of public visibility, the face-to-face sociality found in San'ya is one that has grown increasingly scarce in society at large. Galbraith and Slater write: "Nakane Chie and Ezra Vogel both show ways in which Japan, Inc. was productive of a very particular masculinity structured around economic and social connections that required personal sacrifice to corporate goals and co-workers, and willingness to share collective responsibility. In today's media . . . we encounter these narratives once again, but mostly in their absence: they represent a closeness and connection that especially younger men cannot achieve, and an absence of anything to sacrifice to or for." Galbraith and Slater, "Re-Narrating Social Class."

37. See, for instance, Siegel, *Naming the Witch*; or Morris, *Returns of Fetishism*.

38. I am thinking here of Kathleen M. Millar, who writes of "how life becomes livable through forms of labor commonly defined in terms of redundancy, abandonment, or exhaust" in *Reclaiming the Discarded*; Clara Han, who considers questions of everyday care and sociality under neoliberalism in *Life in Debt*; or Andrea Muehlebach, who addresses neoliberal markets, affect, and ethics in *The Moral Neoliberal*.

39. Spanning from 1945 to 1991, Japan's recovery from World War II and its period of economic high growth have been referred to as the "Japanese economic miracle."

40. By addressing the creative aspects of gambling, I move beyond Malaby's observation that gambling can crystallize "chanceful life into a seemingly more apprehensible form." Malaby, *Gambling Life*, 147. What this book attempts to shows is how gambling—as metaphor and trope—can be mobilized to transform a merely "chanceful life," grounding personhood in experience, time, and mutual recognition. Notably, Clifford Geertz's famous essay on gambling focuses precisely on the Balinese cockfight in terms of social status. Geertz, "Deep Play."

41. See Benjamin, "On Some Motifs," and chap. 3.

42. Grounded in my exposition of manual labor at the construction site, I present an alternative here to theorizations of gambling that have considered its deadening effects, particularly in relation to labor in the service industry, time, and experience. See chap. 3 and Schüll, *Addiction by Design*.

43. See chap. 4 and Spivak, *Can the Subaltern Speak?*

44. See the epilogue and Stryker, "My Words to Victor Frankenstein."

45. Here, I follow the postulate of performance theory that, rather than constituting a preestablished essence or identity, the intelligibility of gender is discursively and performatively created, determining the place of sex, in turn. See Butler, *Gender Trouble*; and, for the discursive constitution of sex as an identifiable difference, Foucault, *Herculine Barbin*. On the influence of performance theory within anthropology, see Morris, "All Made Up."

46. Miyazaki, *Toppamono*, 21.

47. The mythology that was referenced by the conduct of men in San'ya was a specific one, and insofar as it intersected with representations of the yakuza, this mythology was set in opposition to the conduct of actual contemporary yakuza. That is, real yakuza had become driven by self-interest and had lost touch with the virtues embodied by itinerant, honorable outlaw mobsters. For English sources on this mythology, see Kaplan and Dubro, *Yakuza*, "The Honorable Outlaws"; and Buruma, *Behind the Mask*. For an account of the theatricalization of these and similar virtues in theater for the masses (*taishū engeki*), see Ivy, *Discourses of the Vanishing*, "Theatrical Crossings, Capitalist Dreams."

48. As a response to the AIDS epidemic of the 1980s, this "untitled" work by Wojnarowicz is a photograph of a diorama in Washington, DC, depicting the result of a Native American hunting technique. John Sevigny writes as follows of this image: "The

buffalo is an animal so sacred to Americana that it once graced the tails side of the nickel, and it was going off a Southwestern, Spaghetti Western cliff like a lemming, presumably driven on by hunters who nearly pushed the animal to extinction. The photograph goes far beyond representing the death of the American dream. In a simple image, it captures the forced, borderline-psycho disillusionment felt by anyone left of center during an age in which Right was right and homosexual men died because God himself had descended from the heavens to exact His revenge. This is not Death of a Salesman. This is the photographic equivalent of Allen Ginsberg's Howl, an indictment of a sick nation reeling in riches and hubris even as it feasted on the weakest, cast the mentally ill out into the streets, and blamed death on the dying." Sevigny, "Twenty Years Later." I thank the David Wojnarowicz Estate and PPOW, New York, for permission to reproduce this image.

49. Jean-François Lyotard explicates the future anterior in *The Postmodern Condition*, 81.

50. On this seminal distinction between labor and play, see Caillois, *Man, Play and Games*. On gambling and time as a "narcotic," see Benjamin, "Paris, the Capital."

51. See Stryker, "My Words to Victor Frankenstein"; and Stone, "Empire Strikes Back."

52. For more on homeless people in Japan, particularly regarding the implementation of Japanese state policies in turn-of-the-century Japan, see Gill, "Whose Problem?," 192–210. See also Tokyo City Bureau, "Hōmuresu Taisaku."

53. Benjamin, "Destructive Character," 541.

1. SETTING OUT "YAMA"

1. The name *Yama* derives from an alternative reading of the ideograms that compose San'ya. The ideogram for *San* (mountain) can be read as "Ya," while the ideogram for *ya* (valley) can be read as "ma," to create "Yama." As "Yama," San'ya takes on a local connotation: a city of mountains and valleys, or of highs and lows.

2. Oyama Shiro writes: "Looking back, I can say that the first six-year period, during the bubble era, was a golden age for us day laborers. . . . In those days, it simply wasn't possible to step out of my doya in the morning with the intention of finding work and not come away with a job. Indeed, I'd be hailed by several agents who recruited workers off the street on my way to the main drag around Namidabashi intersection, where most of the recruiting takes place." Oyama, *Man with No Talents*, 17.

3. Writing in 1996, Fowler says: "Because it is not being replenished, the pool of men making a living today as day laborers in San'ya has dwindled considerably and the population is growing old. Whereas half or more were still in their thirties or younger in the 1960s, better than half were over fifty in 1990. More than two-fifths of the day-laborer population have lived in San'ya for at least ten years, and a substantial number have made it their home for decades. Those who migrated from the farms to San'ya in the mid-century are sticking it out in the yoseba rather than returning to the provinces. The increase in average age has brought with it an increase in job-related injuries, illness, and the death rate. Yet signs that San'ya has passed its prime notwithstanding, no one is predicting that the yoseba will disappear completely." Fowler, *San'ya Blues*, 42.

4. Except for institutions like the Palace Hotel, which could house hundreds of laborers, the *doya* is usually two stories tall, with a single corridor running along each floor. No larger than 1.5 by 2.5 meters, single rooms flank each side of the corridor, separated by thin wooden walls. Each is equipped with a mini-TV and air-conditioner. Toilets and a common bathing area are shared among residents, who must observe designated bathing hours. Depending on the *doya*, there may also be a gas stove available, but residents must pay for every minute of usage. Electrical sockets are most often blocked, as residents are not allowed to use electrical appliances. So too, many old *doya* have a curfew. The daily price for a room ranges from ¥1,800 to ¥3,000 ($18–$30), the monthly total of

which often exceeds rent for a reasonable apartment. However, the residents on welfare must have permission from their ward to relocate to an apartment, and those who work must have guarantors and be ready to deposit approximately four times the monthly rent (as Japanese real estate agents ask) to move into an apartment.

5. The doya used to be and ostensibly still are run by the local yakuza. To increase profits in the heyday of San'ya, the use of space was maximized to fit four, if not eight or sixteen, men into the bunk beds of a single room; however, with the disappearance of construction work, most doya have since been converted into single-room occupancy. It should also be noted that as men on welfare got older (or if they were seriously ill), the ward would approve their move from a doya into a proper, albeit small apartment. Yet this came with its own set of inconveniences, because the apartment might be far from San'ya, which entailed isolation and transportation costs, and the apartment might not have a bath or shower. All doya, on the other hand, had set bathing times but frequently also a curfew. Most of the guys were still living in doya during the two years that this ethnography takes place. Notably, Tom Gill has written of a variation on the doya in northern Kyushu (the southernmost of Japan's four main islands), namely, the *ninpudashi*: "The word *ninpu* is a fairly coarse Japanese term for a navvy or manual laborer. *Dashi* derives from the verb *dasu*, to produce, give, or supply something. Hence *ninpudashi* are navvy-suppliers. . . . The *ninpudashi* combine the roles of the *yoseba* (casual labor introductions) and the *doya* (cheap, low-grade accommodation). The owner of the *ninpudashi* supplies the worker with a room, either a small *doya*-like individual room, or a larger room shared with several other workers. Meals will generally be provided, though probably at extra cost. He also supplies the worker with employment, activating a network of contacts to find casual work." Gill, "*Yoseba* and *Ninpudashi*," 130–31.

6. Consider the mass-mediated case of the TV personality Yoshimoto Jun'ichi, whose family was accused of "deceitful receipt" (*fusei jukyū*) of welfare in 2012, on account of his high income. In another mass-mediated instance, the mayor of Osaka, Hashimoto Tōru, argued that city bus drivers should have their pay reduced by 38 percent on account idling. Bus drivers, he argued, spent most of their time taking breaks as they waited for their next scheduled trip and should not be paid for this time. See "Nihonkeizai o Boroboro ni Suru Hitobito." Like the conservative US discourse critical of welfare recipients, such rhetoric forms part of a discourse that bashes the so-called abuse of state funds, although resentment is rarely if ever expressed toward state bureaucrats and politicians who ran the economy into the ground to begin with.

7. Like San'ya, the day-laborer district of Osaka, Nishinariku, is located next to the old red-light district and to a Buraku neighborhood. For a comparison of Nishinariku and San'ya during the 1980s and 1990s, see Oyama, *Man with No Talents*, 2–3.

8. Japan's controversial family registry (*koseki*) system allows the state and lawyers to determine whether an individual is of Buraku ancestry, and lawyers have been known to acquire such information illegally. The term *Buraku*, which translates as "community" or "neighborhood," may also be referred to as *hinin*—translated literally as "nonhuman"—or *eta*. For a consideration of the Buraku minority in contemporary Japan, see Hankins, *Working Skin*. As a carryover from premodern times, discrimination against Buraku originally derives from their association with supposedly unsanitary forms of labor involving animals, leather tanning, or death. Thus, there was a profusion of small-scale shoe factories in Imado, the Buraku neighborhood just south of San'ya. According to Hankins: "Present-day Buraku discrimination is primarily based on whether a person lives in a Buraku neighborhood, or whether her or his parents are from such a neighborhood." Hankins, *Working Skin*, 35. See also Shimazaki, *Broken Commandment*; and Nakagami, *Cape*.

9. This crime rate is notably low in comparison to other countries, but this is also because San'ya has become a welfare town with an average age of sixty-four. Jōhoku Wel-

fare Center, "Jigyō Annai: Heisei 28." In a nation that still lauds itself on its "public safety" (*chian*) and in which murder anywhere makes national headline news, both the proximity of murder (of or by an acquaintance) and the fact that these murders go unreported by the media disclose a structure in which San'ya marks a departure from the norm.

10. In observing that "it has rarely been made clear what their status, what the meaning was of this proximity which seemed to assign the same homeland to the poor, to the unemployed, to prisoners, and to the insane," Michel Foucault identifies an "imperative of labor." Confinement, he writes, "constituted one of the answers the seventeenth century gave to an economic crisis that affected the entire Western world: reduction of wages, unemployment, scarcity of coin." Foucault, *Madness and Civilization*, 39–49. For a list of the economic downturns that led a heterogeneous mass of men to concentrate in San'ya, see Fowler, *San'ya Blues*, 15.

11. I invoke Freud's notion of the uncanny here insofar as the death-inducing expendability of men in San'ya—"human garbage" (*ningen no gomi*), as Akira said—discloses the repressed truth of capitalist Japan and, indeed, of capitalism at large. For Freud's elaboration of the movement from the *heimlich*, or homely, to the *unheimlich*, or uncanny, see Freud, "'Uncanny.'" I specifically consider this repression an effect of the commodity form and what Derrida has called its "visor effect," of whose disruptive ghostliness Derrida writes: "This Thing meanwhile looks at us and sees us not see it even when it is there . . . to feel ourselves seen by a look which it will always be impossible to cross, that is the *visor effect* on the basis of which we inherit from the law." Derrida, *Specters of Marx*, 6–7.

12. Oyama writes of the smell of bodies in San'ya's bunkhouses back in the day: "The aforementioned piercing, organic stench, which materializes in a week to ten days, not only has a limited range but also tends to dissipate once it has attacked the olfactory sense. The 'wafting odor' that kicks in after a month's time, on the other hand, is both pervasive *and* persistent. It never seems to let up." Oyama, *Man with No Talents*, 8.

13. See "Yama" Seisaku Jōei Iinkai, *Yararetara Yarikaese*, 18.

14. I refrain from referring to homeless people as the "homeless." For as Robert Desjarlais has pointed out, the negative and spectral invocation of the "homeless" expresses all sorts of normative and murderous intent: "To describe someone as 'homeless' announces a lasting identity. When used, the adjective is lasting and all-encompassing: journalists and others often speak of a 'homeless' woman or man with the same certitude that they identify someone as a doctor, a politician, or a white man. Homelessness denotes a temporary lack of housing, but connotes a lasting moral career. Because this 'identity' is deemed sufficient and interchangeable, the 'homeless' usually go unnamed. The identification is typically achieved through spectral means: one knows the homeless not by talking to them but by seeing them. . . . Homeless figures are presented negatively, as models to be avoided, and thus as illustrations of the value of other ways of being . . . Lest anyone take these ways of making meaning to be inconsequential, without real force in the world, we need only recall the predictable fate of Mr. Corniel, who was portrayed as a leprous lunatic in the wake of his death at the hands of the police in front of the White House, or read about the man set afire in New York City in the summer of 1995, or consider the 'social cleansings' (*limpieza social*) enacted by vigilantes in Colombia, who have killed hundreds of vagrants, criminals, prostitutes, street children, and drug addicts, also known as 'disposables.' These are metaphors to kill by." Desjarlais, *Shelter Blues*, 2–5.

15. *Hanafuda*, or traditional Japanese playing cards, are designed with flowers or leaves denoting each season. Popular games include Koi-Koi or Oicho-Kabu. See the glossary and chap. 3.

16. Like the severed tip of the pinkie, the scar of a knife wound on the cheek may connote yakuza affiliation. Slashing the cheek or severing the pinkie may be undertaken to compensate for infractions against organizational rules.

17. Unlike "group" (*gurūpu*), the *gumi* of Okinawagumi carries the connotation of gang or mob affiliation. I therefore translate this socially recognized moniker for a loose affiliation of individual men as "Okinawa-gang." In fact, many "members" (*membā*) of the Okinawa-gang objected to being referred to as members, although they clearly constituted a gang of sorts—working, drinking, gambling, and fighting together—in their everyday conduct. When I refer to actual yakuza syndicates, however, such as Yamaguchi-gumi or Sakaume-gumi, I retain their proper names in their entirety. The same goes for the proper name of the local yakuza organization, the Kanamachi-ikka, in which *ikka* might be translated as "clan" or "family," or the Sumiyoshi-kai, in which *kai* might be translated as "association."

18. Although *nakama* may be translated variously as "companions," "colleagues," "comrades," or "fellows," I have chosen to go with "buddies" because it conveys the casual, loose character of social intimacy among the guys, without invoking the distant formality of a "friend" (*tomodachi*). Buddies (*nakama*) were first and foremost drinking buddies, but the term was also used to signal inclusion and exclusion, such that someone might note of an absent other that "he is a buddy" (*nakama da*), or if they had had a falling out, that "he is not a buddy" (*nakama jya nai*), even if they were still drinking together as part of the larger group of guys. As I detail later, there were also times when individuals were shunned by the entire group, or rather, by "everyone" (*minna*), and at such times, it would be apt to translate *nakama* as "group," such that these individuals were "excluded from the group" (*nakama hazure*). In short, there was "the buddy," and there were "buddies," each of which referenced the social entity of the group but could be used variously to signal personal intimacy and trust or inclusion within the group at large. It was the *social* character of the group that was at stake in the use of this word: if someone was a buddy, he was invariably one of us. But there was an exception to this terminology of exclusivity, and that was in death. Whether someone had been a buddy or not in life, when they died, they were reincorporated into the fold of the social, as a buddy (*nakama*).

19. Suffixes to Japanese names function widely to indicate hierarchy or intimacy. Strictly speaking, I should have added -*san* to many of the names in this book, to indicate my subordinate status to the person in question, but in the interest of legibility, I have omitted these suffixes. Among the day laborers in San'ya, such hierarchy was primarily a reflection of age. Men of the same age might refer to one another as *dōkyūsei* (classmates). In such cases, they often eliminated the addition of a suffix to the name, referring to the other simply as Saruma or Kentarō. Even the difference of one year in age could prompt someone to add the suffix -*san* to the name—indicating that so-and-so was of senior status—or -*kun* to show that so-and-so was younger. Yet the addition of suffixes—or, for that matter, the choice of using surnames or first names—was equally a matter of the preference of the individual addressed. Suzuki, who was fifty, preferred to be called Suzu-chan by me, who was twenty years younger than him. By adding the suffix -*chan*—usually reserved for children—a certain familiarity was created between Suzu-chan and myself. Akira, who was Suzuki's senior by five years, simply referred to Suzuki by his first name, without any suffixes. Others, like Wakami—who worked under Suzuki—referred to Suzuki as Suzuki-san (surname plus suffix). Such matters were complicated yet further by the fact that many of the workers I knew employed the suffix -*bō*—like -*chan*—to signal intimacy with younger individuals. Hence, Kentarō, who was Akira's senior by one year, referred to Akira by adding the suffix -*bō* to his first name. Akira, in turn, referred to Kentarō by adding -*san* to his surname, but because there was one week of the year when Akira and Kentarō were of the same age—a week during which Akira referred to Kentarō simply as "Kentarō!"— Akira performed their equality to comic effect for everyone by calling "Kentarō!" into line. No one referred to Takeda-san except as Takeda-*san*. If only because *everyone* I knew ad-

dressed these three individuals with the suffix -*san*, I have retained this suffix for Takeda-san; his partner, Nē-san; and the head of Sanyukai, Guy-san.

20. Lévi-Strauss identifies a problem of segregation in the ternary social structure of the Guana in Paraguay, the Bororo of the Mato Grosso, and the Mbaya Caduveo of Brazil. But while the Guana and Bororo had employed a sociological system of binary moieties (and the social synthesis it would create) to resolve or conceal the contradiction of a ternary system of hierarchical castes, each undoing the social whole by turning in upon itself, the Caduveo had no such system in place. Of the Mbaya Caduveo, Lévi-Strauss writes: "This solution never existed among the Mbaya: either they did not know of it (which is unlikely), or, more probably, it was incompatible with their fanaticism. They therefore never had the opportunity of resolving their contradictions or of at least concealing them by means of artful institutions. But the remedy they failed to use on the social level, or which they refused to consider, could not elude them completely; it continued to haunt them in an insidious way. And since they could not become conscious of it and live it out in reality, they began to dream about it. Not in a direct form, which would have clashed with their prejudices, but in a transposed, and seemingly innocuous, form: in their art. If my analysis is correct, in the last resort the graphic art of the Caduveo women is to be interpreted, and its mysterious appeal and seemingly gratuitous complexity explained, as the phantasm of a society ardently and insatiably seeking a means of expressing symbolically the institutions it might have, if its interests and superstitions did not stand in the way." Lévi-Strauss, *Tristes Tropiques*, 196–97.

21. Usually the companion of a senior male individual, the term for the caretaking figure of Takeda-san's partner Nē-san (older sister) draws explicitly on the world of the yakuza. As it was explained to me, matriarchs in the mobster world were not unheard of, and it was rumored that, albeit temporarily, a sister had taken over the Yamaguchi-gumi after its head had passed away. Akira himself related the story of having encountered one of the last yakuza matriarchs in his younger days, when he had been caught and beaten for destroying an outdoor stall (*tekiya*) protected by the local mob. It had been his first and only time to inject meth, and the young Akira had found himself taking the stall apart in a mindless rage. When the moment of reckoning arrived, Akira was presented to the matriarch, who entered the room with thumping footsteps and addressed him with a husky bellow. As it turned out, the big boss deemed that the young Akira had taken the beating well, and he was commended for his grit.

22. In this respect, the guys were no different from salarymen who frequent hostess clubs or snack bars to be waited on by female staff. The guys may have been on a tighter budget and certainly did not have a family or home to return to, but from a structural point of view, their relationship to mama-sans (older female proprietors or managers), waitresses, hostesses, and prostitutes was identical to that of the salaryman. Masculinity could only be asserted on the ground of sexual difference. For an ethnographic consideration of this logic in the context of corporate Japan, see Allison, *Nightwork*.

23. As a street-level labor broker (tehaishi) working within the "territory" (*nawabari*) of the local yakuza organization, the Kanamachi-ikka, Suzuki was official "blood brothers," or more formally, a "sworn brother" (*kyōdaibun*), with one of its members. The relationship between these two men had supposedly been made official through the ritual act of cutting their forearms, joining their bleeding wounds by crossing their arms, and drinking a glass of sake thus.

24. Individuals who had failed to succeed as radical leftists also came to San'ya. Oyama describes one such man: "I believe he was deeply hurt by the fact that the radical leftists he associated with never took him seriously or offered him the kind of position in their infrastructure he felt he deserved. He found himself unable to play the role of the foot

soldier with men young enough to be his children in order to reactivate his political career in San'ya; yet at the same time he couldn't face old age as a common day laborer. Both prospects were equally unbearable to him. Was this not how his despondency manifested itself: in the form of these early-morning bellows in front of the Center?" Oyama, *Man with No Talents*, 50.

25. Welfare recipients were required to declare income so that their welfare could be calibrated accordingly. For more details, see Tokyo City Bureau, "Seikatsu no Fukushi" and chap. 2.

26. For those approved and registered by the ward, the "out-of-work aid" or "unemployment pay" (*abure teate*) system was designed specifically for old day-laborer districts, both to sustain the livelihood of laborers and to maintain them as an available pool of laborers. Thus, laborers had to work to receive out-of-work aid, and workers approved by the ward were given a "pocket notebook" (*techō*) in which to receive stamps from their employers as proof of having worked. See chap. 2 and Oyama, *Man with No Talents*, 25. Ken C. Kawashima writes of the individualizing effects of a similar system for Korean day laborers in interwar Japan. With reference to the so-called Unemployment Emergency Relief Program (UERP), Kawashima says: "In sum, therefore, the implementation of the work book registration system not only functioned to separate unemployed Korean workers from unemployed Japanese workers, but also produced individuals as effects of registration. Registering with the UERP was a mechanical function of marking, coding, stamping, registering, and, most of all, producing labor power in the form of individuals for the purpose of inaugurating them into exploitative regimes of wage labor that the UERP coordinated, specifically (as we will see shortly) in the public works industry." Kawashima, *Proletarian Gamble*, 180.

27. If *tehaishi* refers to the street-level labor broker himself, the noun *tehai* refers to the actual work of brokering, such that one might ask of a tehaishi: "Have you finished tehai?" (*tehai owatta?*). Not surprisingly, the ideograms used to write *tehai* combine "hand" (*te*) with the verb "distribute" (*kubaru*), suggesting the distribution of hands or labor.

28. While the precise etymology of *takobeya* (octopus room) is unclear, the term derives historically from the inhuman conditions under which laborers were caught, like octopi perhaps, and sent to work on the northern borders of Japan, in Hokkaido, as forced laborers. Dating back to the 1880s, the term is associated with colonialism and the forced labor of Koreans, but in San'ya, it referred to conditions of virtual confinement in which individuals were made to work off their debt to the mob, while they were crammed like octopi into a single room, for which they also paid. Notably, there were numerous illegal schemes at work in the underground world of San'ya's homeless people, who were oftentimes approached by shady characters and enticed to get off the streets by moving into a dormitory. The dormitory would be located in the hinterlands of Japan, and the scheme had been designed to divest them of their welfare funds.

29. It was said that there used to be many characters like Yasuko in San'ya: brash, loud, in and out of jail on account of petty misdemeanors. Two or three nonprofit organizations in the environs of San'ya welcomed women.

30. Sanyukai, *Hibi no Dekigoto*.

31. I take some liberty with Lacan, insofar as his understanding of desire is grounded in a theorization of language and of subjectivity as split within language. In Lacanian lingo, the subject desires to occupy the place of desire precipitated by alienation in language and lack. In desiring to be desired, the subject thus desires to occupy the place of "the Other's desire." Lacan, "Subversion of the Subject," 690. For Lacan, the movement of desire is therefore located in the unconscious, which assumes the form of language. However, it should not be forgotten that Lacan's formulation of desire owes to Kojève and

Hegel, in whom the master or the state are dependent on the slave's recognition to maintain their own identity: a dialectic in which the slave is not recognized but is made to satisfy the master's desire by recognizing him. See Weber, *Return to Freud*.

32. Sanyukai, *Hibi no Dekigoto*.

33. See Tokyo City Bureau, "Hōmuresu Taisaku." Supposedly, the number of homeless people within Tokyo was reduced from 5,500 to 2,600 between 2004 and 2008. In the absence of a follow-up study, however, it is likely that the eyesore of blue tents along the Sumida River was simply dispersed.

34. As Lacan writes: "There's no such thing as a sexual relationship" (*il n'y a pas de rapport sexuel*). Lacan, *On Feminine Sexuality*, 5.

35. Oyama expresses a similar sentiment of Christian volunteers in San'ya. He writes:

"What I sense from such people's 'good deeds' (what Christians call putting their love into practice) is utter shamelessness, and I can't help feeling repulsed.

"These Christian volunteers depend in a far more profound way on San'ya—as objects for their 'good deeds' (that is, relief work)—than San'ya men do on the volunteers, yet the famous grandma and her ilk seem all too oblivious to this fact. If, for example, the government were to conduct relief work on a wider scale, San'ya men would no longer need these people; the volunteers, on the other hand, will always require San'ya men as their very own 'needy' and as living proof of their own spiritual redemption. "The fact that these volunteers seem to feel no shame at the hypocrisy of their 'good deeds' is, I believe, a huge failing on their part. Isn't their obliviousness to this fact the reason they are regarded as complete outsiders here in San'ya?" Oyama, *Man with No Talents*, 97.

36. Of an analogous logic of containment and threatening reversal, Foucault writes: "Instituted by the unity of soul and body, madness turned against that unity and once again put it in question. Madness, made possible by passion, threatened by a movement proper to itself what had made passion itself possible." Foucault, *Madness and Civilization*, 89. Here, I am concerned with the threatening *place* that San'ya occupied insofar as it harbored a constitutive negativity in relation to general society. In chapter 4, I return briefly to Foucault's elaboration of "madness" and, specifically, to logics of silence and the internalization of guilt as it applies to the San'ya man.

37. Unfamiliar as it may sound, I have recuperated a nineteenth-century British term for the "unskilled laborer"—navvy—both because contemporary job descriptions do not encompass the range of menial tasks imposed upon the guys and because navvy invokes an unruly temperament that cannot be disassociated from San'ya. Like the labor of the guys at construction sites, the work of navvies once focused on excavation or digging into the earth to build canals, as "navigators," according to Daniel William Barrett. But their "unskilled" character would also allow them to cross boundaries between work that might be described variously today as that of a general laborer, helper, or, quite simply, a laborer. So too, the ideograms for *dokata* (navvy) contain the ideogram for "earth" or "soil" (*tsuchi*) and a dictionary search for *dokata kotoba* (dokata language) turns up "bad language" or "low language"—the very word *dokata* (navvy) carries pejorative connotations. Indeed, navvies of the Victorian age constituted a disorderly and recalcitrant breed of vagrants that threatened the powers that be. In his 1880 *Life and Work among the Navvies*, Barrett cites descriptions of navvies as "the roughest of the rough," "the most uncouth of the human species," "a roving pest to society," and "coarse brutes." Barrett, 31–33. Gregory Dart likewise observes that the mid-nineteenth-century navvy was considered "insubordinate, unruly, and ungovernable" and that they carried the "notorious reputation" of being "the most dangerous type of modern worker." Dart, "Reworking of 'Work,'" 82–83. Thus, the figure of the navvy not only invokes the (literally) lowest, most basic, menial, and brute form of labor, but a type of character. On this note, I make one

final reference to a nineteenth-century text, namely, that of the ex-foreman Denis Pou-lot's typology of workers, as elaborated in *Le Sublime*. For if we follow Poulot, the guys were not just unruly navvies. As if their employers and general society could not quite wrap their minds around *what* these men, they were *sublime*—that is what Poulot ob-serves workers referring to themselves as when they transgressed against the disciplin-ary regimes of the workplace and family. See Cottereau, "Denis Poulot's 'Le Sublime,'" 104–11. I thank Aslı Menevse for this reference.

38. Reminiscent both of the corner at which Akira stood at Sanyukai and the entry-way to the Iroha arcade, where men congregated over drinks, Liebow writes: "The street-corner is, among other things, a sanctuary for those who can no longer endure the experience or prospect of failure. There, on the streetcorner, public fictions support a sys-tem of values which, together with the value system of society at large, make for a world of ambivalence, contradiction and paradox, where failures are rationalized into phan-tom successes and weaknesses magically transformed into strengths." Liebow, *Tally's Corner*, 139.

39. Journal entry from 2012.

2. THE DAY LABORER

Parts of this chapter were originally published as "Gambling, Dignity, and the Nar-cotic of Time in Tokyo's Day-Laborer District, San'ya," *Cultural Anthropology* 37, no. 1 (2022): 150–75, https://orcid.org/0000-0002-0578-2828.

1. Unlike an *onsen*, the *sentō* or local downtown bathhouse is an inexpensive and in-formal affair. They usually cost no more than five hundred yen, and the ward office distributes discount coupons to those on welfare, which can also be purchased at the morning market (see below). The bathhouses themselves usually include baths of vari-ous kinds, be it at different temperatures, a jacuzzi-like area, or an electric bath (*denki-buro*). If their patrons are lucky, there may also be a sauna, a cold bath, and an outdoor bathing area. The locals who frequent these bathhouses know each other, converse, and gossip, and many of them really have no choice but to frequent these institutions because they have no shower or bath at home.

2. In May 2011, the story of an individual from San'ya's counterpart in Osaka, Nishi-nariku, made the news. The person had applied for a job as a dump truck operator in Mi-yagi Prefecture, but upon arrival, he discovered that he had been hired to drive inside the compound of Fukushima Daiichi Nuclear Power Plant. See "Osaka Nishinariku no Rōdōsha." In San'ya, it was said that news of this incident put a stop to flagrantly disin-genuous efforts to contract labor from day-laborer districts.

3. Marx, *Capital*, 340–416. The "exchange of equivalents" masks the process through which the capitalist takes a "portion of the labour of others," arrogating the right "to ap-propriate the unpaid labour of others or its product." It is the *act* of exchange—"*post festum*," Marx says—that creates capital as an "alien power that dominates and exploits," actualizing a machinery of domination. Marx, *Capital*, 729–30, 168, 716. In fact, in *In-tellectual and Manual Labor*, Alfred Sohn-Rethel proposes that commodity exchange is formative of science, mental labor, and the very discipline capital imposes on manual labor. Arguing mainly against Kant, Sohn-Rethel contends that the categories of time and space are not a priori and that the transcendental subject apprehends the world through abstractions that originate in commodity exchange. Sohn-Rethel writes: "What defines the character of intellectual labour in its full-fledged division from all manual labour is the use of non-empirical form-abstractions which may be represented by nothing other than non-empirical, 'pure' concepts. The explanation of intellectual labour and of this division thus depends on proving the origin of the underlying, non-empirical form-

abstractions. This is the task we have undertaken. And we can see that this origin can be none other than the real abstraction of the commodity exchange, for it is of a non-empirical form-character and does not spring from thought." Sohn-Rethel, *Intellectual and Manual Labour*, 66.

4. This work ethic is by no means specific to San'ya or Japanese manual laborers. The book of Genesis extolls, "By the sweat of your brow you will eat your food." Genesis 3:19, NIV.

5. Writing of the 1950s, Miyazaki says: "Compared with nowadays, it was a much more macho era. The idea that a man should live like a man was an omnipresent value—an obsession, if you will—upon which most men modeled their conduct. Evading one's responsibilities or acting in a cowardly fashion was abhorred and disdained. At the same time, there was a deep-rooted belief that a man should live by the sweat of his toil. I think this was something that was more strongly felt in the Kansai region of western Japan. Physical labor, such as construction work, was far more respected than it is today." Miyazaki, *Toppamono*, 39–40.

6. See Tokyo City Bureau, "Seikatsu no Fukushi." Although it was not immediately apparent from the welfare system, everyone in San'ya was aware that declaring income could result in an overall diminution of funds. Like the conservative discourse that vilifies welfare recipients who spend money on alcohol or drugs, this disincentive to report earnings is familiar in the United States, if not in other nations. More importantly, the disincentive to report one's earnings produced a labor force willing to perform undesirable tasks at their own risk, on the black market.

7. Marx, *Capital*, 781. Operated by the ward, out-of-work aid was described by some day laborers as approaching obsolescence. While it had once provided the city as a whole with a steady, readily available supply of workers when construction workers had been in high demand, it no longer fulfilled this function, or at least not as efficiently. Hence, it was said that, in the eyes of the "city" (*shi*)—as opposed to the ward—out-of-work aid constituted an anachronism that had outlived its original function. Workers, of course, made ready use of the system. If they were on good terms with their superiors at the work site, they could receive stamps for individuals who were not working that day. Kentarō carried the stamp books of others to work and had them stamped. To collect their ¥7,500, workers then presented their stamp book at the Tamahime Rōdō Shucchōsho (Tamahime Labor Branch Office) at seven thirty in the morning. Gill provides extensive descriptions of how labor was organized through the Tamahime Rōdō Shucchōsho and the San'ya Labor Center in the early 1990s and by their counterparts in Yokohama's Kotobukichō, namely, the Kotobuki Labor Center Free Employment Introduction Office and the Yokohama Public Employment Stability Office. See Gill, "Sanya Street Life," 276; and *Men of Uncertainty*, 50–54.

8. Miyazaki writes of the construction world in the late 1970s. Though not exactly the world of the *hiyatoi* (day laborer) who moves from tehaishi to tehaishi, he says: "But despite its importance, the industry is for the most part built on the physical labor supplied by marginalized members of society—the poorly educated and the discriminated against. It's a fascinating world to be a part of—boisterous, vibrant, frenetic—but at the same time, one in which old habits are deeply ingrained. The best illustration of the way it works is to think of a pyramid with a handful of giant general contractors at the apex who subcontract the work to those below them. Every industry has its own subcontracting system, but what makes the construction industry unique is the extent of its stratification, with subcontractors feeding off subcontractors, and so on down the line. Tiny sub-sub-subcontractors, who eke out a living by clinging to some part of the pyramid, account for 99 percent of the industry.

"This highly stratified structure is directly reflected in the industry's close-knit system of hierarchical ties. The contractor-subcontractor relationship very much resembles the *oyabun-kobun* (boss-follower) bond in the yakuza world, in that it requires absolute loyalty to the boss. The same is repeated further down the pyramid between subcontractor and sub-subcontractor, and so on. Those in the subordinate position regard the job as something they have been allowed to do." Miyazaki, *Toppamono*, 208.

9. As Engels writes: "It offers him the means of living, but only for an 'equivalent' for his work. It even lets him have the appearance of acting from a free choice, of making a contract with free, unconstrained consent, as a responsible agent who has attained his majority." Engels, *Condition*, 88.

10. Marx, *Capital*, 163–65.

11. Kondo explicates some of the terminology that surrounds the figure of the skilled artisan. She writes: "Prevailing notions of skill among artisans—in the present day as in earlier times—stress physical idioms of technical ability. The aim is to go beyond a purely cognitive level of learning, and to *karada de oboeru*, to learn with the body. A multiplicity of idioms indicate that this is a kind of physical knowledge. An artisans's skill and technique is known as his *ude*, his arm, and to hone a skill is to polish one's arm, *ude o migaku*." Kondo, *Crafting Selves*, 238.

12. I translate *pinhane* here as "finder's fee" because that is how this extraction of absolute surplus value was justified. But it would perhaps be more correct to describe this extraction as the surplus value or excess obtained by skimming off someone else's labor and wages, usually at an unfair percentage. Though the significance of the term applies just as well to the state (consider taxes) and capitalism at large, *pinhane* is associated with sordid labor practices of corrupt companies or the mobster underworld. In gambling terminology, *pin* might refer to "one," and thus, a fraction or slice, and *hane* derives from the verb, *haneru*, which, in this instance, means "to skim off."

13. In this respect, San'ya itself was a symptom of capitalist Japan, hidden from view. Like Makoto, San'ya occupied the place of what Slavoj Žižek describes as an "internal negation" within the order of equivalent exchange: "We have here again a certain ideological Universal, that of equivalent and equitable exchange, and a particular paradoxical exchange—that of the labour force for its wages—which, precisely as an equivalent, functioned as the very form of exploitation. The 'quantitative' development itself, the universalization of the production of commodities, brings about a new 'quality', the emergence of a new commodity representing the internal negation of the universal principle of equivalent exchange. . . . For Marx, this 'irrational' element of the existing society was, of course, the proletariat, 'the unreason of reason itself' (Marx), the point at which the Reason embodied in the existing social order encounters its own unreason." Žižek, *Sublime Object of Ideology*, 17–18.

14. Oyama writes of individuals in San'ya vanishing: "Here a man who had showed up two or three times a week for years on end might suddenly disappear and never again be heard from again. No one in San'ya is going to tell you, 'This is my last day here. I won't be coming to the Center any more. Thanks for everything.' You might ask around about someone ('I haven't seen Mr. So-and-so lately. Do you know what's happened to him?'), but nobody will know a thing, and after a while all talk about him stops. This is the way people around here disappear from the scene." Oyama, *Man with No Talents*, 33.

15. Day laborers clearly occupied the very bottom rung of this vine of subcontractors, which Gill has described in terms of a *keiretsu* system, with origins in prerecessionary Japan: "One of the reasons why big Japanese corporations were able to maintain excellent standards of job security for their employees was because they maintained relatively small workforces. Compared with other capitalist countries, a much larger portion of production was out-sourced: entrusted to smaller companies that stood in a variety

of relationships to the main company. . . . Construction keiretsu were generally vertical; the smaller companies acted as a kind of safety valve for the main company." Gill, "*Yoseba* and *Ninpudashi*," 124.

16. Gill cites a policeman of Yokohama's day-laborer district, Kotobuki: "As far as I know, neither my superiors in the force, nor the local authorities, have any intention to 'clean up' Kotobuki or 'close it down' or whatever. Kotobuki won't change. In my personal view, it would be a bad thing if Kotobuki disappeared. There is a need for such a place. There are good and bad people in every city; there must be a place for bad people to go to. Given that human nature, and therefore cities, are not perfect, it's not a bad idea to concentrate the problems in one place." Gill, "Unconventional Moralities," 249.

17. Journal entry from 2013.

18. Riots by San'ya day laborers against the yakuza, police, and construction subcontractors reached a peak in 1984 and were famously captured in Saitō Mitsuo's documentary, *Yama: Attack to Attack*. During its filming, the director himself was killed by the yakuza. For an account of the production of the documentary and the historical circumstances surrounding the riots, see "Yama," *Yararetara Yarikaese*. For an even earlier account of militant left-wing labor movements in San'ya and Kamagasaki (the day-laborer district of Osaka), see Kama Kyōtō San'ya, *Yararetara Yarikaese*.

19. The yakuza has a longstanding association with nuclear labor, and it is hardly a secret that nuclear labor at Fukushima Daiichi Nuclear Power Plant has been provided by the mob. TEPCO is notorious for its pyramid-like hierarchy, which alleviates its elites of responsibility for subcontracting practices at the bottom rung, where the yakuza provide workers who may (or may not) be in debt. For an account of cutting wages or the *pinhane* (finder's fee) system at nuclear plants and specifically at Fukushima Daiichi Nuclear Power Plant in the 1970s, see Horie Kunio's 1979 classic, *Genpatsu Jipusī*, 85–88. For a contemporary account of relations between the yakuza and nuclear power, see Suzuki, *Yakuza to Genpatsu*.

20. Journal entry from 2013.

21. Of this massification of laborers and the constitutive place of the foreman, Marx writes: "Their unification into one single productive body, and the establishment of a connection between their individual functions, lies outside their competence. . . . An industrial army of workers under the command of a capitalist requires, like a real army, officers (managers) and N.C.O.s (foremen, overseers), who command during the labour process in the name of capital. The work of supervision becomes their established and exclusive function." Marx, *Capital*, 449–50. Frederick Winslow Taylor likewise says: "In almost all of the mechanic arts the science which underlies each act of each workman is so great and amounts to so much that the workman who is best suited to actually doing work is incapable of fully understanding this science, without the guidance and help of those who are working with him or over him, either through lack of education or through insufficient mental capacity." Taylor, *Principles of Scientific Management*, 18.

22. Of the manufacturing division of labor, Marx writes: "The division of labour within society is mediated through the purchase and sale of the products of different branches of industry, while the connection between the various partial operations in a workshop is mediated through the sale of the labour-power of several workers to one capitalist, who applies it as combined labour-power." Marx, *Capital*, 475–76.

23. In 2012, 1,500 people died in accidents at construction sites in Japan. See Japan Construction, "Kensetsugyō ni Okeru."

24. These practices of turning a blind eye to the health conditions of workers are reminiscent of the "cover-up system" (*inpei taisei*) employed by the nuclear industry in Japan to conceal the radiation exposure of workers. See, for instance, Horie, *Genpatsu Jipusī*, 108–10, 169–72; and Suzuki, *Yakuza to Genpatsu*, 143–45, 244–59.

25. *Tobi* (scaffolders) were said to assume complete financial responsibility in the event of accidents at work. For this reason, they were paid around ¥17,500 ($175) per day, approximately ¥5,000 more than other professions in the construction business. Oyama Shiro has described the figure of the *tobi* in the heyday of San'ya. While his description accords with the status of Rikiishi and Norihisa as respected scaffolders in San'ya, it contrasts with the respect given to Kentarō, a former carpenter, and Shōkawa, a former ironworker. Oyama writes: "Tobi are the aristocrats of San'ya. . . . The training required to nurture their skills to a level worthy of their calling and the confidence gained through having those skills recognized by their peers give them a commanding presence and bestow on their countenance a certain poise. All in all, they cut a very dashing figure. There is a certain crispness about their movements and indeed about their entire demeanor. I would imagine that their individual abilities vary considerably, but the best have a truly unmistakable aura about them. . . . Carpenters and ironworkers are not employed as day laborers or as contract laborers, so there are none in San'ya. Here, the word *shokunin*—skilled worker—means only one thing, and that is tobi." Oyama, *Man with No Talents*, 61.

26. As Marx unfolds, the emergence of an "unskilled" class of workers is a consequence of the manufacturing division of labor: "Manufacture therefore develops a hierarchy of labour-powers, to which there corresponds a scale of wages. . . . Every process of production, however, requires certain simple manipulations, which every man is capable of doing. These actions too are now separated from their constant interplay with those aspects of activity which are richer in content. . . . Hence in every craft it seizes, manufacture creates a class of so-called unskilled labourers, a class strictly excluded by the nature of handicraft industry." Marx, *Capital*, 469–70.

27. Traditionally, so-called unskilled labor has been relegated to women at the workplace. As Kondo writes regarding the female composition of part-time workers and the male composition of full-time artisans at a downtown sweets factory in late 1970s Tokyo: "The development of an aesthetic approach to craft work and the teaching of skills to the *male* workers guarded the boundaries of this select group. . . . The artisans, then, excluded women by identifying as a collectivity of full-time, skilled workers. As a collectivity, they could protect their identities by downplaying the many contributions of the women to the work process. Yet these women are also necessary members of the company, who in some ways constituted a threat to artisanal articulations of a skill-based hierarchy." Kondo, *Crafting Selves*, 251–53.

28. Marx viewed the reunification of mental and manual labor as a precondition for a communist or socialist society. He writes: "In a higher phase of communist society, after the subjection of individuals to the division of labour, and thereby the antithesis between mental and physical labour, has disappeared . . . only then can the limited horizon of bourgeois right be wholly transcended, and society can inscribe on its banner: from each according to his abilities, to each according to his needs!" Marx, "Critique," 214–15. See also Llorente, "Analytical Marxism."

29. Sohn-Rethel writes as follows of the division of mental from manual labor under monopoly capitalism: "The division directly involved in the managerial authority over the monopolistic labour process is the one between the technical and organisational intelligentsia and the manual work-force. As this division springs from the foundations from which monopoly capitalism itself arises, the stability of monopoly capitalism virtually depends on the relations between these two forces, the mental and manual, remaining safely divided. Should the division be changed into an alliance, the authority of the management would be in jeopardy." As a science, moreover, mental labor seeks to maximize production: "Modern science is not aimed at helping society in her relations

with nature. It studies nature only from the viewpoint of capitalist production. . . . It can be said that objects over which capital can exercise control must be cast in the form of a commodity. It is the exact truth of exact science that it is knowledge of nature in commodity form." Sohn-Rethel, *Intellectual and Manual Labor*, 157, 132.

30. Under capitalism, Sohn-Rethel writes, "physical production has lost its direct social cohesion and can form a viable totality only by the intermediary of a network of exchange under the rule of private property. As capital it controls production . . . Individual labour is in full control only in the small-scale individual production of peasants and artisans. Only then is production based on the individual unity of head and hand. This artisan mode of production is ousted by capitalist production." Sohn-Rethel, 78. As an attribution of value, the exchange of wages for labor achieves a social synthesis insofar as it reincorporates manual labor within a totality. But the *form* of this exchange is inherently alienating because it dispossesses the laborer of the products of their labor, feeding the power of capital to repeat this process, and because, in exchange, "the action is social, the minds are private," such that the wage negates and isolates the interiority of the worker within a solipsistic world of their own. Sohn-Rethel, 29.

31. I cite from Marx: "But what was at first merely a starting-point becomes, by means of nothing but the continuity of the process, by simple reproduction, the characteristic result of capitalist production, a result which is constantly renewed and perpetuated. On the one hand, the production process incessantly converts material wealth into capital, into the capitalist's means of enjoyment and his means of valorization. On the other hand, the worker always leaves the process in the same state as he entered it—a personal source of wealth, but deprived of any means of making that wealth a reality for himself. . . . The worker himself constantly produces objective wealth, in the form of capital, an alien power that dominates and exploits him; and the capitalist just as constantly produces objective wealth which is abstract, exists merely in the physical body of the worker, and is separated from its own means of objectification and realization; in short, the capitalist produces the worker as wage-labourer. This incessant reproduction, this perpetuation of the worker, is the absolutely necessary condition for capitalist production." Marx, *Capital*, 716.

32. In "Machinery and Large-Scale Industry," Marx says: "It is not the worker who employs the conditions of his work, but rather the reverse, the conditions of work employ the worker. However, it is only with the coming of machinery that this inversion first acquires a technical and palpable reality. Owing to its conversion into an automaton, the instrument of labour confronts the worker during the labour process in the shape of capital, dead labour, which dominates and soaks up living labour-power. The separation of the intellectual faculties of the production process from manual labour, and the transformation of those faculties into powers exercised by capital over labour, is, as we have already shown, finally completed by large-scale industry erected on the foundation of machinery. The special skill of each individual machine-operator, who has now been deprived of all significance, vanishes as an infinitesimal quantity in the face of the science, the gigantic natural forces, and the mass of social labour embodied in the system of machinery, which, together with those three forces, constitutes the power of the 'master'." Marx, *Capital*, 548–49.

33. For a discussion of this future-anterior mode of temporality, see Lyotard, *Postmodern Condition*, 81.

34. Freud, *Beyond the Pleasure Principle*, 30. Freud wrote of this "protective shield against stimuli" in specific relation to modern warfare, mechanization, and machinery. Writing after World War I, he theorized trauma or the compulsion to repeat unpleasurable experiences as the effect of a penetration of this "shield." Freud wrote: "Living substance is

suspended in the middle of an external world charged with the most powerful energies; and it would be killed by the stimulation emanating from these if it were not provided with a protective shield against stimuli. It acquires the shield in this way: its outermost surface ceases to have the structure proper to living matter, becomes to some degree inorganic and thenceforward functions as a special envelope or membrane resistant to stimuli. In consequence, the energies of the external world are able to pass into the next underlying layers, which have remained living, with only a fragment of their original intensity; and these layers can devote themselves, behind the protective shield, to the reception of the amounts of stimuli that have been allowed through it." Freud, 30. And Marx himself comes close to describing such a shield insofar as the shutting out, deadening, or etiolation of undesirable elements demands increased "attention" on the task at hand from the worker. Marx says: "Apart from the exertion of the working organs, a purposeful will is required for the entire duration of work. This means close attention. The less he is attracted by the nature of the work and the way in which it has to be accomplished, and the less, therefore, he enjoys it as the free play of his own physical and mental powers, the closer his attention is forced to be." Marx, *Capital*, 284. In *Railway Journey*, Wolfgang Schivelbusch illuminates how the repression of the specter of accidents constitutes a hallmark of modernity.

35. As I detail, the etiolation of material stimuli is demanded of the laborer by the exchange relation, in which they sell their labor for wages. Sohn-Rethel writes: "Exchange empties time and space of their material contents and gives them contents of purely human significance connected with the social status of people and things." Sohn-Rethel, *Mental and Manual Labour*, 48.

36. Journal entry from 2012.

37. Of slacking or "soldiering," Taylor writes: "Underworking, that is, deliberately working slowly so as to avoid doing a full day's work, 'soldiering,' as it is called in this country, 'hanging it out,' as it is called in England, 'ca canae,' as it is called in Scotland, is almost universal in industrial establishments, and prevails also to a large extent in building trades; and the writer asserts without fear of contradiction that this constitutes the greatest evil with which the working people of both England and America are now afflicted." Taylor, *Principles of Scientific Management*, 3.

38. *Geta* are traditional Japanese footwear, wooden and heavy like clogs but held by a thong like flip-flops.

39. I follow Lukács here, who writes that, as "it stamps its imprint upon the whole consciousness of man," the commodity form finally penetrates consciousness with intellectual labor. Thus reified, the journalist, lawyer, or intellectual laborer sells their minds and souls as commodities, while mistakenly believing their products proceed from a singular self. Lukács, "Reification and the Consciousness," 100, 172.

40. Lukács proposes that the "*self-consciousness of the commodity*" hinges on a contingent moment when the dialectical antinomy between subject and object reaches its limit in the proletariat—a moment that marks the arrival of contingency into history, when the fetishism of the commodity gives way to "relation between men" and mutual recognition. Lukács, "Reification and the Consciousness," 168–69.

41. Of dying in the name of a "master signifier," Jacques Alain-Miller writes of a "death that is risked or a death that is wished for or a death that is assumed, and which is related to the transcendence of the signifier." Miller, "On Shame," 19. And to explicate the constitutive character of shame to this master signifier, Miller cites Lacan: "He explains it, indirectly, 'Henceforth, as subjects, you will be pinned down by signifiers that are only countable signifiers and which will efface the singularity of S1.' They have begun to transform the singularity of S1 into units of value. The master signifier is the singular unit of value, which cannot be quantified, which will not fit into a calculus in which everything is weighted. This is the context in which he proposes to 'make ashamed,' which has noth-

ing to do with guilt. Making ashamed is an effort to reinstate the agency of the master signifier." Miller, 23.

42. In the name of "scientific management," Taylor asserts the "self-evident fact that maximum prosperity can exist only as a result of the determined effort of each workman to turn out each day his largest possible day's work." Taylor, *Principles of Scientific Management*, 4.

43. Rikiishi was a *tobi* (scaffolder) by profession. On this note, Miyazaki writes of scaffolders in the late 1970s: "The world of the *tobi* (scaffolder) is certainly a rowdy one, and scrapping was a daily occurrence. Among such men was a special breed known as the heavy-duty scaffolder. Incredibly strong, they balanced steel girders on their shoulders as they flew along scaffolding high above the ground. They were reckless, devil-may-care types that you would think had been born to fight." Miyazaki, *Toppamono*, 207.

44. Of "labor power," Anson Rabinbach writes that it "represents the quantitative aspect of labor under capitalism." He cites Engels, pointing out a Marxist truism, namely, that labor power "is, in our present-day capitalist society, a commodity like every other commodity, but a very peculiar commodity. It has, namely, the peculiarity of being a *value-creating force* (my italics), the source of value, and moreover, when properly treated, the source of more value than it possesses itself." Rabinbach, *Human Motor*, 74. See also Marx, *Capital*.

45. Sohn-Rethel writes: "Time and space rendered abstract under commodity exchange are marked by homogeneity, continuity and emptiness of all natural and material content, visible or invisible (e.g. air) . . . The exchange abstraction excludes everything that makes up history, human and even natural history. The entire empirical reality of facts, events and description by which one moment and locality of time and space is distinguished from another is wiped out. Time and space assume thereby that character of absolute historical timelessness and universality which must mark the exchange abstraction as a whole and each of its features." Sohn-Rethel, *Intellectual and Manual Labour*, 48–49.

46. I draw here on Marx's chapters in *Capital* "The Sale and Purchase of Labour-Power" and "The Working Day."

47. Rabinbach writes of chronophotographic images in *Human Motor*, 104–19.

48. Consisting of a repetitive isolation of movements, this compartmentalization recalls the analogous relationship that Benjamin describes between factory work and gambling: "the ivory ball that rolls into the *next* compartment, the *next* card . . .". Benjamin, "On Some Motifs in Baudelaire," 179. See also Natasha Dow Schüll, *Addiction by Design*, 203–207.

49. Ernst Bloch, *Heritage of Our Times*, 97. The capitalist mode of production produces the obsolescence of older forms of labor, prompting Bloch to note that: "a merely awkward man who for this very reason falls short of the demands of his position or little position is simply backward in himself. But what if in addition, through the continuing effect of ancient peasant origin for instance, as a type from earlier times he does not fit into a very modern one? Various years in general beat in the one which is just being counted and prevails. Nor do they flourish in obscurity as in the past, but contradict the Now; very strangely, crookedly, from behind." Bloch, *Heritage of Our Times*, 97. As a critique of the times, Bloch identified the nostalgia for such non-contemporaneous elements as fascism. But it was also precisely in their subjugation and incompletion that he recognized their revolutionary potential: "It is only thus that the non-past, because never wholly become, and hence lastingly subversive and utopian contents in the relations of human beings to human beings and to nature are of use: these contents are as it were the gold bearing rubble in the course of the previous work processes and their work-based superstructures." Bloch, *Heritage of Our Times*, 116.

50. Okabayashi Nobuyasu, "San'ya Blues," track A1 on *San'ya Blues*, Victor SV-1028, 1968, LP Record.

3. GAMBLING

Parts of this chapter were originally published as "Gambling, Dignity, and the Narcotic of Time in Tokyo's Day-Laborer District, San'ya," *Cultural Anthropology* 37, no. 1 (2022): 150–75, https://orcid.org/0000-0002-0578-2828.

1. As the JRA (Japan Racing Association) writes on their website, the acronym WINS was introduced in 1987 to make the term "off-track betting hall" (*jōgai kachiuma tōhyōken hatsubaisho*) more familiar to fans. Easier to remember and easier to say, WINS (pronounced "uinzu" in Japanese) clearly references the English word *win* but is also said to stand for "WINning Spot" and "Weekend IN Spot." As an off-track betting hall, WINS is not specific to Asakusa. A WINS hall can be found in virtually every city of median size or larger in Japan, and there were several WINS halls in Tokyo. These halls, therefore, were not places where actual horse races could be seen but ones in which horse races from across the country were screened on TVs. Japan Racing Association, "Beginner's Guide (JRA)."

2. For the uninitiated, the "betting card" refers to the blank piece of paper riddled with numbers and circles that you fill out to place your bet. To place your bet, you insert this betting card into one of the machines that line the walls of WINS and pay the amount you indicated on the betting card; in return, the machine issues your "gambling ticket." If you lose, you shred the ticket. If you win, you insert your ticket back into a machine, and—voila—out comes your winnings. In Japanese, the "betting card" is called a *māku kādo* (literally, a "mark card"), and in the case of horse racing, the "gambling ticket" or "horse racing ticket" is called a *baken* (literally, "horse ticket").

3. The experience of boat, bicycle, and horse racing was mediated by the TV screen. On very rare occasions, someone might venture to the actual racetrack, but this was rather something everyone had done at some point in the past and could tell of but did not do anymore. Instead, they fixated on the TV screen or moved between TV screens at WINS, standing to see the main races. I do not dwell on the technological aspect of gambling here, but the up-close experience of gambling on screens immersed gamblers in the medium of transmission, foreclosing critical distance. Precipitated by moving from screen to screen, from race to race, the affect generated by gambling recalls the euphoria that Fredric Jameson has identified with postmodern aesthetics of surface, pastiche, and *écriture* as "radical difference." Jameson, *Postmodernism*, 29–31. Rotating between TV screens facilitated a shameless enjoyment that Jacques Lacan has associated with both the commensurable value form of the commodity and the absence of a reciprocating gaze on TV. See Lacan, *Television*; and Miller, "On Shame."

4. Located next to an amusement park and the Tokyo Dome (formerly the Korakuen Stadium for baseball, constructed in 1937 and demolished in 1987), Korakuen refers to the WINS gambling hall in Suidōbashi, Tokyo. Unlike WINS in Asakusa and other parts of the city, this location allowed gamblers to bet on horses throughout the week.

5. See Japan Racing Association, "Beginner's Guide (JRA)."

6. It is as if the winning numbers have already been decided and all the gambler has to do is get them right. The excess of abstract numbers in the newspapers recalls the "signifier surfeit" that Claude Lévi-Strauss writes of regarding a fundamental "contradiction" in language by which "there is always a non-equivalence or 'inadequation' between the total system of signifiers and any given signified." A "supplementary ration" is needed to achieve complementarity, and the ability to achieve this resides in the magical effectivity of the copula: to *be*. Lévi-Strauss, *Introduction to the Work*, 62–64. In this way, the gambler hopes that his gambling ticket *is* the floating signifier of the winning ticket.

7. Dating back to premodern Japan, the lottery (*takara kuji*) translates literally as a combination of "treasure" (*takara*) and "raffle" or "draw" (*kuji*), and flower cards (*hanafuda*) translates as a combination of "flower" (*hana*) and "cards" (*fuda*). Unlike the Western card deck, the flower card deck is composed of twelve suits of four, making a total of forty-eight cards. Each suit is represented by a traditional drawing of a flower or leaf known to sprout in a specific month of the year (at least before climate change), which gives that card its value. Hence, cherry blossoms (*sakura*) signify March and the value of "3," while pine (*matsu*) signifies January and the value of "1." There are no actual number indications on the cards, save for the images, and the complexity of the deck allows for an array of games because some cards in specific suits are further marked with a red ribbon, a poetry ribbon, a purple ribbon, or animals—a crane, a bush warbler, a cuckoo, butterflies, a boar, geese, a deer, a swallow, or a Chinese phoenix—which can be combined in different ways. Then there is the so-called "Rainman" (*Ono no Michikaze*) card, the chrysanthemum poetry cup (*Kiku no Sakazuki*) card, and so on. Depending on the game, there are also nicknames for various values that emerge, including "pig" (*buta*) for zero—consider Akira's use of this word in chapter 4—or *pin* for "one," which recalls *pinhane*, in which a *pin*, percentage, or slice is skimmed by the tehaishi. Notably, the individual who ran the one-man gambling operation by the entryway to the Iroha arcade, Gīn, was also nicknamed *Pin*.

8. Insofar as the initial "hook" of a "near miss" is concerned, the appeal of gambling in San'ya may even be likened to that of slot machines. But this is also where the affinities end, because the manual laborer's desire for self-constitution through a narrative form of experience contrasts with the asocial "self-liquidation" realized in the "machine zone" by gamblers at slot machines, as Natasha Dow Schüll illuminates in relation to people seeking an escape from the relentless vagaries of human relations in the service industry. Whereas Schüll explicates the asocial dimensions of the gambler's desire to reach a "zero state" at slot machines, the San'ya gambler discloses the initial thrill and social aspect of gambling. See Schüll, *Addiction by Design*, 96–97, 221–27.

9. See Matome, "Kyōtei de 30 Oku."

10. Immanuel Kant writes of the mathematical sublime as "that which is great beyond all comparison." Kant, *Critique of the Power*, 132.

11. Although I move on to theorize the restorative aspect of gambling as an experience of contingency, my reference to the "real" opens to a consideration of gambling as repetition compulsion in the psychoanalytic sense. In this respect, the "real" does not refer to reality in the colloquial sense but to a constitutive exclusion that organizes the imaginary and symbolic dimensions of our everyday worlds and, in so doing, operates as an object cause of desire. In gambling, the repetition, coincidence, and contiguity of signifiers precipitate and release a certain excess or residue of the "real," which Samuel Weber explicates as "residing at the innermost core of the imaginary insofar as the latter is constituted by an ambivalence and a conflict that, precisely, resists imaginary representation, and in so doing goads it on." Weber, *Return to Freud*, 106.

12. Roger Caillois makes this seminal distinction between labor and "play," as "an occasion of pure waste." Caillois, *Man, Play and Games*, 5.

13. Readers of Benjamin will note that I push back against his rather hopeless presentation of gambling as an analog to factory work, particularly in "On Some Motifs in Baudelaire." Insofar as Benjamin pointed out an identity between factory work and gambling, rather than an analog (as I argue), Gerda Reith is right to say that he mistakenly equates the drudgery of work with the thrill of gambling, for even in the self-liquidation that Schüll identifies at slot machines, it begins with the seduction of a "near miss." Gerda Reith, *The Age of Chance*, 137–38. But when Benjamin writes that the "contact between his motor stimuli and 'fate'" must stay intact for the gambler, he undercuts the oft-cited,

seeming identity he makes between the "drudgery" of factory work and gambling. See Benjamin, "Notes on a Theory of Gambling," 298. Schüll argues convincingly for an asocial merging of machine, body, and consciousness—the "machine zone"—at slots in Las Vegas, in which "near misses" truly appear to induce a deadened state of Freudian repetition compulsion. Yet, in the words of Schüll's interlocutor, Mollie, a winning streak at slots is deceptively similar to Benjamin's description of motor-connectivity to fate: "this vibration between what I *want* and what *happens*" must remain intact. Schüll, *Addiction by Design*, 171.

14. Of such experience, Erving Goffman observed that the gambler must "expose himself to time, to seconds and minutes ticking off outside his control." Goffman, "Where the Action Is," 261.

15. Benjamin writes: "When a winning number is clearly predicted but not bet on, the man who is not in the know will conclude that he is in excellent form and that next time he just needs to act more promptly, more boldly. Whereas anyone familiar with the game will know that a single incident of this kind is sufficient to tell him that he must break off instantly. For it is a sign that the contact between his motor stimuli and 'fate' has been interrupted." Benjamin, "Notes on a Theory," 298.

16. Journal entry from 2012.

17. I hold off here on a detailed description of each of these games. Suffice it to say that their rules are almost endlessly complicated, not least because, like mahjong, each of these games has regional variations that differ, for instance, in the Kansai region of Osaka from the Kantō region of Tokyo.

18. Himself an incorrigible gambler, Dostoyevsky writes of such repetition in roulette: "It seemed as though fate were urging me on. This time, as luck would have it, a circumstance occurred which, however, is fairly frequent in the game. Chance favours red, for instance, ten or even fifteen times in succession. I had heard two days before that in the previous week red had turned up twenty-two times in succession; it was something which had never been remembered in roulette, and it was talked about with amazement. Every one, of course, abandoned red at once, and after the tenth time, for instance, scarcely any one dared to stake on it. But none of the experienced players staked black either. The experienced gambler knows what is meant by this 'freak of chance.' It would mean that after red had won sixteen times, at the seventeenth time the luck would infallibly fall on black. Novices at play rush to this conclusion in crowds, double and treble their stakes, and lose terribly." Dostoyevsky, "Gambler," 489.

19. Here the repetition and coincidence of numbers approaches what Richard Klein and William B. Warner, drawing on Jung, have described as "significant coincidence," which "may be defined as a conjuncture of events so unlikely or implausible that to call it accident seems less reasonable than to assume some intentional, motivated connection." Klein and Warner, "Nuclear Coincidence," 6. On the repetition of numbers, see also Freud's essay, "'Uncanny,'" 213–14.

20. In an analog to off-track betting floors, Caitlin Zaloom expands on the importance to financial traders of "learning not to calculate." Zaloom, *Out of the Pits*, 151.

21. Of this motor connectivity, Benjamin says: "No one has so many chances of betting on a winning number as someone who has just made a significant win. This means that the correct sequence is based not on any previous knowledge of the future but on a correct physical disposition, which is increased in immediacy, certainty, and uninhibitedness by every confirmation, such as is provided by a win." Benjamin, "Notes on a Theory," 298.

22. The gesture of the sketch follows Benjamin's observation that the gambler must use "their hands sparingly, in order to respond to the slightest innervations." Benjamin, "Notes on a Theory," 297. On gambling, Benjamin, and "innervation," Miriam Bratu Hansen writes: "Entwined with the multiple meanings of *Spiel*, is the already mentioned concept of

innervation. This term broadly refers to a nondestructive, mimetic incorporation of the world—which Benjamin explored, over the course of a decade, through exemplary practices such as writing and reading, yoga, eroticism, children's play, experiments with hashish, Surrealism, and cinema. In an unpublished fragment written around 1929–30, 'Notes on a Theory of Gambling' (... des *Spiels*), Benjamin states that the decisive factor in gambling is 'the level of motor innervation.' ... In other words, rather than relying on the master sense of vision, say, by 'reading' the table, let alone an 'interpretation of chance' (*AP*, p. 513), gambling turns on a '*bodily* presence of mind,' a faculty that Benjamin elsewhere attributes to 'the ancients.' In marginal cases of gambling, this presence of mind becomes 'divination—that is to say, one of the highest, rarest moments in life.'" Hansen, "Room-for-Play," 9–10.

23. Benjamin writes: "The gambler's basic approach must, so to speak, adumbrate the subtlest network of inhibitions, which lets only the most minute and unassuming innervations pass through its meshes." Benjamin, "Notes on a Theory," 297.

24. Of the winning streak in roulette, Dostoyevsky writes: "Black won. I don't remember my winnings after, nor what I staked on. I only remember as though in a dream that I won, I believe, sixteen thousand florins; suddenly three unlucky turns took twelve thousand from it; then I staked the last four thousand on *passe* (but I scarcely felt anything as I did so: I simply waited in a mechanical senseless way)—and again I won; then I won four times running. I only remember that I gathered up money in thousands; I remember, too, that the middle twelve won most often and I kept to it. It turned up with a sort of regularity, certainly three or four times in succession, then it did not turn up twice running and then it followed three or four times in succession. Such astonishing regularity is sometimes met with in streaks, and that is what throws inveterate gamblers who calculate with a pencil in their hands out of their reckoning. And what horrible ironies of fate happen sometimes in such cases!" Dostoyevsky, "Gambler," 488.

25. It is "at the critical moment of danger (of missing his chance)," Benjamin writes, "that a gambler discovers the trick of finding his way around the table, of reading the table." Benjamin, "Notes on a Theory," 297.

26. It is at games like craps, roulette, and at off-track betting parlors for horses that the social and vertiginous dimensions of gambling in San'ya can be encountered in other contexts. On the vertigo (*ilinx*) of gambling, see Roger Caillois, *Man, Play, and Games*, 24. For a description of off-track betting parlors in the United States, see Holly Kruse, *Off-Track and Online*. For a consideration of the "negative valuation" of horse gambling in Fiji, see Presterudstuen, "Horse Race Gambling." Schüll also observes the exhilaration of craps in *Addiction by Design*, 18.

27. Benjamin writes: "Furthermore, one should note the factor of danger, which is the most important factor in gambling, alongside pleasure (the pleasure of betting on the right number)." Benjamin, "Notes on a Theory," 298. At slot machines, this seduction quickly gives way to the drudgery of the "zone." Schüll, *Addiction by Design*, 96–97.

28. Quoted in Benjamin, *Arcades Project*, 498.

29. Freud, *Beyond the Pleasure Principle*, 30. See also chap. 2.

30. The newspapers enabled gamblers to "isolate what happens from the realm in which it could affect the experience." Benjamin, "On Some Motifs," 158.

31. For a similar explication of the heads-up display in online poker, which "releases players" from keeping notes, see Schüll, "Online Poker," 570–74.

32. In exchange value, Marx writes, the commodity does not contain "an atom" of use value or quality, which is to say that, in itself, the money form cannot provide the ground for the qualitative, singular reputation of an individual. Marx, *Capital*, 128.

33. Scanlan, *Horse God Built*, 160–64. Even today, uncashed winning tickets from Secretariat's 1973 Belmont race can be purchased online.

34. The necessity of secrecy, of conferring a guise of singularity on bets, recalls Derrida's observation that the signature is haunted by a constitutive iterability—an iterability that must be repressed for the signature to appear singular. In their abstract form, numbers are considered not only repeatable but identical. Derrida, "Signature Event Context," 20.

35. Riku's comment recalls Malaby's observation that gambling can crystallize a "chanceful life into a seemingly more apprehensible form." Malaby, *Gambling Life*, 147.

36. As a compartmentalization of time, Benjamin writes that because "each operation at the machine is just as screened off from the preceding operation as a *coup* in a game of chance is from the one that preceded it, the drudgery of the laborer is, in its own way, a counterpart to the drudgery of the gambler. The work of both is equally devoid of substance." Benjamin, "On Some Motifs," 177.

37. Benjamin, "On Some Motifs," 163. Robert Desjarlais offers a pointed critique of this notion of "experience" (*erfahrung*), of which he also notes that its "temporal integration" is achieved through narrative, much as the guys told stories of their big wins. Tied to normative notions of personhood, the question of "experience" for Desjarlais concerns who the category excludes by default. Desjarlais writes: "Experience builds toward something more than a transient, episodic succession of events. The intransience of experience ties into the fact that it has a lasting and memorable effect on the person who undergoes it. 'To undergo an experience with something,' Heidegger writes, '—be it a thing, a person, or a god—means that this something befalls us, strikes us, comes over us, overwhelms and transforms us.' . . . Experience transforms: it 'does not leave him who has it unchanged,' or so says Gadamer in his specification of a 'genuine experience' (*erfahrung*). To have an experience or to learn by experience suggests an education that can accrue in certain skills or knowledge, though this education hinges on a flux of subjective reflections that other kinds of learning (such as operant conditioning) do not. The Oxford English Dictionary notes that, since the sixteenth century, experience has involved 'knowledge resulting from actual observation or from what one has undergone.' Experience is thus fodder for the kind of psychological developments or becomings that have characterized ideas of personhood in Europe since the Old Testament at least." Desjarlais, *Shelter Blues*, 16–17.

38. Benjamin writes: "Perhaps the special achievement of shock defense may be seen in its function of assigning to an incident a precise point in time in consciousness at the cost of the integrity of its contents. This would be the peak achievement of the intellect; it would turn the incident into a moment that has been lived (*Erlebnis*)." Benjamin, "On Some Motifs," 163.

39. Such punctuated bursts of intensity recall the repetitive temporality of Geertz's Balinese cockfight, a "process that reoccurs rather than a continuous one." Geertz, "Deep Play," 447–48.

40. Time, for Benjamin, remains to be actualized as a "*durée*"—which Bergson described as "past and present melting into one another." Cited in Reith, *Age of Chance*, 136.

41. See chap. 2 for my discussion of the deadening effects of manual labor on time and the body.

42. Connecting gambler to flaneur, and time to space, Benjamin observes that gambling "converts time into a narcotic," creating a "phantasmagoria of time." Benjamin, "Paris, the Capital," 12.

43. Benjamin, "On Some Motifs," 193–94. Susan Buck-Morss has pointed out the transformative possibilities of such "impotent rage": "Action is the sister of the dream." Buck-Morss, *Dialectics*, 270.

44. Although I cite here from the above passage in Benjamin's essay, "On Some Motifs in Baudelaire," Benjamin's full exposition of the disintegration of aura under modern conditions of reproducibility can be found in "The Work of Art in the Age of

Mechanical Reproducibility." Over against technologies of reproduction (consider photography) and the commensurability of all things under the commodity form—everything has a price—I write of "aura" in terms of its incommensurable character within a modern world of abstraction.

45. The "jackpot," Rizzo writes, is "not possible because no empirically giveable prize is adequate to it." Rizzo, "Compulsive Gambling," 266.

46. Welfare recipients were given "ranks" (*kyū*) corresponding to their health status. Those in the "A rank" (*A kyū*), of which Akira was one, received more than others. Akira typically transformed this rank into the positive sign—albeit to be kept hush-hush—of his secure place within the welfare system. See Tokyo City Bureau, "Seikatsu no Fukushi."

47. It was in this manner that, by incurring excessive debts through gambling, the stakes and significance of gambling had been amplified to involve "esteem, honor, dignity, respect," as Clifford Geertz once wrote of the pain and pleasure of "deep play." Geertz, "Deep Play," 455. Moreover, in these eminently social dimensions, gambling in San'ya recalls the "character" that Erving Goffman once depicted as a compensation for the routinized predictability of office work among male casino gamblers in his "Where the Action Is" (1967).

48. That credit constitutes the social reputation of a man should recall any number of ruminations on debt and the social form of Marcel Mauss's gift, in which "the productivity of debt can also be understood in terms of a primary relation that puts debtor-creditor relations at the very base of social relations more generally. . . . This approach implies that debt is productive of something and that the productivity of debt is not necessarily revealed in those moments where disorder confronts order. Debt breaks with the logic of exchange not because it subverts it, but rather because it induces deferred exchange." Roitman, "Unsanctioned Wealth," 212–13.

49. Of this conjunction between shameless enjoyment, the commodity as a commensurable form of value, and TV, see Lacan, *Television*; and Miller, "On Shame."

50. Malaby notably writes of "concealment and revelation" in gambling insofar as these logics establish and protect "an intimate sphere." Malaby, *Gambling Life*, 33.

51. Asides from the myth that the term *yakuza* derives from a premodern outlaw imitating the flashy character of an onstage *yakusha* (actor), it is generally recognized that the term comes from the three unlucky gambling numbers: *ya* (eight), *ku* (nine), and *za* (three). As in gambling, "yakuza" refers to a no-good character, down on his luck. For English sources on the yakuza and gambling, see Miyazaki, *Toppamono*; Saga, *Confessions of a Yakuza*; and Kaplan and Dubro, *Yakuza*. There also exists an abundance of untranslated Japanese texts on the yakuza. Two examples are the classical autobiographical texts by the third "foreman" (*kumichō*) of the Yamaguchi-gumi, Taoka Kazuo, *Yamaguchigumi Sandaime* (The third foreman of the Yamaguchi-gumi), and the mobster who became an actor, Andō Noboru, *Yakuza to Kōsō* (Yakuza and battle). Taoka Kazuo writes specifically of gambling in *Yamaguchigumi Sandaime*, 49–56. Moreover, Taoka had assumed a mythical place in the imaginary of former mobsters like Akira, much like Takeda-san. Akira recounted how there had been a queue of men lining up to give blood for Taoka Kazuo when he was lying on his deathbed. When I asked Akira whether he had read Taoka's autobiography, his response was a dismissive no. Why should he have to, when he knew what the man stood for in real life?

52. See "Seikatsu Hogo de Kyōtei?"

53. See "Kyōtei de Nomi."

54. Operating as a "point de capiton," the term *kuni* (state/nation) stitches together and gives sense to the reportage. See Lacan, "Subversion of the Subject," 681.

55. As it was explained to me, this ritual of passing around an *itchō* (single) block of tofu, or more literally, to "take the edges off" or "the corners off" (*tōfu no kado o otosu*) a

246 NOTES TO PAGES 112-114

block of tofu upon someone's "release from prison" (*shussho*), is common practice in the yakuza world. The tofu itself is served without soy sauce or dressing, in its pure state, as if to cleanse the "stomach" (*hara*) or make it white. In this instance, Shōkawa was asked to finish the block of tofu. But this is not always required, because the main point of the ritual is to take the rough edges off someone who has been incarcerated, making them amenable to life on the outside.

56. This is my inadequate translation of the title. Jōji, *Hei no Naka*. The novel was turned into a film bearing the same title in 1987.

57. To explicate the practices that underpin the claim to masculinity, I draw here on the psychoanalytic concept of the "Thing." In San'ya, being an otoko or performing its values was constitutively threatened. For as Žižek points out, as an obsessive object of identification, the "Thing" does not just constitute a point of symbolic identification but consists in a specific organization of jouissance (enjoyment) in relation to the "real" and can never be fully claimed as one's own. As such, Žižek says, "It appears as what gives plenitude and vivacity to our life, and yet the only way we can determine it is by resorting to different versions of an empty tautology; all we can say about it is, ultimately, that the Thing is 'itself', 'the real Thing', 'what it really is about', and so on." Indeed, much as the abuse of yakuza iconography triggered rage among a group of men who identified the "real yakuza" as someone who looked out for the weak (like Robin Hood?), Žižek writes that "what we conceal by imputing to the Other the theft of enjoyment is the traumatic fact that *we never possessed what was allegedly stolen from us*." Žižek, "Eastern Europe's Republics," 52–54.

58. *BEGIN*, "Shimanchu nu Takara," track 1 on *Begin no Shimauta*, Imperial Records (13) TECN-20798, 2002, compact disc.

59. Obon refers to the Buddhist festival of ancestors, held across Japan during three days in mid-August and celebrated with traditional dances, outdoor food stalls (*tekiya*), and such.

60. For more on this traditionalist notion of "shame" (*haji*), see chap. 5.

61. Derrida identifies the nostalgic discourse of emancipation through drugs (or, for that matter, gambling) as a "phantasm of reappropriation," as a dream of the impossible "restoration of an 'ego,' of a self, or of the self's own body." Yet he is quick to point out that the discourse of prohibition also seeks to achieve this plenitude, justifying itself by referring to such a restoration: "Depending on the circumstances (tirelessly analyzed, whether macroscopically or microscopically) the discourse of 'interdiction' can be justified *just as well or just as badly* as the liberal discourse." And this entails that the discourses of prohibition and emancipation are mutually constitutive, and that each threatens the other as "the trace of the third": "the third as destructuring structuration of the social bond." Derrida, "Rhetoric of Drugs," 239, 241–42, 251. For more on upstanding society and its constitutive relation to "drugs," see Ronell, *Crack Wars*.

62. Lest he lose the "very *stakes* [he] hoped to *win*," Akira maintained what Derrida described as a "*respect* for death" in the Hegelian dialectic, necessary to signification, because if he was to succeed in imposing himself on others and being recognized on his own terms, limits had to be placed on a "negativity *without reserve*." Charging "headlong into death pure and simple" entailed surrendering signification itself. At the limit of loss, gambling threatened to undo the Hegelian dialectic by "uncovering the limit of discourse and the beyond of absolute knowledge." Derrida, "From Restricted to General," 255–61. Notably, limiting and harnessing this negativity recalls the point at which the slave represses what Kojève described as the "liquefaction of every stable-support," thereby overcoming the condition of slavery. Kojève, *Introduction*, 20–21.

63. Georges Bataille has written of *expenditure* with reference to "unproductive forms" of activity in which "the accent is placed on a *loss* that must be as great as possible in or-

der for that activity to take on its true meaning." Of gambling, he says that it "can be considered to be a real *charge* of the passions unleashed by competition and that, among a large number of bettors, it leads to losses disproportionate to their means; these even attain such a level of madness that often the only way out for gamblers is prison or death." Bataille, "Notion of Expenditure," 118–20. Indeed, it was said of Matsuda that, to escape his underworld creditors, he had probably gotten himself into jail.

64. On "addiction," see my discussion of Derrida's essay "The Rhetoric of Drugs," in the introduction and the endnotes above.

65. This denigrating gaze is one that dovetails with the discourse on *ikizurasa* (pain of life)—see Allison, *Precarious Japan*.

66. Of a constitutive divide between "us" and "them," Kathleen Stewart writes of a social worker in Appalachia: "Although she had worked daily with clients from the camps, she had never herself ventured out to this place that began five miles from her doorstep in a protected middle-class enclave. For her it was an imagined landscape beyond the pale—a place given over to dirt and violence, lack and excess." Stewart, *Space on the Side*, 67.

4. FORBEARANCE

1. Rabson provides historical context to the migration of Okinawan youth to the Japanese mainland: "Even before the official transfer to Japanese administration on May 15, 1972, an increasing number of Okinawans began traveling to the mainland, especially youth seeking opportunities for work and study. Job prospects remained bleak in an Okinawan economy still heavily dependent on expenditures of the U.S. military, and more than 6,000 left for work on the mainland in 1971. Factories and other employers had begun fourteen years earlier, in 1957, to recruit Okinawans, mostly in their teens and early twenties, through agents who organized transportation and job placements in what were called 'group hirings' (*shūdan shūsoku*) for work in mainland cities." Rabson, *Okinawan Diaspora*, 189.

2. As it is also called in English, the itai-itai disease was so named in early twentieth-century Toyama Prefecture when cadmium poisoning caused individuals to experience constant pain. As it turned out, Mitsui Mining and Smelting Co. had been releasing the chemical into a river that proceeded to poison local water and food.

3. For a depiction of the incendiary conflicts that arose between subcontractors (for work) in the late 1970s, see Miyazaki, *Toppamono*, 210–12.

4. Joining the mob did not secure Akira employment free from discrimination. As Miyazaki writes of one mob member in the 1980s: "Most hit men involved in yakuza battles in Kansai were from Okinawa, making their way by offering their bodies as shooting targets. Kuniba was one of them. It was the only way for outsiders like him to get ahead, given the way the Kansai yakuza world is dominated by locals." Miyazaki, *Toppamono*, 365. In fact, Akira's moment of glory in the mob came when he was released from his stint in jail as a "substitute" (*migawari*), and eight hundred members from various syndicates gathered to pay their respects. It was an achievement of which he would say, "It's not like everyone can do it" (*dare demo dekiru wake jya nai*). However, these words were undercut by the regret Akira expressed over the incident in which he was found guilty of killing a man and that led to his life in the mob: "Why'd he have to die from being hit" (*nande nagutte shinun dayo*).

5. It is no coincidence that the word *forbearance* appears in one of Akira's favorite songs, "Otoko," by Tsuruta Kōji. Also famous as an actor in yakuza movies and as Miyamoto Musashi's adversary, Sasaki Kojirō, Tsuruta's song gives poignant expression to the struggles of masculinity and failing to live up to a mother's expectations. With the phrase—"Write the letter of forbearance/and hold back the tears"—the song emphasizes the need for self-reliance under conditions of severe hardship. Tsuruta Kōji, "Otoko,"

track 1 on *Otoko/Kizudareke no Jinsei*, Victor SV-2173, 1971, LP Record. I thank Harumi Osaki for her help with this song.

6. The ideogram for "forbearance" (*nin*) is most often used with another kanji to spell *nintai*, which translates either as "endurance," "perseverance," "forbearance," or "patience." *Nintai* is almost synonymous with the word *gaman*, which likewise translates as "patience," "endurance," "perseverance," "tolerance," "self-control," or "self-denial." I translate the *nin-* of *nintai* as "forbearance" because forbearance foregrounds the virtuous character of the conduct I describe. As the kanji is drawn from Tsuruta Kōji's song "Otoko," a citation is apposite from Ian Buruma's orientalist tract, *Behind the Mask* (a book in which he himself translates *gaman* as "forbearance"): "Tsuruta Koji has the melancholy, haunted look of a man who has seen it all but still, somehow, manages to keep going, like an ageing courtesan or a seasoned gambler who sticks to the old rules in a bad new world where everyone plays dirty. . . . His heyday as a *yakuza* star is now over, but he still appears on television as a singer of noble gangster stories or sentimental wartime ballads, sometimes dressed in full naval uniform. Fan magazines and record-jacket notes never cease to inform us that Tsuruta was on the list to be a kamikaze pilot. . . . Suffering is very much part of his image. Mishima wrote about him that 'he makes the beauty of *gaman* shine brightly.' Indeed, Tsuruta is all *gaman*. The main thing he suffers from is being an anachronism. A typical beginning of a Tsuruta film shows him coming out of jail after several years, dressed in a kimono. He finds the world a changed place: his old friends wear suits now and work for construction companies taking kick-backs and bribing politicians. He is of course appalled and appeals to his friends' sense of *yakuza* honour and humanity." Buruma, *Behind the Mask*, 177.

7. Junichi Saga writes: "So you see, if you aren't powerful, somebody's going to come barging into your turf. And if you can't shove him out again, you've had it. So you mustn't ever show weakness. Suppose you get into a fight with a guy from some other gang: whatever happens, you must squash him. If you let yourself get hurt without hurting him back, then it doesn't matter what happens to you, *we're* the ones who're going to suffer." Saga, *Confessions of a Yakuza*, 81.

8. Mauss writes: "Societies have progressed in so far as they themselves, their subgroups, and lastly, the individuals in them, have succeeded in stabilizing relationships, giving, receiving, and finally, giving in return. To trade, the first condition was to be able to lay aside the spear. From then onwards they succeeded in exchanging goods and persons, no longer only between clans, but between tribes and nations, and, above all, between individuals. Only then did people learn to create mutual interests, giving mutual satisfaction, and, in the end, to defend them without resort to arms." Mauss, *Gift*, 105–6. For a similar logic in which exchange supplants warfare, see Lévi-Strauss's chapter, "A Writing Lesson," in *Tristes Tropiques*.

9. As Derrida writes: "The gift is not a gift, the gift only gives to the extent that it *gives time*. The difference between a gift and every other operation of pure and simple exchange is that the gift gives time. *There where there is gift, there is time*." Derrida, *Given Time*, 41.

10. "Between equal rights, force decides." Marx, *Capital*, 344.

11. As the third foreman of Japan's largest yakuza syndicate, the Yamaguchi-gumi, Taoka Kazuo observes: "This thing called gambling is a battle to read the opponent's hand." Taoka, *Yamaguchigumi Sandaime*, 52.

12. Describing an underground character, Miyazaki refers to similar values: "As he spoke, Mr. Uchida kept nodding to himself. To him, even a bad reputation was good publicity. It never occurred to him that press coverage like this would dirty my name. To him, the opposite was true: 'You stood up for yourself all the way in your fight with the police, and you won through in the end. That earns you respect.'

"Mr. Uchida only cares about the principles at stake. He rejects anything that doesn't add up to him, whether he hears it from a general contractor or a yakuza.

"Many times I've heard him tell a yakuza, 'You're full of shit. Get lost!'"

"This didn't have the kind of consequences you might expect, however. Yakuza knew he wouldn't hesitate to kill someone if he felt it was justified, and I think they respected him for that. Indeed, he had been sent to prison thirteen times for standing his ground. No one could deny the formidable spirit of a man who matched words with deeds." Miyazaki, *Toppamono*, 277.

13. As Mauss explicates, a gift cannot be returned right away, because such a return would amount to an annulment and therefore a rejection of the gift. And a gift cannot simply be returned in the same form but must bear a mark of difference across time. Mauss writes: "In every possible form of society, it is in the nature of a gift to impose an obligatory time limit or term. By definition, even a meal shared in common, a distribution of kava, or a talisman that one takes away, cannot be reciprocated immediately." Mauss, *Gift*, 45. So too, Derrida comments on the necessity of a gift to bear a mark of difference: "So we were saying that, quite obviously, if the donee gives back the same thing, for example an invitation to lunch (and the example of food or of what are called consumer goods will never be just one example among others), the gift is annulled. It is annulled each time there is restitution or counter-gift." Derrida, *Given Time*, 12.

14. As opposed to the closed system Marcel Mauss observes in the economy of gifting, Derrida points to a constitutive excess that propels circulation. Derrida writes: "For finally, the overrunning of the circle by the gift, if there is any, does not lead to a simple, ineffable exteriority that would be transcendent and without relation. It is this exteriority that sets the circle going, it is this exteriority that puts the economy in motion. It is this exteriority that *engages* in the circle and makes it turn." Derrida, *Given Time*, 30. He continues: "An essential exaggeration marks this process. Exaggeration cannot be here a feature among others, still less a secondary feature. The problem of the gift has to do with its nature that is *excessive in advance, a priori exaggerated*." Derrida, *Given Time*, 38.

15. Miyazaki writes of similar virtues in his autobiography: "Basically my father was utterly indifferent to my schooling and never said a word on anything educational. But there was one precept he used to drum into me like crazy: act like a man. His definition of manliness was to protect the weak, one's juniors, and friends in trouble, even if it meant putting your body between them and danger. Also, stand up to the strong when they try and push you about, never back down, and never make excuses." Miyazaki, *Toppamono*, 38.

16. Barthes, "World of Wrestling."

17. Pro wrestling recalls the extravagance and celebration of "character" that Susan Sontag identified with "camp," of which she writes that it consists in "artifice as an ideal, theatricality." Sontag, *Notes on "Camp,"* 288. But as Henry Jenkins III writes, pro wrestling also invokes a melodramatic script in which "stories hinge upon fantasies of upward mobility, yet ambition is just as often regarded in negative terms, as ultimately corrupting. Such a view of ambition reflects the experience of people who have worked hard all of their lives without much advancement and therefore remain profoundly suspicious of those on top. Wrestling speaks to those who recognize that upward mobility often has little to do with personal merit and a lot to do with a willingness to stomp on those who get in your way. Virtue, in the WWF moral universe, is often defined by a willingness to temper ambition through personal loyalties, through affiliation with others, while vice comes from putting self-interest ahead of everything else." Jenkins, "Never Trust a Snake," 45. Pro wrestling intersects with other melodramatic forms of theater and theatricality in Japan, of which *taishū engeki* (theater for the masses) is most conspicuous

for its invocations of itinerancy and yakuza characters fighting it out for justice. See Ivy, "Theatrical Crossings, Capitalist Dreams."

18. As Barthes says, wrestlers must "succeed in imposing an immediate reading of their inner nature," in "emptying out of interiority to the benefit of its exterior signs." Barthes, "World of Wrestling," 18–19.

19. There exists an abundance of literature on "bullying" (*ijime*) in Japan, particularly as it unfolds among kids, although the phenomenon extends beyond the educational system into the adult workplace. See, for instance, Kamata, *Ijime Shakai no Kodomotachi*; or Naitō, *Ijime no Kōzō*. For English sources, see Yoneyama, *Japanese High School*; or Naito and Gielen, "Bullying and *Ijime*."

20. Here, I argue against René Girard's elaboration of the relation between ritual sacrifice and sociality and, specifically, against his claim that violence is simply grounded in "the reality of human relationships." Girard, *Violence and the Sacred*, 260. Moreover, the absence of the state and of the violence of state recognition in Girard's exposition recall the structure of the "ban" that Agamben develops in *Homo Sacer*. Of this "ban," Agamben writes: "*The originary relation of law to life is not application but Abandonment. The matchless potentiality of the nomos, its originary 'force of law,' is that it holds life in its ban by abandoning it. . . . A critique of the ban will therefore necessarily have to put the very form of relation into question, and to ask if the political fact is not perhaps thinkable beyond relation and, thus, no longer in the form of a connection.*" Agamben, *Homo Sacer*, 29. I argue that it is a specific relation or connection to the state that achieves the social expulsion and death of San'ya and that forces the circulation of violence to remain within San'ya. Through state recognition, in which the San'ya man is negated in just about every aspect of his person—since he gives himself to be recognized in accordance with state demands rather than imposing himself upon the state—the violence of this relation was materialized daily, be it at the workplace (in the wage), hospital, welfare office, or with the police. Ultimately, the state wields the threat of death over its subjects.

21. Of such disposability in the 1990s, Oyama observes: "That San'ya's true homeless are the older men who have been wholly excluded from the labor market is apparent from the resistance that they, as former laborers, put up when confronting this ultimate degradation. Those who *can* somehow remain in the labor pool will spare no effort to do so when facing such a crisis. It is only these older men, therefore—men whose final resistance has met with defeat—who are to be counted among the truly homeless." Oyama, *Man with No Talents*, 74. Fowler also describes San'ya in the 1990s, noting that "an increasing number of doya are affordable only to the young and able-bodied day laborers physically capable of working at least every other day. Their number is dwindling, however. As noted above, San'ya's population is aging rapidly along with the nation's as a whole, with one important difference. The day laborer's life average age, in the early fifties as of 1990, is approaching his average life expectancy. . . . The final resting place for many of these men, who are too old to do hard labor but too young for welfare, is typically the street." Fowler, *San'ya Blues*, 47.

22. The temporary staffing agency (*haken gaisha*) has indeed superseded the role of day-laborer districts in providing a flexible pool of laborers. With the temp agency, workers do not meet face-to-face after work. Nor do they see their agent, who simply texts them with an address in the morning, and many are known to sleep in internet cafes or to pass their nights at a twenty-four-hour McDonalds. For a broad overview, see Allison, *Precarious Japan*.

23. Bataille observes: "The true luxury and the real potlatch of our times falls to the poverty-stricken, that is, to the individual who lies down and scoffs. A genuine luxury requires the complete contempt for riches, the somber indifference of the individual who refuses work and makes his life on the one hand an infinitely ruined splendor, and on the

other, a silent insult to the laborious lie of the rich. Beyond a military exploitation, a religious mystification and a capitalist misappropriation, henceforth no one can rediscover the meaning of wealth, the explosiveness it heralds, unless it is in the splendor of rags and the somber challenge of indifference." Bataille, *Accursed Share*, 76–77.

24. Bataille writes: "The man of high rank is originally an explosive individual (all men are explosive, but he is explosive in a privileged way)." Bataille, *Accursed Share*, 75.

25. Journal entry from 2013. Like *toshikoshi* soba (year-crossing soba), *osechi ryōri* are traditional foods eaten during the New Year holiday. They consist of a variety of *osechi*, or dishes served in bento-like boxes, stacked on top of each other.

26. Mary Douglas has described a type of social power comparable to that attributed to Takeda-san. Of a power derived from disorder, Douglas says: "Ritual recognises the potency of disorder. In the disorder of the mind, in dreams, faints and frenzies, ritual expects to find powers and truths which cannot be reached by conscious effort. Energy to command and special powers of healing come to those who can abandon rational control for a time . . . In these beliefs there is a double play on inarticulateness. First there is a venture into the disordered regions of the mind. Second there is the venture beyond the confines of society. The man who comes back from these inaccessible regions brings with him a power not available to those who have stayed in control of themselves and of society." Douglas, *Purity and Danger*, 95–96.

27. David E. Kaplan and Alec Dubro describe the outlaw character in Japanese literature: "Like Goro Fujita's novels of seventy years later, Hasegawa's stories portrayed men of questionable backgrounds who fought as hard as they gambled, yet maintained a philosophy of supporting the underdog and never troubling the common folk. Above all, they remained loyal to those who helped them. A virtuous traveler would be willing to sacrifice his life for the oyabun who for one day had opened the gang's home to him.

"The aggressive yet compassionate outlaw, useless to mainstream society but willing to stand up for the common man—these are the essential components of the yakuza legend. It is a tradition inherited not only from the machi-yakko but from the samurai as well, and it spread through the feudal underworld." Kaplan and Dubro, *Yakuza*, 16–17.

28. Either someone in the group had filled in Takeda-san's paperwork for him, and not knowing how to write his name in ideograms (names with the same pronunciation can be written a number of different ways using Japanese ideograms, kanji), this person had written his name with the syllabic alphabet. Or Takeda-san had been indifferent—it is not uncommon to write one's name with syllables in Japanese, as a courtesy to someone who may not be able to read the ideograms with which one's name is written (for instance, if one is putting one's name down for a restaurant queue).

29. Miyazaki, *Toppamono*, 424.

30. In this instance, "gang" is a literal translation of the Japanese *gyangu*, which comes from the English word, and should be differentiated from the "gang" of "Okinawa-gang," which derives from the yakuza-affiliated word *gumi*. See chap. 1. The scandalous character of the Okinawa-gang resided in the fact that they were neither here nor there. While they used yakuza terminology to describe their relations, at the end of the day, they were simply "buddies" (*nakama*)—somewhere in between a *gyangu* and a *gumi*.

31. Oyama writes of such "gangs" (*gyangu*): "I refer to the frequent outbreaks of crime involving thieves (some working by stealth, some violently) called *mogaki*, who went after laborers returning to San'ya fresh from their jobs at a hanba. By the time these laborers, who had worked for a ten- or fifteen-day stretch, arrived back in San'ya, they were already well in their cups; once here they'd lose all inhibition and drink away until finally they sank, plastered, to the street, with their work bags as pillows. In their pockets were the earnings—ten or fifteen days' worth—that they'd received from their hanba jobs. . . . Such men would become the targets of *mogaki*, who stole about at night in packs of twos and

threes. *Mogaki* would lift valuables from the pockets of men who had passed out drunk; any victim who was awakened by the commotion would first be beaten to a pulp and then robbed. Members of a San'ya labor union formed by radicals used to band up and go on patrol late at night in order to lend a hand to potential victims." Oyama, *Man with No Talents*, 84–85.

32. Miyazaki writes of the figure of the "elder sister" (*nē-san*) in the yakuza world of old: "While yakuza like to talk of *otoko no hanamichi* ('man's glorious path'), 'manliness,' 'honor,' and the like, the fact is that beneath its macho exterior there is a matriarchal aspect to the yakuza world and maternal principles exert a powerful influence. Men adhered to a code of 'take my good name and you take my life,' and were extremely conscious of face and obligation. Moreover, many would die young, either killed in gangland strife or burned out by debauchery and dissipation. To help them cope, they needed the emotional anchor provided by something maternal.

"The yakuza world wouldn't be complete without its 'mother' figures. These women would heal the pain caused by the deaths of menfolk by recounting the exploits of the fallen and transforming their lives into the stuff of legend. Actually, the women often grew quite fed up with how stupid men could be, but would sing their praises anyway— and it was this kind of support that would encourage the men to take leaps into the unknown. So while on the surface it was a typically male-dominated world, the existence of women in the underworld counted for a great deal, in both spiritual and material ways. I am under the impression that there were many times when my father was dancing unknowingly to my mother's tune." Miyazaki, *Toppamono*, 21–22.

33. See chap. 1 for more on contemporary discrimination against the Buraku minority, Japan's outcaste class whose work has traditionally been associated with animals, leather tanning, and death.

34. There was no overcoming the constitutive stain of the "outlaw" (*autorō*), which, rather than assert a code of honor of its own, gave credence to the shamefulness with which San'ya was regarded.

35. For Matsuda, on the other hand, it was precisely "alcohol" (*sake*) that ruined the accountability of men. How many times had he castigated Akira for drinking to the point of self-destruction! Indeed, Matsuda might have disappeared for days on end, but he could never be found drunk.

36. In San'ya, the phrase "an eye for an eye" (*yararetara yarikaese*) can be traced back to the early 1980s confrontation between San'ya laborers, led by the then powerful Sōgidan labor union, and the state, yakuza, and labor subcontractors. With the transformation of San'ya into a "welfare town" (*fukushi no machi*), the phrase seems to have come to signify reciprocity among laborers themselves. See "Yama," *Yararetara Yarikaese*; Kama Kyōtō San'ya, *Yararetara Yarikaese*; and Yamaoka, *Yama: Yararetara Yarikaese*. Stuart Dowsey traces the emergence of the phrase to an even earlier moment in the Chūkaku-ha movement of the late 1960s: "The government has resorted to increasing the strength of the riot police in order to suppress the university struggle and the anti-Ampo struggle, so in order to cope with this the Chukaku have elected to follow the old Biblical adage 'An eye for an eye, a tooth for the tooth!'" Dowsey, *Zengakuren*, 233. For a description of "denunciation sessions" conducted by militant leftist unions in the 1980s, see Oyama, *Man with No Talents*, 98–99.

37. I draw here on Theodor W. Adorno's seminal essay "The Meaning of Working Through the Past," in which Adorno warns of fascism from "*within* democracy." Submission to the labor market, Adorno writes, requires the negation of "autonomous subjectivity," predisposing individuals to "renounce their self" in an identification with the status quo of "power as such." Adorno, "Meaning of Working Through," 90, 98–99.

38. The discourse of the otoko intersected with an imperialist and colonialist discourse that purports that the Imperial Japanese Army liberated the hundreds of thousands of "comfort women" (*jūgun ianfu*) that prostituted themselves for the Japanese army during World War II. According to this fascist discourse, these women were not systematically and forcibly conscripted as prostitutes for the Imperial Japanese Army but willingly offered themselves to their Japanese liberators, leaving behind their families. In the context of the Greater East Asia Co-Prosperity Sphere (a.k.a. Japanese imperialism during World War II) and contemporary disavowals by the Japanese state of atrocities committed during World War II, this discourse of saving women echoes Gayatri Chakravorty Spivak's sentence: "White men are saving brown women from brown men" Spivak, *Can the Subaltern Speak?*, 48–49.

39. For a factual account of the connection between the right wing and yakuza in postwar Japan, see Kaplan and Dubro, *Yakuza*.

40. See "Yama," *Yararetara Yarikaese*, 25–26.

41. "Yama," 15–17. Saitō observed that the camera functioned as a "weapon" (*buki*) for day laborers by exposing the conditions of their exploitation by the state, subcontractors, and mob. He was shot with a live camera raised to his eye. Although the title of Saitō's documentary could also be translated as "Yama: An Eye for an Eye," it was screened outside Japan as *Yama—Attack to Attack*. Saitō's film recalls Kazuo Hara's 1987 documentary, *The Emperor's Naked Army Marches On*, in which the protagonist, Okuzaki Kenzō, confronts his former World War II officers with the guilt of ordering the execution of two other men in his unit so that they could be eaten. Hara, *Camera Obtrusa*.

42. Regarding the murder of this policeman, see 6.9 Rally Executive Committee.

43. In this case, *-chan* operates as a suffix expressing endearment. Recall my elaboration of suffixes in San'ya in chap. 1.

44. Translated as *The Anatomy of Dependence*, Takeo Doi argued that Japanese culture predisposes individuals to seek indulgence from institutions and persons of authority within their select group. See Doi, *Anatomy of Dependence*.

45. Having learned the "computer" (*pasakon*) and "internet" (*intānetto*), Akira was to read what his crush had to say of his conduct, not in person but on Sanyukai's homepage, under "Hibi no Dekigoto" (Daily events):

A Relationship of Growing Together

A gentleman who is always smiling, a gentleman who cracks jokes and gives everyone a good time, a gentleman who is there together, and kindly helps out with this and that. There are times when such a gentleman suddenly stops showing up, and gets angry at some instant with an incredibly threatening attitude. Or rather, a gentleman who has special difficulty communicating. At such times, I think of the life that person led until encountering him at Sanyukai.

A heart's wound that still has not healed, a shadow power that nothing can be done about, that cannot be controlled with one's own power. There are such things for anyone. But I am sometimes startled by the fact that that of the gentleman far exceeds our imagination. Being thrown away by someone important, betrayed, being made unnecessary, being insulted . . . if in the same position, anyone would surely become the same way.

When the gentleman who disappeared comes back, or comes to his senses and takes on things with a serious mind, or when he opens his heart more than before, there is a big happiness that spreads out. Being glad and sad by turns, we are waiting for that day to come again, and believe in it before we know it. Every day, we do not know what will happen. Every individual has their unique rhythm and time. That is why every day is important. Because every individual gradually becomes an indispensable person, as we are changed through our interactions with each other.

46. I cite here from Michel Foucault's chapter "The Birth of the Asylum," for what is fundamentally at stake in Akira's confrontation with Sanyukai is an attribution and organization of guilt. Nor should it be forgotten that, albeit in earlier chapters of *Madness and Civilization*, Foucault observes that an economic imperative informs the designation of those who are to be confined as "mad," and by this point in Akira's relationship with Sanyukai, he had been deemed not only useless but troublesome. Thus, Akira was simply ignored. Writing of the loosening of chains and the consignment of relations in the asylum to "silence," Foucault says: "Henceforth, more genuinely confined than he could have been in a dungeon and chains, a prisoner of nothing but himself, the sufferer was caught in a relation to himself that was of the order of transgression, and in a non-relation to others that was of the order of shame. The others are made innocent, they are no longer persecutors; the guilt is shifted inside, showing the madman that he was fascinated by nothing but his own presumption. . . . The language of delirium can be answered only by the absence of language, for delirium is not a fragment of dialogue with reason, it is not language at all; it refers, in an ultimately silent awareness, only to transgression. And it is only at this point that a common language becomes possible again, insofar as it will be one of acknowledged guilt." Foucault, *Madness and Civilization*, 261–62.

47. For an in-depth, ethnographic consideration of the death-inducing effects of social expulsion and medical misdiagnosis, see, for instance, Biehl, *Vita*.

5. DISINTEGRATION

1. Marx, *Capital*, 272.

2. Fowler writes: "Whether resolutely or resignedly, the men leave something behind by coming here: jobs, families, creditors, prison records, gangster connections, failed businesses—the list is perhaps nearly as long as the combined roster of the area's two hundred lodging houses. They may indeed gain anonymity and freedom of movement, but the price they pay for these is very dear: a loss of contact with the outside world. It is a price that newcomers pay perhaps more willingly than veterans of the yoseba; the latter know the tally of loneliness adds up over the years with compound interest." Fowler, *San'ya Blues*, 16.

3. I draw here on Marx's "The Eighteenth Brumaire of Louis Bonaparte," in which a mode of production blocks lateral relations and the realization of a "common interest"—as opposed to the "general interest" of capital, emblematized in the revenant figure of Bonaparte, the emperor. Marx, "Brumaire," 115–16.

4. The family registry (*koseki*) refers to the state-endorsed family registry and provides the grounds for discrimination by preserving such information as Buraku background or parental marriage status.

5. On *haji*, see Benedict, *Chrysanthemum and the Sword*; and Ukai, "Future of an Affect." Ukai observes how Benedict's text has become a classic in Japan, serving as a point of identification. He writes: "At the end of *Orientalism*, Edward Said criticized the conservatives in the Arabic world, saying that the serious problem today is that people or the ruling class of the people who are represented by Orientalism themselves deepen their complicity with Orientalism, equally or more so than the 'representation' or 'creation' of the Orient by the West. This situation is consistent with post-war Japan." Ukai, "Future of an Affect," 17.

6. A term that would secure the inscrutability of "Japanese culture," it is not surprising that *haji* was interpreted by an American anthropologist, Ruth Benedict. While the term has emerged as a point of identification for Japanese culture more generally, *haji*

carries anachronistic connotations and is generally not used outside of specific circles, be they right-wing or traditionalist. In San'ya, *haji* was described with virtually the same terms that Benedict used to explicate the normative force of shame among "the Japanese": "A failure to follow their explicit signposts of good behavior, a failure to balance obligations or to foresee contingencies is a shame (*haji*). Shame, they say, is the root of virtue. A man who is sensitive to it will carry out all the rules of good behavior. 'A man who knows shame' is sometimes translated as 'virtuous man,' sometimes 'man of honor.'" Benedict, *Chrysanthemum and the Sword*, 224.

7. The 1983 gangster movie *Ryūji* refers to its main character as "a man of legend" (*densetsu no otoko*). As much as Japanese literature, films, TV shows, shame culture, or karaoke, the myth of the yakuza is constituted through the gaze of the West and, specifically, through the gaze of the United States. See, for instance, Sydney Pollack's cult classic 1984 movie, *The Yakuza*; Kaplan and Dubro, *Yakuza*; or, more recently, Adelstein, *Tokyo Vice*.

8. In this respect, not much has changed since the early 1990s, when Gill wrote: "Who can get social security? A doctor's letter stating that the bearer has a long-term illness or disability preventing him from working usually guarantees the success of an application: but people who are old or weak but lack any specific disabling condition must rely on the discretion of local officials." Gill, "Sanya Street Life," 278.

9. As an obsessive object of identification, I draw here on the psychoanalytic concept of the "Thing." See Žižek, "Eastern Europe's Republics," 51–53. In the context of Japan, see Ivy, "Mourning the Japanese Thing." See also chap. 3.

10. Although there are many versions of the *mujin kō*, pooling club, or rotating savings and credit association, Geertz sums up the *mujin kō* as I saw it: "The basic principle upon which the rotating credit association is founded is everywhere the same: a lump sum fund composed of fixed contributions from each member of the association is distributed, at fixed intervals and as a whole, to each member of the association in turn. Thus, if there are ten members of the association, if the association meets weekly, and if the weekly contribution from each member is one dollar, then each week over a ten-week period a different member will receive ten dollars (i.e., counting his own contribution). If interest payments are calculated, by one mechanism or another, as part of the system, the numerical simplicity is destroyed, but the essential principle of rotating access to a continually reconstituted capital fund remains intact." Geertz, "Rotating Credit Association," 243. See also Ardener, "Comparative Study."

11. Like the lottery, the *mujin kō* has premodern origins and has been considered a form of gambling, as its success depends on the reliability of its members. In some of its iterations, the individual who takes the pot home was even decided by a draw. But the *mujin*, which translates as "inexhaustible" (*mujin*), followed by "compassion" or "traditional cooperative" (*kō*), has historically functioned as financial aid for the poor or as a bank for people without credit. Moreover, as an underground institution designed to protect its members against destitution, the *mujin* has been subject to regulation by the Japanese state and the Ministry of Finance. Tetsuo Najita provides an exhaustive genealogy of the *mujin kō*, grounded as it is in practices and discourse connected to figures like Miura Baien or Ninomiya Sontoku. Najita writes: "Based on commoner or commensense epistemology, commoners wrote and published in the hope that other commoners would read and reflect on how ordinary people were able to control knowledge and overcome poverty. Such efforts were intrinsic to ethical practice and not demeaning to human virtue. The issues addressed here were fundamentally about trust and contract relations that could save lives by means of initiatives taken without any expectation of political benevolence. Everyone in the community understood that as a matter of common sense, as many people as possible had to join in this self-help effort. . . . Except for scholars

like Baien, who will be discussed later, this remains a history without names, primarily one about social thinking and action and not about scholarly debates that abounded in Tokugawa times. Mine also is a history that discusses the theme of organization and practice in the form of economic insurance confraternities known as *kō*, termed most commonly as cooperatives of 'inexhaustible compassion' (*mujin kō*) and of trust like that between 'mother and child' (*tanomoshi kō*)." Najita, *Ordinary Economies in Japan*, 16–17. See also Embree, *Suye Mura*.

12. While the *mujin kō* or *tanomoshi kō* has become relatively rare on the Japanese mainland, it continues to thrive in Okinawa, where it is known as the *moai*. Whether the practice of the *mujin kō* in San'ya derived from the Okinawan identity of many of its members, from a historical practice specific to San'ya, or from a combination of the two, I do not know. Writing of Okinawa, Christopher T. Nelson describes the affective, commemorative, and social power of the *moai*: "As they make whatever sacrifices they need to make and come together to recreate the *moai*, as they share this deceptively ordinary moment together again, they experience once more the pain, the pride, and the pleasure in that act. As they look to each of the moments that extend into the past, they know what they can hope for in the future: To be known and valued, to be in the company of those upon whom they rely. It is a kind of creative dialectic. They seize the opportunity to remember who they are and what they can do, to make the most of this moment—of all moments. In doing so, they mobilize capacities and practices that can move beyond this moment, to transform their lives and their worlds in new ways." Nelson, "They Were Right," 140.

13. Of the *moai*, Nelson writes: "As romanticized as it might be in popular culture, most Okinawans know that the *moai* can be inadequate to the challenges that threaten the everyday. The *moai* can even become oppressive mechanisms in which unpleasant or exploitative relationships are reproduced and renewed. Every Okinawan knows stories about *moai* that have careened out of control, demanding greater and greater contributions from members until many broke under the weight of financial obligation. Some became speculative, vehicles for the valorization of capital rather than mutual support. Others collapsed as members proved themselves unworthy of friends' trust, slipping away with their winnings and breaking the cycle of reciprocity." Nelson, 134.

14. Perhaps on account of my friendship with Akira, of which Akira said that Guysan was jealous, the head of the NPO had taken to giving me the cold shoulder, particularly so after I stopped volunteering.

15. Translated as "you," *omae* can be a particularly condescending form of address, as it was in this case.

16. Oyama, himself a day laborer, writes of a similar encounter with doctors: "He didn't stop writing in his file even when I sat in the chair right in front of him. I waited for the exam to begin, but he didn't stop writing even then, so finally, unable to bear the silence, I launched into a catalog of my symptoms. The doctor still didn't lay eyes on me, however; he simply continued scribbling in his file. He seemed to realize that I'd been talking only when I had finished, at which point he whispered something to the nurse standing next to him. She escorted me out of the room to an area where I could have my blood pressure recorded and produce a urine sample. . . . Later, when she finally called me back into the room, there he was, with his nose still in a file. At this point the form he was filling out seemed to be on my behalf; he handed the completed form to the nurse. 'That's all now; we'll get you your medicine,' she said, and ushered me out of the room. During the entire exam, the doctor did not look at me or speak to me even once.

"I paid this doctor more than ten visits altogether, with virtually the same scenario playing itself out every time." Oyama, *Man with No Talents*, 102.

17. Like *omae* above, *anata* (you) can operate as a condescending form of address.

18. Journal entry from 2013.

19. Alexandre Kojève writes of this "negating-negativity" as an "absolute liquefaction of every stable-support." See Kojève, *Introduction to the Reading of Hegel*, 21–23.

20. As Julia Kristeva explicates it, abjection borders on the primal and therefore does not concern itself with secondary elaborations of subjectivity. Rather than "*Who* am I?," the abject asks, "*Where* am I?" Kristeva, *Powers of Horror*, 8.

21. Journal entry from 2013. People from Okinawa have long suffered from being unable to readily travel home. Rabson observes how, during the US occupation of Okinawa (1945–1972), the "military imposed strict regulations on travel, businesses, and currency transfers that hindered communication. People on the mainland were unable to reach Okinawa in time to be with critically ill relatives, help with child care when parents were called away unexpectedly, or provide other essential support in family emergencies. 'When my grandfather was dying, my father couldn't get a passport to return to Okinawa,' recalls Osaka resident Kinjō Yūji. 'So he went by ship as far as Yoron Island [at the southern tip of Japanese jurisdiction], then sailed in a *sabani* fishing boat all the way to Okinawa. But the shore patrol arrested him there and took him back to Japanese territory, so he couldn't say goodbye to his dying father.'" Rabson, *Okinawan Diaspora*, 156.

22. Members of the Okinawa-gang were intimately familiar with suicide by disembowelment. Akira attempted suicide in this manner. Shōkawa's father had taken his life this way. And when I traveled with Akira to Miyakojima in 2015, he discovered that one of his childhood friends had passed away by "cutting the stomach" (*hara o kitta*). On account of this act, this friend was remembered with a grin by another acquaintance, accompanied by the words "he had grit" (*konjō atta*). While I cannot generalize beyond the men I knew, suicide by disembowelment was no cause for surprise among the guys. At the same time, suicide by disembowelment is most uncommon in Japan, where the most common way to commit suicide is hanging. The Ministry of Health, Labour, and Welfare does not offer any statistic on suicide by disembowelment and refers instead to suicide by use of a "sharp object," which composed 2.5 percent of total suicides in 2017. See Izumi, "Tōkei de Miru Nihonjin"; and the Ministry of Health, Labour, and Welfare, "Jisatsu no tōkei."

EPILOGUE

1. Marx observed that capital accumulation not only mandates a reserve army of labor but that it produces a pauperism sustained by the state. See Marx, *Capital*, "So-Called Primitive Accumulation." For a historical account that considers Okinawa within this framework, elucidating the resistances raised by the people of Okinawa to capitalist processes of dispossession, subsumption, and surplus extraction, especially in early modern Miyakojima, see Matsumura, *Limits of Okinawa*. For an account of the manner in which the Japanese state has sought to transform the people of Okinawa into a reserve army of labor, see Tomiyama, *Okinawajin*. Lastly, in *The Okinawan Diaspora*, Rabson provides a history of the expropriation of Okinawa and of the conditions that have forced generations of Okinawans to emigrate to mainland Japan in search of work.

2. Writing in 2012, Rabson observes of Okinawa: "Along with Japanese government investment, a steadily growing tourist industry has brought economic growth to Okinawa, although mainland corporations have been criticized for building oceanfront resorts that damage the environment, and for siphoning most of the profits back to the mainland. While living standards have improved conspicuously since the occupation years, Okinawa remains the Japanese prefecture with the lowest per capita income (75 percent the national average) and the highest unemployment rate (twice the national average)." Rabson, *Okinawan Diaspora*, 36.

3. Insofar as these ironic acts were legible to those around Kentarō and not necessarily to those in places of authority, consider the "periformative" as Eve Kosofksy Sedgwick's develops this concept in *Touching, Feeling*.

4. Places like San'ya constitute a breakdown in the mirroring structure to which Louis Althusser attributes the force of ideology. See Althusser, "Ideology and Ideological State."

5. This statement is not atypical. Rabson recounts the story of "a resident of Osaka in his forties [who] didn't learn from his migrant parents about his Okinawan ethnicity until he was eight. He recalled feeling ashamed of it for many years, but later developed a pride that motivated him to say 'I am not Japanese.'" Rabson, *Okinawan Diaspora*, 215.

6. I circle back to Wojnarowicz and to the violence that *any* kind of exclusive identification entails, be it in masculinity, in being a "man," an otoko, or in what Wojnarowicz describes as the "ONE-TRIBE NATION." Wojnarowicz writes: "Words can strip the power from a memory or an event. Words can cut the ropes of an experience. Breaking silence about an experience can break the chains of the code of silence. Describing the once indescribable can dismantle the power of taboo. To speak about the once unspeakable can make the INVISIBLE familiar if repeated often enough in clear and loud tones. To speak of ourselves—while living in a country that considers us or our thoughts taboo—is to shake the boundaries of the illusion of the ONE-TRIBE NATION. To keep silent is to deny the fact that there are millions of separate tribes in this illusion called AMERICA. To keep silent even when our individual existence contradicts the illusory ONE-TRIBE NATION is to lose our own identities. BOTTOM LINE, IF PEOPLE DON'T SAY WHAT THEY BELIEVE, THOSE IDEAS AND FEELINGS GET LOST. IF THEY ARE LOST OFTEN ENOUGH, THOSE IDEAS AND FEELINGS NEVER RETURN." Wojnarowicz, *Close to the Knives*, 153.

7. Journal entry from 2013.

8. In "Hate Crimes and Violence against the Transgendered," Tarynn M. Witten and A. Evan Eyler write, "Crimes of violence and victimization against transsexual, transgendered and cross-dressing persons are often characterized as either the action of individuals (males) who do not live within the rules of society, or as being somehow provoked by victims through their deviancy with regard to gender expectation. In each case, these arguments are simply extensions of the traditional discourse regarding violence against women: either the perpetrator is a 'mad dog' (i.e. a criminally deviant male) or the victim 'asked for it' (via exhibiting the 'provocative behavior' of failing to conform to gender role expectations)." Witten and Tyler, "Hate Crimes and Violence," 461.

9. Susan Stryker observes: "Those who commit violence against transgender people routinely seek to excuse their own behavior by claiming they have been unjustly deceived by a mismatch between the other's gender and genitals. State and society do similar violence to transgender people by using genital status, rather than public gender or subjective gender identity, as the fundamental criterion for determining how they will place individuals in prisons, residential substance abuse treatment program, rape crisis center, or homeless shelter." Stryker, "(De)Subjugated Knowledges," 10. Commenting on the constructed character of the order of sex, Rosalind C. Morris writes: "The constructedness of bodies becomes most visible when it deviates from the expectations of the dominant ideology. . . . Ambiguity is the taboo of medicalized bodies, the impermissible threat against which hormone therapies and surgical intervention are marshalled so relentlessly." Morris, "All Made Up," 570. I thank Tommy Birkett for many of these sources and for commenting on this section.

10. See Knight, "LGBT Bullying and Exclusion." See also McLelland and Suganuma, "Sexual Minorities." For an older take on theater and the theatricality of cross-dressing in Japan, see Robertson, "Politics of Androgyny."

11. Stryker writes of the transformative potential of "transgender rage": "[It] furnishes a means of disidentification with compulsorily assigned subject positions. It makes pos-

sible the transition from one gendered subject position to another possible by using the impossibility of complete subjective foreclosure to organize an outside force as an inside drive and vice versa. Through the operation of rage, the stigma itself becomes the source of a transformative power." Stryker, "My Words to Victor Frankenstein," 253.

12. Of the threat of constructedness and the normative violence it triggers, Stryker writes: "Confronting the implications of this constructedness can summon up all the violation, loss, and separation inflicted by the gendering process that sustains the illusion of naturalness. My transsexual body literalizes this abstract violence. As the bearers of this disquieting news, we transsexuals often suffer for the pain of others, but we do not willingly abide the rage of others directed against us. And we do have something else to say, if you will but listen to the monsters: the possibility of meaningful agency and action exists, even within fields of domination that bring about the universal cultural rape of all flesh." Stryker, 254.

13. Many former members of the Matsuda-group did indeed go to work at Fukushima Daiichi Nuclear Power Plant.

14. Thus, Sandy Stone writes of "the force of an imperative—a natural state toward which all things tend—to deny the potentialities of mixture, acts to preserve 'pure' gender identity." Stone, "Empire Strikes Back," 226.

15. Miyazaki, *Toppamono*, 221.

16. Journal entry from 2012.

17. I translate the "general" (*ippan*) of "general society" (*ippan shakai*) as "ordinary" (*ippan*) or "ordinary folk" (*ippan no hito*).

Bibliography

Abe, Jōji. *Hei no Naka no Korinai Menmen* [Incarcerated and incorrigible]. Tokyo: Shinpūsha, 2004.

Adelstein, Jake. *Tokyo Vice: An American Reporter on the Police Beat in Japan.* New York: Pantheon Books, 2009.

Adorno, Theodor. "The Meaning of Working Through the Past." In *Critical Models: Interventions and Catchwords,* 89–103. Translated by Henry W. Pickford. New York: Columbia University Press, 1998.

Agamben, Giorgio. *Homo Sacer: Sovereign Power and Bare Life.* Translated by Daniel Heller-Roazen. Stanford, CA: Stanford University Press, 1998.

Allison, Anne. *Nightwork: Sexuality, Pleasure, and Corporate Masculinity in a Tokyo Hostess Club.* Chicago: Chicago University Press, 1994.

Allison, Anne. *Precarious Japan.* Durham, NC: Duke University Press, 2013.

Althusser, Louis. "Ideology and Ideological State Apparatuses (Notes towards an Investigation)." In *Lenin and Philosophy and Other Essays,* 127–86. Translated by Ben Brewster. New York: Monthly Review, 2001.

Amamiya, Karin. *Ikisasero! Nanminka Suru Wakamonotachi* [Survive! The refugeeization of young people]. Tokyo: Ōtashuppan, 2007.

Andō, Noboru. *Yakuza to Kōsō* [Yakuza and battle]. Tokyo: Tokuma Bunko, 1993.

Arai, Andrea. "Killing Kids: Recession and Survival in Twenty-First Century Japan." *Postcolonial Studies* 6, no. 3 (2003): 367–79. https://doi.org/10.1080/1368879032000162211.

Ardener, Shirley. "The Comparative Study of Rotating Credit Associations." *Journal of the Royal Anthropological Institute of Great Britain and England* 94, no. 2 (July–December 1964): 201–29.

Barrett, Daniel William. *Life and Work among the Navvies.* London: Wells Gardner, Darton, 1880.

Barthes, Roland. "The World of Wrestling." In *Mythologies,* 15–25. Translated by Richard Howard and Annette Lavers. New York: Hill and Wang, 2012.

Bary, Brett de. "Sanya: Japan's Internal Colony." In *The Other Japan: Postwar Realities,* edited by E. Patricia Tsurumi, 112–18. Armonk, NY: M. E. Sharpe, 1988.

Bataille, Georges. *The Accursed Share.* Vol. 1. Translated by Robert Hurley. New York: Zone Books, 1988.

Bataille, Georges. "The Notion of Expenditure." In *Visions of Excess: Selected Writings, 1927–1939,* 116–29. Translated by Allan Stoekl. Minneapolis: University of Minnesota Press, 1985.

Benedict, Ruth. *The Chrysanthemum and the Sword.* New York: First Mariner Books, 2005.

Benjamin, Walter. *The Arcades Project.* Translated by Howard Eiland and Kevin McLaughlin. Cambridge, MA: Belknap Press of Harvard University Press, 1999.

Benjamin, Walter. "The Destructive Character." In *Reflections,* edited by Peter Demetz, 301–3. Translated by Edmund Jephcott. New York: Harcourt Brace Jovanovich, 1978.

Benjamin, Walter. "Notes on a Theory of Gambling." *Selected Writings: Volume 2, Part 1, 1927–1930*, edited by Michael W. Jennings, Howard Eiland, and Gary Smith, 297–98. Translated by Rodney Livingstone et al. Cambridge, MA: Harvard University Press, 1999.

Benjamin, Walter. "On Some Motifs in Baudelaire." In *Illuminations*, edited by Hannah Arendt, 155–200. Translated by Harry Zohn. New York: Schocken Books, 1968.

Benjamin, Walter. "Paris, the Capital of the Nineteenth Century (Exposé of 1935)." In *The Arcades Project*, 3–13. Translated by Howard Eiland and Kevin McLaughlin. Cambridge, MA: Belknap Press of Harvard University Press, 1999.

Benjamin, Walter. "The Work of Art in the Age of Mechanical Reproducibility." In *Illuminations*, edited by Hannah Arendt, 217–52. Translated by Harry Zohn. New York: Schocken Books, 1968.

Bestor, Theodore C. *Neighborhood Tokyo*. Stanford, CA: Stanford University Press, 1989.

Biehl, João. *Vita: Life in a Zone of Abandonment*. Berkeley: University of California Press, 2005.

Bloch, Ernst. *Heritage of Our Times*. Translated by Neville and Stephen Plaice. Oxford: Polity, 1991.

Borovoy, Amy. *The Too-Good Wife: Codependency and the Politics of Nurturance in Postwar Japan*. Berkeley: University of California Press, 2005.

Bourgois, Philippe. *In Search of Respect: Selling Crack in El Barrio*. Cambridge: Cambridge University Press, 2002. https://doi.org/10.1017/CBO9780511808562.

Buck-Morss, Susan. *The Dialectics of Seeing: Walter Benjamin and the Arcades Project*. Cambridge, MA: MIT Press, 1989.

Buruma, Ian. *Behind the Mask: On Sexual Demons, Sacred Mothers, Transvestites, Gangsters, and Other Japanese Cultural Heroes*. New York: Pantheon Books, 1984.

Butler, Judith. *Gender Trouble: Feminism and the Subversion of Identity*. New York: Routledge, 1990.

Caillois, Roger. *Man, Play, and Games*. Translated by Meyer Barash. Chicago: University of Illinois Press, 2001.

Cottereau, Alain. "Denis Poulot's 'Le Sublime'—a Preliminary Study of Daily Life and Workers' Resistance in Paris in 1870." In *Voices of the People: The Politics and Life of 'La Sociale' at the End of the Second Empire*, edited by Adrian Rifkin and Roger Thomas, 99–177. Translated by John Moore. New York: Routledge & Kegan Paul, 1988.

Dart, Gregory. "The Reworking of 'Work.'" *Victorian Literature and Culture* 27, no. 1 (1999): 69–96. https://doi.org/10.1017/S1060150399271045.

Derrida, Jacques. *Given Time: 1. Counterfeit Money*. Translated by Peggy Kamuf. Chicago: Chicago University Press, 1992.

Derrida, Jacques. "From Restricted to General Economy: A Hegelianism without Reserve." In *Writing and Difference*, 251–77. Translated by Alan Bass. Chicago: University of Chicago Press, 1978.

Derrida, Jacques. "The Rhetoric of Drugs." In *POINTS . . . Interviews, 1974–1994*, edited by Elisabeth Weber, 228–54. Translated by Michael Israel. Stanford, CA: Stanford University Press, 1995.

Derrida, Jacques. "Signature Event Context." In *Limited Inc*, 1–24. Translated by Samuel Weber and Jeffrey Mehlman. Evanston, IL: Northwestern University Press, 1988.

Derrida, Jacques. *Specters of Marx: The State of Debt, the Work of Mourning, and the New International*. Translated by Peggy Kamuf. New York: Routledge Classics, 1994.

Desjarlais, Robert. *Shelter Blues: Sanity and Selfhood among the Homeless*. Philadelphia: University of Pennsylvania Press, 1997.

Doi, Takeo. *The Anatomy of Dependence*. Translated by Ted Bester. Tokyo: Kodansha International, 1971.

Dore, Ron P. *City Life in Japan: A Study of a Tokyo Ward*. New York: Routledge, 2013.

Dostoyevsky, Fyodor. "The Gambler." In *Great Short Works of Fyodor Dostoyevsky*, 379–520. Translated by Constance Garnett. Princeton: Perennial Classics, 1968.

Douglas, Mary. *Purity and Danger*. New York: Routledge, 1966.

Dowsey, Stuart J. *Zengakuren: Japan's Revolutionary Students*. Berkeley: Ishi, 1970.

Embree, John. *Suye Mura: A Japanese Village*. Chicago: University of Chicago Press, 1939.

Engels, Friedrich. *The Condition of the Working Class in England*. New York: Oxford University Press, 1993.

Foucault, Michel. *Herculine Barbin: Being the Recently Discovered Memoirs of an Eighteenth Century Hermaphrodite*. Translated by Richard McDougall. New York: Pantheon, 1980.

Foucault, Michel. *Madness and Civilization: A History of Insanity in the Age of Reason*. Translated by Richard Howard. New York: Vintage Books, 1988.

Fowler, Edward. *San'ya Blues: Laboring Life in Contemporary Japan*. Ithaca, NY: Cornell University Press, 1996.

Freud, Sigmund. *Beyond the Pleasure Principle*. Translated by James Strachey. New York: W. W. Norton, 1961.

Freud, Sigmund. "The 'Uncanny.'" In *Writings on Art and Literature*, edited by Werner Hamacher and David E. Wellbery, 193–233. Translated by James Strachey. Stanford, CA: Stanford University Press, 1997.

Galbraith, Patrick W., and David H. Slater. "Re-Narrating Social Class and Masculinity in Neoliberal Japan." *ejcjs* 7 (Sept. 30, 2011). http://www.japanesestudies.org.uk /articles/2011/SlaterGalbraith.html.

Geertz, Clifford. "Deep Play: Notes on the Balinese Cockfight." In *The Interpretation of Cultures*, 435–75. New York: Basic Books, 1973.

Geertz, Clifford. "The Rotating Credit Association: A 'Middle Rung' in Development." *Economic Development and Cultural Change* 10, no. 3 (April 1962): 241–63.

Genda, Yūji. *A Nagging Sense of Job Insecurity: The New Reality Facing Japanese Youth*. Translated by Jean Connell Hoff. Tokyo: International House of Japan, 2005.

Gill, Tom. *Men of Uncertainty: The Social Organization of Day Laborers in Contemporary Japan*. Albany: State University of New York Press, 2001.

Gill, Tom. "Sanya Street Life under the Heisei Recession." *Japan Quarterly* 41:270–86.

Gill, Tom. "Unconventional Moralities, Tolerance and Containment in Urban Japan." In *Morals of Legitimacy: Between Agency and the System*, edited by Italo Pardo, 229–56. New York: Berghahn Books, 2001.

Gill, Tom. "Wage Hunting at the Margins of Urban Japan." In *Lilies of the Field: Marginal People Who Live for the Moment*, edited by Sophie Day, Evthymios Papataxiarchis, and Michael Stewart, 119–36. Oxford: Westview, 1999.

Gill, Tom. "Whose Problem? Japan's Homeless People as an Issue of Local and Central Governance." In *The Political Economy of Governance in Japan*, edited by Glenn Hook, 192–210. London: Routledge, 2005.

Gill, Tom. "*Yoseba* and *Ninpudashi*: Changing Patterns of Employment on the Fringes of the Japanese Economy." In *Globalization and Social Change in Contemporary Japan*, edited by J. S. Eades, Tom Gill, and Harumi Befu, 123–42. Melbourne: Trans Pacific Books, 2000.

Girard, René. *Violence and the Sacred*. Translated by Patrick Gregory. Baltimore: Johns Hopkins University Press, 1977.

Goffman, Erving. "Where the Action Is." In *Interaction Ritual: Essays on Face-to-Face Behavior*, 147–270. New York: Pantheon Books, 1967.

Hammering, Klaus K. Y. "Gambling, Dignity, and the Narcotic of Time in Tokyo's Day-Laborer District, San'ya." *Cultural Anthropology* 37, no. 1 (2022): 150–75. https://orcid.org/0000-0002-0578-2828.

Han, Clara. *Life in Debt: Times of Care and Violence in Neoliberal Chile.* Berkeley: University of California Press, 2012.

Hankins, Joseph D. *Working Skin: Making Leather, Making a Multicultural Japan.* Berkeley: University of California Press, 2014.

Hansen, Miriam Bratu. "Room-for-Play: Benjamin's Gamble with Cinema." *October* 109 (2004): 3–45. https://doi.org/10.1162/0162287041886511.

Hara, Kazuo. *Camera Obtrusa: The Action Documentaries of Hara Kazuo.* Translated by Pat Noonan and Takuo Yasuda. New York: Kaya, 2009.

Hirose, Takashi. *Genshiro Jigen Bakudan: Daijishin ni Obieru Nihon Rettō* [Nuclear reactor time bomb: The Japanese archipelago that fears a major earthquake]. Tokyo: Diamondsha, 2010.

Horie, Kunio. *Genpatsu Jipusī* [Nuclear gypsy]. Tokyo: Gendai Shokan, 2011.

Horie, Kunio, and Shigeru Mizuki. *Fukushima Genpatsu no Yami* [The darkness of the Fukushima nuclear plant]. Tokyo: Asahi Shinbun Shuppan, 2011.

Hubert, Henri, and Marcel Mauss. *Sacrifice: Its Nature and Functions.* Translated by W. D. Halls. Chicago: University of Chicago Press, 1964.

Ivy, Marilyn. *Discourses of the Vanishing: Modernity, Phantasm, Japan.* Chicago: University of Chicago Press, 1995.

Ivy, Marilyn. "Mourning the Japanese Thing." In *In Near Ruins: Cultural Theory at the End of the Century,* edited by Nicholas B. Dirks, 93–118. Minneapolis: University of Minnesota Press, 1998.

Iwata, Masami. *Gendai no Hinkon: Wākingu pua/Hōmuresu/Seikatsuhogo* [Poverty today: Working poor / homeless / welfare]. Tokyo: Chikuma Shoten, 2007.

Izumi, Kōtaro. "Tōkei de Miru Nihonjin no Jisatsu to Tasatsu: Mijika na Hōhō kara Odoroki no Shudan Made" [Japanese murder and suicide from a statistical perspective: Familiar means to surprising techniques]. *Diamond Online,* December 19, 2017. https://diamond.jp/articles/-/153462?page=3.

Jameson, Fredric. *Postmodernism, or The Cultural Logic of Late Capitalism.* Durham, NC: Duke University Press, 1991.

Japan Construction Occupational Safety and Health Association. "Kensetsugyō ni Okeru Rōdō Saigai Hassei Jōkyō" [The prevalence of accidents in the construction industry]. 2023. http://www.kensaibou.or.jp/data/statistics_graph.html.

Japan Racing Association. "Beginner's Guide (JRA)." In *Horse Racing in Japan: A Guide to Thoroughbred Racing in Japan,* 2023. https://japanracing.jp/en/racing/go_racing/guide/.

Jenkins III, Henry. "'Never Trust a Snake': WWF Wrestling as Masculine Melodrama." In *Steel Chair to the Head,* ed. Nicholas Sammond, 33–66. Durham: Duke University Press, 2005. https://doi.org/10.1215/9780822386827-003.

Jōhoku Labor and Welfare Center. "Jigyō Annai: Heisei 28" [Summary of activities: Heisei 28]. 2016. https://www.fukushizaidan.jp/401johoku/jigyouannai/.

Kama Kyōtō San'ya Gentōi Henshūiinkaihen. *Yararetara Yarikaese: Jitsuroku, Kamagasaki, San'ya Kaihō Tōsō* [An eye for an eye: A record of the Kamagasaki, San'ya liberation fight]. Tokyo: Tahata Shoten, 1974.

Kamata, Satoshi. *Ijime Shakai no Kodomotachi* [Children in a bullying society]. Tokyo: Kodansha Bunko, 1998.

Kant, Immanuel. *Critique of the Power of Judgement.* Edited by Paul Guyer. Translated by Paul Guyer and Eric Matthews. Cambridge: Cambridge University Press, 2000.

Kaplan, David E., and Alec Dubro. *Yakuza: Japan's Criminal Underworld.* Berkeley: University of California Press, 2003.

Kawashima, Ken C. *The Proletarian Gamble: Korean Workers in Interwar Japan.* Durham, NC: Duke University Press, 2009.

Klein, Richard, and William B. Warner. "Nuclear Coincidence and the Korean Airline Disaster." *Diacritics* 16, no. 1 (1986): 2–21. https://doi.org/10.2307/464647.

Knight, Kyle. "'The Nail that Sticks Out Gets Hammered Down': LGBT Bullying and Exclusion in Japanese Schools." Human Rights Watch, May 5, 2016. https://www.hrw.org/report/2016/05/05/nail-sticks-out-gets-hammered-down/lgbt-bullying-and-exclusion-japanese-schools.

Kojève, Alexandre. *Introduction to the Reading of Hegel: Lectures on the Phenomenology of Spirit.* Translated by James H. Nichols. Ithaca, NY: Cornell University Press, 1980.

Kondo, Dorinne. *Crafting Selves: Power, Gender, and Discourses of Identity in a Japanese Workplace.* Chicago: University of Chicago Press, 1990.

Kristeva, Julia. *Powers of Horror: An Essay on Abjection.* Translated by Leon S. Roudiez. New York: Columbia University Press, 1982.

Kruse, Holly. *Off-Track and Online: The Networked Spaces of Horse Racing.* Cambridge, MA: MIT Press, 2016.

"Kyōtei de Nomi Kōi Kyaku no Taihan ga Seikatsu Hogo" [Illegal bookmaking with boat gambling, most of the customers on welfare]. NHK News, October 22, 2012. http://b.hatena.ne.jp/entry/www3.nhk.or.jp/news/html/20121022/k10015919051000.html.

Lacan, Jacques. "The Mirror Stage as Formative of the Function of the *I* as Revealed in Psychoanalytic Experience." In *Écrits: The First Complete Edition in English,* 75–81. Translated by Bruce Fink. New York: W. W. Norton, 2006.

Lacan, Jacques. *The Seminar of Jacques Lacan: On Feminine Sexuality, the Limits of Love and Knowledge, Book XX.* Translated by Bruce Fink. New York: W. W. Norton, 1998.

Lacan, Jacques. "The Subversion of the Subject and the Dialectic of Desire in the Freudian Unconscious." In *Écrits: The First Complete Edition in English,* 671–702. Translated by Bruce Fink. New York: W. W. Norton, 2006.

Lacan, Jacques. *Television: A Challenge to the Psychoanalytic Establishment,* edited by Joan Copjec. Translated by Dennis Hollier, Rosalind Krauss, Annette Michelson, and Jeffrey Mehlman. New York: W. W. Norton, 1990.

Lévi-Strauss, Claude. *Introduction to the Work of Marcel Mauss.* Translated by F. Baker. London: Routledge & Kegan Paul, 1987.

Lévi-Strauss, Claude. *Tristes Tropiques.* Translated by John and Doreen Weightman. New York: Penguin Books, 1992.

Liebow, Elliot. *Tally's Corner: A Study of Negro Streetcorner Men.* Lanham, MD: Rowman & Littlefield, 1967.

Llorente, Renzo. "Analytical Marxism and the Division of Labor." *Science and Society* 70, no. 2 (April 2006): 232–51. https://doi.org/10.1521/siso.2006.70.2.232.

Lukács, Georg. "Reification and the Consciousness of the Proletariat." In *History and Class Consciousness,* 83–222. Translated by Rodney Livingstone. Cambridge, MA: MIT Press, 1971.

Lyotard, Jean-François. *The Postmodern Condition: A Report on Knowledge.* Translated by Geoff Bennington and Brian Massumi. Minneapolis: University of Minnesota, 1984.

Malaby, Thomas M. *Gambling Life: Dealing in Contingency in a Greek City.* Chicago: University of Illinois Press, 2003.

Marx, Karl. *Capital.* Vol. 1. Translated by Ben Fowkes. New York: Vintage, 1997.

Marx, Karl. "Critique of the Gotha Program." In *Marx: Later Political Writings*, edited and translated by Terrell Carver, 208–26. New York: Cambridge University Press, 1996.

Marx, Karl. "The Eighteenth Brumaire of Louis Bonaparte." In *Marx: Later Political Writings*, edited and translated by Terrell Carver, 31–127. New York: Cambridge University Press, 1996.

Matsumura, Wendy. *The Limits of Okinawa: Japanese Capitalism, Living Labor, and Theorizations of Community*. Durham, NC: Duke University Press, 2015.

Matsuzawa, Tessei. "Street Labour Markets, Day Labourers and the Structure of Oppression." In *The Japanese Trajectory: Modernization and Beyond*, edited by Gavan McCormack and Yoshio Sugimoto, 147–63. Cambridge: Cambridge University Press, 1988.

Mauss, Marcel. *The Gift: The Form and Reason for Exchange in Archaic Societies*. Translated by W. D. Halls. New York: Routledge Classics, 2002.

McLelland, Mark, and Katsuhiko Suganuma. "Sexual Minorities and Human Rights in Japan: An Historical Perspective." *International Journal of Human Rights* 13, no. 2–3 (2009): 329–43. https://doi.org/10.1080/13642980902758176.

Millar, Kathleen M. *Reclaiming the Discarded: Life and Labor on Rio's Garbage Dump*. Durham, NC: Duke University Press, 2018.

Miller, Jacques-Alain. "On Shame." In *Jacques Lacan and the Other Side of Psychoanalysis*, edited by Slavoj Žižek, 11–28. Durham, NC: Duke University Press, 2006. https://doi.org/10.1215/9780822387602-002.

Ministry of Health, Labour, and Welfare. "Jisatsu no tōkei" [Suicide statistics]. 2023. https://www.mhlw.go.jp/toukei/saikin/hw/jinkou/tokusyu/suicide04/index.html.

Miyazaki, Manabu. *Toppamono*. Translated by Kotan Publishing. Tokyo: Kotan, 2005.

Morris, Rosalind C. "All Made Up: Performance Theory and the New Anthropology of Sex and Gender." *Annual Reviews* 24 (1995): 567–92. https://doi.org/10.1146/annurev.an.24.100195.003031.

Muehlebach, Andrea. *The Moral Neoliberal: Welfare and Citizenship in Italy*. Chicago: University of Chicago Press, 2012.

Mutō, Ruiko. *From Fukushima to You* [Fukushima kara Anata e]. Translated by Emma Parker. Tokyo: Otsuki Shoten, 2012.

Naitō, Asao. *Ijime no Kōzō—Naze Hito ga Kaibutsu ni Narunoka* [The structure of bullying—why people become monsters]. Tokyo: Kodansha Shinsho, 1984.

Naito, Takashi, and Uwe P. Gielen. "Bullying and *Ijime* in Japanese Schools: A Sociocultural Perspective." In *Violence in Schools: Cross-Cultural and Cross-National Perspectives*, edited by Florence Denmark, Herbert H. Krauss, Robert W. Wesner, Elizabeth Midlarsky, and Uwe P. Gielen, 169–90. New York: Springer Science & Business Media, 2005.

Najita, Tetsuo. *Ordinary Economies in Japan: A Historical Perspective, 1750–1950*. Berkeley: University of California Press, 2009.

Nakagami, Kenji. *The Cape and Other Stories from the Japanese Ghetto*. Translated by Eve Zimmerman. Berkeley, CA: Stone Bridge, 1999.

Nelson, Christopher T. *Dancing with the Dead: Memory, Performance, and Everyday Life in Postwar Okinawa*. Durham, NC: Duke University Press, 2008.

Nelson, Christopher T. "They Were Right about the Stars: Reading a History of War and Occupation in the Streets of Koza." In *Spaces of Possibility: In, Between, and Beyond Korea and Japan*, edited by Clark W. Sorensen and Andrea Gervutz Arai, 109–44. Seattle: University of Washington Press, 2016.

"Nihonkeizai o Boroboro ni Suru Hitobito" [The people who put the Japanese economy in tatters]. *Livedoor*, November 28, 2011. http://blog.livedoor.jp/nnnhhhkkk/archives /65711840.html.

"Osaka Nishinariku no Rōdōsha/Miyagiken no Untenshu no Kyūjin ni Taiō Suru to Fukushima Genpatsu e Tsureteikareru" [Laborers from Nishinariku, Osaka, respond to job posting for a driver in Miyagi prefecture only to be taken to Fukushima nuclear plant]. Rocket News 24, May 9, 2011. http://rocketnews24.com/2011/05/09/%E5%A4 %A7%E9%98%AA%E8%A5%BF%E6%88%90%E5%8C%BA%E3%81%AE%E5%8A %B4%E5%83%8D%E8%80%85-%E5%AE%AE%E5%9F%8E%E7%9C%8C%E3%81 %AE%E9%81%8B%E8%BB%A2%E6%89%8B%E3%81%AE%E6%B1%82%E4%BA %BA%E3%81%AB%E5%BF%9C/.

Oyama, Shiro. *A Man with No Talents*. Translated by Edward Fowler. Ithaca, NY: Cornell University Press, 2005.

Pine, Jason. *The Art of Making Do in Naples*. Minneapolis: University of Minnesota Press, 2012.

Presterudstuen, Geir Henning. "Horse Race Gambling and the Economy of 'Bad Money' in Fiji." *Oceania* 84, no. 3 (2014): 256–71. https://doi.org/10.1002/ocea.5059.

Rabinbach, Anson. *The Human Motor: Energy, Fatigue, and the Origins of Modernity*. Berkeley: University of California Press, 1992.

Rabson, Steve. *The Okinawan Diaspora in Japan: Crossing the Borders Within*. Honolulu: University of Hawai'i Press, 2012.

Rancière, Jacques. *The Philosopher and His Poor*, edited by Andrew Parker. Translated by John Drury, Corinne Oster, and Andrew Parker. Durham, NC: Duke University Press, 2003.

Reith, Gerda. *The Age of Chance: Gambling and Western Culture*. London: Routledge, 1999.

Rizzo, James. "Compulsive Gambling, Diagrammatic Reasoning, and Spacing Out." *Public Culture* 16, no. 2 (2004): 265–88. https://doi.org/10.1215/08992363-16-2-265.

Roberson, James E., and Nobue Suzuki. *Men and Masculinities in Contemporary Japan: Dislocating the Salaryman Doxa*. New York: Routledge, 2003.

Robertson, Jennifer. "The Politics of Androgyny in Japan: Sexuality and Subversion in the Theater and Beyond." *American Ethnologist* 19, no. 3 (1992): 419–42. https://doi .org/10.1525/ae.1992.19.3.02a00010.

Roitman, Janet. "Unsanctioned Wealth: or, the Productivity of Debt in Northern Cameroon." *Public Culture* 15, no. 2: 211–37. https://doi.org/10.1215/08992363-15-2-211.

Ronell, Avital. *Crack Wars: Literature Addiction Mania*. Chicago: University of Illinois Press, 2004.

Seidensticker, Edward. *Low City, High City: Tokyo from Edo to the Earthquake*. Cambridge, MA: Harvard University Press, 1991.

Saga, Junichi. *Confessions of a Yakuza*. Translated by John Bester. New York: Kodansha International, 1989.

Sanyukai. "Hibi no Dekigoto" [Daily events]. Accessed Sept. 30, 2019. http://sanyukai .or.jp/katsudou.html.

Scanlan, Lawrence. *The Horse God Built: The Untold Story of Secretariat, the World's Greatest Race Horse*. New York: Thomas Dunne Books, 2007.

Schivelbusch, Wolfgang. *Railway Journey: The Industrialization of Time and Space in the Nineteenth Century*. Berkeley: University of California Press, 1986.

Schüll, Natasha Dow. *Addiction by Design: Machine Gambling in Las Vegas*. Princeton, NJ: Princeton University Press, 2012.

Schüll, Natasha Dow. "Online Poker and the Software of Self-Discipline." *Public Culture* 28, no. 3 (2016): 563–92. https://doi.org/10.1215/08992363-3511550.

Sedgwick, Eve Kosofksy. *Touching, Feeling.* Durham, NC: Duke University Press, 2003.
"Seikatsu Hogo de Kyōtei? Nomiya Yōgi de Yamaguchigumi Kumiinra Taiho, Tokyo, San'ya" [Boat gambling with welfare? Yamaguchi-gumi members arrested under suspicion of illegal bookmaking, Tokyo, San'ya]. Sankei News, October 22, 2012. http://sankei.jp.msn.com/affairs/news/121022/crm12102213090009-n1.htm.
Sevigny, John. "Twenty Years Later: David Wojnarowicz's Buffalo Photograph." *Guernica,* July 25, 2009. https://www.guernicamag.com/john_sevigny_twenty_years_late/.
Shimazaki, Toson. *The Broken Commandment.* Translated by Kenneth Strong. Tokyo: University of Tokyo Press, 1977.
Siegel, James T. *Naming the Witch.* Stanford, CA: Stanford University Press, 2006.
6.9 Rally Executive Committee. "6.9 Kekki 30 Nen, Towaretsuzukeru Yoseba, Kangoku, Hinkon . . . Shūkai Hōkokushū" [6.9 Rally 30 years on, continuing to examine the yoseba, jail, poverty . . . symposium report]. Saitama: Shūkai Jikkō Iinkai, 2010.
Sohn-Rethel, Alfred. *Intellectual and Manual Labour: A Critique of Epistemology.* Translated by Martin Sohn-Rethel. London: MacMillan, 1978.
Sontag, Susan. "Notes on 'Camp.'" In *Against Interpretation and Other Essays,* 275–92. New York: Picador, 2001.
Spivak, Gayatri Chakravorty. "'Can the Subaltern Speak?' Revised Edition, from the 'History' Chapter of *Critique of Postcolonial Reason.*" In *Can the Subaltern Speak? Reflections on the History of an Idea,* edited by Rosalind C. Morris, 21–80. New York: Columbia University Press, 2010.
Stevens, Carolyne S. *On the Margins of Japanese Society: Volunteers and the Welfare of the Urban Underclass.* London: Routledge, 1997.
Stewart, Kathleen. *A Space on the Side of the Road: Cultural Politics in an "Other" America.* Princeton, NJ: Princeton University Press, 1996.
Stone, Sandy. "The Empire Strikes Back: A Posttransexual Manifesto." In *The Transgender Studies Reader,* edited by Susan Stryker and Stephen Whittle, 221–35. New York: Routledge, 2006. https://doi.org/10.1215/02705346-10-2_29–150.
Stryker, Susan. "My Words to Victor Frankenstein above the Village of Chamounix: Performing Transgender Rage." In *The Transgender Studies Reader,* edited by Susan Stryker and Stephen Whittle, 244–56. New York: Routledge, 2006. https://doi.org /10.1215/10642684-1-3-237.
Suzuki, Tomohiko. *Yakuza to Genpatsu* [Yakuza and nuclear power]. Tokyo: Bungeishunju, 2011.
Taoka, Kazuo. *Yamaguchigumi Sandaime: Taoka Kazuo Jiden* [The third foreman of the Yamaguchi-gumi: The Autobiography of Taoka Kazuo]. Tokyo: Tokuma Bunko, 2009.
Taylor, Frederick Winslow. *The Principles of Scientific Management.* New York: Dover, 1998.
Tokyo City Bureau of Social Welfare and Public Health. "Hōmuresu Taisaku" [Preventing homelessness]. 2023. http://www.fukushihoken.metro.tokyo.jp/seikatsu/rojo /homelesstaisaku.html.
Tokyo City Bureau of Social Welfare and Public Health. "Seikatsu no Fukushi" [Welfare]. 2023. http://www.fukushihoken.metro.tokyo.jp/.
Tomiyama, Ichirō. *Kindainihonshakai to Okinawajin* [Modern Japanese society and Okinawan people]. Tokyo: Nihon Keizai Hyōronsha, 1991.
Tsukuda, Tsutomu. *Dakara San'ya ga Yamerarenē* [This is why I cannot quit San'ya]. Tokyo: Gentosha Bunko, 2008.
Ukai, Satoshi. "The Future of an Affect: The Historicity of Shame." In *Specters of the West and the Politics of Translation,* edited by Naoki Sakai and Yukiko Hanawa, 3–36. Translated by Sabu Kohso. Hong Kong: Hong Kong University Press, 2001.

Walkerdine, Valerie. "Video Replay: Families, Film and Fantasy." In *Formations of Fantasy*, edited by Victor Burgin, James Donald, and Cora Kaplan, 167–99. London: Methuen, 1986.

Weber, Samuel. *Return to Freud: Jacques Lacan's Dislocation of Psychoanalysis*. Translated by Michael Levine. Cambridge: Cambridge University Press, 1991.

Witten, Tarynn M., and A. Evan Tyler. "Hate Crimes and Violence against the Transgendered." *Peace Review* 11, no. 3 (1999): 461–68.

Wojnarowicz, David. *Close to the Knives: A Memoir of Disintegration*. New York: Vintage Books, 1991.

"Yama" Seisaku Jōei Iinkai. *Yama: Yararetara Yarikaese* [Yama: Attack to attack]. Saitama: "Yama" Seisaku Jōei Iinkai, 1986.

Yamaoka, Kyōichi. *Yama: Yararetara Yarikaese* [Yama: An eye for an eye]. Tokyo: Gendaikikashitsu, 1996.

Yano, Christine R. "The Burning of Men: Masculinities and the Nation in Japanese Popular Song." In *Men and Masculinities in Contemporary Japan*, edited by James E. Roberson and Nobue Suzuki, 77–90. New York: Routledge, 2003.

Yoneyama, Shoko. *The Japanese High School: Silence and Resistance*. London: Routledge, 2007.

Yuasa, Makoto. *Hanhinkon: "Suberidai Shakai" kara no Dasshutsu* [Reverse poverty: Escape from a "sliding down society"]. Tokyo: Iwanami Shinsho, 2008.

Zaloom, Caitlin. *Out of the Pits: Traders and Technology from Chicago to London*. Chicago: University of Chicago Press, 2006.

Žižek, Slavoj. "Eastern Europe's Republics of Gilead." *New Left Review* 128 (1990): 50–62.

Žižek, Slavoj. *The Sublime Object of Ideology*. New York: Verso, 2008.

\

Index

Rabinbach, Anson, 239n44, 239n47
Rabson, Steve, 223n30, 247n1, 257n2, 258n5
racism, 15, 143–44
radiation exposure, 7–8
rank system, 245n46
recognition, 104–17, 178. *See also* dignity;
state recognition
reputation, 39–41, 61, 104–17
research methodology, 19–21
reserve army of labor, 48
right-wing political ideologies, 12, 20–21,
108, 143–45, 255n6
Rizzo, James, 245n45
rotating savings and credit association
(ROSCA). See *mujin kō*
Ryūji (film), 255n7

sacrifice, as term, 5, 220n10
sakura, 213, 216, 241n7
Sanja Kensetsu, 54–55
Sankei News (publication), 109–10
"San'ya Blues" (song), 82, 205
San'ya district, overview, 1–17, 22–25,
194–200, 219nn2–4, 220n6. *See also*
Yama, as term
Sanyukai, 31, 32–43, 115–16, 147–61, 180–81,
186–88, 202–3
scaffolding work, 39, 49, 62, 67, 68, 71, 73,
74–75, 217, 236n25. *See also* construction
work; *tobi*
schizophrenia misdiagnosis, 18, 160–61
Schüll, Natasha Dow, 240n8, 241n13
Secretariat (horse), 99, 243n33
Seichō Corporation, 68
seimeisen, 202, 203, 208
seiza, 128, 209, 216
self-liquidation, 240n11, 240n13
self-recrimination, 13, 193. *See also* shame
and shamelessness
self-responsibility, 71, 182, 186
sentō, 10, 216, 232n1
sex industry, 8, 143–44, 198
sexism, 15
shabu. *See* meth
shame and shamelessness, 13, 36, 37, 164–65,
178, 193, 222n29, 252n34
shatei, 30, 165, 216
shifting labor, 48–51
shigoto, 23
shikatanai, 204–5
shinjiyūshugi, 7, 15, 204, 221n15, 224n38
Shinjuku Ni-chōme district, Tokyo, 199
Shirahige Hospital, 173–75, 181

Shiro, Oyama, 225n2
shussho, 216, 246n55
skilled artisan, 77, 234n10
Skytree, 57–58
slacking, 78–79, 81, 226n6, 238n37
smells, 23, 25, 26, 173, 227n12
smoking, 76
sociality, 2, 13, 29, 119–47, 224n36. *See also*
individualism
Sōgidan, 26, 31, 146, 147, 149, 182, 252n36
Sohn-Rethel, Alfred, 67, 232n3, 236n29,
237n30, 238n35, 239n45
Sontag, Susan, 249n17
sōpurando (sōpu), 216
Spivak, Gayatri Chakravorty, 15, 144,
253n38
state recognition, 13, 17, 180, 193–94.
See also recognition
Stewart, Kathleen, 247n66
stigmatization, 8, 24, 194, 220n7
Stone, Sandy, 259n14
Stryker, Susan, 15, 197, 258n9, 258n11
Sugawara Bunta, 3
suicide and suicide attempts, 19, 39, 142, 179,
181, 184–85, 188, 192, 193, 195, 200–203,
213. *See also* premature death
suji o tōsu, 152–53, 216
Sumiyoshi-kai, 198, 216, 228n17

taishū engeki, 16
Taitō Ward, 48–49
Takakura, Ken, 3
takara kuji, 87. *See also* gambling
Takeo Doi, 253n44
Takeshi Kitano, 4
takidashi, 31, 216
takobeya, 32, 216–17, 230n28
Tamahime park, 6
Tanba Tetsurō, 3
Taoka Kazuo, 248n11
tattoos, 10, 26–27, 42
Taylor, Frederick Winslow, 235n21, 238n37,
239n42
tehai, 31, 51, 162, 170
tehaishi, 31, 49–52, 209, 217, 230n27, 233n8,
241n7
tekiya, 141, 215, 217, 229n21, 246n59
tekkinya, 49, 217
temporality, 13
Tenjima Company, 32, 48
"Thing," as concept, 246n57
This Is Why I Cannot Quit San'ya (Tsukada), 9
3K work, 8, 17

Studies of the Weatherhead East Asian Institute

Columbia University

Selected Titles

(Complete list at: weai.columbia.edu/content/publications)

Afterlives of Letters: The Transnational Origins of Modern Literature in China, Japan, and Korea, by Satoru Hashimoto. Columbia University Press, 2023.

Republican Vietnam, 1963–1975: War, Society, Diaspora, edited by Trinh M. Luu and Tuong Vu. University of Hawai'i Press, 2023.

Territorializing Manchuria: The Transnational Frontier and Literatures of East Asia, by Miya Xie. Harvard East Asian Monographs, 2023.

Takamure Itsue, Japanese Antiquity, and Matricultural Paradigms that Address the Crisis of Modernity: A Woman from the Land of Fire, by Yasuko Sato. Palgrave Macmillan, 2023.

Rejuvenating Communism: Youth Organizations and Elite Renewal in Post-Mao China, by Jérôme Doyon. University of Michigan Press, 2023.

From Japanese Empire to American Hegemony: Koreans and Okinawans in the Resettlement of Northeast Asia, by Matthew R. Augustine. University of Hawai'i Press, 2023.

Building a Republican Nation in Vietnam, 1920-1963, edited by Nu-Anh Tran and Tuong Vu. University of Hawai'i Press, 2022.

China Urbanizing: Impacts and Transitions, edited by Weiping Wu and Qin Gao. University of Pennsylvania Press, 2022.

Common Ground: Tibetan Buddhist Expansion and Qing China's Inner Asia, by Lan Wu. Columbia University Press, 2022.

Narratives of Civic Duty: How National Stories Shape Democracy in Asia, by Aram Hur. Cornell University Press, 2022.

The Concrete Plateau: Urban Tibetans and the Chinese Civilizing Machine, by Andrew Grant. Cornell University Press, 2022.

Confluence and Conflict: Reading Transwar Japanese Literature and Thought, by Brian Hurley. Harvard East Asian Monographs, 2022.

Inglorious, Illegal Bastards: Japan's Self-Defense Force During the Cold War, by Aaron Skabelund. Cornell University Press, 2022.

Madness in the Family: Women Care, and Illness in Japan, by H. Yumi Kim. Oxford University Press, 2022.

Uncertainty in the Empire of Routine: The Administrative Revolution of the Eighteenth-Century Qing State, by Maura Dykstra. Harvard University Press, 2022.

Outsourcing Repression: Everyday State Power in Contemporary China, by Lynette H. Ong. Oxford University Press, 2022.

Diasporic Cold Warriors: Nationalist China, Anticommunism, and the Philippine Chinese, 1930s–1970s, by Chien-Wen Kung. Cornell University Press, 2022.

Dream Super-Express: A Cultural History of the World's First Bullet Train, by Jessamyn Abel. Stanford University Press, 2022.

The Sound of Salvation: Voice, Gender, and the Sufi Mediascape in China, by Guangtian Ha. Columbia University Press, 2022.

Carbon Technocracy: Energy Regimes in Modern East Asia, by Victor Seow. The University of Chicago Press, 2022.

Milton Keynes UK
Ingram Content Group UK Ltd.
UKHW031056150924
448265UK00002B/14